Beginning Python Visualization

Crafting Visual Transformation Scripts

Shai Vaingast

Apress®

Beginning Python Visualization: Crafting Visual Transformation Scripts

Copyright © 2009 by Shai Vaingast

ISBN-13 (pbk): 978-1-4302-1843-2

ISBN-13 (electronic): 978-1-4302-1844-9

Printed and bound in the United States of America 9 8 7 6 5 4 3 2 1

Trademarked names may appear in this book. Rather than use a trademark symbol with every occurrence of a trademarked name, we use the names only in an editorial fashion and to the benefit of the trademark owner, with no intention of infringement of the trademark.

Lead Editors: Frank Pohlmann, Michelle Lowman
Technical Reviewer: C. Titus Brown
Editorial Board: Clay Andres, Steve Anglin, Mark Beckner, Ewan Buckingham, Tony Campbell,
    Gary Cornell, Jonathan Gennick, Michelle Lowman, Matthew Moodie, Jeffrey Pepper,
    Frank Pohlmann, Ben Renow-Clarke, Dominic Shakeshaft, Matt Wade, Tom Welsh
Project Manager: Kylie Johnston
Copy Editor: Ami Knox
Associate Production Director: Kari Brooks-Copony
Production Editor: Kelly Winquist
Compositor: Dina Quan
Proofreader: Liz Welch
Indexer: Julie Grady
Artist: April Milne
Cover Designer: Kurt Krames
Manufacturing Director: Tom Debolski

Distributed to the book trade worldwide by Springer-Verlag New York, Inc., 233 Spring Street, 6th Floor, New York, NY 10013. Phone 1-800-SPRINGER, fax 201-348-4505, e-mail orders-ny@springer-sbm.com, or visit http://www.springeronline.com.

For information on translations, please contact Apress directly at 2855 Telegraph Avenue, Suite 600, Berkeley, CA 94705. Phone 510-549-5930, fax 510-549-5939, e-mail info@apress.com, or visit http://www.apress.com.

Apress and friends of ED books may be purchased in bulk for academic, corporate, or promotional use. eBook versions and licenses are also available for most titles. For more information, reference our Special Bulk Sales–eBook Licensing web page at http://www.apress.com/info/bulksales.

The information in this book is distributed on an "as is" basis, without warranty. Although every precaution has been taken in the preparation of this work, neither the author(s) nor Apress shall have any liability to any person or entity with respect to any loss or damage caused or alleged to be caused directly or indirectly by the information contained in this work.

The source code for this book is available to readers at http://www.apress.com.

This book is dedicated to my wife, Orna Vaingast.

Contents at a Glance

Contents

■CHAPTER 7   Math Games 221

■CHAPTER 8   Science and Visualization 249

About the Author

SHAI VAINGAST has been an engineer, an engineering manager, and a director of engineering since 1993. He has worked in the defense industry and in the medical device industry while being heavily involved with data processing and visualization. He has several patents.

About the Technical Reviewer

C. TITUS BROWN is a professor of Computer Science and Engineering and Microbiology and Molecular Genetics at Michigan State University, where he studies developmental biology. Dr. Brown has been using Python for about a decade, and he is the author of several Python bioinformatics packages as well as several testing tools. You can visit his blog at `ivory.idyll.org/blog/`.

Acknowledgments

I'd like to thank the following individuals for their contribution to the book (in alphabetical order): Shai Ayal, C. Titus Brown, Ehud Cohen, Bryan Crouse, Kylie Johnston, Michelle Lowman, Rich Lundeen, Frank Pohlmann, Ami Saguy, Sam Saguy, Janet Vaingast, Motty Vaingast, Orna Vaingast, and Arnon Zeira.

Introduction

I was always drawn to math and computers, ever since I was a kid playing computer games on my Sinclair ZX81. When I attended university, I had a special interest in numerical analysis, a field that I felt combines math and computers ideally. During my career, I learned of MATLAB, widely popular for digital signal processing, numerical analysis, and feedback and control. MATLAB's strong suits include a high-level programming language, excellent graphing capabilities, and numerous packages from almost every imaginable engineering field. But I found that MATLAB wasn't enough. I worked with very large files and needed the ability to manipulate both text and data. So I combined Perl, AWK, and Bash scripts to write programs that automate data analysis and visualization. And along the way, I've developed practices and ideas involving the organization of data—for example, ways to ensure file names are unique and self-explanatory.

With the increasing popularity of the Internet, I learned of GNU/Linux and the open source movement. I made an effort to use open source software whenever possible, and so I've learned of GNU-Octave and gnuplot, which together provide excellent scientific computing functionality. That fit well on my Linux machine: Bash scripts, Perl and AWK, GNU-Octave and gnuplot.

Knowing I was interested in programming languages and open source software, a friend suggested I give Python a try. My first impression was that it's just another programming language: I can do most anything I need with Perl and Bash, resorting to C/C++ if things got hairy. And I'd still need GNU-Octave and gnuplot, so what's to gain? Eventually, I did learn Python and discovered that it is far better than my collection of tools. Python provides something that is extremely appealing: it's a one-stop shop—you can do it all in Python.

I've shared my enthusiasm with friends and colleagues. Many who expressed interest with the ideas of data processing and visualization would ask, "Can you recommend a book that teaches the ideas you're preaching?" And I would tell them, "Of course, numerous books cover this subject!" But they didn't want numerous books, just one, with information distilled to focus on data analysis and visualization. I realized there wasn't such a title, and this was how the idea for this book originated.

Who This Book Is For

Although this book is about software, the target audience is not necessarily programmers or computer scientists. The reader's main line of work is research or R&D, in his or her field of interest, be it astrophysics, signal and image processing, or biology. The audience includes

- Graduate and PhD students in exact and natural sciences (physics, biology, and chemistry) working on their thesis, dealing with large experimental data sets. The book also appeals to students working on purely theoretical projects, as they require simulations and means to analyze the results.

- R&D engineers in the fields of electrical engineering (EE), mechanical engineering, and chemical engineering: engineers working with large sets of data from multiple sources. In EE more specifically, signal processing engineers, communication engineers, and systems engineers will find the book appealing.

- Programmers and computer enthusiasts, unfamiliar with Python and the GNU/Linux world, willing to dive into a new world of tools.

- Hobby astronomers and other hobbyists who deal with data and are interested in using Python to support their hobby.

The book can be appealing to these groups for different reasons. For scientists and engineers, the book provides the means to be more productive in their work, without investing a considerable amount of time learning new tools and programs that constantly change. For programmers and computer enthusiasts, the book can serve as an appetizer, opening up their world to Python. And because of the unique approach presented here, they might share the enthusiasm the author has for this wonderful software world. Perhaps it will even entice them to be part of the large and growing open source community, sharing their own code.

It is assumed that the reader does have minimal proficiency with a computer; namely he or she must know how to manipulate files, install applications, view and edit files, and use applications to generate reports and presentations. Background in numerical analysis, signal processing, and image processing, as well as programming, is of help, but not required.

This book does not intend to serve as an encyclopedia of programming in Python and the covered packages; nor does it try to be complete. It serves as an introduction to data analysis and visualization in Python and covers most of the topics associated with that field.

How This Book Is Structured

The book is designed so that you can easily skip back and forth as you engage topics.

Chapter 1 is a case study introducing the topics discussed throughout the book: data analysis, data management, and, of course, data visualization. The case study involves reading GPS data, analyzing it, and plotting it along with relevant annotations (direction of travel, speed, etc.). A fully functional Python script will be built from the ground up, complemented with lots of explanations. The fruit of our work will be an eye-catching GPS route.

If you're new to data analysis and visualization, consider reading Chapter 2 first. The chapter describes how to set up a development environment to perform the tasks associated with data analysis and visualization in Python, including the selection of an OS, installing Python, and installing third-party packages.

If you're new to Python, your next stop should be Chapter 3. In this chapter, I swiftly discuss the Python programming language. I won't be overly rehashing basic programming paradigms; instead I'll quickly overview the Python programming building blocks.

Regardless of your Python programming experience, I highly encourage you to read Chapter 4 before proceeding to the next chapters. Organization is the key to successful data analysis and visualization. This chapter covers organizing data files, pros and cons of different file formats, file naming conventions, finding data files, and automating file creation. The ideas in Chapter 4 are used throughout the book.

From here on out you have several options. If you intend to process text and data files, proceed to Chapter 5. Chapter 5 covers text files from all aspects: I/O operations, string processing, the csv module, regular expressions, and localization and internationalization. If Chapter 5 leaves you wanting to know more about file processing, proceed to Chapter 10. Chapter 10 includes advanced file processing topics: binary files, command-line arguments, file and directory manipulation, and more. Both Chapters 5 and 10 are complemented with numerous examples.

If graphs and plots are your heart's desire, skip directly to Chapter 6. In Chapter 6 I examine matplotlib and explore its capabilities.

If you're interested in the numerical aspects of data, it is advised you read Chapter 7 first. Chapter 7 discusses the basic building blocks for scientific computing. Chapter 8 builds on Chapter 7 and includes more advanced topics such as numerical analysis and signal processing.

Image processing is an important aspect of data processing. Chapter 9 deals with tools available as part of the Python Imaging Library (PIL) package and shows how to further expand the package and perform more complex image processing tasks.

Chapter 10 covers advanced file processing topics including binary files and random access, object serialization, command-line parameters, file compression, and more.

Finally, the Appendix provides additional source code listings used in the book.

Downloading the Code

The source code for this book is available to readers at www.apress.com in the Source Code section of this book's home page. Please feel free to visit the Apress web site and download all the code there. You can also check for errata and find related titles from Apress.

Contacting the Author

You can contact me at shai.vaingast@gmail.com.

■ ■ ■

## CHAPTER 1

Navigating the World of Data Visualization

A Case Study

As an engineer, I work with data all the time. I parse log files, analyze data, estimate values, and compare the results with theory. Things don't always add up. So I double-check my analysis, perform more calculations, or run simulations to better understand the results. I refer to previous work because the ideas are similar or sometimes because they're dissimilar. I look at the graphs and realize I'm missing some crucial information. So I add the missing data, but it's noisy and needs filtering. Eventually, I realize my implementation of the algorithm is poor or that there is a better algorithm with better results, and so back to square one. It's an iterative process: tweak, test, tweak again until I'm satisfied with the results.

Those are the tasks surrounding research and development (R&D) work. And to be honest, there's no systematic method. Most of the time, research is organized chaos. The emphasis, however, should be on organized, not chaos. Data should be analyzed and presented in a clear and coherent manner. Sources for graphs well understood and verified to be accurate. Algorithms tested and proven to be working as intended. The system should be flexible. Introducing new ideas and challenging previous methods should be easy and testing new ideas on current data fast and efficient.

In this book I will attempt to address all the topics associated with data processing and visualization: managing files and directories, reading files of varying formats, performing signal processing and numerical analysis in a high-level programming language similar to MATLAB and GNU-Octave, and teaching you Python, a rich and powerful programming language, along the way.

In a nutshell, *Beginning Python Visualization* deals with the processing, analysis, manipulation, and visualization of data using the Python programming language. The book covers the following:

- Fundamentals of the Python programming language required for data analysis and visualization

- Data files, format, and organization, as well as methods and guidelines for selecting file formats and storing and organizing data to enable fast, efficient data processing

- Readily available Python packages for numerical analysis, signal and image processing, graphing and plotting, and more

Gathering Data

We spend a considerable time recording and analyzing data. Data is stored in various formats depending on the tools used to collect it, the nature of the data (e.g., pictures vs. sampled analog data), the application that will later process the data, and personal preferences. Data files are of varying sizes; some are very large, others are smaller but in larger quantities. Data organization adds another level of complexity. Files can be stored in directories according to date, grouped together in one big directory or in a database, or adhere to a different scheme altogether. Typically, the number of data files or the amount of data per file is too large to allow skimming or browsing with an editor or viewer. Methods and tools are required to find the data and analyze it to produce meaningful results.

Case Study: GPS Data

You just got a USB GPS receiver for your birthday! You'd like to analyze GPS data and find out how often you exceed the speed limit and how much time you spend in traffic. You'd like to track data over a year, or even longer.

Some hardware background: most USB GPS receivers behave as serial ports (this is also true for Bluetooth GPS devices). What this means is that once a GPS is connected, and assuming it's installed properly, reading GPS data is as simple as opening the COM port associated with the GPS and reading the values. GPS values are typically clear text values: numbers and text. Of course, if you're planning on recording data from your car, it would make a lot of sense to hook it up to a laptop rather than a desktop.

We would like to record, analyze, and visualize the GPS data, in Python. First things first: recording GPS data.

■**Note** If you wish to follow along with the remainder of the chapter by means of issuing the commands yourself and viewing the results, you might first want to refer to Chapter 2 and set up Python on your system. That being said, it's not necessary, and you can follow along to get an understanding of the book and its purpose. In fact, I encourage you to come back to this chapter and read it again after you've had more experience with Python.

Python is an interpreted programming language. What this means is each command is first read and then executed, in contrast to compiled programming languages, where the entire program is evaluated (compiled) and then executed. One of the important features of interpreted programming languages is that it's easy to run them interactively. That is, perform a command, examine the results, perform more commands, and examine more results, and so on. The ability to run Python interactively is very useful, and it allows you to examine topics as you learn them.

It's also possible to run Python scripts, that is, noninteractively, and there are several ways to do that. You can run scripts from the interactive Python prompt by issuing the command execfile('scriptname.py'). Or you can enter python scriptname.py at the command-line interface of your operating system. If you're using IPython, you can issue the command run scriptname.py instead; and if you're running IDLE, the Python GUI, you can open the script and press F5 to execute it. The .py extension is a common convention that distinguishes Python scripts from other files.

Back to recording GPS data. To be able to access the serial port from Python, we'll be using the pySerial module. PySerial, as the name suggests, allows seamless access to serial ports. To use pySerial we must first read the module to memory, that is, import it using the import command. If all goes well, we'll be presented with the Python prompt again.

```
>>> import serial
```

Note To distinguish between interactive sessions and Python scripts, when code starts with >>>, it means that the code was run on Python interactively. In case the ellipsis symbol (...) appears, it means that this is a continuation of a previously interactively entered command. Lines of text following the symbols ... or >>> is Python's response to the issued command. A code listing that does not start with >>> is a script written in an editor, and in order to execute it you will have to save it under scriptname.py (or some other name) and execute it as described previously.

Scanning Serial Ports

Next, we need to find the serial port parameters: the *baud rate* and the *port number*. The baud rate is a GPS parameter, so it's best to consult the GPS manual (not to worry if you can't find this information, I'll discuss later how to "guess" what it is). As for the port number, this is determined by your operating system. If you're not sure how to find the port number, or if the port number keeps changing when you plug and unplug your GPS, you can use the short program in Listing 1-1 to identify active serial ports.

Listing 1-1. *Scanning Serial Ports with scanport.py*

```
import serial

found = False
for i in range(64):
    try:
        ser = serial.Serial(i)
        ser.close()
        print "Found COM", i+1
        found = True
```

```
    except serial.serialutil.SerialException:
        pass

if not found:
    print "No ports found, make sure GPS is connected."
```

■Note   Short programs are typically referred to as *scripts*.

Run scanport.py and note the result:

```
>>> execfile('scanport.py')
Found COM 5
```

This is a rather quick introduction to Python! First, let's dissect scanport.py line by line. The first line, import serial, loads the pySerial module. We then assign to the Boolean variable found the value False; this variable will be used as an indication of whether a serial port was found or not. We proceed with the for loop: the loop goes over the values between 0 and 63 as implied by range(64) (most systems have less than 64 virtual COM ports). The function range(N) returns a list of values from 0 to N-1. Our approach to seeing what ports are available is rather simple: try and open the port, and if all goes well, that port is a candidate. If it was not possible to open the port, just ignore that port. And so this is exactly how it's coded!

This is a common motto in Python: It's Easier to Ask Forgiveness than Permission, or EAFP. The idea is this: Try and perform an operation. If all goes well, great. If not, handle it with the except clause, or more figuratively, ask forgiveness. This is eloquently coded with the try/except mechanism.

In our case, the function that's most likely to fail (raise an exception) is the one that tries to open a nonexistent port: ser = serial.Serial(i). The function Serial() is part of the serial module (notice case sensitivity). To access functions within modules, you specify the module name, dot (.), and the function name. So to call the function Serial() within the module serial, write serial.Serial(). The function Serial() takes one parameter: the port number. Python, like C, starts counting at 0, so remember to subtract 1 from your virtual COM port when passing a parameter to the function. My GPS turned out to be connected to COM5, so a call to serial.Serial(4) will allow me access to the GPS. If the port is successfully opened, no exception is raised, and the opened port is associated with the variable ser.

The next line in the try block, ser.close(), tries to close the port. Closing the port renders it accessible to other applications, including your own. If you neglect to close the port, Python will close it for you once the variable associated with it, ser, is no longer in use. We also print out a message saying the port is a good candidate and set the found flag to True.

If the block of commands under try fails, the block of commands under except is executed assuming the except condition is met. In our case, if an exception occurred, and if the exception is of type serial.serialutil.SerialException, which means the port could not be opened, we want to simply disregard it. This is done using the pass statement, which does nothing.

Lastly, once the for loop is complete, and in case no port was found, a message indicating that is printed.

■Note The indentation (tabs) in Python is important because it groups commands together. This is also true when using Python in an interactive mode. All lines with the same indentation are considered one block. Python's indentation is equivalent to C/C++ curly braces—{ }.

Recording GPS Data

Let's start gathering data. Enter code in Listing 1-2 and record it in the file record_gps.py.

Listing 1-2. *record_gps.py*

```
import time, serial

# change these parameters to your GPS parameters
ser = serial.Serial(4)
ser.baudrate = 4800
fmt = "../data/GPS-%4d-%02d-%02d-%02d-%02d-%02d.csv"

filename = fmt % time.localtime()[0:6]
f = open(filename, 'wb')
while True:
    line = ser.readline()
    f.write(line)
    print line,
```

This time, we've imported another module: time. The time module provides access to date and time functions, and we'll use those to name our GPS data files. We also introduce an important notion here, comments! Comments in Python are denoted by the # sign and are similar to C++ double slash notation, //. Everything from that point onward is considered a remark. If the # sign is at the beginning of a line, then the entire line is a remark, usually describing the next line or block of code. The exception to the # sign indicating a remark is if it is quoted inside a string, as follows: "#".

Don't forget to change the port number to point at your serial port (minus 1) and set the proper baud rate. Determining the baud rate is not complex either—best to consult the manual. Mine turned out to be 4800, but if you're not sure, you can tweak this parameter. The script record_gps.py will print the output from the GPS on screen so you can change the baud rate value (in multiples of 2, for example 4800, 9600, and so on) until you see some meaningful results (i.e., text and numbers).

Running record_gps.py (I'll get to how it works soon) yields GPS data:

```
>>> execfile('record_gps.py')
$GPRMC,140053.00,A,4454.1740,N,09325.0143,W,000.0,128.7,300508,001.1,E,A*2E
$GPGGA,140053.00,4454.1740,N,09325.0143,W,1,09,01.1,00289.8,M,-030.7,M,,*5E
$GPGSA,A,3,21,15,18,24,26,29,06,22,,03,,,02.0,01.1,01.7*04
$GPGSV,3,1,12,21,75,306,40,15,59,075,46,18,57,269,49,24,56,115,46*79
$GPGSV,3,2,12,26,48,059,43,29,27,188,48,06,25,308,41,22,18,257,33*7D
$GPGSV,3,3,12,08,14,060,,03,11,320,32,09,06,144,,16,04,311,*7C
```

```
$GPRMC,140054.00,A,4454.1740,N,09325.0143,W,000.0,128.7,300508,001.1,E,A*29
$GPGGA,140054.00,4454.1740,N,09325.0143,W,1,09,01.1,00289.8,M,-030.7,M,,*59
$GPGSA,A,3,21,15,18,24,26,29,06,22,,03,,,02.0,01.1,01.7*04
```

Data is being recorded to file as it is displayed. When you wish to stop viewing and recording GPS data, press Ctrl+C. If you're running in an interactive Python, once you issue Ctrl+C, be sure to close the serial port, or you won't be able to rerun the script record_gps.py. To close the port, issue the following command:

```
>>> ser.close()
```

It's also a good idea to close the file:

```
>>> f.close()
```

Let's turn back so I can explain how record_gps.py works. The heart of the script lies in the following lines of code:

```
while True:
    line = ser.readline()
    f.write(line)
    print line,
```

This is a straightforward implementation. The first line, while True:, instructs that the following block should be run indefinitely, that is, in an infinite loop. That's why you need to press Ctrl+C to stop recording. The next three lines are then executed continuously. What we do is read a line of text from the serial port, store it to file, and print it to screen. Reading GPS data is carried out by the command line = ser.readline(). Writing that data to a file for later processing is done by f.write(line). Printing the data to screen so the user has some visual feedback is done with print line,. The reason for the comma following line is to suppress an extra line break.

Data Organization

Let's turn to selecting file format, file naming conventions, and data location. Now there isn't a good solution that fits all, but the methodologies and ideas are simple. The method I'll use here is based on file names. I'll show you how to name data files in a way that lends itself easily to automatic processing later on.

File Format

A file format is a set of rules describing the contents of a file. For the GPS problem, we'll choose the Comma Separated Values (CSV) file format. CSV files are text files with values separated by commas. For example:

```
$GPGSV,3,2,12,06,43,096,37,07,41,291,38,16,39,052,32,27,34,291,34*76
$GPGSV,3,3,12,19,26,152,35,08,06,280,,10,00,337,,00,00,000,*74
$GPRMC,233547.32,A,4455.6446,N,09329.3400,W,030.1,272.5,040608,001.1,E,A*2E
$GPGGA,233547.32,4455.6446,N,09329.3400,W,1,06,02.8,00299.0,M,-030.7,M,,*5A
```

CSV is a popular format recognized by most spreadsheets and database applications and, of course, text editors, seeing as they're really just text files. As it turns out, the data the GPS outputs is already comma separated, so all that's required is to save this information to a file, as is.

File Naming Conventions

We turn to selecting proper file names for our data files. File names should be unique so that files won't be accidentally overwritten. File names should be descriptive, that is, tell us something about the contents. Lastly, we'd like the file name extension to tell us how to view the file. The latter is typically achieved by selecting a proper extension, in our case, `.csv`. Here are the naming conventions I chose for this example:

- File names holding GPS data will start with the text "GPS-".

- Next is the date and time in ISO format with the separating colons omitted and a hyphen between the date and time: YYYY-mm-dd-HH-MM-SS, where YYYY stands for year, mm for month, dd for day, HH for hours, MM for minutes, and SS for seconds. In case a value is one digit and two digits are required, values will be padded with zeros, for example, the month of May will be denoted by 05, not 5. For additional information regarding the ISO format, refer to ISO 8601, "Data elements and interchange formats— Information interchange—Representation of dates and times" (`http://www.iso.org`).

- All files will have a `.csv` extension.

Following these conventions, a file name might look like this:

```
GPS-2008-05-30-09-10-52.csv
```

Data Location

This is where we store data files:

- All data files are stored in directory `data`. All scripts are stored in directory `src`. Both directories are under the same parent directory `Ch1`. So a relative path from `src` to `data` is `../data`.

- It's a good idea to also add a `Readme.txt` file. Readme files are clear text files describing the contents of a directory, in as much detail as deemed reasonable: the data source, data acquisition system, person in charge of data gathering, reason for gathering the data, and so on. Here's an example:

```
Data recorded from a USB GPS receiver, connected to a Lenovo laptop T60.
Data was gathered via the serial port stored to clear text files (CSV).
Measurements were taken to estimate speed and time spent in traffic.
Gathered by Shai Vaingast.
Date: throughout 2008, see file timestamps.
```

Data Analysis

Once data is organized and accessible in files, the next step is to extract information. Information can be a value, a graph, or a report pertaining to the problem at hand.

The idea is to use Python's scripting abilities and the wide range of readily available packages to write a fully automated application to process, analyze, and visualize data. Scripts are small pieces of code that are written relatively quickly in a high-level programming language. The key word here is productivity, the ability to change and test algorithms and extract results fast. Scripts might not be highly efficient in terms of processing speed, but written properly, they should not slow down running times. For example, a script might generate graphs or search the hard drive for data files, analyze log files, and extract the maximum and minimum temperatures, or in our case, analyze GPS data.

Back to our GPS case study. The following is the algorithm we'll follow:

1. Compile a list of all the data files.

2. For each file

    a. Read the data.

    b. Process the data.

    c. Plot the data.

Walking Directories

To compile a list of all the files having GPS data, we'll use the function os.walk() provided with the module os, which is part of the Python Standard Library. To use os, we issue import os.

```
>>> import os
>>> for root, dirs, files in os.walk('../data'):
...     print root, dirs, files
...
../data [] ['GPS-2008-05-30-09-00-50.csv', 'GPS-2008-05-30-09-10-52.csv',
'Readme.txt']
```

■**Note** To be able to change directories within the Python interpreter, first issue import os. Then, to change to a directory, issue os.chdir(directory_path). To list directory contents, you can use os.listdir(directory_path). Some interpreters like IPython let you use, among other enhancements, shell-like commands such as cd and ls, which add considerably to usability.

The function os.walk() iterates through the directory data and its subdirectories recursively, looking for files and folders, storing the results in variables root, dirs, and files. The second line prints out the root directory for our search, in our case ../data (notice the relative path), then the subdirectories, and lastly the files themselves, in a list. I've only recorded two data files, but as time progresses, more data is added to this folder, and the number can

increase substantially. Since we have no subdirectories in folder data, the output corresponding to dirs should be an empty list, which is denoted by [].

os.walk() is a bit of an overkill here. In our case, directory data doesn't have any subdirectories, and we could have just as easily listed the contents of the directory using the
os.listdir() function call, as follows:

```
>>> os.listdir('../data')
['GPS-2008-30-05-09-00-50.csv', 'GPS-2008-30-05-09-10-52.csv', 'Readme.txt']
```

However, os.walk() is very useful. It's not uncommon to have files grouped together in
directories and within those directories subdirectories holding more files. For example, you
might want to group files in accordance with the GPS that recorded the data. Or if another
driver is recording GPS data, you might want to put that data in a separate subdirectory within
your data directory. In those cases, os.walk() is exactly what's needed.

Now that we have a list of all the files in directory data, we turn to process only those
with the .csv extension. This is done using the endswith() function, which checks whether a
string ends with "csv". Files that do not end with "csv" are skipped using the continue statement: continue instructs the for loop to skip current execution and proceed to the next
element. Files that do end with "csv" are read and processed. We also introduce a function to
create a full file name path from the directory and the file name, os.path.join(), as shown in
Listing 1-3.

Listing 1-3. *Processing Only CSV Files*

```
for filename in files:
    # create full file name including path
    cur_file = os.path.join(root, filename)
    if filename.endswith('csv'):
        y = read_csv_file(cur_file)
    else:
        continue

    # only files with the .csv extension from here on
```

Reading CSV Files

Our next step is to read the files. Again, we turn to Python's built-in modules, this time the csv
module. Although the CSV file format is quite popular, there's no clear definition, and each
spreadsheet and database employs its own "dialect." The files we'll be processing adhere to
the most basic CSV file dialect, so we'll use the default behavior of Python's csv module. Since
we'll be reading several CSV files, it stands to reason to define a function to perform this task.
Listing 1-4 shows this function.

Listing 1-4. *A Function to Read CSV Files*

```
def read_csv_file(filename):
    """Reads a CSV file and returns it as a list of rows."""
```

```
data = []
for row in csv.reader(open(filename)):
    data.append(row)
return data
```

The first line defines a function named read_csv_file(). CSV file support is introduced with the csv module, so we have to import csv before calling the function. The function takes one variable, filename, and returns an array of rows holding data in the file. What I mean by this is that every line read is processed and becomes a list, with every comma-separated value as one element in that list. The function returns an array of such lists. For example:

```
>>> import csv
>>> x = read_csv_file('../data/GPS-2008-06-04-09-03-45.csv')
>>> len(x)
3683
>>> x[10]
['$GPGSV', '3', '3', '12', '29', '10', '040', '', '16', '01', '302', '', '26', '01',
'037', '', '00', '00', '000', '*72']
>>> x[1676]
['$GPGSV', '3', '1', '12', '21', '86', '258', '43', '18', '66', '286', '20', '15',
'50', '059', '45', '24', '44', '126', '43*72']
```

len(x) lets us know the size of the array of lists. It's also a crude way for us to ensure that data was actually read into the array.

The second line in the function is called a *docstring*, and it is characterized by three quotes (""") surrounding the text in the following manner: """dosctring""". In this case, a docstring is used to document the function, that is, what it does. Issuing the command help(funcname) yields its docstring:

```
>>> help(read_csv_file)
Help on function read_csv_file in module __main__:

read_csv_file(filename)
    Reads a CSV file and returns it as a list of rows.
```

You should use help() extensively. help() can be invoked with functions as well as modules. For example, the following invokes help on module csv:

```
>>> help(csv)
Help on module csv:

NAME
    csv - CSV parsing and writing.

FILE
    /usr/lib/python2.5/csv.py

MODULE DOCS
    http://www.python.org/doc/current/lib/module-csv.html
```

DESCRIPTION
> This module provides classes that assist in the reading and writing
> of Comma Separated Value (CSV) files, and implements the interface
> described by PEP 305. Although many CSV files are simple to parse,
> the format is not formally defined by a stable specification and
> is subtle enough that parsing lines of a CSV file with something
> like line.split(",") is bound to fail. The module supports three
> basic APIs: reading, writing, and registration of dialects.

Next in our dissection is the line data = [] which declares a variable named data and initializes it as an empty list. data will be used to store the values from the CSV file.

The csv module helps us read CSV files by automating a lot of the tasks associated with reading CSV files. I will discuss CSV files and the csv module in Chapters 4 and 5, so here I'll only provide an overview.

These are the operations to perform in order to read CSV files using the csv module:

1. Open the file for reading.

2. Create a csv.reader object. The csv.reader object has functions that help us read CSV files.

3. Using the csv.reader object, read the data from the file, a row at a time.

4. Append every row to variable data.

5. Close the file.

Let's try this, a step at a time:

```
>>> f = open('../data/GPS-2008-06-04-09-03-45.csv')
>>> cr = csv.reader(f)
>>> for row in cr:
...     print row
...
 ['$GPGSA', 'A', '3', '21', '18', '15', '24', '', '22', '', '', '', '', '', '',
'03.5', '02.2', '02.7*09']
['$GPGSV', '3', '1', '12', '21', '86', '267', '39', '18', '66', '286', '44', '15',
'51', '060', '43', '24', '45', '125', '30*7A']
['$GPGSV', '3', '2', '12', '06', '28', '300', '33', '22', '27', '265', '31', '03',
'18', '312', '27', '29', '15', '185', '31*7C']
['$GPGSV', '3', '3', '12', '09', '15', '138', '31', '16', '00', '301', '', '19',
'00', '332', '', '00', '00', '000', '*70']
['$GPRMC', '140706.24', 'A', '4455.6241', 'N', '09328.0519', 'W', '011.4', '152.7',
'040608', '001.2', 'E', 'A*25']
['$GPGGA', '140706.24', '4455.6241', 'N', '09328.0519', 'W', '1', '04',
'03.0','00295.1', 'M', '-030.7', 'M', '', '*51']
['$GPGSA', 'A', '3', '21', '18', '15', '24', '', '', '', '', '', '', '', '', '08.9',
'03.0', '08.4*04']
>>> f.close()
```

First we open the data file and assign it to variable f. The opened file can now be referred to by the variable f. Next, we create a csv.reader object, cr. We associate the csv.reader object, cr, with the file f. We then iterate through every row of the csv.reader object and print that row. Lastly, we close the file by calling f.close(). It is considered good practice to close the file once you're done with it, but if you neglect to do so, Python will close the file automatically once the variable f is no longer in use.

One of the things that you can do in Python is cascade functions. This means you can call functions on results of other functions. This process can be repeated several times. Cascading (usually) adds clarity and produces more elegant scripts. In our case, since variable f isn't really important to us, we discard it after we attach it to a csv.reader object; so instead of the preceding code, we can write the following:

```
>>> cr = csv.reader(open('data/CB401-2005-06-21-013504.csv'))
>>> for row in cr:
...     print row
```

The same holds true for variable cr, so if we're feeling particularly brave, we can use this script:

```
>>> for row in csv.reader(open('data/CB401-2005-06-21-013504.csv')):
...     print row
```

While the script might be shorter, there's no performance gain. It is therefore suggested that you cascade functions only if it adds clarity; there's a good chance you'll be editing this code later on, and it's important to be able to understand what's going on. In fact, not cascading functions might be useful at times because you might need access to intermediate variables (such as f and cr in our case).

The csv.reader object converts each row we read into a row of fields, in the form of a list. That row is then appended to a list of rows, data. This is also the value returned by the function.

■**Note** By now you've seen the dot symbol (.) used several times, and it might be a bit confusing, so an explanation is in order. The dot symbol is used to access function members of modules as well as function members of objects (classes). You've seen it in member functions of modules, such as csv.reader(), but also for objects, such as f.read(). In the latter, it means that the file object has a member function read() and that function is called to operate on variable f. To access these functions, we use the dot operator. We'll touch on this again in Chapter 3. Lastly, we use the ellipsis symbol (...) to denote line continuation when interactively entering commands in Python.

Analyzing GPS Data

Let's take a closer look at the GPS data.

- Each row seems to start with a text header stamp, beginning with the characters $GP.

- There are several header stamps, for example, $GPGSA and $GPRMC.

- Following the header are additional values, most of which are numeric.

Not being GPS savvy, I looked up the GPS format on the Internet. It turns out the format is known as NMEA 0183. NMEA stands for the National Marine Electronics Association; see http://www.nmea.org for more information. The NMEA 0183 data format is described at http://www.gpsinformation.org/dale/nmea.htm. There are a lot of header stamps in the format, and some might hold useful information for our task.

As mentioned earlier, several $GP header stamps appear in our data files, but which ones exactly are of relevance is a different question. First, it would be nice to know which header stamps from the NMEA standard are even present in our data files. One option would be to open the files, look for the headers, and jot down every new header once we see it. Another, of course, would be to use Python to do that for us.

Python is a very high-level programming language. As such, it has built-in support for *dictionaries* (also known as associative arrays in Perl), which are data structures that have a one-to-one relationship between a key and a value, very much like real dictionaries. Traditional dictionaries, however, often have several values for a key, that is, several interpretations (values) for one word (key). You can easily implement this in Python's using the dictionary object as well by assigning a list value to a key. That way you can have several entries per one key, because the key is associated with a list that can hold several values. In reality, it's still a one-to-one relationship. But enough about that for now, I'll cover dictionaries in more detail in future chapters. What we want to do here is use a dictionary object to hold the number of times a header is encountered. Our key will be the GPS header stamp, and our value will be a number, indicating occurrence. We'll increment the value whenever a key is encountered, as shown in Listing 1-5.

Listing 1-5. *Function* `list_gps_commands()`

```
def list_gps_commands(data):
    """Counts the number of times a GPS command is observed.

Returns a dictionary object."""

    gps_cmds = dict()
    for row in data:
        try:
            gps_cmds[row[0]] += 1
        except KeyError:
            gps_cmds[row[0]] = 1

    return gps_cmds
```

Some notes about this function. First, the docstring spans multiple lines, which is one of the key benefits of docstrings. Docstrings will display all the spaces and line breaks as shown in the function itself. Next we initialize a variable, `gps_cmds`, to be our dictionary. We then process every list in the GPS data: we only care about the first element of every row, as that's the value that holds the GPS header stamps. We then increment the value associated with the key: `gps_cmds[row[0]] += 1`. We use the += operation to increment the value by 1, similar to how it's done in C (Python, however, does not use the ++ operator). If the key does not exist, which will happen whenever we encounter a new header stamp, an exception will be raised. We catch the exception with our `except KeyError` statement. In case of an exception, we set the dictionary value associated with the key to 1.

The function `list_gps_commands()` can be written even more compactly using the dictionary method `get()`; see Chapter 3 for details.

Let's analyze some GPS data:

```
>>> x = read_csv_file('../data/GPS-2008-05-30-09-00-50.csv')
>>> list_gps_commands(x)
{'$GPGSA': 282, '$GPGSV': 846, '$GPGGA': 282, '$GPRMC': 283}
```

Turns out there are four distinct GPS headers being generated by my GPS. Of those, only two interest me: $GPGSV, which holds the number of satellites in view (Hey! It's really important!), and $GPRMC, which holds location and velocity information.

So what we'd like to do is code a function that takes the GPS data and, whenever the header field is $GPGSV or $GPRMC, extracts the information and stores it in numerical arrays that will be easier to manipulate later on. Numerical arrays are introduced with the NumPy module, so we have to issue `import numpy`. Since we'll be using a lot of the functionality of NumPy, SciPy, and matplotlib, an easier approach would be to issue `import pylab`, which imports all these modules, as follows:

```
>>> from pylab import *
```

■ **Note**   The name PyLab comes from Python and MATLAB. PyLab provides MATLAB-like functionality in Python.

Extracting GPS Data

In the case of a $GPGSV header, the number of satellites is the fourth entry. In case of a $GPRMC header, we have a bit more interesting information. The second field is the timestamp, the fourth field is the latitude, the sixth field is the longitude, and the eighth field is the velocity. Again, turn to the NMEA 0183 format for more details. Table 1-1 summarizes the fields and their values in a $GPRMC line.

Table 1-1. *$GPRMC Information (Excerpt)*

Field Name	Index	Format
Header	0	$GPRMC (fixed)
Timestamp	1	hhmmss.ss
Latitude	3	DDMM.MMM
Longitude	5	DDDMM.MMM
Velocity	7	VVV.V

Some caveats regarding the information in $GPRMC. We first turn to the timestamp of an arbitrary line:

```
>>> x[12]
['$GPRMC', '140055.00', 'A', '4454.1740', 'N', '09325.0143', 'W', '000.0', '128.7',
'300508', '001.1', 'E', 'A*28']
```

In this output, the timestamp appears as '140055.00'. This follows the format hhmmss.ss where hh are two digits representing the hour (it will always consist of two digits—if the hour is one digit, say 7 in the morning, a 0 will be added before it), mm are two digits representing the minute (again, always two digits), and ss.ss are five characters (four digits plus the dot) representing seconds and fractions of seconds. (There's also a North/South field as well as an East/West field. Here, for simplicity, we assume northern hemisphere, but you can easily change these values by reading the entire $GPRMC structure.)

■**Note** In the ISO time format, we've used HHMMSS to denote hours minutes and seconds. Here we follow the convention in NMEA, which uses hhmmss.ss for hours, minutes, and seconds and sets DD and MM to angular degrees and minutes.

The timestamp string is a bit hard to work with, especially when plotting data. The first reason is that it's a string, not a number. But even if you translated it to a number, the system does not lend itself nicely to plotting because there are 60 seconds in a minute, not a 100. So what we want to do is "linearize" the timestamp. To achieve this, we translate the timestamp as seconds elapsed since midnight, as follows: T = hh * 3600 + mm * 60 + ss.ss.

The second issue we have is that hh, mm, and ss.ss are strings, not numbers. Multiplying a string in Python does something completely different from what we want here. So we have to first convert the strings to numerical values, in our case, float, because of the decimal point in the string representing the seconds. This all folds nicely into the following:

```
>>> row = x[12]
['$GPRMC', '140055.00', 'A', '4454.1740', 'N', '09325.0143', 'W', '000.0', '128.7',
'300508', '001.1', 'E', 'A*28']
>>> float(row[1][0:2])*3600+float(row[1][2:4])*60+float(row[1][4:6])
50445.0
```

The operator [ ] denotes the index, so row[1] is the second field of row (counting starts at zero) which is a string. The first two characters of a string are denoted by [0:2]; this is known as *string slicing*. So to access the first two characters of the first field, we write row[1][0:2]. Upcoming chapters will include more about strings and methods of slicing them.

Next we tackle latitude and longitude. We face the same issue as with the timestamp, only here we deal with degrees. Latitude follows the format DDMM.MMM where DD stands for degrees and MM.MMM stands for minutes. We decide to use degrees this time. To translate the latitude into decimal degrees, we need to divide the minutes by 60:

```
>>> row = x[12]
['$GPRMC', '140055.00', 'A', '4454.1740', 'N', '09325.0143', 'W', '000.0', '128.7',
'300508', '001.1', 'E', 'A*28']
>>> float(row[3][0:2])+float(row[3][2:])/60.0
44.902900000000002
```

For latitude information we require the fourth field, hence row[3]. This example also introduces another notation, [2:], which means the slice of the string from the third character until the end. Also notice that the code uses 60.0 and not 60. When dividing by 60, it's implied that you want an integer division; dividing by 60.0 means you want a floating-point division, which is to say you care about the information past the decimal point. However, seeing as we already specified that we want the information as a floating-point number as indicated by the float() conversion, the result will be a floating point regardless. Still, it's good practice to let Python know what kind of division you really want.

Here are some examples to further illustrate the point:

```
>>> 100/60
1
>>> 100/60.0
1.6666666666666667
>>> float(100)/60
1.6666666666666667
```

Longitude information is similar to latitude with a minor difference: longitude degrees are three characters instead of two (up to 180 degrees, not just up to 90 degrees) so the indices to the strings are different.

Listing 1-6 presents the entire function to process GPS data.

Listing 1-6. *Function process_gps_data()*

```python
from pylab import *

# constant definitions
NMI = 1852.0

def process_gps_data(data):
    """Processes GPS data, NMEA 0183 format.

Returns a tuple of arrays: latitude, longitude, velocity [km/h],
time [sec] and number of satellites.
See also: http://www.gpsinformation.org/dale/nmea.htm."""

    latitude   = []
    longitude  = []
    velocity   = []
    t_seconds  = []
    num_sats   = []

    for row in data:
        if row[0] == '$GPGSV':
            num_sats.append(float(row[3]))
        elif row[0] == '$GPRMC':
            t_seconds.append(float(row[1][0:2])*3600 + \
                float(row[1][2:4])*60+float(row[1][4:6]))
            latitude.append(float(row[3][0:2]) + \
```

```
        float(row[3][2:])/60.0)
    longitude.append((float(row[5][0:3]) + \
        float(row[5][3:])/60.0))
    velocity.append(float(row[7])*NMI/1000.0)

return (array(latitude), array(longitude), \
    array(velocity), array(t_seconds), array(num_sats))
```

Some notes about the process_gps_data() function:

- NMI is defined as 1852.0, which is one nautical mile in meters and also one minute on the equator. The reason the constant NMI is not defined in the function is that we'd like to use it outside the function as well.

- We initialize the return values latitude, longitude, velocity, t_seconds, and num_sats by setting them to an empty list: []. Initializing the lists creates them and allows us to use the append() method, which adds values to the lists.

- The if and elif statements are self-explanatory: if is a conditional clause, and elif is equivalent to saying "else, if." That is, if the first condition didn't succeed, but the next condition succeeds, execute the following block.

- The symbol \ that appears on the several calculations and on the return line indicates that the operation continues on the next line.

- Lastly, the return value is a tuple of arrays. A *tuple* is an immutable sequence, meaning you cannot change it. So tuple means an unchangeable sequence of items (as opposed to a list, which is a mutable sequence). The reason we return a tuple and not a two-dimensional array, for example, is that we might have different lengths of lists to return: the length of the number of satellites list may be different from the length of the longitude list, since they originated from different header stamps.

Here's how you call process_gps_data():

```
>>> y = read_csv_file('../data\\GPS-2008-05-30-09-00-50.csv')
>>> (lat, long, v, t, sats) = process_gps_data(y)
```

The second line introduces sequence unpacking, which allows multiple assignments. Armed with all these functions, we're ready to plot some data!

Data Visualization

Our next step is to visualize the data. We'll be relying on the matplotlib package heavily. We've already imported matplotlib with the command from pylab import *, so there's no additional importing needed at the moment. It's time to read the data and plot the course.

Our first problem is that the information is given in latitude and longitude. Latitude and longitude are spherical coordinates, that is, those are points on a sphere, the earth. But we want a map-like plot, which uses Cartesian coordinates, that is, x and y. So first we have to transform the spherical coordinates to Cartesian. We'll use the quick-and-dirty method shown in Listing 1-7 to do this, one that's actually quite accurate as long as the distances traveled are small relative to the radius of the earth.

Listing 1-7. *"Quick-and-Dirty" Spherical to Cartesian Transformation*

```
x = longitude*NMI*60.0*cos(latitude)
y = latitude*NMI*60.0
```

To justify this to yourself, consider the following reasoning: As you go up to the North Pole, the circumference at the location you're at gets smaller and smaller, until at the North Pole it's zero. So at latitude 0º, the equator, each degree (longitude) means more distance traveled than at latitude 45º. That's why x is a function of the longitude value itself but also of the latitude: the greater the latitude, the smaller a longitude change is in terms of distance. On the other hand, y, which is north to south, is not dependent on longitude.

The next thing to understand is that the earth is a sphere, and whenever we plot an x-y map, we're only really plotting a projection of that sphere on a plane of our choosing, hence we denote it by (px,py), where p stands for "projection." We'll take the southeastern-most point as the start of the GPS data projection: (px,py) = (0,0). This translates into the code shown in Listing 1-8.

Listing 1-8. *Projecting the Traveled Course to Cartesian Coordinates*

```
py = (lat-min(latitude))*NMI*60.0
px = (long-min(longitude))*NMI*60.0*cos(D2R*latitude)
```

Some things to note:

- Variables py and px are arrays of floating-point values. We now operate on entire arrays seamlessly. This is part of the NumPy package.

- D2R is a constant equal to $\pi/180$, converting degrees to radians.

- To set the y-axis at the minimum latitude and the x-axis at the minimum longitude, we subtract the minimum latitude and minimum longitude values from latitude and longitude values, respectively.

GPS Location Plot

Now the moment we've been waiting for, plotting GPS data. To be able to follow along and plot data, be sure to define the functions read_csv_file() and process_gps_data() as previously detailed and set the file name variable to point to your GPS data file. I've suppressed matplotlib responses so that the code is cleaner to follow.

```
>>> filename = 'GPS-2008-05-30-09-00-50.csv'
>>> y = read_csv_file('../data/'+filename)
>>> (lat, long, v, t, sats) = process_gps_data(y)
>>> px = (long-min(long))*NMI*60.0*cos(D2R*lat)
>>> py = (lat-min(lat))*NMI*60.0
>>> figure()
>>> gca().axes.invert_xaxis()
>>> plot(px, py, 'b', label='Cruising', linewidth=3)
>>> title(filename[:-4])
>>> legend(loc='upper left')
>>> xlabel('east-west (meters)')
```

```
>>> ylabel('south-north (meters)')
>>> grid()
>>> axis('equal')
>>> show()
```

Figure 1-1 shows the result, which is rather pleasing.

Figure 1-1. *GPS data*

We've used a substantial number of new functions, all part of the matplotlib package: plot(), grid(), xlabel(), legend(), and more. Most of them are self-explanatory:

- xlabel(string_value) and ylabel(string_value) will print a label on the x- and y-axis, respectively. title(string_value) is used to print a caption above the graph. The string value in the title is the file name up to the end minus four characters (so as to not display ".csv"). This is done using string slicing with a negative value, which means "from the end."

- legend() prints the labels associated with the graph in a legend box. legend() is highly configurable (see help(legend) for details). The example plots the legend at the top-left corner.

- grid() plots the grid lines. You can control the behavior of the grid quite extensively.

- plot() requires additional explanation as it is the most versatile. The command plot(px, py, 'b', label='Cruising', linewidth=3) plots px and py with the color blue as specified by the character 'b'. The plot is labeled "Cruising" so later on, when we call the legend() function, the proper text will be associated with the data. Finally, we set the line width to 3.

- The function axis() controls the behavior of the graph axis. Normally, I don't call the axis() function because plot() does a decent job at selecting the right values. However, in this case, it's important to visualize the data properly, and that means to have both x- and y-axes with equal increments so the graph is true to the path depicted. This is achieved by calling axis('equal'). There are other values to control axis behavior as described by help(axis).

- Lastly, gca().axes.invert_xaxis() is a rather exotic addition. It stems from the way we like to view maps and directions. In longitude, increasing values are displayed from right to left. However, in mathematical graphs, increasing values are typically displayed from left to right. This function call instructs the x-axis to be incrementing from right to left, just like maps.

- When you're done preparing the graph, calling the show() function displays the output.

Matplotlib, which includes the preceding functions, is a comprehensive plotting package and will be explored in Chapter 6.

Annotating the Graph

We'd like to add some more information to the GPS graph: we'd like to know where we've stopped and where we were speeding. For this we use the function find(), which is part of the PyLab package. find() returns an array of indices that satisfy the condition, in our case:

```
>>> STANDING_KMH = 10.0
>>> SPEEDING_KMH = 50.0
>>> Istand = find(v < STANDING_KMH)
>>> Ispeed = find(v > SPEEDING_KMH)
>>> Icruise = find((v >= STANDING_KMH) & (v <= SPEEDING_KMH))
```

We also calculate when we're cruising (i.e., not speeding nor standing) for future processing.

To annotate the graph with these points, we add another plot on top of our current plot, only this time we change the color of the plot, and we use symbols instead of a solid blue line. The combination 'sg' indicates a green square symbol (g for green, s for square); the combination 'or' indicates a red circle (r for red, o for circle). I suggest you use different symbols for standing and speeding, not just colors, because the graph might be printed on a monochrome printer. The function plot() supports an assortment of symbols and colors; consult with the interactive help for details. The values we plot are only those returned by the find() function.

```
>>> plot(px[Istand], py[Istand], 'sg', label='Standing')
>>> plot(px[Ispeed], py[Ispeed], 'or', label='Speeding!')
>>> legend(loc='upper left')
```

Figure 1-2 shows the outcome.

Figure 1-2. *GPS data with additional speed information*

We'd also like to know the direction the car is going. To implement this, we'll use the text() function, which allows the writing of a string to an arbitrary location in the graph. So to add the text "Hi" at location (10, 10), issue the command text(10, 10, 'Hi'). One of the nice features of the text() function is that you can rotate the text at an arbitrary angle. So to plot "Hi" at location (10, 10) at 45 degrees, you issue text(10, 10, 'Hi', rotation=45). Our implementation of heading information involves rotating the text ">>>" at the angle the car is heading. We'll only do this ten times so as not to clutter the graph with ">" symbols. Calculating the direction the car is heading at a given point, i, is shown in Listing 1-9.

Listing 1-9. *Calculating the Heading*

```
dx = px[i+1]-px[i]
dy = py[i+1]-py[i]
heading = arctan(dy/dx)
```

Instead of actually using the function arctan(dy/dx), we'll use the function arctan2(dy, dx). The benefits of using arctan2() over arctan() are twofold: 1) there's no division that might cause a divide-by-zero exception in case dx is zero, and 2) arctan2() preserves the angle from –180 degrees to 180 degrees, whereas arctan() produces values between 0 degrees and 180 degrees only. The following code adds the direction symbols:

```
>>> for i in range(0, len(v), len(v)/10-1):
...     text(px[i], py[i], ">>>", \
...         rotation = arctan2(py[i+1]-py[i], -(px[i+1]-px[i]))/D2R, \
...         ha='center')
```

Figure 1-3 shows the resulting graph.

Figure 1-3. *GPS graph with heading*

Velocity Plot

We now turn to plotting a graph of the speed. This is a lot simpler:

```
>>> figure()
>>> t = (t-t[0])/60.0
>>> plot(t, v, 'k')
>>> plot([t[0], t[-1]], [STANDING_KMH, STANDING_KMH], '-g')
>>> text(t[0], STANDING_KMH, \
...     " Standing threshold: "+str(STANDING_KMH))
>>> plot([t[0], t[-1]], [SPEEDING_KMH, SPEEDING_KMH], '-r')
>>> text(t[0], SPEEDING_KMH, \
...     " Speeding threshold: "+str(SPEEDING_KMH))
>>> grid()
>>> title('Velocity')
>>> xlabel('Time from start of file (minutes)')
>>> ylabel('Speed (Km/H)')
```

We start by opening a different figure with the figure() command. We proceed by changing the timescale units to minutes, a value easier for most humans to follow than seconds. Selecting the proper units of measurement is important. Most people will find it easier to follow the sentence "I drove for 30 minutes" as opposed to "I drove for 1800 seconds." We also set the time axis to start at t[0]. Next we plot the velocity as a function of time, in black. Good graphs require annotation, so we choose to add two lines describing the thresholds for standing and speeding as well as text describing those thresholds. To generate the text, we combine the text "Standing threshold" with the threshold value (after casting it to a string) and use the + operator to concatenate strings. Last, of course, are the title, x and y labels, and grid. Figure 1-4 shows the final result.

Figure 1-4. *Velocity over time*

Subplots

We'd also like to display some statistics. But before we do that, it would be preferable to combine all these plots (GPS, velocity, and statistics) into one figure. To do this, we use the subplot() function. subplot() is a matplotlib function that divides the plot into several smaller sections called subplots and selects the subplot to work with. For example, subplot(1, 2, 1) informs subsequent plotting commands that the area to work on is 1 by 2 subplots and the currently selected subplot is 1, so that's the left side of the plot area. subplot(2, 2, 2) will choose the top-right subplot; subplot(2, 2, 4) will choose the lower-right subplot. A selection I found most readable in this scenario is to have the GPS data take half of the plot area, the velocity graph a quarter, and the statistics another quarter.

Text

Sometimes, the best way to convey information is using text, not graphics. We'll be limiting our work to the statistics quarter for this section. Our first task is to get rid of the plot frame and the x and y ticks. We just want a plain canvas to display text on. This is achieved by issuing the following:

```
>>> subplot(2, 2, 4)
>>> axis('off')
```

The first call to subplot() selects our region of work as the lower-right quarter. The second line removes the axes and hides the frame box.

It's time to calculate some statistics. It appears that GPS data is being sent in regular intervals, typically one second. So to calculate the time spent standing, in seconds, we calculate the length of the vector Istand. Likewise, to calculate the time speeding, we can calculate the length of Ispeed. To estimate how much these were in percent values, we divide the length of the Istand and Ispeed vectors by the length of the velocity vector and multiply by 100. To calculate the average speed, we use the mean() function, which is part of PyLab.

We also would like to calculate the total distance traveled. The distance can be calculated as the sum of the distances between each two consecutive data points. The function diff() returns a vector of the differences of the input vector.

```
>>> diff([1, 4, 0, 2])
array([ 3, -4,  2])
```

This is really useful because now to calculate the distance we can do the following:

```
>>> sum(sqrt(diff(px)**2+diff(py)**2))
1652.1444099624528
```

which in turn yields the total distance traveled.

To automate the whole process of printing the statistics, we store the text to be printed in the variable stats, a list of strings. We also use a method of formatting strings similar to C's printf() function, although the syntax is a bit different. %s indicates a string; the %f indicates a floating point number, in our case %.1f indicates a float with one digit after the decimal point; and %d indicates an integer. The following generates the statistics text:

```
>>> Total_distance = float(sum(sqrt(diff(px)**2+diff(py)**2))/1000.0)
>>> Stand_time  = len(Istand)/60.0
>>> Cruise_time = len(Icruise)/60.0
>>> Speed_time  = len(Ispeed)/60.0
>>> Stand_per   = 100*len(Istand)/len(v)
>>> Cruise_per  = 100*len(Icruise)/len(v)
>>> Speed_per   = 100*len(Ispeed)/len(v)
>>> stats=['Statistics', \
...     '%s' % filename, \
...     'Number of data points: %d' % len(y), \
...     'Average number of satellites: %d' % mean(sats), \
...     'Total driving time: %.1f minutes:' % (len(v)/60.0), \
...     '    Standing: %.1f minutes (%d%%)' % \
...     (Stand_time, Stand_per), \
...     '    Cruising: %.1f minutes (%d%%)' % \
...     (Cruise_time, Cruise_per), \
...     '    Speeding: %.1f minutes (%d%%)' % \
...     (Speed_time, Speed_per), \
...     'Average speed: %d km/h' % mean(v), \
...     'Total distance traveled: %.1f Km' % Total_distance ]
```

To print the text on the canvas, we again use the text() function, in a for loop, iterating over every string of the stats list.

```
>>> for index, stat_line in enumerate(reversed(stats)):
...     text(0, index, stat_line, va='bottom')
...
>>> plot([index-.2, index-.2])
>>> axis([0, 1, -1, len(stats)])
```

We've introduced two new functions. One is reversed(), which yields the elements of stats, in reversed order. The second is enumerate(), which returns not just each row in the stats array but also the index to each row. So when variable stat_line is assigned the value 'Average speed...', the variable index is assigned the value 8, which indicates the ninth row in stats. The reason we want to know the index is that we use it as location on the y-axis. Lastly, the vertical alignment of the text is selected as bottom as suggested by the parameter va='bottom' (va is short for vertical alignment).

Tying It All Together

Finally, Listing 1-10 shows the combined code to analyze and plot all GPS files in directory data.

Listing 1-10. *Script gps.py*

```
from pylab import *
import csv, os

# constant definitions
STANDING_KMH = 10.0
SPEEDING_KMH = 50.0
NMI = 1852.0
D2R = pi/180.0

def read_csv_file(filename):
    """Reads a CSV file and returns it as a list of rows."""

    data = []
    for row in csv.reader(open(filename)):
        data.append(row)
    return data


def process_gps_data(data):
    """Processes GPS data, NMEA 0183 format.

Returns a tuple of arrays: latitude, longitude, velocity [km/h],
time [sec] and number of satellites.
See also: http://www.gpsinformation.org/dale/nmea.htm.
    """
```

```
    latitude    = []
    longitude   = []
    velocity    = []
    t_seconds   = []
    num_sats    = []

    for row in data:
        if row[0] == '$GPGSV':
            num_sats.append(float(row[3]))
        elif row[0] == '$GPRMC':
            t_seconds.append(float(row[1][0:2])*3600 + \
                float(row[1][2:4])*60+float(row[1][4:6]))
            latitude.append(float(row[3][0:2]) + \
                float(row[3][2:])/60.0)
            longitude.append((float(row[5][0:3]) + \
                float(row[5][3:])/60.0))
            velocity.append(float(row[7])*NMI/1000.0)

    return (array(latitude), array(longitude), \
        array(velocity), array(t_seconds), array(num_sats))


# read every data file, filter, and plot the data
for root, dirs, files in os.walk('../data'):
    for filename in files:
        # create full file name including path
        cur_file = os.path.join(root, filename)
        if filename.endswith('csv'):
            y = read_csv_file(cur_file)
        else:
            continue

        # only files with the .csv extension from here on

        # process GPS data
        (lat, long, v, t, sats) = process_gps_data(y)

        # translate spherical coordinates to Cartesian
        py = (lat-min(lat))*NMI*60.0
        px = (long-min(long))*NMI*60.0*cos(D2R*lat)

        # find out when standing, speeding, or cruising
        Istand = find(v < STANDING_KMH)
        Ispeed = find(v > SPEEDING_KMH)
        Icruise = find((v >= STANDING_KMH) & (v <= SPEEDING_KMH))
```

```python
# left side, GPS location graph
figure()
subplot(1, 2, 1)

# longitude values go from right to left,
# we want increasing values from left to right
gca().axes.invert_xaxis()

plot(px, py, 'b', label=' Cruising', linewidth=3)
plot(px[Istand], py[Istand], 'sg', label=' Standing')
plot(px[Ispeed], py[Ispeed], 'or', label=' Speeding!')

# add direction of travel
for i in range(0, len(v), len(v)/10-1):
    text(px[i], py[i], ">>>", \
        rotation = arctan2(py[i+1]-py[i], \
            -(px[i+1]-px[i]))/D2R, ha='center')

# legends and labels
title(filename[:-4])
legend(loc='upper left')
xlabel('east-west (meters)')
ylabel('south-north (meters)')
grid()
axis('equal')

# top-right corner, speed graph
subplot(2, 2, 2)

# set the start time as t[0]; convert to minutes
t = (t-t[0])/60.0
plot(t, v, 'k')

# plot the standing and speeding threshold lines
plot([t[0], t[-1]], [STANDING_KMH, STANDING_KMH], '-g')
text(t[0], STANDING_KMH, \
    " Standing threshold: "+str(STANDING_KMH))
plot([t[0], t[-1]], [SPEEDING_KMH, SPEEDING_KMH], '-r')
text(t[0], SPEEDING_KMH, \
    " Speeding threshold: "+str(SPEEDING_KMH))
grid()

# legend and labels
title('Velocity')
xlabel('Time from start of file (minutes)')
ylabel('Speed (Km/H)')
```

```
        # right-side corner, statistics data
        subplot(2, 2, 4)

        # remove the frame and x-/y-axes. we want a clean slate
        axis('off')

        # generate an array of strings to be printed
        Total_distance = float(sum(sqrt(diff(px)**2+diff(py)**2)) \
            /1000.0)
        Stand_time  = len(Istand)/60.0
        Cruise_time = len(Icruise)/60.0
        Speed_time  = len(Ispeed)/60.0
        Stand_per   = 100*len(Istand)/len(v)
        Cruise_per  = 100*len(Icruise)/len(v)
        Speed_per   = 100*len(Ispeed)/len(v)
        stats=['Statistics', \
        '%s' % filename, \
        'Number of data points: %d' % len(y), \
        'Average number of satellites: %d' % mean(sats), \
        'Total driving time: %.1f minutes:' % (len(v)/60.0), \
        '     Standing: %.1f minutes (%d%%)' % \
        (Stand_time, Stand_per), \
        '     Cruising: %.1f minutes (%d%%)' % \
        (Cruise_time, Cruise_per), \
        '     Speeding: %.1f minutes (%d%%)' % \
        (Speed_time, Speed_per), \
        'Average speed: %d km/h' % mean(v), \
        'Total distance traveled: %.1f Km' % Total_distance ]

        # display statistics information
        for index, stat_line in enumerate(reversed(stats)):
            text(0, index, stat_line, va='bottom')

        # draw a line below the "Statistics" text
        plot([index-.2, index-.2])

        # set axis properly so all the text is displayed
        axis([0, 1, -1, len(stats)])
show()
```

Figure 1-5 shows the final results.

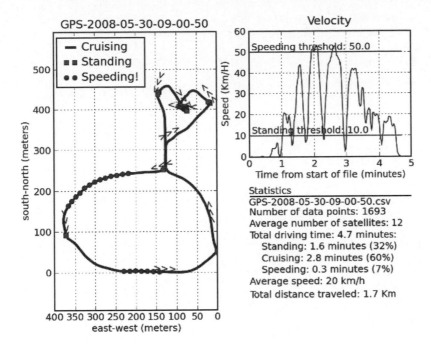

Figure 1-5. *Output of gps.py on some GPS data*

Final Notes and References

The GPS problem described here is research in nature: a computation, an intermediate result, not an end product. Research, or R&D work, especially feasibility studies, requires rapid responses. This means using readily available tools as much as possible and combining them to get the job done. If those tools are inexpensive, or free, that's yet another reason to use them.

Throughout the book, we will examine different packages and modules and see how they may be used to perform data analysis and visualization. The theme we'll be using is open software, including software published under the GNU Public License (GPL) and the Python Software Foundation (PSF) license. Examples of these tools include GNU/Linux and, of course, Python.

There are several benefits to developing data analysis and visualization scripts in Python:

- Developing and writing code is quick, appealing for research work.

- Readily available packages further increase productivity and ensure accurate results.

- Scripts introduce automation. Modifying an algorithm is easily done.

Scripts will be numerous and explained in detail, and I aim to cover most of the issues you are likely to encounter in the real world. Examples include scripts to deal with binary files, to combine data from different sources, to perform text parsing, to use high-level numerical algorithms, and much more. Scripts will be written in Python: some will be simple one-liners, others more complex. Special attention will be given to data visualization and how to achieve pleasing results in Python.

If you'd like to read more about Python in general (and not necessarily for data analysis and visualization), the Python official web site is an excellent resource:

- Python Programming Language—Official Website, `http://www.python.org`

CHAPTER 2

■ ■ ■

The Environment
Tools of the Trade

In the previous chapter we've seen a case study involving the collection, analysis, and visualization of GPS data. Unless you're already familiar with Python and the packages we've used, you should read this chapter and build yourself a development environment.

Analyzing and visualizing data requires several software tools: a text editor to write code, Python to run and test the scripts, and perhaps a tool to present the results.

I've decided to break the discussion of software tools into two categories: general-purpose software components and specific software components. The general-purpose software components are merely a recommendation on my part on tools I think improve productivity. If you're already comfortable with another software package, by all means use it over the one suggested here. The specific software components category, on the other hand, is composed of tools required to run the examples in the book. To clarify, whenever a component is a required component, it is clearly mentioned.

The following is a suggested list of software components that I feel provides a solid development environment.

General software components:

- An operating system (OS)

- A text editor

- An image viewer

- Tools for presenting and viewing the results

- A version control system

Specific software components:

- Python with its built-in packages

- Additional Python packages for data analysis and visualization

This chapter introduces the different software components in a linear fashion, that is, it builds things from the ground up—first the OS, then Python and Python packages, and lastly, supporting software components.

Although the chapter is organized in a linear fashion, feel free to skip the general software components section if you already know what applications you'll be using. You should, however, ensure you have the specific components (Python and additional packages) properly installed; code presented in the book assumes that is the case.

Operating Systems

The development environment is built upon an operating system. There are several options to choose from: UNIX-based operating systems (including GNU/Linux, Mac OS X, and others) and Windows. Of those, we'll focus on Linux and Windows. As for Mac OS, since it is a UNIX-based operating system, most of the discussions regarding Linux apply to it as well. The Python web site (http://www.python.org) is an excellent resource for all things Python, including supported operating systems.

GNU/Linux

Linux is a generic term that describes UNIX-like operating systems based on the Linux kernel. A Linux distribution is a collection consisting of the Linux kernel along with additional software packages that together provide a full OS. Most distributions provide more than a basic OS functionality; they provide additional software packages such as multimedia applications, games, office productivity suites, and much more. A considerable portion of the packages in most Linux distributions is based on the GNU project (http://www.gnu.org), hence the term GNU/Linux.

There is a large number of Linux distributions (distros) available today, including

- *Fedora project*: http://www.fedoraproject.org
- *Debian*: http://www.debian.org
- *Ubuntu*: http://www.ubuntu.com
- *Gentoo*: http://www.gentoo.org

Most of these are excellent distributions, so if you plan on going the Linux route, spend some time to acquaint yourself with these distributions to decide on the one that best suits your needs (or should I say best fits your personality?).

It is especially important that you know how to install applications in the Linux distribution of your choice. Most distributions come with a package management tool (e.g., rpm/Yum on Fedora, apt-get/APT on Debian, and emerge/Portage on Gentoo) that enables downloading applications and installing them on your Linux OS. Typically, package management tools synchronize with an online repository and enable downloading and upgrading software. They also take care of any version conflicts and perform the actual installation tasks such as copying files and updating system information.

As a general rule, opt for using your Linux distribution's built-in package management tool to install the software components discussed in this chapter, Python and packages included, over a manual install; this will ensure a stable Linux system.

In case a software application of your liking is not available via the package management tool of your Linux distribution, you still have the option of manually installing that application. This is not a trivial task and requires some Linux expertise. That being said, in the case of

Python packages, a manual install is straightforward, and an example will be provided later in the chapter in section "Manually Installing a Python Package."

Windows

Of the Windows versions available today, any version from Windows XP upward should be fine; previous flavors of Windows are growing obsolete, so support for applications running on older versions of Windows is limited. That being said, most applications still do run on older versions of Windows; however, you should check with the packages' online documentation.

Unlike Linux, after selecting Windows as the OS, there's still a decision to be made, and that is what exact environment Python will be running on. There are three main options to choose from:

- Stand-alone (natively)
- Cygwin
- Virtual machines (VMs)

Stand-Alone (Natively)

Unless you have a strong reason against it, this should be your preferred choice if you intend on using Windows: installing Python natively without an additional environment. Python comes as an executable file with an installer application. After downloading, double-click the executable and install Python (more on Python installation shortly). Most other packages we'll be dealing with also come bundled in this fashion, so installing them should be simple as well.

In case you'd like to install a package that doesn't come with an installer, you'll have to consult with that package's documentation. By the way, regardless of whether you choose a stand-alone approach or one of the other methods suggested next (or Linux), there are bound to be packages that require a manual installation, so knowing how to do a manual package install is of value.

Cygwin

Cygwin (http://www.cygwin.com) is an environment that runs in Windows and provides UNIX-like functionality. It is an excellent software product even if you are a devoted Windows user.

Cygwin comes with a GUI installer that runs on Windows named Cygwin Net Release Setup Program (setup.exe) that allows picking and installing software packages. The Cygwin installer is actually a package management tool just like any other package management tool in most Linux distributions. As you browse through the list of packages, you'll realize there's an extensive selection to choose from; however, that should not deter you. Install the default options knowing you can always go back and add or remove applications; it's as simple as rerunning the Cygwin installer. After installing Cygwin, run it via Start ➤ All Programs ➤ Cygwin ➤ Cygwin Bash Shell.

Cygwin provides a great number of additional open source software packages, including Python. If you want additional functionality—Bash shell, SSH, editors, viewers, version control systems, X functionality, and more—then Cygwin is an excellent choice. The downside is that it is a bit more complex for a less-experienced user than the stand-alone approach presented earlier. There's also a small performance hit using Cygwin compared with a native installation.

For example, on my computer, a simple for loop summing values was 20 percent slower in Python on Cygwin compared with a native Python installation.

■**Note** Cygwin treats drives differently from Windows as it follows a UNIX directory structure. If you installed Cygwin under c:\cygwin, then this directory is usually denoted as the topmost directory: /. To access directories outside c:\cygwin, use the following notation: /cygdrive/disk. For example, if a file is located in c:\data, it is accessible in Cygwin as /cygdrive/c/data.

Virtual Machines

The third option, which is a bit more exotic, is running a virtual machine (VM). A virtual machine allows the user to run a Linux OS (or another OS for that matter) in the host operating system, which is in this case Windows or Mac OS. This option is for the more experienced user: installing and configuring a VM is not an easy task.

On Windows, there are several VMs available today including the open source Cooperative Linux (coLinux, http://www.colinux.org) and the commercial VMware (http://www.vmware.com), which has a free version as well. A popular VM on Mac OS is Parallels (http://www.parallels.com), which allows for running both Linux and Windows alongside Mac OS.

■**Tip** Running a virtual machine might be a good option in case you just want to try out Linux in general but don't want to go the full route of installing an OS. If that is the case, there is also the option of running a live CD, which basically means booting a full-fledged Linux OS from CD-ROM. There's quite a large number of live CDs available today, with one of the well-known ones being Knoppix (http://www.knoppix.net).

INSTALLING COLINUX

As mentioned, installing a Linux VM in Windows is not a trivial task. The process involves several steps that require Linux and networking expertise. Here's a set of steps to install coLinux in Windows XP:

1. First, install coLinux with an image of the Linux distribution of your choice.

2. Set up Internet connectivity on the target OS (Linux) so that you can download and update packages. Update and install packages as needed.

3. Set up a networking connection between the host OS and the target OS so you can transfer data files.

VM packages nowadays, both commercial and open source, automate these tasks and make the installation a lot more user friendly.

One of the downsides of using a VM is that you pay a price in performance. That being said, VM implementations and the increasing power of computing have made this a relatively small price to pay.

Choosing an Operating System

From a data analysis and visualization perspective, Linux is a perfect match. The main reason is that Linux comes with a strong command-line interface (CLI) compared with Windows, which relies heavily on a graphical user interface (GUI).

Working with a significant number of files, CLI wins hands down. Consider renaming a large number of files, say, pictures you took on your last vacation. Most cameras generate files that follow a sequential naming scheme: DSB00001.jpg, DSB00002.jpg, and so forth, which is rather cryptic. You, on the other hand, would like to rename these files to something a bit more informative, such as Vacation2007-09-20-NNNNN.jpg, where NNNNN is the running index. So a file named DSB00002.jpg will now be named Vacation2007-09-20-00002.jpg. You can perform this task with both a GUI and a CLI:

- With the GUI approach, this means a task of point, click, and rename for each and every file. While this might be perfectly reasonable for a small number of pictures, as the number increases, this becomes a tedious task.

- The CLI approach is to write a command to rename all the files. If you're familiar with Bash, you might issue the following:

  ```
  $ for fn in DSB*.jpg; do mv $fn ${fn/DSB/Vacation2007-09-20-}; done
  ```

  (There are lots of ways to do it with a CLI, and this is just one I prefer. I will not be discussing Bash in the book.) Again, for a small number of pictures, this seems like overkill; however, once the number of files increases, this is the better approach.

Of course, renaming files is a simple task, one that Windows supports via its command prompt as well (which is the Windows version of a CLI), but even this simple task is not trivial in Windows, unless you install additional software or write some code to perform the task (although recent versions of Windows also introduce shell capabilities enabling both GUI and CLI interfaces). For more complex data management tasks, a CLI-centric approach is much better than a GUI. An operating system built around CLI is usually a better choice for managing data files.

■**Tip** There isn't a right or wrong, whatever OS you choose—the concepts (and code) presented in this book will work just fine.

Here are some things to consider when choosing an OS:

- Linux is a stable and able operating system. The benefits of using Linux include low cost (typically, none), solid CLI, and an active and supportive community. The main disadvantage with Linux is that if you're not familiar with the OS, there is a learning curve, although with today's distributions the curve has leveled off significantly. Also, support for hardware isn't as all-encompassing as is the case in Windows. This might prove a serious disadvantage if your work involves using an already existing piece of hardware that isn't supported in Linux to generate data.

- Windows is a widely popular operating system. Most users have experienced working in Windows to some degree, so the learning curve is very shallow, if any. Support for hardware is very good; most hardware vendors target Widows as their primary OS. The drawbacks of using Windows are lack of a strong CLI and cost of the OS and additional software applications.

- MacOS is gaining popularity: it combines the GUI experience with UNIX power. Although relatively new in the data analysis and visualization scene, due to those two traits, I have a feeling you'll see more and more of Mac OS being used. Mac OS downsides as I view them are cost and support for legacy hardware.

Table 2-1 summarizes the aforementioned pros and cons.

Table 2-1. *Linux, Windows, and Mac OS as Development Environments for Data Processing and Visualization*

	Linux	Windows	MacOS
CLI	Very good (native)	Good (with Python)	Very good (native)
Applications	Full (mostly free)	Full (possible additional cost)	Full (possible additional cost)
Learning curve	Steep	Gentle	Gentle
Cost	Low	Medium	Medium
Hardware support	Good	Very good	Medium
Stability	Very good	Very good	Very good

Then Again, Why Choose? Using Several Operating Systems

The nice thing about Python is that it eliminates the operating system from the equation. Python is a complete environment, with a "batteries-included" approach: you should be pretty much good to go, out of the box, after installing Python; the standard library provides full functionality. What that means is that all of a sudden, Windows has a strong CLI as well: the Python interpreter.

With that in mind, the selection of an OS becomes more of a personal preference than anything else. I have both Linux and Windows and use both for data analysis and visualization: my Linux machine is a stationary home server so I can't use it to record GPS data when driving; my laptop runs Windows and does that for me.

If you require more UNIX-like functionality than Python provides but would still like to use Windows, opt for Cygwin as discussed previously. Cygwin provides a host of GNU tools ported to Windows. In fact, I use Cygwin's X server and connect to my Linux machine if I'd like some interactive work-plotting data (the Linux machine is tucked under the desk and has no monitor).

If you plan on using both Windows and Linux to analyze data on the same computer, that is, dual-booting, think about how you're going to transfer data between the Linux and Windows partitions. There are several ways: having a shared partition that both Linux and Windows can handle (FAT32, NTFS on some), transferring files through a USB device, or even networking to another machine. Each has its benefits, but remember that you might be dealing with a large number of files, so it would be best if you could access the data on a shared resource.

■**Caution** Installing an OS is a time-consuming task, taking twice as long if you intend to dual-boot. You should consult with the Linux documentation of your distribution on how to best achieve dual-booting, and especially on what OS (Linux or Windows) you should install first. Dual-booting is an advanced topic and is not suggested for the beginner.

Using a dual-boot system can be annoying at times, especially since you have to reboot to switch operating systems. Not to mention that the installation process is a bit risky: there could be scenarios of lost data due to repartitioning of the hard disk (which can be avoided, if you know what you're doing). This is exactly why a VM is a good alternative: data is safe from repartitions, and actual reboots are not required. My PC is strong enough to run Linux as a VM in Windows with excellent performance. If you'd like to use this setup, again, think about how you're going to share data between the host OS and the target OS. A common (and good) approach is to transfer files using a virtual network interface.

On Mac OS, the need for these solutions is somewhat less required; Mac OS is already a UNIX-like OS.

The Python Environment

By now you should've already selected and installed the OS of your choice. You should also be comfortable with downloading and installing packages. It's now time to install Python. This section discusses the installation of Python and Python packages to enable programming data analysis and visualization scripts. A more detailed discussion on using Python both in an interactive shell and as a stand-alone application will be given in Chapter 3. In this chapter, I'll be covering Python distributions, Python IDEs, and Python packages.

Versions

The book covers Python version 2.5 and should work on version 2.4 as well. As a general rule, you should opt for the most updated Python version. Unfortunately, that's not always possible:

- Some operating systems, for example the Gentoo Linux distribution, rely heavily on Python for system administration, and upgrades require extensive testing to ensure the system is stable. So although a new release of Python becomes available, you might not be able to use it yet. There are workarounds to that such as installing several versions of Python on one machine; again, refer to your Linux distribution for further information, as this topic is beyond the scope of this chapter.

- At the time of writing, Python 2.6 was released. However, not all the packages used in the book have caught up yet, so I've had to stick with Python 2.5. We already know Python 3.0 is in the making, and a lot of the information regarding the upcoming changes can already be viewed on the Python web site (`http://www.python.org`). When applicable, I've tried to cover the differences between Python 2.6 and Python 3.0.

■**Tip** Always make sure you're downloading and installing a version of a package that is compatible with the version of Python you're using. Some packages keep older versions if you need them for compatibility reasons.

Python

You can download a Python implementation for your specific OS from `http://www.python.org/download/`. Read carefully and select the package that fits your OS. Again, if you're running a Linux OS, opt for using that system's package management tool over downloading and installing from the Python web site. The same applies for Cygwin: use the Cygwin installer if you can. On Windows, the common practice is to use the Python binaries distributed with an installer from the preceding URL.

You can install Python from source code, that is, download the source code and compile it on your OS. Personally, I have not found a reason to do this other than to satisfy my curiosity that the code does indeed compile properly.

If you are wondering about Jython (an implementation of Python written purely in Java, see `http://www.jython.org`) and IronPython (an implementation of Python on Microsoft's .NET platform, see `http://www.codeplex.com/Wiki/View.aspx?ProjectName=IronPython`), I'm afraid they're not good options for this book. A lot of the code and examples rely heavily on packages that do not run on Jython or IronPython.

Python Distributions with Scientific Packages

Another option is to use a Python distribution that already bundles a significant number of the Python packages we'll be using. Enthought Python Distribution (EPD, `http://www.enthought.com/`) and Python(x,y) (`http://www.pythonxy.com/`) provide Python distributions that should prove a good option if you don't want the hassle of installing individual packages. Opt for this option if you can't wait to be past the installation phase and up and running code.

■**Tip** If you choose the distribution from Enthought or Python(x,y), you can skip the sections related to SciPy, NumPy, matplotlib, and IPython later in the chapter. Both these distributions include those packages out of the box.

Python Integrated Development Environments

An integrated development environment (IDE) is, simply put, an application that helps programmers write code. Typically an IDE is composed of the language engine (Python), an editor, a debugger, documentation, and possibly additional productivity tools. While it is by all means possible to use Python without an IDE, using one will greatly increase your productivity and will enable a faster learning pace.

There is a wealth of Python IDEs, and a rather extensive list is provided in the books *Python in a Nutshell: A Desktop Quick Reference* and *Beginning Python: From Novice to Professional* (see the references at the end of this chapter). In this chapter, we'll limit our discussion to IDLE and IPython (which isn't really an IDE, more of a Python shell enhancement).

IDLE

IDLE (`http://www.python.org/doc/2.6/library/idle.html`) is a cross-platform Python GUI IDE. If you installed from Windows binaries, IDLE is automatically installed; access it via Start ➤ All Programs ➤ Python 2.5 ➤ IDLE (Python GUI). IDLE is a capable IDE with the following features: seamless integration with the Python interpreter, an editor, a debugger, and a help system. It's an excellent environment to get up and running, especially if you're new to programming.

One of the benefits of using IDLE is that you can write code in an editor, specifically designed for Python, and then quite easily execute it in IDLE by pressing F5. With a CLI approach, you'd have to invoke Python with the file you'd like to execute (more on this in Chapter 3).

IPython

As you start working with a CLI, you'll realize there are some things you'd really like enhanced. IPython (`http://ipython.scipy.org/`) provides an enhanced interactive Python shell and is highly recommended mostly because data analysis and visualization is interactive in nature. IPython is supported on most platforms. Here's a short list of the added features that come with IPython:

- Tab completion, which involves completion of variables, functions, methods, attributes, and file names. Tab completion is achieved with the GNU Readline library (`http://tiswww.case.edu/php/chet/readline/rltop.html`) and is highly addictive. It's very hard to go back to a regular CLI after you've been exposed to GNU Readline.

- Command history capabilities: issue the command `history` for a full account of the commands you've recently typed. You can copy and paste those into a Python script and save time and effort.

- Seamless integration with system shell: you can use `ls -l` or `cd /home/user`, for example.

- Colored output.

■**Note** IPython is not required but is highly recommended. The code in the book will work without IPython as well as with it.

IPython comes bundled with an installer for Windows and is available on most package management tools as well on Linux and Cygwin. Depending on your OS, you might need to install GNU Readline; on Windows, you'll also need to install PyReadline (`http://ipython.scipy.org/moin/PyReadline/Intro`). Consult with IPython's installation documentation.

■**Note** IPython should be installed after Python, GNU Readline, and PyReadline are installed.

CHARACTER COMPLETION WITH GNU READLINE

Character completion with GNU Readline is a welcomed addition to an interactive CLI. With IPython, character completion can be used to complete

- Names of variables

- Names of methods and attributes

- File names

To invoke character completion, start by spelling out the first few characters of the word you wish to write and then press the Tab key to have GNU Readline try and complete the word for you. The following is from IPython:

```
In [1]: s = "A string"
In [2]: s.is
s.isalnum s.isalpha s.isdigit s.islower s.isspace s.istitle s.isupper
In [2]: s.is
```

After typing **s.is**, the user pressed the Tab key and was presented with a list of options. Had the user spelled the word `s.isd` and pressed Tab, the entire `s.isdigit` would have appeared automatically at the prompt.

The way GNU Readline works is that it tries to complete the word by searching for a variable, function, method, attribute, or file name that matches the typed characters. In case of one option, that word is automatically spelled out at the prompt. In case of several options, all the options are displayed. To select which of the options you'd rather have completed, supply the next character and then press Tab again. In case of no matches to the typed word, nothing happens.

You can also use the character completion feature to explore methods and attributes of a class, or any other namespace for that matter. In the following listing, the Tab key is pressed after a. is entered (notice the dot).

```
In [1]: a = dict()


In [2]: a.
a.__class__          a.__hash__         a.__setattr__      a.itervalues
a.__cmp__            a.__init__         a.__setitem__      a.keys
a.__contains__       a.__iter__         a.__str__          a.pop
a.__delattr__        a.__le__           a.clear            a.popitem
a.__delitem__        a.__len__          a.copy             a.setdefault
a.__doc__            a.__lt__           a.fromkeys         a.update
a.__eq__             a.__ne__           a.get              a.values
a.__ge__             a.__new__          a.has_key          a.pdf
a.__gctattribute__   a.__reduce__       a.items
a.__getitem__        a.__reduce_ex__    a.iteritems
a.__gt__             a.__repr__         a.iterkeys
```

Scientific Computing

A significant portion of the book is dedicated to the processing of data prior to visualization. Two packages help us achieve that end: NumPy and SciPy. NumPy will be discussed in Chapter 7, and SciPy will be reviewed in Chapter 8. These two packages, combined with matplotlib (more on this package shortly) behave similarly to most high-end math packages such as the open source GNU Octave (http://www.octave.org) and the commercial MATLAB (http://www.mathworks.com). In fact, there's even a name for these three packages working together: PyLab, which is a combination of Python and MATLAB. A portal for SciPy and NumPy is located at http://www.scipy.org.

SciPy, NumPy, and matplotlib are all open source software packages and are required to run the code presented in the book.

NumPy

NumPy provides a powerful N-dimensional array that is the basis for most of the data processing we'll perform. You've already seen it in action in the GPS example in Chapter 1. NumPy also provides additional numerical capabilities: linear algebra, Fourier transforms, and more.

NumPy is a mature and stable package and can be downloaded and installed from http://numpy.scipy.org/. NumPy will be discussed in Chapter 7 and Chapter 8.

SciPy

SciPy builds on top of NumPy and adds additional scientific computing tools. These include numerical integration, differential equations, interpolation, signal processing, optimization, linear algebra, and more.

Even if you're not interested in scientific computing, I encourage you to give SciPy a try—it provides additional utility functions to NumPy that are very useful and used extensively in the book.

SciPy can be downloaded and installed from http://www.scipy.org/ and will be reviewed in Chapter 8.

■**Note** SciPy relies on NumPy and should be installed after NumPy is installed.

Plotting

Visualization is the final step, displaying data graphically to the audience, portraying an idea, and capturing information efficiently and elegantly. We now turn to two packages that allow easy plotting and graphing.

Matplotlib

Plotting throughout the book will rely heavily on the matplotlib package, maintained at http://matplotlib.sourceforge.net/. Matplotlib is a 2-D plotting package that interfaces well with NumPy and SciPy. The package is cross-platform and works on Linux, Windows, and Mac OS.

Matplotlib can produce both interactive and hard-copy plots using various engines. You can therefore use it both for interactive work, which is very useful in the early stages of an algorithm design; or you can use it in an automatic mode, for example, batch processing, to plot results to, say, a shared directory or a web server.

Matplotlib is both simple to use and highly customizable, yielding an excellent package for our purposes. It allows a range of 2-D plot types and has excellent graph annotation capabilities.

■**Tip** Matplotlib has some additional toolkits available, out of which the one that is of interest especially in light of Chapter 1 is the basemap toolkit. The basemap toolkit allows working with map projections. I will not be covering the basemap toolkit in this book.

Gnuplot

An alternative package suggested here is gnuplot (http://www.gnuplot.info/). Gnuplot is a widely popular plotting package that has been ported to numerous platforms including Linux, Windows, and Mac OS. This renders gnuplot a very good graphing and plotting package. Gnuplot also supports both interactive and hard-copy graphs.

One of the benefits of gnuplot over matplotlib is 3-D graph support. If you require such capabilities, opt for gnuplot.

In order to use gnuplot interactively from the Python CLI, a software package to connect the two is required. I have used the Gnuplot.py package (`http://gnuplot-py.sourceforge.net/`) to do so with good results.

■Note   To use gnuplot from Python, be sure to install both gnuplot and Gnuplot.py. After installing Gnuplot.py, you'll have to set the variable `Gnuplot.GnuplotOpts.gnuplot_command` to point to the location of the gnuplot binary executable. Alternatively, you can edit a configuration file to permanently set this variable; consult with Gnuplot.py's documentation. In Windows, you'll also require `pgnuplot.exe`, which is a part of gnuplot for Windows and allows sending commands to wgnuplot (the Windows version of the gnuplot application).

As mentioned previously, most of the examples in the book rely on matplotlib, so you'll need to modify the code if you wish to use gnuplot solely. Unless you have a strong reason not to use matplotlib, or that gnuplot is already installed on your system and heavily used, I suggest you stick with matplotlib.

Image Processing

Image processing provides the final piece of the puzzle. It is an important part of data visualization and will be discussed extensively in Chapter 9. We'll be using the Python Imaging Library (PIL) to provide image processing support.   *285*

Python Imaging Library

The Python Imaging Library (`http://www.pythonware.com/products/pil/`) enhances Python with excellent image processing capabilities. PIL supports most popular image file formats and provides a wealth of functions for manipulating image data. PIL, combined with NumPy, provides a very capable image processing environment for Python.

Additional Python Packages

Numerous Python packages are available, and more are being written every day. The following are good sources of information on Python packages:

- *The Python Package Index*: `http://pypi.python.org/pypi`
- *SourceForge*: `http://www.sourceforge.net`

PySerial

In Chapter 1 we used pySerial to capture GPS data through the serial port. PySerial is available at `http://pyserial.wiki.sourceforge.net/pySerial`.

■**Note** In Windows, you will also need to install the Python Win32 Extensions (win32all) from `http://python.net/crew/mhammond/win32/Downloads.html` as well as possibly a real-time library. Consult the pySerial and Python Win32 Extensions documentation.

Example: Manually Installing a Python Package

As mentioned previously, some Python packages do not come with a stand-alone installer. In that case, you'll have to perform a manual install. Not to worry, this is easier than it sounds.

As a general rule, it's best to read the documentation and follow the instructions. That being said, most Python packages require a similar set of steps to install:

1. Download the package.

2. Unpack the package to a temporary directory. Most packages are distributed as compressed files, with extensions such as `.tar.gz` or `.zip`, or even self-extracting `.exe` files. You'll need to unpack the package to a temporary directory. (Occasionally, files having the extension `.tar.gz` are downloaded as `.tar.tar`. If that is the case, rename the file with the extension `.tar.gz` and continue to unpack as you normally would.)

3. Run `python setup.py install` in the temporary directory. Of course, this has to be done after Python is installed and working properly on your system.

The following documents the steps I took to install pySerial on Cygwin:

```
$ tar zxvf pyserial-2.4.tar.gz
$ cd pyserial-2.4
$ python setup.py install
```

The first command unpacks the downloaded file to a newly created directory named `pyserial-2.4`; the creation of the new directory is done automatically by the application tar and is reported to the user. In case you're running Windows (and not Cygwin), you can use a native Windows utility, such as 7-Zip (`http://www.7-zip.org/`), to unpack the files; the tar application is available in Linux and usually comes preinstalled with the OS. The second command changes directory to the temporary directory. The third command performs the installation and ensures the package is properly installed.

You can also use the setuptools package (which includes the easy_setup tool), available from `http://peak.telecommunity.com/DevCenter/setuptools`, for better control over installing and maintaining packages, especially packages that depend on other packages. Another benefit of the package is that you can also install Python packages without worrying about root (superuser) permissions.

Installation Summary

Table 2-2 summarizes the Python packages discussed previously and indicates which software is required to run the examples in the book.

Table 2-2. *Package Installation Summary*

Software/Package	Functionality	Required?
Python	Python programming language	Yes
IDLE	Python IDE	No
IPython, Readline	Python CLI enhancements	No
NumPy	N-dimensional arrays and math package	Yes
SciPy	Scientific tools	Yes
Matplotlib	Plotting and graphing package	Yes
Gnuplot, gnuplot.py	Plotting and graphing package	No
PIL	Python Imaging Library	Partial (Chapter 9)
PySerial	Serial interface	Partial (Chapter 1)

Additional Applications

By now you should have a working development environment that includes the OS of your choice, Python, and Python packages. We now turn to additional software applications to complete an environment for developing and running data analysis and visualization scripts in Python.

This section suggests tools to augment the development environment from the open source software world. While there are excellent commercial applications as well, I will not be covering those. The suggested applications are perfectly good for me, but you might have your own preference, even an application that's not mentioned here. By all means, use your favorite; this section is mostly intended for those who require some starting points.

Editors

The number one tool in a developer's arsenal is a text editor. Think of it as your Swiss Army knife: it can be used to read, write, or modify scripts, view data files, as a scratchpad for ideas, as a clipboard for intermediate copy and paste, and more. Basic text editors will soon frustrate you as some are limited in the size of files they can edit, others do not allow several open files, and yet others are missing syntax highlighting or bookmark capabilities.

Selecting the Proper Editor for You

Editors play a major role in your development environment. There's a bit of a learning curve with a new editor, so consider the following points when you select a text editor or switch from your current one.

- *Ease of use*: This one is obvious. Is the editor easy to use and intuitive? Is there a learning curve, and if so, how long will it take you to master?

- *Multiple file editing*: You might be dealing with a considerable number of script files or even examining data files in the editor. Having one application deal with all these files removes clutter from your desktop and is generally easier to handle.

- *Maximum file size*: What's the largest file you can open in the editor? Again, useful when you'd like to view large data files.

- *Syntax highlighting*: Syntax highlighting is a feature that displays reserved or specific syntax of a programming language in a different color or font so that the code is easier to view. Most editors that support syntax highlighting have built-in support for several programming languages, including Python. This feature is handy as it will highlight possible syntax errors as well as make the code more readable.

- *Line numbering*: Errors and warnings typically return line information where they occurred. Therefore, being able to know what line caused an error without counting lines is important. Some editors also support a jump-to-line command, which can be useful if your code is long. Lastly, line numbers are helpful when communicating with another person.

- *Most recently used files list*: This is a nice feature that allows you to easily access one of the files you've recently viewed or edited, without specifying its full path.

- *Bookmarks*: Bookmarks allow easy navigation and are especially useful with large files.

- *Macro support and macro recording*: Macros and the ability to record and play back macros can boost productivity (see the sidebar "Recording Macros").

- *Autocompletion*: This feature is similar to character completion, described previously in the sidebar "Character Completion in Readline" (but usually with a different keystroke, such as Ctrl+space). It can boost productivity but requires some getting used to.

- *Other features*: The preceding is a list of features I consider important. You might have different needs and different requirements, so jot them down and use those to select the proper editor for you.

RECORDING MACROS

Macro recorders are a quick and effective way to perform automation without actually writing code. Suppose you want to combine every two consecutive lines in a file into one line with && symbols in between. This is not easily done with a search and replace (unless your search and replace also supports new-line characters). Of course, you could write a Python script to do this, but let's suppose in this particular case there's no point in automation simply because you'll only do it once. This is exactly where you would use a macro recorder.

First, move your cursor to the beginning of the file (or press Ctrl+Home on some editors to get there). Now start your macro recorder and perform the following actions: press End to reach the end of the line, press Del to delete the line separator and combine the two lines into one long line, type **&&**, move down one line with the down arrow, and press Home to get to the beginning of the next line. Stop your macro recorder to finish the recording of your macro. This sequence combines two lines into one, adding && in between. Note that I've used the keyboard and not the mouse; this is important, as most macro recorders in editors don't support mouse recording.

Next, run the macro N times where N is the number of lines in the file divided by 2 (remember you combine two lines per run). Or you can run that macro for each pair of lines you want to combine. Some editors have the option to run the macro to the end of file. The following figure shows a macro recorder in Notepad++.

The macro is highly reliant on the location of the cursor. If you move the cursor to the end of the file and run the macro, you might get some unintended results.

A Short List of Text Editors

Table 2-3 presents a short list of some popular text editors. Use this table as a starting point in selecting an editor. This is by all means not a comprehensive list of available editors, so shop around and use the Internet to find more.

Table 2-3. *Short List of Open Source Editors*

Editor	OS/Environment	Notes
Notepad++ http://notepad-plus.sourceforge.net/	Windows	Has all the features described previously in the chapter and more. Downside: available only in Windows, sorry Linux folks.
SciTE Scintilla Text Editor http://www.scintilla.org/SciTE.html	Windows, X	A very good text editor, especially if you're developing on both Windows and X: you can use one editor for both platforms. Lacks in the number of open files and macro recording capabilities.
GNU Emacs http://www.gnu.org/software/emacs/	Windows, Linux, X, Cygwin, Mac OS	A very rich editor. Runs on most any platform including text-based CLI (Linux), X, and Windows as well as Cygwin. Has a bit of a learning curve if you're new to Emacs.
Vim http://www.vim.org	Windows, Linux, X, Cygwin, Mac OS	A very rich editor that runs on most any platform; has most of the features described previously and more (e.g., hex editor).
GNU Nano http://www.nano-editor.org/	Linux, Cygwin, DOS	A text-based (nongraphical) lightweight editor. Missing some features but makes up for that in size and performance. A good candidate when writing code over a telnet or SSH connection.

A BINARY EDITOR

At times it proves useful to edit binary files as well (see Chapter 10 for discussion of binary files). Binary files typically cannot be viewed nor edited using regular editors (with maybe the exception of Vim). Hexedit (http://people.mandriva.com/~prigaux/hexedit.html) is a useful utility that allows editing of binary files. It displays the hex values as well as their ASCII representation (if such is available) and allows editing of both the hexadecimal and ASCII values. I wouldn't recommend writing binary files in hexedit, rather using it to tweak or modify binary files. Hexedit is available with most Linux distributions as well as Cygwin. To invoke hexedit, issue the following:

```
$ hexedit filename
```

While in hexedit, pressing F1 will bring up a help screen. To exit hexedit without saving, press Ctrl+C.

Spreadsheets

Spreadsheets are excellent tools for data processing and visualization. The ease in which a user can import data from various file formats, organize it, and generate graphs is outstanding.

CSV, a most useful file format, is supported by virtually all spreadsheet applications. CSV files are used extensively in data analysis and visualization, and being able to edit them easily is a great benefit of spreadsheets.

Most spreadsheets come equipped with additional tools such as linear regression, statistical computations, financial functions, and more. A more experienced user may be able to use macros to automate tasks or to update results when new data is entered. Because of these features, spreadsheets will definitely complement your development environment.

Spreadsheets are not ideal for data processing. They're designed with an interactive point-and-click (GUI) user in mind, which makes them less natural at script automation. They're also limited in the amount of data they can process—you typically have to open the entire file in the spreadsheet, and with large files that's an issue. Lastly, they lack inherent documentation—it's hard to capture and document the steps you took to reach a result.

Therefore, we will not be using spreadsheets in this book; however, I will mention their usage when appropriate. For example, it is of value to know how to export and import data to and from spreadsheets.

The following are open source spreadsheet applications:

- Gnumeric (http://www.gnome.org/projects/gnumeric/) is part of the GNOME desktop environment project.

- Calc (http://www.openoffice.org/) is part of the OpenOffice.org project and is available on most platforms.

Word Processors

Finally, it might be of value to write a report or a presentation, displaying the results of your work. And you might want to publish the results in HTML or PDF format. Again, several open source applications are available, most notably the following:

- AbiWord (http://www.abisource.com/) is a word processing application available for Windows, GNU/Linux, and Mac OS.

- Write (http://www.openoffice.org/) is part of the OpenOffice.org project and is available on most platforms.

Image Viewers

If you plan on performing image processing tasks, an image viewing utility is required. Even if you're not really performing an image processing task, for example, generating a hard-copy graph in known file formats such as PNG and JPG, an image viewing utility is still a must.

Windows has built-in support for most popular image formats. On Linux, both GNOME and KDE desktop environments come with built-in image viewers. Plus, it's possible to open an image using a web browser both on Windows and Linux, as browsers also support most image formats.

Point of the matter: no need to install anything. Use your OS image viewer or web browser.

Version Control Systems

Version control systems (VCSs) enable management of several revisions of a document (or documents) with full history, tagging, and date capabilities. Most packages also support several developers working together simultaneously on the same file.

A VCS allows going back to a previous working version, or checking the difference between the current version and an older one, or even viewing a version of the document based on date. It might hold such information as who edited the file or the tag assigned to the document to mark its status.

A VCS is increasingly recognized as a required tool for a team of developers. But there's also a case to be made for even one developer. These management systems are growing in popularity and for a good reason: they save time and help manage software projects. For this reason, they're good software to enhance your development environment.

The downside of using a VCS is that it's not trivial to master and perhaps should be postponed until after you're comfortable with your programming environment. To help offset the complexity involved with VCSs, some also provide a GUI front end.

WORKING WITH A VERSION CONTROL SYSTEM

In a nutshell, working with a version control system can be described as follows:

1. **Check-out** the project: create a local copy of the most updated version of the documents.

2. **Modify** your local copy: edit source code, fix bugs, and add features.

3. **Review** your changes: make sure the right files are modified.

4. **Commit** changes: save the changes you've made in the version control repository.

When you check out a document from the VCS repository, the system ensures you have the most updated version to work with. This is typically done once, and from here on you edit your local copy. You then modify your document, and once you're satisfied with the results, review the changes. Reviewing the changes can be done by performing a `diff` of the file you have with the copy in the repository. You then commit your changes (also known as checking in) and possibly add a description of the changes. Subsequent modifications follow steps 2 through 4.

The version control system notifies you in case of a conflict. For example, suppose you checked out version 1 of the document, but by the time you wish to commit your changes, another developer has already checked in his version of the document: the system will alert you of a possible conflict, because you're trying to update a document which is now version 2, whereas you were working on version 1.

The system also maintains a full history of the project. So even if you're the only person working on a project, the ability to go back to previous versions of the project is as simple as checking out an older revision. Most systems allow checking out of documents based on date, revision, or even a tag that you've previously supplied. Because the system maintains such a complete history, most developers feel that you should commit changes as often as possible— you won't be negatively affecting "good" releases.

One final note: if you can, choose to use text files over binary files. Performing a `diff` on text files is supported by most VCS systems and is a valuable tool. With the binary version of the file (e.g., an executable), a `diff` yields very little information other than that the current version is not identical to the one in the repository.

Here's a set of commands I often use, working on a local copy I'm continually editing, once I'm done editing my local copy. With Mercurial, I issue

```
$ hg status
$ hg commit filename
$ hg push
$ hg update
```

The first command checks the status of the project: which files are modified. The second and third commands check in the local copy and update the repository (where Mercurial stores the files). The last command ensures I have the most updated version of the project in my local directory.

In CVS, I follow a similar set of commands:

```
$ cvs diff
$ cvs commit
$ cvs update
```

Here are some pointers to several open source VCS software applications:

- CVS (http://www.nongnu.org/cvs/) is a widely popular system with several graphical user interfaces including web-based ones.

- Subversion (http://subversion.tigris.org/) is another widely popular system available on most platforms.

- Mercurial (http://www.selenic.com/mercurial/wiki/) is a lightweight VCS package designed for distributed projects.

Example: Directory Structure for the Book

In the process of writing this book, I've used a VCS system to control the documents, images, source code, and data for each chapter. I've used the following directory structure: each chapter has a directory of its own named ChXX, with XX being the chapter number. Within each directory corresponding to a chapter, I've added four additional directories named doc, data, images, and src. My actual writing was placed in directory doc; my data files in directory data; images (such as those embedded in documents) in directory images; and source code in directory src.

```
Book
    Ch1
        data
        images
        src
        doc
    Ch2
        data
        images
        src
        doc
    ...
```

Another side benefit of this directory structure is that it is helpful in envisioning how a project will look. If there's something important you realized in the first piece of code (in my case, the first chapter) but it doesn't really belong there, simply dump the ideas and code in the relevant directory for future processing.

> **■Tip** This directory structure is also apparent in the source code listing. Since the source code resides in directory ChXX/src, and data files reside in directory ChXX/data, the relative path to directory data is ../data. Similarly, the relative path to directory images is ../images.

The reason I decided on using a VCS system for the book is quite simple. I've handed over documents of various revisions to editors, I've revisited others, and I've sent reviewers yet a different version. Some would return responses to a revision that I've already updated, and so I had to know what document they've edited. If you think about it, in a sense, there were really several developers for one document, and managing them all is a lot easier with a version control system.

Licensing

Most of the software described in the chapter is open source and free (with the obvious exception of Windows and other commercial packages: MATLAB and VMware, to name a couple). That being said, there are limitations on what you can do with open source software, especially if you intend on distributing your applications. Several software licenses exist, and I urge you to read each and every one. The same applies for commercial software: ensure you read the license agreement.

The following is a list of some of the license agreements of the software described in this chapter. It is neither complete nor comprehensive, and the licenses might change with time, so be sure to check the most recent license documentation.

- *GNU licenses, including GPL and LGPL, which cover a substantial number of the packages described in this chapter*: http://www.gnu.org/licenses/licenses.html

- *Linux distributions licenses*: Refer to the respective web page of the distribution of your choice

- *Cygwin*: Refer to the license documents installed in Cygwin, usually under c:\cygwin\usr\share\doc\common-licenses as well as http://www.redhat.com/software/cygwin/

- *VMware*: http://www.vmware.com/

- *Python*: http://www.python.org/psf/license/

- *Enthought (EPD)*: http://www.enthought.com/products/epdlicense.php

- *IPython*: http://ipython.scipy.org/

- *Matplotlib*: http://matplotlib.sourceforge.net/users/license.html

- *SciPy and NumPy*: http://www.scipy.org/License_Compatibility

- *Python Imaging Library (PIL)*: http://www.pythonware.com/products/pil/license.htm

- *PySerial*: http://pyserial.svn.sourceforge.net/

- *Python Windows extensions (win32all)*: refer to the license agreement as part of the package.

- *Scintilla and SciTE*: http://scintilla.sourceforge.net/License.txt

- *Subversion*: http://subversion.tigris.org/

Final Notes and References

By now you should have a full development environment, one that provides all the tools of the trade. Experiment with your environment, get accustomed to it; in the following chapters you'll be using it extensively.

The following provide additional useful information in building a Python development environment should you want to investigate some more:

- *Beginning Python: From Novice to Professional, Second Edition,* by Magnus Lie Hetland (Apress, 2008)

- *Python in a Nutshell: A Desktop Quick Reference, Second Edition* by Alex Martelli (O'Reilly, 2006)

## CHAPTER 3

Python for Programmers
The Building Blocks

Python is a very readable language. Assuming you've had some previous experience in programming, you should be able to read the code presented in the book without much trouble; you'll understand what's going on.

That being said, the book would be incomplete without coverage of the Python programming language. From a book-design perspective, it stands to reason that this chapter appears in the beginning. But that shouldn't bind you; feel free to skip it and come back to it later.

Furthermore, this chapter does not cover the full extent of the language. Some Python topics that I felt were not crucial for data analysis and visualization were left out of scope. If you would like to learn more about the Python programming language, I've listed several books in the "Final Notes and References" section at the end of the chapter; these books are all Python oriented and should prove valuable resources.

Now to the chapter itself: I'll be taking you quickly through the Python building blocks and complement the discussion with short examples. We'll start by going through the basics of invoking and using Python interactively and noninteractively, entering expressions, and running scripts. We then look at the basic building blocks of most modern programming languages: data types, structures, variables, printing, flow control, and functions. We continue with a brief discussion of object-oriented programming (OOP) and finalize with a discussion of modules and packages.

What Is Python?

Python is an open source, object-oriented, high-level programming language. This is a rather vague definition; if you're looking for a more accurate one, have a look at `http://www.python.org/` and `http://www.python.org/about/`. That being said, I think it's easier to show what Python is, rather than try and define it. This really is the purpose of this book in a narrow sense: using Python effectively for data analysis and visualization and not just learning Python for the purpose of knowing the language.

Python seemed to have developed a culture around it. You'll find such notions as "Pythonic" or "Easier to Ask Forgiveness than Permission" (EAFP) or the "batteries included" approach—all of which shows that Python is more than just a programming language.

It is rumored that many developers first use the language as a simple tool to solve a specific problem, but with time they are absolutely captivated to the point they start writing haikus in Python. I'm afraid I'm not that artistic, so you won't be seeing any haikus in here.

Here are the language features I view as the most important for the topics presented in the book:

- *Open source*: Yes, I view this as one of the fundamental aspects about Python. Python, and its packages, have been developed by an active community. The language evolves and changes, providing a dynamic environment built on discussion, on actual needs, on real problems people have to solve. I think this approach ensures a good language that hopefully will withstand the test of time.

- *Ease of learning*: It's easy to learn Python, especially if you're familiar with other programming languages—Python combines the best of several programming languages and programming paradigms in one.

- *"Batteries included"*: Python includes a great number of libraries as part of the standard library (several will be explored in this book). Additional packages can be installed and used seamlessly. You should be able to do most, if not all, of the work associated with data analysis and visualization without ever leaving the Python environment.

- *Versatility*: Python is versatile in that it supports both the early stages of development, as a rapid application development tool, and later phases of the project, when more structured programming paradigms are required.

- *Interactive nature*: More about this in the next section.

Interactive Python

The ability to run Python interactively, with a command-line interface (CLI), is an envious ability. The CLI allows both understanding of the workings of the programming language as well as your code as you write it. It's not a new concept, and personally, the first programming environment I ever used was also interactive in nature: Basic in Sinclair's ZX-81 (see `http://en.wikipedia.org/wiki/Zx-81` for some nostalgia). At times, when I write C code, I just wish I could do the same . . .

The interactive nature of Python is elegantly introduced in Guido van Rossum's "Python Tutorial" available at `http://docs.python.org/tut/tut.html` (Guido van Rossum is Python's creator). Nevertheless, here's a short introduction to running Python interactively, from a data analysis and visualization perspective.

Invoking Python

How you invoke Python depends on your platform:

- In Windows, assuming you've installed the binaries, click Start ➤ All Programs ➤ Python 2.5 ➤ Python (command line) or IDLE (Python GUI) if you prefer a GUI environment. You might have a newer version by now.

- In Windows, under Cygwin, start a Cygwin bash shell and issue the following command:

  ```
  $ python
  ```

- In Linux, open a terminal and issue the same command:

  ```
  $ python
  ```

To exit Python, either press Ctrl+D or enter

```
>>> exit()
```

Entering Commands

After starting Python in interactive mode, you're presented with version information along with a short list of introductory commands, help, copyright, credits, and license, and the Python prompt >>>.

■**Note** Whenever you encounter the >>> prompt in any listings in the book, it is meant to indicate that the command was issued interactively with the Python interpreter, and you should try it yourself by repeating the same commands in your Python interpreter. Similarly, when you encounter three dots (...) at the beginning of a line of code, it means that this is a continuation of the text entered interactively in the previous line.

Issue any of the these commands by entering the command name and pressing Enter (from now on, I'll refrain from mentioning to press Enter or discussing how to erase characters; I assume you know how to use a CLI). Here's the output from issuing the help command:

```
>>> help
Type help() for interactive help, or help(object) for help about object.
```

Python's CLI allows entering statements and evaluating expressions. Some basic ones are described here. Try them to get a feel for the interactive nature of Python:

```
>>> 1+2+3+4+5+6+7+8+9
45
>>> 22*2
44
>>> a = 4
>>> a*4
16
>>> 'a'*4
'aaaa'
>>> sqrt(a)
Traceback (most recent call last):
  File "<stdin>", line 1, in <module>
NameError: name 'sqrt' is not defined
```

The first couple of lines use Python to do basic arithmetic. One of the nice benefits of using interactive Python as opposed to using a calculator is that you can edit your previous entries very easily. Plus, you can retrace your steps and find a typo. But that's hardly the reason for using Python, just an added bonus.

The third line is an assignment: we assign the value 4 to the variable a. The next line prints out the value of a times 4. You'll learn more about variables, functions, and statements soon, but for now, let's examine the interactive environment and get you up to speed on how to work with it efficiently.

The following line shows Python's string capabilities. A string is typically enclosed in quotes, so the next command multiplies the string 'a' by 4. Which is exactly that: 'a' multiplied four times results in 'aaaa'—pretty cool.

The last line shows what happens when the interpreter encounters a problem: it raises an exception and reports the reason back to the user. In this particular case, the interpreter doesn't know of the function sqrt(); this can be easily remedied if we import the function by issuing from math import sqrt, but that's reserved for later.

The Result Variable

Whenever Python executes a statement, the result is stored in a special variable named _. This is useful when you're doing some manual calculations:

```
>>> 1+2+3+4+5+6+7+8+9
45
>>> _
45
>>> _ + 10
55
>>> _
55
>>> _ / 5
11
```

The result variable keeps on being updated, as shown in this example, so bear that in mind.

The Interactive Help System

The interactive help system is a valuable tool both when learning the language and when programming. Python has a considerable number of functions, modules, and packages, so a help system is a must. As the name suggests, the help system is an interactive system. Invoking it is straightforward (notice the required empty parentheses):

```
>>> help()
```

Enter quit to exit the system. Enter a function name to read about it (e.g., execfile).

If you enter sqrt, the help system will respond that there's no documentation regarding sqrt. The reason for this is that sqrt is part of the math module, and to view its help information you'll have to enter math.sqrt instead. Refer to the "Modules and Packages" section later in this chapter for discussion about modules.

You can also view specific function help (noninteractively) using help(function):

```
>>> help(execfile)
Help on built-in function execfile in module __builtin__:

execfile(...)
    execfile(filename[, globals[, locals]])

    Read and execute a Python script from a file.
    The globals and locals are dictionaries, defaulting to the current
    globals and locals.  If only globals is given, locals defaults to it.
```

In reality what happens when you issue the command help(function) is that that function's *docstring* is printed. More about docstrings in the "Defining Functions" section later in this chapter.

Moving Around

At times, it's of value to know how to change the current working directory within the Python interpreter. This is especially important if the code and data are located in different directories; it might be easier to just switch to another directory as the situation requires.

Suppose you defined a function that accepts a file name as input, reads it, and does some processing. Furthermore, this function was defined interactively, as you were using the interpreter. Now you'd like to run this function on some files, but the path to these files is long and cumbersome. This is a situation where it'd be much easier to switch to the directory where the files reside and execute the function with the relatively shorter file name, that is, excluding the path.

Module os provides us with this functionality. You've already seen the os module in Chapter 1, but this time we use it to move around the interpreter:

```
>>> import os
>>> os.getcwd()
'/home/shai/python'
>>> os.listdir('.')
['src', 'data']
>>> os.chdir('src')
>>> os.getcwd()
'/home/shai/python/src'
>>> os.chdir('/home/shai/python/data')
>>> os.getcwd()
'/home/shai/python/data'
>>> os.chdir('../src')
>>> os.getcwd()
'/home/shai/python/src'
>>> os.listdir('/home/shai/python/data')
['GPS-2008-06-05-13-02-56.csv']
```

In this listing I've used several functions. The first line imports the os module, containing functions required to move around. I've then used several functions from the os module:

- The function os.listdir(path) lists directory contents. The function must be supplied with a string argument. If the string argument is an empty string ('') or a string with a single dot in it ('.'), the function will return the contents of the current directory.

- To figure out what's your current working directory, issue the command os.getcwd(). This function takes no arguments.

- Finally, I've shown the usage of the os.chdir(path) function. The function accepts one string as an argument and, depending on the string, changes directories accordingly. The function accepts both relative directory paths (such as '../src') as well as full directory paths ('/home/shai/python/data').

■**Tip** In IPython (see Chapter 2), you can use the commands cd, ls, and pwd as you would in any Linux shell instead of using the os module functions (it's faster to type!).

Running Scripts

The interactive environment can only get you so far. Eventually, you will want to write programs (scripts) and run them either noninteractively or from within the Python interpreter.

There could be various reasons to write scripts, and most are due to the fact that you might perform a task more than once. Say the accountants in your company use nonlinear depreciation equations, and being their favorite programmer they ask you for a personal favor, so you decide to write a web-based depreciation calculator. Or the clinical people in your medical device company often require access to log files that are large and require processing, so they ask you to write an end-of-day report per patient summarizing the day's events based on those log files, or . . . and the list goes on and on.

The path I typically follow is that I use the interactive environment in parallel to coding the script. That is, I run Python interactively, run a few statements, assign some variables, plot some graphs; if things look good, I copy over the commands I issued to an editor where my script resides.

■**Tip** In IPython you can issue the command history to view a list of recently entered commands.

The benefit of coding interactively is that you can examine the variables and data structures of your code, without additional debugging tools. If the script raises an exception, you now have at your fingertips all the variables and data structures: you can reproduce the error and possibly fix the bug.

Once your script is ready (well it's never really *ready*, let's just agree that it's ready to be test-driven), you have several options to run it:

- Run the script from the GUI environment: running IDLE (Python GUI), select File ➤ Open and choose the script to run. This will open the Python script in the IDLE editor (if it's already open, there's no need to reopen it). To run the script, press F5 or select Run Module from the Run menu. The output should appear in the Python GUI shell.

- Run the script from Python's CLI. Using `execfile('path/to/filename.py')` is my favorite option when developing. The reason I prefer this method over the GUI environment is that I like editing my code in an editor that is not part of an IDE.

Tip If you're using IPython, you could issue the command `run path/to/filename.py` instead of `execfile('filename.py')`; the benefits are 1) you can use character completion to select the file name, and 2) you can supply command-line parameters to the script: `run path/to/filename.py param1 param2`.

- Invoke the script from the shell or a command window (noninteractive mode).

  Even though you might have developed your script in interactive Python, it's a good idea to test your script in a shell as well, especially if you're distributing your code for others to use: they might not want to run the code interactively. To run the script from a Linux shell or Cygwin, use this command:

  `$ python path/to/filename.py`

  Or in Windows:

  `c:\python25\python.exe path\to\filename.py`

  In Windows, you could also set the PATH variable to include the Python directory path, in this case, `c:\python25`, so invoking the script will not require a full path to the Python executable:

  ```
  path=%path%;c:\python25
  python path\to\filename.py
  ```

- Finally, it's also possible to enjoy both worlds: interactive and noninteractive mode! This is done by running the script with the `-i` switch, which opens up a Python shell *after* the script has run and lets you examine variables, interactively:

  `$ python -i somescript.py`

Tip Since the backslash character (\) has a special meaning in strings (we'll get to that later) and is also used as a path separator in Windows, it's best to use the slash (/) character whenever you're working with file names and file paths. If you can, opt to use relative paths (e.g., `../data` instead of `c:\data`); your code will be portable across operating systems and much easier to read.

That's it. I think we're ready for the language itself now.

Data Types

Python data types are similar to data types in other programming languages; you'll see here strings and numbers just as you would in, say, Basic. But there are some niceties you should know about even in those basic data types, for example, the long data type supports infinite integer precision.

Numbers

We'll start off with numbers. Python natively supports int, long, float, and complex.

Int and Long

The data type *int* is equivalent to C's long data type, and its precision is system dependent. I run a 32-bit machine, so on my system, int defaults to a 4-byte integer. This means the maximum int I can represent on my system is $2^{31}-1$, and the minimum is -2^{31}. If you're uncertain of the bit count on your system or if your code might be running on different platforms (e.g., both 32-bit and 64-bit platforms), you can use the following to determine the maximum int value:

```
>>> import sys
>>> sys.maxint
2147483647
```

The data type *long* provides infinite integer precision. It's not limited by the platform. However, there is a price to be paid: performance. Long integer numbers are denoted in Python with a trailing L character:

```
>>> 2**70
1180591620717411303424L
>>> 2**700
52601359015483735072409898828801286655503398028231738594982809030687321
54297080822113666536277588451226982968856178217713019432250183803863127
81477065188084995522367112844459819166375788432271727129325173578137
6L
```

I've introduced the operator power, denoted by **, so 2**70 is 2^{70}. Once you leave the int range (4 bytes on a 32-bit machine, 8 bytes on a 64-bit machine), that is, your calculation extends to a number greater than sys.maxint, Python automatically converts the number to a long integer value, giving it infinite precision. So if your plan was to use an int, make sure you didn't accidentally cast it into a long. Here's a possible pitfall:

```
>>> 2**31-2
2147483646L
```

As you can see, the result is a long, denoted by the trailing L. But surely this number is less than sys.maxint! The problem is that the first calculation, 2^{31}, already exceeded sys.maxint, and now any future computations are performed in infinite precision, denoted by the trailing L.

Once a number is long, it will keep on being treated as long unless you specifically convert it back to an int using the int() function, assuming the number indeed can be represented as an int.

Personally, I haven't used `long` all that much. I typically use integer values when counting things (for example, in loops) and $2^{31}-1$ is more than enough. However, had I required such a large number, I'd have to jump through a series of hoops in, say, C, but in Python it's a lot easier (not effortless, but still easier).

WHY NOT EFFORTLESS?

This is a bit off-topic and is an advanced discussion that assumes some knowledge of Python.

The reason it's not effortless doing infinite precision with integers is that a lot of the functions we're used to working with in Python return `int`, and not `long`. To illustrate this problem, suppose you'd like to compute a sum of numbers from 1 to N, where N is greater than 2^{32} (yes, there are easier ways but I'm trying to make a point here). A typical approach would be to use a `for` loop with an `xrange()` iterator as follows:

```
>>> total = 0
>>> for x in xrange(1000):
...     total += x
...
>>> total
499500
```

Note that I've used a variable named `total` and not `sum` because sum is a built-in function in Python.

Now the problem lies with the call to `xrange()`—the iterator accepts only `int` values. So if you were to replace the number 1000 with, say, `2**32`, you'd get an error:

```
>>> xrange(2**32)
Traceback (most recent call last):
  File "<stdin>", line 1, in <module>
OverflowError: long int too large to convert to int
```

which means you'd have to resort to other techniques such as (caution: this is a long run)

```
>>> x, total = 0, 0
>>> while(x < 2**33):
...     x += 1
...     total += x
```

It's definitely doable in Python, but it's not effortless. That said, doing the same in C is even harder.

Other Useful Bases

Bases that are powers of 2 are native to computing systems. One byte is 2^8 as opposed to, say, a power of the decimal system. For this reason, the ability to convert values to and from bases that are powers of 2 (such as the hexadecimal base or the octal base) to the decimal system is important.

Hexadecimal values are denoted with a leading 0x. Thus, 0x20 is 32 (decimal). You can use both capital and noncapital letters for digits A–F:

```
>>> 0xaB
171
>>> 0xff
255
```

Octal values are denoted with a leading 0 (that's a zero, not the character O). Thus 020 is 16 (decimal):

```
>>> 020
16
```

Regardless of how you enter numbers, that is, what base you've used, they're still retained as numbers in Python. Should you want to look up the different base representation, use the oct() and hex() function calls. Both these functions return a string:

```
>>> hex(100)
'0x64'
>>> oct(100)
'0144'
```

You can also perform any other base conversion using the function int(str[, radix]), which returns a number, not a string. In case radix isn't specified, it is assumed to be 10:

```
>>> int('100')
100
>>> int('100', 3)
9
```

The argument to the function int() is a string and not a number. So in case you'd like to convert 101 in base 3 to a decimal value, write int('101', 3) or int(str(101), 3). The latter is more useful if you'd like to use a variable, that is, int(str(variable), base).

It's possible to use higher bases than hexadecimal (base 16), using an increasing number of letters from the alphabet as the new digits for the base. In base 17, the character g is added; in base 18, the character h is used, and so on. So the number 'ggg' in base 17 should be 17^3–1:

```
>>> int('ggg', 17)
4912
>>> 17**3-1
4912
```

This support for bases is up to value 36, corresponding with the letter "z".

Comparisons

You can compare values using the regular operators: > and < for greater than and less than, respectively. Equality checks are done using a double equal sign (==) to differentiate from the assignment symbol denoted by a single equal sign (=). Inequality is !=, and you can also use >= and <= for greater-than-or-equal and less-than-or-equal comparisons.

```
>>> 2*3 > 5
True
>>> 2*3 != 5
True
```

Some comparisons are not allowed, for instance, comparing a complex number (described in the next section) with an integer value:

```
>>> 1+1j > 2
Traceback (most recent call last):
  File "<stdin>", line 1, in <module>
TypeError: no ordering relation is defined for complex numbers
```

Bitwise Operations

Bitwise operators are similar to C's bitwise operators as shown in Table 3-1.

Table 3-1. *Bitwise Operations*

Operator	Description	Example
~	Bitwise not	~0x0ff+0x100 returns 0.
<<	Shift left	1<<8 returns 256.
>>	Shift right	256>>2 returns 64.
^	Bitwise exclusive OR (XOR)	0xff ^ 0xf0 returns 15 (0x0f).
&	Bitwise AND	0xff & 0x0f returns 15 (0x0f).
|	Bitwise OR	0x0f | 0xf0 returns 255 (0xff).

Augmented Assignments

Augmented assignments introduce the operators +=, -=, *=, /=, %=, **= , <<=, >>=, &=, ^=, and |=. This is notation is similar to C/C++ syntax. That is, instead of writing a = a+1, you can write a += 1. Similarly, instead of writing a = a>>1, you can write a >>= 1. Please note that Python does not support the increment operator ++.

Float and Complex

Floating-point values have been around for quite some time, and there's no escaping them. Python's *float* data type is equivalent to C's double, so it's really more accurate than C's float (C's float has fewer bytes than C's double).

Floating-point values are represented with a dot or with the e or E character denoting exponential notation. So if you want to ensure your value is a float, either add a leading dot (or dot zero, or e/E) or explicitly do so with the function float():

```
>>> 2.0
2.0
>>> 2
2
>>> float(2)
2.0
>>> 1e3
1000.0
```

The reason specifying a float is important is that you might get an integer operation where you really want a floating-point operation.

```
>>> 2/3
0
>>> 2./3
0.66666666666666663
>>> 2/3.
0.66666666666666663
>>> 2.0/3.0
0.66666666666666663
>>> float(2)/3
0.66666666666666663
>>> float(2/3)
0.0
```

Note In Python 3.0, 2/3 will return a floating-point value; for an integer division, use 2//3 instead. See http://www.python.org/dev/peps/pep-0238/ for more details.

In the first operation and the last operation, the division is integer division, returning the value 0. As a general rule, whenever a floating-point number is introduced, any integers (both int and long) are converted to a float, and from that point onward the calculation continues with floating-point values. This is also known as *promotion* or *coercion*; long and int are promoted to a float.

You can force a value into a floating-point value by using the float() function. This works on strings as well as numbers, as long as the conversion is possible.

The *complex* data type represents complex numbers and is composed of two floating-point values, one representing the real part and one representing the imaginary part. The imaginary part is appended with the trailing letter j (or J). Accessing the real and imaginary parts is possible using the .imag and .real attributes, as follows:

```
>>> a = 1+2j
>>> a.real
1.0
>>> a.imag
2.0
```

You can use most any operator on complex numbers just as you would on floating-point numbers. Once a computation involving a complex number is encountered, the remaining computation will remain a `complex`, that is, integers and floating-point values are promoted to complex values. You can convert a number to a complex number using the `complex(real[, imag])` function. In case `imag` is provided, it holds the imaginary value of the complex number:

```
>>> complex(10)
(10+0j)
>>> complex(10, 2)
(10+2j)
```

The `complex` data type as well as examples on using it will be discussed in Chapter 7.

Strings

Per the classic Python definition, strings are an immutable sequence of characters. This means a *string* is a sequence of characters, and it is unchangeable: you can't change the characters. I know that this might seem odd at first: you're probably thinking, "How do I work with strings if I can't modify them?" The answer is that you create new strings based on your current string.

Expressing Strings

There are several ways to express a string: single quotes, `'string'`; double quotes, `"string"`; and triple-double-quotes, `"""string"""` (phew), to name a few. And there are even more: raw strings denoted by the letter r such as `r"string"` and Unicode strings denoted by the letter u, for example, `u"unicode"`.

To express a basic string, use single quotes as follows:

```
>>> 'split'
'split'
```

In case your string has a quote in it, you'll have to escape it with a backslash (\):

```
>>> 'it\'s a split'
"it's a split"
```

The reason we escaped the quote that's part of the word `it's` is so that the quote before the letter s won't terminate the string.

Single quotes and double quotes are interchangeable. Therefore, we could've achieved the same result, without escaping the quote that's part of the word `it's`, by replacing the enclosing quote (the ones at the beginning and end) with double quotes:

```
>>> "it's a split"
"it's a split"
```

But what if we wanted a string that actually does have the backslash before the quote as well—a string that looks exactly like this: it\'s a split? Well, one option is to escape the backslash as well as the quote:

```
>>> 'it\'\\s a split second'
"it'\\s a split second"
>>> print 'it\'\\s a split second'
it'\s a split second
```

Notice how the interpreter represents that string differently from how it's printed.

Well, this pattern can keep on going, making things harder to understand. Instead, we could use a raw string:

```
>>> r"it\'s a split second"
"it\\'s a split second"
>>> print r"it\'s a split second"
it\'s a split second
```

A raw string means that everything following the character r and the starting quote and before the ending quote should be taken literally. Have Python escape what needs escaping and return a proper string back to me!

■**Note** Raw strings will be used extensively in regular expressions so as not to escape special meaning characters on several levels. See Chapter 5 for details.

Strings can also span multiple lines with a backslash:

```
>>> "it's a \
... split second"
"it's a split second"
```

This obviously could bring about more disasters—what if you *really* wanted that backslash to appear, as well as the line break? Not to worry, time to use triple-double-quotes (or triple-single-quotes, they're interchangeable):

```
>>> print """it's a \
... split second"""
it's a \
split second
```

If all this sounds too confusing, you're in good company. To acquaint yourself with these caveats, launch Python interactively and experiment!

I haven't talked about Unicode strings here; I'll touch on that in Chapter 5.

String Operations

So what can you do with strings? Table 3-2 lists some operations that can be performed on strings, along with examples. In the examples, I've selected strings that don't require escaping so they're easier to follow, but the same can be applied to any string expression described previously.

Table 3-2. *String Operations*

Operator	Description	Example
Adding and Multiplying		
str1+str2	Concatenates strings str1 and str2.	'split '+'second' returns 'split second'.
str*n	Concatenates the str string n times.	'second '*3 returns 'second second second '.
Indexing and Slicing		
n and m are positive integer values less than the length of str. Negative values are counted from the end of the string.		
s[n]	Retrieves the nth character of s	'split'[3] returns 'i'.
s[n:m]	Retrieves a string slice from nth character to the mth character, excluding the mth character. If n or m are negative, they are counted from the end of the string.	split second'[6:12] returns 'second'. 'split second'[-6:-2] returns 'seco'.
s[:m]	Equals s[n:m] with n=0.	'split second'[:3] returns 'spl'.
s[n:]	Retrieves a string slice from the nth character to the end.	'split second'[6:] returns 'second'.

You can check whether a character is in a string using the in operator:

```
>>> 'd' in 'abcde'
True
```

or count the number of characters in a string using the len() function:

```
>>> len('abcde')
5
```

Both in and len() operate on other sequences, as you'll soon see.

I'll discuss strings (including Unicode strings and raw strings) in more detail in Chapter 5.

Booleans

I've postponed discussion of *Boolean* values until after you've seen some other data types because Booleans values shine in the context of other data types. Booleans can take two values: True (1) or False (0).

```
>>> a = True
>>> a > 1
False
>>> a == 1
True
>>> bool(5)
```

```
True
>>> type(a)
<type 'bool'>
```

You can cast a value to a Boolean by using the bool() function. Empty strings, as well as other empty sequences, and the value zero of any form are considered False:

```
>>> bool(0)
False
>>> bool(5)
True
>>> bool("")
False
>>> bool("s")
True
```

Logical Operations

Logical operations and, or, and not operate on Booleans. I assume you know how to use them. Let's see if you know the answer to the following . . .

```
>>> 5 > 1 and ((4 < 3) or 2+4 < 5 and not 6 < 2)
```

Data Structures

Python, being a high-level programming language, also provides additional, more complex, data types, which I refer to as *data structures*. These include lists, tuples, dictionaries, and sets, to name a few. Data structures make the programming experience a lot more enjoyable.

Python documentation does not necessarily differentiate between data types and data structures the way I have. My purpose in this distinction is to split the discussion into two categories: simple *data types*, which you're likely to encounter in popular programming languages (such as C), and more complex data types, or *data structures*, which you're likely to see in higher-level programming languages such as Python and Perl. Regardless of the classification presented in this chapter, both are built-in data types as far as Python is concerned.

In a sense, you've already been exposed to data structures: strings and complex numbers. The string is an immutable sequence, hardly a "simple" data type. By comparison, the C programming language does not support a native string data type, rather an array of characters, which is to show that strings aren't really all that basic. But a string is still limited—it's a sequence of characters. What about sequences of other objects? And what about mutable (changeable) sequences?

Not to worry, Python provides those as well. A *list* in Python is a mutable sequence of arbitrary data types. A *tuple* is quite similar to a list, only that it's immutable.

We'll also talk about some more complex data structures that can make programming yet more entertaining. You've already seen a *dictionary* object in Chapter 1, and we'll explore that data structure as well as the *set* object. Python is also an object-oriented-programming language; therefore, a discussion of the *class* object will be presented after we have talked about *functions*.

Lastly, there are also additional native data types and structures in Python, but most of them will be left out of the scope for this book; they're not a must for data analysis and visualization (with the possible exception of *file* data types, which will be discussed in Chapter 5).

Lists

A *list* is a mutable sequence of objects. A list is denoted by brackets:

```
>>> [1, 'hey', 1+2j]
[1, 'hey', (1+2j)]
```

You can also create a list using the list() function. This is useful when converting different sequences to a list, say, from a string:

```
>>> list('some text')
['s', 'o', 'm', 'e', ' ', 't', 'e', 'x', 't']
```

A list can be modified. You can add another element to a list by using the + operator. The + operator concatenates lists, so you have to supply another list:

```
>>> [1, 'hey', 1+2j] + ['hey', 'hey']
[1, 'hey', (1+2j), 'hey', 'hey']
```

The following, however, will fail, since you cannot add an integer to a list:

```
>>> [1, 2, 3] + 2
Traceback (most recent call last):
  File "<stdin>", line 1, in <module>
TypeError: can only concatenate list (not "int") to list
```

The proper way to do this would be to form another list, made solely of the value 2:

```
>>> [1, 2, 3] + [2]
[1, 2, 3, 2]
```

If you're looking to add the value 2 to each and every element of the list [1, 2, 3], that is, to modify the list to [3, 4, 5], you'll get the details in the sections "The for Statement" and "List Comprehensions" later in this chapter.

A list is an object too, so you can also have a list inside a list:

```
>>> [[1, 2], [3, 4]]
[[1, 2], [3, 4]]
```

Now things get trickier, both in describing the object and in actually performing operations. Say you'd like to add another list, [5, 6], to the preceding example. How exactly would you like to add it? Should the updated list be [[1, 2], [3, 4], [5, 6]] or [[1, 2], [3, 4], 5, 6] or [[[1, 2], [3, 4]], [5, 6]] (which really is shamelessly tricky)?

The way I like to describe the data structure [[1, 2], [3, 4]] is as a list of rows. The first row is [1, 2] and the second row is [3, 4].

Here are some of the things you can do to concatenate lists:

```
>>> [[1, 2], [3, 4]] + [5, 6]
[[1, 2], [3, 4], 5, 6]
```

```
>>> [[1, 2], [3, 4]] + [[5, 6]]
[[1, 2], [3, 4], [5, 6]]
```

The first line adds the elements 5 and 6. The second line adds the row [5, 6].

Another option is to use a variable to hold the list, L, and use the append() and extend() methods:

```
>>> L = [[1, 2], [3, 4]]
>>> L.append([5, 6])
>>> L
[[1, 2], [3, 4], [5, 6]]
>>> L.extend([7, 8])
>>> L
[[1, 2], [3, 4], [5, 6], 7, 8]
```

The method append() adds an item to the list, in this case the list [5, 6]. The method extend() adds elements from the sequence one by one to the list, in this case, the elements 7 and 8. It's a bit hard to follow at first, but experiment with lists interactively to get a feel for how to use them properly.

Lists can also be indexed, similarly to strings:

```
>>> L = [['hey', '1'], [2, 3, 4], '']
>>> L[0]
['hey', '1']
>>> L[1]
[2, 3, 4]
>>> L[1][1]
3
```

The last statement, L[1][1], requires some explanation. The statement L[1] returns the second element in the list (indices start at 0, so index 1 is the second element). For our purposes, let's mentally assign L[1] to variable M. But variable M is a list as well: [2, 3, 4]. So clearly we can index M as well: M[1] is 3. Instead of doing those two steps, we can write this more compactly as L[1][1].

Lists much like strings can also be sliced:

```
>>> L = [['hey', '1'], [2, 3, 4], '']
>>> L[:-1]
[['hey', '1'], [2, 3, 4]]
>>> L[2:]
['']
```

You can check whether an item is in a list using the in operator:

```
>>> 'hey' in ['hey', 'hey', 'split', 'second']
True
```

You can count the number of elements in a list using the len() statement:

```
>>> len([['hey', '1'], [2, 3, 4], ''])
3
```

Since lists are mutable, they can be reassigned:

```
>>> L = [['hey', '1'], [2, 3, 4], '']
>>> L[1] = [4, 5, 6]
>>> L
[['hey', '1'], [4, 5, 6], '']
```

or have items removed using the del statement:

```
>>> L = [['hey', '1'], [2, 3, 4], '']
>>> del L[0]
>>> L
[[2, 3, 4], '']
```

Lists also have methods, functions that operate only on list objects such as append() and extend(), shown previously. To use a method, follow the list object with a dot and the function name with parentheses and parameters within (empty ones in case of no parameters):

```
>>> L = ['hey', 'hey', 'split', 'second']
>>> L.count('hey')
2
>>> L.sort()
>>> L
['hey', 'hey', 'second', 'split']
```

I've used the methods count(), which counts the occurrences of an item in a list, and sort(), which sorts a list. Table 3-3 describes the list methods along with some examples. In the examples, assume that L is ['second', 'second', 8].

Table 3-3. *List Methods*

Method	Description	Example
append(obj)	Adds an element to the end of a list.	L.append('hey') changes L to ['second', 'second', 8, 'hey'].
count(val)	Returns the number of times val appears in the list.	L.count('second') returns 2.
extend(iterable)	Adds elements to the list from iterable (more on iterators and iterables later in this chapter).	L.extend(xrange(2)) changes L to ['second', 'second', 8, 0, 1].
index(val, [start, [stop]])	Returns the first index of val in the list. If start is supplied, this method returns the first index that is greater than start; if stop is supplied, the index also has to be less than stop.	L.index('second') returns 0. L.index('second', 1) returns 1. L.index('second', 2, 3) raises an exception x not in list.
insert(n, obj)	Inserts an object at index n.	L.insert(2, 'me') changes L to ['second', 'second', 'me', 8].

Continued

Table 3-3. *Continued*

Method	Description	Example
pop([n])	Returns the nth element in the list and removes it. If n is not supplied, this method returns the last element.	L.pop() returns 8, and the modified list is ['second', 'second']. L.pop(-3) returns 'second', and the modified list is ['second', 8].
remove(val)	Removes the first occurrence of val in x.	L.remove('second') changes L to ['second', 8].
reverse()	Reverses the list.	L.reverse() modifies L to [8, 'second', 'second'].
sort()	Sorts the list. You can supply a sort function to the list; see help(list.sort).	L.sort() modifies L to [8, 'second', 'second'].

Tuples

A *tuple* is an immutable (unchangeable) sequence of objects. A tuple is denoted by parentheses and can be created using the tuple() function:

```
>>> (1, 2, 3)
(1, 2, 3)
>>> tuple('hey')
('h', 'e', 'y')
```

Tuples don't necessarily require parentheses; merely adding a comma suggests the expression is a tuple:

```
>>> 1, 2
(1, 2)
>>> 1,
(1,)
>>> (1)
1
```

The expression (1) is not a tuple: it's the value 1 within parentheses, which is treated simply as 1.

Tuples behave similarly to lists, with the exception of modification: you can't modify a tuple. But you can create a new one based on an existing one:

```
>>> tuple([1, 2, 3])
(1, 2, 3)
>>> _ * 2
(1, 2, 3, 1, 2, 3)
```

In the first statement, I've created a tuple based on a list. Note that tuple(1, 2, 3) would raise an exception, because the function tuple() expects one argument, not three. In the preceding code I passed a list as an argument: [1, 2, 3]. I could've also written tuple((1, 2, 3)), effectively achieving the same thing: the first outer set of parentheses in the expression is the function parentheses; the inner one is the tuple parentheses. In the second statement listed, I've created a second tuple based on the first one, by multiplying the result variable.

Tuples can contain different data types and data structures:

```
>>> ([1, 2], (3, 4))
([1, 2], (3, 4))
```

The preceding is a tuple containing a list and a tuple.

Tuples can also be indexed, similarly to lists and strings. Remember that indexing requires brackets, not parentheses:

```
>>> ([1, 2], (3, 4))[0]
[1, 2]
>>> ([1, 2], (3, 4))[1]
(3, 4)
>>> ([1, 2], (3, 4))[1][0]
3
```

A tuple can be sliced, generating a new tuple:

```
>>> ([1, 2], (3, 4))[1:]
((3, 4),)
```

However, tuples cannot be reassigned:

```
>>> a = (['hey', '1'], '')
>>> a[0] = 0
Traceback (most recent call last):
  File "<stdin>", line 1, in <module>
TypeError: 'tuple' object does not support item assignment
```

But the lists within them *can* be changed, since lists are mutable:

```
>>> a = (['hey', '1'], '')
>>> a[0][0] = 'wow'
>>> a
(['wow', '1'], '')
```

Checking whether an item is in a tuple can be done using the in operator:

```
>>> 1 in (2, 3)
False
```

Finally, it's common practice to use tuples to perform multiple assignments, also known as unpacking:

```
>>> a, b = 1, 2
>>> a + b
3
```

Dictionaries

Dictionaries are mutable sequences that connect a *key* with a *value*. The key must be unique, whereas the value need not be. I like to use a phonebook analogy when I think about dictionaries. Every phone number (key) has but one entry (value) associated with it, usually a person; however, one person (value) can have several phones (keys). The key and value objects can be most data types, with the exception of some (e.g., another dictionary).

There are several ways to create a dictionary: using the dict() function with a sequence of (key, value) tuples or using the curly braces ({}) with colons separating keys and values:

```
>>> dict((('split', 8), ('second', 1)))
{'second': 1, 'split': 8}
>>> {'split':8, 'second':1}
{'second': 1, 'split': 8}
```

There are many parentheses in the first expression: the outermost are the parentheses for the function dict(), the innermost are specific tuple pairs, and the ones in between denote a tuple of tuples, because dict() can only accept one argument. A more readable approach would be to pass dict() a list of tuples, instead of a tuple of tuples:

```
>>> dict([('split', 8), ('second', 1)])
{'second': 1, 'split': 8}
```

Retrieving values from a dictionary is achieved using brackets:

```
>>> D = dict([('split', 8), ('second', 1)])
>>> D['split']
8
```

Checking for membership in a dictionary is done using the in operator, which defaults to checking against the keys of the dictionary, not the values. If you wish to check against the values, use the values() method:

```
>>> D = dict([('split', 8), ('second', 1)])
>>> 'split' in D
True
>>> 8 in D
False
>>> 8 in D.values()
True
```

Changing values and assigning new values is done using brackets as well:

```
>>> D = dict([('split', 8), ('second', 1)])
>>> D['python'] = 'snake'
>>> D
{'python': 'snake', 'second': 1, 'split': 8}
>>> D['python'] = 'programming language'
>>> D
{'python': 'programming language', 'second': 1, 'split': 8}
```

In the preceding example, the second assignment to the key 'python' has overwritten the previous value, 'snake', with the value 'programming language'.

If you think about it, real-world dictionaries may have several entries for one key: the word "Python" can mean the Python snake or the Python programming language. This behavior can be mimicked in Python dictionaries as well; simply have the value contain a list:

```
>>> D = dict()
>>> D['python'] = ['snake', 'programming language']
>>> D
{'python': ['snake', 'programming language']}
```

Dictionaries are implemented using a hashing algorithm. This means that retrieving a value from a key is extremely efficient. There's a lot of information regarding hashing algorithms and hashing functions on the Internet, so look that up if you're interested in knowing how they work. There's also good discussion on specific Python dictionary implementation in the *Python Cookbook* (see "Final Notes and References"). Used properly, a dictionary can simplify your code and make it a lot more efficient. In Chapter 4, I present an example of using a dictionary to locate duplicate files on a hard drive.

Table 3-4 lists dictionary member functions. In the examples in the table, assume D is {'second': 1, 'split': 8}.

Table 3-4. *Dictionary Methods*

Method	Description	Example
Functions		
clear()	Removes all items from the dictionary.	D.clear() changes D to {}.
copy()	Returns a shallow copy of D (see the "Variables" section later in the chapter).	D2 = D.copy().
fromkeys(K[, v])	Creates a dictionary from keys K. If v is provided, all values are set to v.	{}.fromkeys(['split', 'second'], 8) returns {'second': 8, 'split': 8}.
get(k[, def])	Returns the value associated with key k. If k is not in the dictionary, this method returns def if provided.	D.get('first', 1) returns 1.
has_key(k)	Returns True if k is a key.	D.has_key('na') returns False.
items()	Returns key-value tuples. In a sense this is the opposite of dict().	D.items() returns [('second', 1), ('split', 8)].
keys()	Returns the list of keys.	D.keys() returns ['second', 'split'].
pop(k[, def])	Returns the value associated with key k and removes it from the dictionary. If k is not in the dictionary, this method returns def if provided; otherwise, it raises an exception.	D.pop('split') returns 8 and changes D to {'second': 1}.
popitem()	Returns an arbitrary key-value tuple and removes the pair from the dictionary.	D.popitem() returns ('second', 1) and changes D to {'split': 8}.

Continued

Table 3-4. *Continued*

Method	Description	Example
setdefault(k[, def])	Returns the value associated with the key k. If k is not in the dictionary, this method returns def if provided and sets D[k] to def.	D.setdefault('hey', 6) returns 6 and changes D to {'second': 1, 'split': 8, 'hey': 6}.
update(e)	Updates the dictionary with data from dictionary e.	See the upcoming example in this section.
values()	Returns the list of values.	D.values() returns [1, 8].

Iterators

Iterators will be discussed later in the chapter. For reference purposes, I've listed dictionary iterator methods in this table.

iteritems()	Returns an iterator holding key-value pairs.	
iterkeys()	Returns an iterator holding the dictionary keys.	
itervalues()	Returns an iterator holding the dictionary values.	

While most of these member functions are easy to follow (with the exception of iterators, which we'll soon get to), I'd like to talk about two member functions that I feel require more explanation: update() and get().

The method update() updates the dictionary with key-value pairs from another dictionary. For ease of discussion, I'll refer to the function call D1.update(D2). In case a key exists in both dictionaries D1 and D2, the value associated with the key in the dictionary D1 is updated with the value from dictionary D2. If a key from D2 does not exist in D1, it is added to D1 along with its value. The following illustrates this behavior:

```
>>> D1 = {'second': 1, 'split': 8}
>>> D2 = {'second': 3, 'hey': 7}
>>> D1.update(D2)
>>> D
{'second': 3, 'split': 8, 'hey': 7}
```

The value associated with the key 'second' was updated, and the key-value pair 'hey': 7 was added.

The next member function I want to talk about is get(). At first, this seems rather odd; how is get() different from simply accessing the key using brackets? The difference is that if you use brackets and the key is not in the dictionary, a KeyError exception is raised. The function get() allows checking whether a key is in a dictionary and as a side product also returns a default value. A good way to show how this is useful is perhaps with an example.

Consider the function list_gps_commands() presented in Chapter 1 (I've removed the docstring), shown here in Listing 3-1.

Listing 3-1. *Function* `list_gps_commands()`

```
def list_gps_commands(data):
    gps_cmds = dict()
    for row in data:
        try:
            gps_cmds[row[0]] += 1
        except KeyError:
            gps_cmds[row[0]] = 1
    return gps_cmds
```

To further illustrate the example, let's build a short list of GPS commands (L) to later sort in a dictionary so you can try the example for yourself. First, we execute a set of commands similar to those detailed in the function `list_gps_commands()`:

```
>>> L = ['$GPGSA', '$GPGSV', '$GPGSV', '$GPGSV', '$GPRMC', '$GPGGA']
>>> D1 = dict()
>>> for elem in L:
...     try:
...         D1[elem] += 1
...     except KeyError:
...         D1[elem] = 1
...
>>> D1
{'$GPGSA': 1, '$GPGSV': 3, '$GPGGA': 1, '$GPRMC': 1}
```

The approach is simple. We first try to access a key in the dictionary. If the key exists, we increment the count. If the key doesn't exist, an exception is raised, which means it's a new entry, so we set it to 1.

A second approach is to check whether a key exists in a dictionary using the `in` statement and then follow up with an `if` sentence, as follows:

```
>>> L = ['$GPGSA', '$GPGSV', '$GPGSV', '$GPGSV', '$GPRMC', '$GPGGA']
>>> D2 = dict()
>>> for elem in L:
...     if elem in D2:
...         D2[elem] += 1
...     else:
...         D2[elem] = 1
...
>>> D2
{'$GPGGA': 1, '$GPGSA': 1, '$GPGSV': 3, '$GPRMC': 1}
```

It's also possible to use the `has_key()` member function in a similar manner.

A much more elegant approach would be to use the `get()` method with a default value of 0:

```
>>> L = ['$GPGSA', '$GPGSV', '$GPGSV', '$GPGSV', '$GPRMC', '$GPGGA']
>>> D3 = dict()
>>> for elem in L:
```

```
...       D3[elem] = D3.get(elem, 0)+1
...
>>> D3
{'$GPGSA': 1, '$GPGSV': 3, '$GPGGA': 1, '$GPRMC': 1}
```

I chose the first approach in Chapter 1 because I think it's clearer to those unfamiliar with the language. However, the last approach presented here is a clear winner in my mind.

Sets

Our last data structure for now will be a *set*. Sets are sequences of unique items. To create a set, use the set() function:

```
>>> set(['split', 'second'])
set(['second', 'split'])
>>> set(['split', 'second']*8)
set(['second', 'split'])
```

If you pass a duplicate to the set() function, it will not be added to the set. This is shown in the second statement where a list multiplied by 8 is passed as an argument.

In a sense, you've already been introduced to sets: the keys in a dictionary form a set since they are unique items.

Set operations are a bit different from the previous sequences you've seen. They are derived from the math operations and include intersection, union, and differences, to name a few:

```
>>> S1 = set(['split', 'second'])
>>> S2 = set(['split', 8])
>>> S1 | S2
set([8, 'second', 'split'])
>>> S1.union(S2)
set([8, 'second', 'split'])
>>> S1 & S2
set(['split'])
>>> S1 - S2
set(['second'])
>>> S1.difference(S2)
set(['second'])
>>> S2.difference(S1)
set([8])
```

The operator | is equivalent to the member function union(). The operator & is equivalent to the member function intersection(). The operator – is equivalent to the member function difference(), and much like regular subtraction, the order is important: S1-S2 is different from S2-S1.

Table 3-5 lists some set functions. In the examples, assume S1 equals set([8, 'hey']).

Table 3-5. *Set Methods*

Method	Description	Example
add(obj)	Adds obj to the set.	S1.add(9) changes S1 to set([8, 9, 'hey']).
clear()	Removes all elements from the list.	S1.clear() changes S1 to set([]).
copy()	Returns a shallow copy of S1 (see a discussion of shallow copy in the "Variables" section later in the chapter).	S2 = S1.copy().
difference(S2)	Returns the difference of two sets. This is equivalent to S1-S2.	S1.difference(set([8])) returns set(['hey']).
difference_update(S2)	Similar to difference() but modifies the list (not merely returns a copy).	S1.difference_update(set([8])) changes S1 to set(['hey']).
discard(v)	Removes the element v from the set. If v is not in the set, nothing happens (no exception is raised).	S1.discard(8) changes S1 to set(['hey']).
intersection(S2)	Returns the intersection of S1 and S2. This is equivalent to S1 & S2.	S1.intersection(['hey']) returns set(['hey']).
intersection_update(S2)	Similar to intersect() but modifies the set (not merely returns a copy).	S1.intersection_update(['hey']) changes S1 to set(['hey']).
issubset(S2)	Returns True if S1 is a subset of S2 (all elements of S1 appear in S2).	S1.issubset(set(['hey',8, 'na'])) returns True.
issuperset(S2)	Returns True if S1 is a superset of S2 (all elements of S2 appear in S1).	S1.issuperset(set([8])) returns True.
pop()	Returns an arbitrary element and removes it from the set.	S1.pop() returns 8 and changes S1 to set(['hey']).
remove(val)	Removes val from the set. If val is not in the set, this method raises an exception.	S1.remove('hey') changes S1 to set([8]).
symmetric_difference(S2)	Returns the symmetric difference. This is equivalent to (S1-S2) | (S2-S1).	S2 = set(['jude','hey']). S1.symmetric_difference(S2) returns set([8, 'jude']).
symmetric_difference_update(S2)	Similar to symmetric_difference() but modifies the set (not merely returns a copy).	
union(S2)	Returns the union of S1 and S2 (all unique elements that appear in both sets).	S1.union(set(['na', 8])) returns set([8, 'na', 'hey']).
update(S2)	Similar to union() but modifies the set (not merely returns a copy).	S1.update(set(['na', 8])) changes S1 to set([8, 'na', 'hey']).

I find I use sets much less than dictionaries. However, using sets at times can be quite elegant. Consider the example shown in our previous discussion about dictionaries that enumerates GPS commands. Now suppose you don't care how many times a GPS command appears, only what types of GPS commands exist. Then this is easily done with a set:

```
>>> L = ['$GPGSA', '$GPGSV', '$GPGSV', '$GPGSV', '$GPRMC', '$GPGGA']
>>> S = set(L)
>>> S
set(['$GPGSA', '$GPGSV', '$GPGGA', '$GPRMC'])
```

Variables

Next topic of our discussion is *variables*. Variables in Python are similar to variables in most other programming languages. Variable names can consist of characters, digits, and an underscore, but they have to start with a character or an underscore and must not contain spaces. I recommend you avoid odd variable names such as _02 (which is a legitimate variable name) as it might lead to some confusing code. Consider _02 = 3; that just doesn't look right.

An important concept regarding variables of data structures in Python is that of binding. When you assign variable b to be equal to variable a, which we'll suppose is a list, Python does not copy the contents of a to b. Rather, it sets both a and b to refer to the same object. This is to achieve speed and performance.

```
>>> a = [1, 2]
>>> b = a
>>> b[0] = 'hey'
>>> a
['hey', 2]
>>> b
['hey', 2]
```

In case you do want a real copy of the data structure, and not merely another reference, you have several options:

- Some data structures provide the copy() method, such as dictionaries.

- In some cases, you can create another item using the constructor, for example, L2 = list(L1).

- You can use the copy module from the standard library:

```
>>> import copy
>>> a = [1, 2]
>>> b = copy.copy(a)
>>> b[0] = 0
>>> a, b
([1, 2], [0, 2])
```

Note In case a variable is a more complex structure (e.g., a list of rows), it's not enough to use `copy.copy()`, as the newly constructed list still points to the rows in the original list. In this case, you might want to use `copy.deepcopy()` instead. For more information about shallow copy, deep copy, and lazy copy, see `http://en.wikipedia.org/wiki/Object_copy`.

Statements

We now turn to Python statements. You've already seen the use of statements, but here I'll cover more ground by talking about statements I haven't discussed yet. Python is a rich language that keeps evolving, so I will not be covering the entire language here. But the statements I cover should be enough to get you going.

I've split the discussion into three statement categories: printing, user input, and flow control. We'll have some off-track discussions about comments, iterators, and list comprehensions as well.

Printing

One of the basic statements in most programming languages is the `print` statement. You can use `print` to display Python objects:

```
>>> print(2**100)
1267650600228229401496703205376
>>> print(1+1j)
(1+1j)
>>> print(0x20)
32
>>> print "String"
String
>>> print(['short list'])
['short list']
>>> print(('a', 'tuple'))
('a', 'tuple')
>>> print dict([('hey', 'jude'), (8, 1)])
{8: 1, 'hey': 'jude'}
>>> print set([1, 2, 1])
set([1, 2])
```

Tip The function `pprint` from module pprint provides an alternative to the `print` statement, one that formats the output in a "prettier" fashion, such as avoiding word breaks. This is especially useful if you're displaying large data structures. To use it, `import pprint` and issue the command `pprint.pprint(object)`.

Suppressing Line Breaks

If you follow a print command with a comma, the next print statement will continue on the same line after printing a space:

```
>>> for i in [1, 2, 3]:
...     print i
...
1
2
3
>>> for i in [1, 2, 3]:
...     print i,
...
1 2 3
```

Format Specifications

The print statement is similar to C's printf() function in that it accepts format specifications in the form %[flags][w][.pre]type. Other than the % and type fields, all parameters are optional. The simplest use of the format specifications is with the % operator, as follows:

```
>>> print "%d" % 2**4
16
```

If more than one specifier is present, provide a tuple after the % operator:

```
>>> print "%d: %s=%d" % (1, 'hey', 8)
1: hey=8
```

The operator % is present after the string to be printed and before the tuple containing the values to be formatted.

■Note The function printf() (on which print is based) is a complex function with a considerable number of options and parameters. This section is quite detailed and should provide most of your daily programming needs. However, should you wish to explore print and printf() some more, a good source of information is the prinft() manual page (also known as the man page). In any Linux (or Cygwin) prompt, enter man 3 printf for an accurate overview. This is C-level documentation, but C programming skills are not required.

There are several values type can have, but only one is allowed in each specification (e.g., the format specifier %sd will be interpreted as a string, followed by the character 'd'). Table 3-6 provides a distilled list of types.

Table 3-6. *Print Format Specification Types*

Character	Type
d	Integer
e, E	An engineering notation of a floating-point number with e or E, respectively (mantissa and exponent are always present).
f	Floating-point number
g	Floating-point number in either f or e form, omitting trailing zeros and the decimal point if it's not needed
o	Octal
s	String
x, X	Hexadecimal (lowercase), hexadecimal (uppercase)

■**Note** Starting from Python 3.0, print becomes a function and not a statement, and to use print you'll have to add parentheses: print(obj).

We now turn to optional flags in the format specifier.

The value flags can take several of the following values: 1) a number, specifying the number of characters to left-align, 2) the character +, specifying that in case of a numeric value, the sign must be present (either + or -), 3) the character -, specifying that the text should be left-aligned, 4) the character #, which modifies behavior of some numeric types (out of the scope of this discussion—refer to the documentation), and 5) the character 0, used to left-pad values with zeros. Here are some examples:

```
>>> print "%d" % 2
2
>>> print "%5d" % 2
    2
>>> print "%+5d" % 2
   +2
>>> print "%-+5d**" % 2
+2   **
>>> print "%05d" % 2
00002
```

The value w specifies minimum width. If the width of the object to print is less than w, the output is left-padded with spaces. If it is greater than w, the value is displayed as is:

```
>>> print "%10s" % 'Really long string'
Really long string
>>> print "%10s" % 'shorter'
   shorter
```

The value pre is preceded with a dot and specifies the *maximum* number of decimal points in floating-point numbers, the *maximum* number of characters to print in a string, or the *minimum* number of digits in integers:

```
>>> print "%.2f, %.3s, %.4d" % (1.0/3, 'this will be truncated', 1)
0.33, thi, 0001
```

You can mix and match format specifiers. Here's a print statement that makes use of several format specifiers:

```
>>> print "%+08.3f" % (1.0/9)
+000.111
```

The + character forces the sign to appear in the output, the digit 0 takes care of the zero padding, the digit 8 forces the output to be at least eight characters long (the plus symbol, three digits, the dot symbol, and three more digits), the dot followed by 3 ensures at most three digits are displayed, and lastly the character f announces that this is a floating-point number.

Employing print in this manner is especially useful when you want to create text output that's properly aligned and can be displayed in a report.

Format specifiers, with the use of the % operator, can also be used to format strings, not only print them:

```
>>> s = "%+08.4f" % (1.0/3)
>>> s
'+00.3333'
```

User Input

We complement our output (printing) discussion with some input discussion, specifically, user input. Other sorts of input, for example, files and command-line parameters, will be discussed in future chapters.

User input in Python is done using the raw_input([prompt]) function. The function prints the prompt string, reads a string from the standard input, and returns it, stripped of end-of-line characters. The prompt argument is optional:

```
>>> s = raw_input("How many times? ")
How many times? 7
>>> print "split "*s
Traceback (most recent call last):
  File "<stdin>", line 1, in <module>
TypeError: can't multiply sequence by non-int of type 'str'
>>> print "split "*int(s)
split split split split split split split
```

The function raw_input() returns a string, thus even though I've input a numeric value, the function returns the string "7". I've converted the string to a number using the int() function.

In Windows, it's common to see raw_input() at the end of a script. This ensures that the command window stays open, waiting for user input and displaying the results of running the script. The default behavior in Windows is that this box is automatically closed, preventing the user from reading the output, and so raw_input() overrides this behavior.

Comments

Comments start at the symbol # provided it's not part of a string:

```
>>> print "Some text" # This is a comment
Some text
>>> # This entire line is a comment
...
>>> print "Text after this sign # is not a comment"
Text after this sign # is not a comment
```

Flow Control

Flow control statements control the behavior of a script. Python provides several flow control statements, some similar to other programming languages. Typically, a flow control statement is followed by a block, which is indented to the left.

if, elif, else

The if statement follows this syntax:

```
if Condition1:
    Block1
elif Condition2:
    Block2
elif Condition3:
    Block3
.
.
.
else:
    ElseBlock
```

Behavior is as follows: if Condition1 evaluates to True, the code in Block1 is executed. Block1 can be more than one line long and must be indented to the same level. If Condition1 is False, Condition2 is evaluated, causing Block2 to be executed if it is True. This continues on to Block3, and so forth. If none of the conditions are met, the ElseBlock is executed.

The statements if, elif, and else should be left-aligned. Statements in each block should be left-aligned as well, but further in than the if clause. The colon after the if, elif, and else statements is required. Here's an example:

```
>>> if 3 > 10:
...     print "Checked whether 3 is greater than 10"
...     print "It is!"
... elif ord('A') == 65:
...     print "Ordinal of 'A' is 65"
```

```
... else:
...     print "All failed, nothing works"
...
Ordinal of 'A' is 65
```

Other than the if statement, all other statements (elif, else) are optional. In case of a short if statement, you can write the block on the same line as the if statement:

```
>>> if 's' < 't': print "Yeap"
...
Yeap
```

Conditions can be more complex and can include conditionals such as and and or:

```
>>> x = 25
>>> if x > 20 and x%2 == 1:
...     print "Odd *and* over 20!"
...
Odd *and* over 20!
```

The pass Statement

The pass statement does nothing, and can be used as a placeholder, for example, in multiple if assignments:

```
>>> x = 0.2
>>> if x < 0.1:
...     print "Too small"
... elif x < 0.3:
...     pass
... elif x > 0.5:
...     print "large"
... else:
...     print "huge"
...
>>>
```

As you can see, nothing happened, which is exactly what I wanted.

Exceptions: try, else, and finally

Exceptions are Python's mechanism of dealing with runtime issues. You've already seen exceptions reported and also how to catch them, that is, prevent them from halting program execution, in Chapter 1.

You can catch, or intercept, exceptions before they stop program execution with the following syntax:

```
try:
    TryBlock
except [ExceptionType1]:
```

```
    ExceptBlock1
except [ExceptionType2]:
    ExceptBlock2
finally:
    FinallyBlock
```

If an exception happens someplace inside the TryBlock, ExceptBlock1 is executed. In case ExceptionType1 is specified, only exceptions that are of type ExceptionType1 are caught. You can have several except clauses to deal with different types of exceptions. The FinallyBlock is optional and executed after both the try and except section have completed execution.

First, let's see an exception in action, without catching it:

```
>>> str = 'second '
>>> n = '7'
>>> print str*n
Traceback (most recent call last):
  File "<stdin>", line 1, in <module>
TypeError: can't multiply sequence by non-int of type 'str'
```

The reason for this exception is that the operator * doesn't know how to multiply 'second ' by '7' (it does know how to do 'second '*7, but that's a different statement).

As you can see, the exception that was raised was a TypeError exception. Let's catch it and print it:

```
>>> str = 'second '
>>> n = '7'
>>> try:
...     print str*n
... except TypeError, e:
...     print "Exception caught!"
...     print e
... finally:
...     print "This will be run regardless"
...
Exception caught!
can't multiply sequence by non-int of type 'str'
This will be run regardless
```

We've caught the exception in the except block, plus we printed what the exception was in the second print line. Lastly, the code in the finally block was executed. Let's run it again, this time without triggering an exception:

```
>>> str='second '
>>> n = 7
>>> try:
...     print str*n
... except TypeError, e:
...     print "Exception caught!"
...     print e
... finally:
```

```
...       print "This will be run regardless"
...
second second second second second second second
This will be run regardless
```

As you can see, the code in the finally block was executed regardless of whether the exception was raised or not.

Now let's trigger an exception that's not of the TypeError exception. I'll modify the line print str*n to print 1/0, which raises a different exception:

```
>>> try:
...       print 1/0
... except TypeError, e:
...       print "Exception caught!", e
...
Traceback (most recent call last):
  File "<stdin>", line 2, in <module>
ZeroDivisionError: integer division or modulo by zero
```

This time, the exception wasn't caught by the code (it didn't print "Exception caught!") and was handled by the interpreter because it wasn't of type TypeError.

If you don't specify an exception condition, all exceptions are caught:

```
>>> try:
...       print 1/0
... except:
...       print "Exception caught!"
...
Exception caught!
```

As a general rule, try to make your exception specific, that is, try to specify the exception condition. If the list of exceptions is too long, maybe wide-range exception catching (i.e., without a condition) is a better approach.

Exceptions are a fundamental part of flow control. The EAFP concept is built around the idea that it's at times simpler to just try to perform an operation, later catching the exception in case of an issue.

Exceptions can occur deep within your code. For instance, say function1() calls function2(), which calls function3(). Now let's suppose an exception occurred in function3(). In case function3() doesn't handle the exception with the try/except mechanism, the exception moves to function2(). If function2() doesn't handle the exception, function1() has a chance. And finally, if function1() doesn't handle the exception, the interpreter will issue an exception and print the cause.

In the preceding scenario, in case function3() does handle the exception, it will not resurface in function2(). However, if you wish to catch an exception *and* pass it to the calling function, you can do that. That's left out of the scope of this discussion; refer to the online documentation for more details at http://docs.python.org/reference/executionmodel.html under the section Exceptions.

You can also raise exceptions of your own. This is of value if you write code and want to ensure it's being used properly. Suppose your algorithm only works on odd numbers; a good approach would be to check whether a parameter passed to the algorithm is odd, and if not, raise an exception:

```
>>> n = 6
>>> if not n%2 == 1:
...     raise ValueError, "value must be odd"
...
Traceback (most recent call last):
  File "<stdin>", line 2, in <module>
ValueError: value must be odd
```

In the preceding example, I've used an existing exception, ValueError. You can create exceptions of your own or use existing exceptions. For more details and a list of existing exceptions, refer to Python's online documentation: http://docs.python.org/library/exceptions.html.

Iterators

Before we move to the for statement, I'd like to cover an important concept, *iterators*. Iterators are objects that return an element one at a time, instead of returning a full sequence. An object that can be iterated over is known as *iterable*. Using iterators is more memory efficient than using a sequence. For example, the function range(1000) creates a list of a thousand values, whereas the iterator xrange() creates an iterator object that consumes much less memory: calls to xrange() yield the values from zero to 1000, excluding the value 1000, one at a time.

Python relies heavily on iterators and provides a great number of iterators that work on data structures I've covered. Iterators are best understood in the context of the for statement, so let's now take a look at this statement.

The for Statement

The for statement is one of the most versatile statements in Python. The statement follows the following syntax:

```
for element in sequence:
    ForBlock
```

In case of a one-line block, the ForBlock can appear on the same line as the for statement. Indentation rules for blocks are the same as those described in the if statement (and for any block for that matter—they must be indented to the same level).

The for statement assigns element to be a value from sequence and executes the ForBlock. This happens for all the values in sequence:

```
>>> for elem in ['hey', 'jude', 8]:
...     print elem,
...
hey jude 8
```

If you're interested in a format similar to that of C's for function, use the range() function:

```
>>> for x in range(10):
...     print x,
...
0 1 2 3 4 5 6 7 8 9
```

The for statement can also operate on an iterator. The function xrange() creates an iterator object, whereas the function range() creates a list. Both can be used in the context of a for statement:

```
>>> for x in range(5):
...     print
...     for y in xrange(5):
...         print "%4d" % (x*5+y),
...
```

```
 0    1    2    3    4
 5    6    7    8    9
10   11   12   13   14
15   16   17   18   19
20   21   22   23   24
```

In the preceding example, I've used both xrange() and range(), effectively yielding the same result. Also, as the preceding code suggests, for loops can be nested.

The for statement shines in the context of iterators. Let's cover a few.

The reversed(seq) iterator returns one element at a time from a sequence in reversed order:

```
>>> for x in reversed(['split', 'second']): print x,
...
second split
```

The iterator enumerate(seq) returns both the index to the item in the sequence and the item, as a tuple:

```
>>> for i, elem in enumerate(['split', 8, 'second']): print i, "-->", elem
...
0 --> split
1 --> 8
2 --> second
```

Some data structures provide iterators themselves. The iterator iteritems() returns a (key, value) tuple and is used to iterate over items in a dictionary:

```
>>> d = {'split':8, 'second':1}
>>> for k, v in d.iteritems(): print k, "-->", v
...
second --> 1
split --> 8
```

List Comprehensions

List comprehensions is a topic I've postponed until after we talked about the for statement. They really do apply to lists, but they're rather hard to explain unless you understand for statements. List comprehensions are an efficient method to create lists from lists, but with a slightly different notation than a regular for loop. List comprehensions follow this syntax:

```
[f(x) for x in list if condition]
```

The condition clause is optional:

```
>>> [x*x for x in range(10) if x > 5]
[36, 49, 64, 81]
>>> [x**2 for x in range(6, 10)]
[36, 49, 64, 81]
```

You can also write a nested list comprehension, similar to nested for loops:

```
>>> [(x, y) for x in range(3) for y in range(3)]
[(0, 0), (0, 1), (0, 2), (1, 0), (1, 1), (1, 2), (2, 0), (2, 1), (2, 2)]
```

You'll encounter numerous uses of list comprehensions throughout the book.

The while Statement

The while statement complements for loops and is best used in case a condition has to occur before the loop is terminated. You've seen the while statement in use in Chapter 1, which allows recording of GPS data until a Ctrl+C is pressed, and also previously in this chapter. The while syntax is as follows:

```
while condition:
    WhileBlock
```

As long as condition evaluates to True, the WhileBlock is executed:

```
>>> import random
>>> while random.random() < 0.9: print "*",
...
* * * * * * * * * * * * * * * * * * * * * * * * * *
```

This example will print a star as long as a random number between 0 and 1 is less than 0.9. I've used the function random() from module random (see Chapter 7).

Statements break and continue

The statements break and continue are used to modify behavior within a loop or a block. The statement break exits a flow control block, and the statement continue stops execution of the block but picks up on the next iteration.

```
>>> for x in range(5):
...     if x == 3: break
...     print x,
...
```

```
0 1 2
>>> for x in range(5):
...     if x == 3: continue
...     print x,
...
0 1 2 4
```

In the first for statement, I've used the statement break when x is equal to 3, effectively terminating the for loop. In the second for statement, I've merely skipped execution of the block in case x is equal to 3, suppressing the print statement, but resuming on the next value.

Some Built-in Functions

Let's now turn to built-in Python functions that weren't covered in any of the previous sections. By built-in, I mean functions that do not require any import command prior to using them. Table 3-7 presents these functions, in alphabetical order.

Table 3-7. *Some Python Built-in Functions*

Statement	Description	Example
all(s)	Returns True if all elements of s are not False.	all(['hi', 2]) returns True. all(['', 2]) returns False.
any(s)	Returns True if some elements of s are True.	any(['', 2]) returns True. any([]) returns False.
chr(n)	Returns the ASCII value of n.	chr(65) returns 'A'.
cmp(x, y)	Returns -1 if x < y, 0 if x == y, and 1 if x > y.	cmp('a', 'bc') returns -1. cmp(2, 1) returns 1.
ord(ch)	Returns the ordinal value of ch. This is the inverse of chr(n).	ord('A') returns 65. ord(chr(80)) returns 80.
range([i,]j[, k])	Returns a list starting at i (if supplied, default is zero), ending right before j, with an increment step of k (if supplied; default is 1).	range(5) returns [0, 1, 2, 3, 4]. range(2, 5) returns [2, 3, 4]. range(2, 5, 2) returns [2, 4]. range(5, 2, -2) returns [5, 3].
sorted(s)	Returns sequence s, sorted.	sorted('hey') returns ['e', 'h', 'y'].
sum(s)	Returns sum of elements in s.	sum(range(10)) returns 45.
type(obj)	Returns the type of obj.	type(1j) returns <type 'complex'>.
zip(s1[, s2])	Returns a list of tuples, each composed of elements at the same location in the sequences. s2 is optional.	zip(range(2), ['hey', 'jude']) returns [(0, 'hey'), (1, 'jude')]. zip(range(2)) returns [(0,), (1,)].

Some of these functions are very useful. For example, have a look at the Newton fractal example in Chapter 7 for an interesting use of the zip()function.

Defining Functions

Functions are a convenient way to reuse code. Functions in Python are similar to procedures, subroutines, and functions in other programming languages. There's no distinction between a function that returns a value and a function that does not—both are considered functions. (In some programming languages, if a function doesn't return a value, it is named differently: procedure or subroutine, for example.)

Functions are declared as follows:

```
def funcname(arguments):
    FunctionBody
```

The keyword def defines a start of a function. The name of the function is funcname; arguments are optional:

```
>>> def f1():
...     print "F1"
...
>>> f1()
F1
>>> def f2(n):
...     print "F2"*n
...
>>> f2(10)
F2F2F2F2F2F2F2F2F2F2
```

I've defined two functions: f1() and f2(). Function f1() requires no parameters, while function f2() requires one parameter. Using the functions (calling them) requires the addition of a set of parentheses.

You can also specify optional parameters using an assignment in the list of arguments in the function name, as follows:

```
>>> def f3(n, s="F3"):
...     print s*n
...
>>> f3(2)
F3F3
>>> f3(2, 'F4!')
F4!F4!
```

In the first call to f3(), the default value of s is "F3". In the second call, that value is assigned the string 'F4!'.

Functions can return values using the return statement:

```
>>> def f5(n):
...     return "f5"*n
...
```

```
>>> f5(3)
'f5f5f5'
>>> a = f5(3)
>>> a
'f5f5f5'
```

The return statement doesn't necessarily have to appear at the end of the function; however, the function ends execution when it reaches a return.

Functions are typically documented with docstrings (which are bold in the following code):

```
>>> def f6(n=1, s="f6"):
...     """Returns a string composed of the string s, repeated n times.
...
...     n and s are both optional."""
...     return s*n
...
>>> help(f6)
Help on function f6 in module __main__:

f6(n=1, s='f6')
    Returns a string composed of the string s, repeated n times.

    n and s are both optional.

>>> f6()
'f6'
>>> f6(2, 'f7')
'f7f7'
```

The benefit of using a docstring immediately after the function declaration is that executing help(funcname) returns the docstring, which is an excellent way to document a function.

Generators

Generators are functions used to create iterators. The main difference between a generator and a regular function is that generators return one element at a time using the yield statement, while functions return one element using the return statement (it could be a sequence or tuple, but it's essentially one object).

```
>>> def odd(s):
...     """A generator function to iterate through odd elements of s."""
...     i = 0
...     while(i < len(s)):
...         yield s[i]
...         i += 2
...
>>> for i in odd(['hey', 'split', 'second', 8]):
```

```
...      print i,
...
hey second
```

In the preceding example, I've defined an iterator named odd() that yields the odd elements in a list (i.e., the first, third, fifth, and so forth). I've implemented the iterator using a while loop and proper indexing.

There are also other methods I could've used to implement the iterator, but it's important to understand that the motivation behind using an iterator is that of efficiency. A different implementation could be one that makes use of the indexing operator with a step value of 2, as follows:

```
>>> def odd(s):
...      """A generator function to iterate through odd elements of s"""
...      for elem in s[::2]:
...          yield elem
```

While this might look like more elegant code, in my mind it's not as good. The reason is that the for loop creates an entire list (albeit half the size), and in case of large lists, this is not memory efficient. The first implementation, on the other hand, is quite memory efficient.

It's also possible to implement the function odd() using a for loop instead of a while loop, in which case I would suggest using the iterator xrange() (over a list comprehension) to avoid creating additional large data structures.

Generator Expressions

Generator expressions, or *genexps*, are a compact method to implement simple generators. Generator expressions follow this syntax:

```
(f(x) for element in sequence if condition)
```

In a sense, they are very similar to list comprehensions, with the difference being that they are iterators and not lists, and hence are more memory efficient. Here's an implementation of the odd() generator function using a genexp:

```
>>> L = ['hey', 'split', 'second', 8]
>>> odd = (x for x in L[::2])
>>> for i in odd:
...      print i,
...
hey second
```

or in one big line:

```
>>> L = ['hey', 'split', 'second', 8]
>>> for i in (x for x in L[::2]):
...      print i,
...
hey second
```

If I were a bit more conscious about memory usage, I'd notice that I've created another list in the for loop: L[::2], which probably is not a good idea (from a memory-conscious application). A different approach is to use the xrange() iterator as follows:

```
>>> L = ['hey', 'split', 'second', 8]
>>> odd = (L[i] for i in xrange(0, len(L), 2))
>>> for elem in odd:
...     print elem,
...
hey second
```

This might be a bit less clear, but it is a more memory-conscious implementation. Alternatively, you could also use the enumerate() iterator, iterating over list elements and only printing an element if the index is odd. Deciding whether an index is odd or even can be done using the modulo (%) operator, which returns the remainder from dividing by a number, in our case 2:

```
>>> L = ['hey', 'split', 'second', 8]
>>> odd = (elem for i, elem in enumerate(L) if not (i % 2))
>>> for elem in odd:
...     print elem,
...
hey second
```

Opt for using genexps over list comprehensions if you just want to iterate over items and don't require the list itself. Unless you're using really large data structures (on the order of scale of the memory you have in your computer), using either is fine.

Object-Oriented Programming

Per the description I've given of the Python language in the beginning of the chapter, you can deduce that Python is an object-oriented programming language. You've already seen this. For example, the data structure list, whose methods are in essence member functions, is an object.

The purpose of this section is to quickly (very quickly!) go over the syntax of object-oriented programming and to show how to implement a basic object. The reason I won't be covering OOP in detail is that this book mostly deals with using objects, rather than coding them. If you'd like to know more about coding an object, refer to the online Python documentation and the references at the end of this chapter.

The basic data structure to implement object-oriented programming in Python is a *class*. Classes have functions, called *methods*, and variables, called *attributes*. Listing 3-2 shows a simple class named Odd that implements the odd functionality, that is, retrieves odd elements.

Listing 3-2. *Listing of odd.py*

```
class Odd:
    def __init__(self, s=[]):
        self.sequence = s
    def odd(self):
        return self.sequence[::2]
```

The first line defines a class named Odd. From here, functions and variables indented per the usual block rules denote functions and variables belonging to class Odd.

I've defined two functions. The first function is the *constructor* __init__ (double underscores on both sides). The constructor function is called whenever an object is instantiated, or created. To instantiate a class object, call the Odd class with parentheses. Here are some ways you can instantiate the Odd class object (be sure to execute the preceding script first):

```
>>> odd1 = Odd()
>>> odd2 = Odd('a string')
>>> odd3 = Odd(['hey', 'split', 'second', 8])
```

The implementation I chose is that in case a parameter is provided, the variable self.sequence is assigned this parameter. An important note here is the use of the argument self: the word self is a convention and not a reserved word. Whenever you call a class property or method, the argument self is passed automatically but not spelled out. That is, to instantiate an Odd object, you enter Odd(s) and not Odd(self, s). By passing the argument self (hidden), Python identifies one created object from another. The analogy I like to use is that self is similar to C++'s this statement.

Another important concept here is that of scope. Had I not used the notation self.sequence and written sequence instead, the local variable sequence, that is, local to the function (and not the class), would have been updated. Once the function returned, that variable would have disappeared. To ensure that the class variable sequence is updated (and not the function's local variable), I've used the notation self.sequence.

The second function I defined is odd(), which returns the odd elements in a sequence. To call the function, use the dot operator after the Odd object, as follows:

```
>>> odd3 = Odd(['hey', 'split', 'second', 8])
>>> odd3.odd()
['hey', 'second']
```

So far, I've only shown methods, but the class Odd also contains a variable: sequence. To access this variable, you can use the dot operator as well:

```
>>> odd3 = Odd(['hey', 'split', 'second', 8])
>>> odd3.sequence
['hey', 'split', 'second', 8]
```

There's a lot more to object-oriented programming in Python, including most of the concepts that appear in other object-oriented programming languages such as inheritance and operator overloading, to name a couple. Again, the references at the end of the chapter should prove valuable resources should you need to learn more about object-oriented programming and design in Python.

Modules and Packages

One of Python's strong suits is the extensive number of packages readily available. You've seen how to install packages in Chapter 2; now it's time to see how to use them.

A module is a set of functions and data structures. In essence, it is similar to a class. Accessing modules is performed using the module's namespace, followed by a dot to access functions and variables. Packages are collections of modules. Accessing modules within packages is performed using the dot operator.

It's also of value to know that it's possible to extend Python with modules from C and C++. From a Python user's perspective, you just import a module and use it as is, regardless of whether it was written in another programming language.

The import Statement

The import statement loads a module, effectively allowing us to access the functions and variables within the module. You can issue the import statement in several ways:

```
import module
import module as name
from module import function
from module import function as name
from module import *
```

The first method, import module, loads a module with its namespace. To access the module functions, use module.function(). The second method loads the module but renames it, so to use its functions, use name.function(). The third statement imports only one function from the module; to access it simply use its name: function(). You can have multiple functions imported in this manner by separating the functions with commas. The fourth statement is identical to the third, only the name of the function is now name; to call the function, enter name(). Lastly, the last import statement loads all functions from a module; to access the functions you enter their name (without the module name). Here are some examples:

```
>>> import math
>>> math.pi
3.1415926535897931
>>> math.sqrt(4)
2.0
>>> import math as m
>>> m.pi
3.1415926535897931
>>> m.sqrt(4)
2.0
>>> from math import sqrt
>>> sqrt(4)
2.0
>>> from math import sqrt as square_root
>>> square_root(4)
2.0
>>> from math import *
>>> sin(0)
0.0
```

Whether you'll be loading the entire module or just some pieces of the module is totally up to you (and a function of the amount of memory you have). At times, though, it's easier to load entire modules, and yet at other times it's important to be able to load modules with their namespace, for example, when two modules have the same function names (such as modules math and cmath).

Modules Installed in a System

Before you start importing modules and reading about their functions, it would be valuable to know what modules are currently installed and available in your system. Don't forget that the Python Standard Library is vast, with a substantial number of modules and packages to choose from. Maybe a function you're looking for already exists in the standard library? Of course, you can refer to the online documentation, but you can also refer to the interactive help system.

Invoke the interactive help system by entering `help()`. At the help prompt, enter `modules`. This will provide a list of available modules in your system. Enter `help(module)` to read more about that module.

The dir Statement

Another useful statement is the `dir` statement, which lists the contents of a specific object (for example, a class) but in this context, it lists the methods and properties of a module as well:

```
>>> import math
>>> dir(math)
['__doc__', '__name__', 'acos', 'asin', 'atan', 'atan2', 'ceil', 'cos', 'cosh',
'degrees', 'e', 'exp', 'fabs', 'floor', 'fmod', 'frexp', 'hypot', 'ldexp', 'log'
, 'log10', 'modf', 'pi', 'pow', 'radians', 'sin', 'sinh', 'sqrt', 'tan', 'tanh']
```

This is very useful if you're exploring the functions in a module or if you forgot the exact name of a function.

Final Notes and References

It is far beyond the scope of this chapter and this book to cover the entire Python programming language. However, this chapter should get you up and running, and you'll be able to follow through with the rest of the book with very little need for additional references. That being said, one of the purposes of the book is to introduce the language and provide additional resources should you want to expand your knowledge.

I have found the following references of value, and I hope you find them useful as well:

- "The Python Tutorial" by Guido van Rosso, `http://docs.python.org/tutorial/index.html`

- The Python Standard Library, `http://docs.python.org/library/index.html`

- *Beginning Python: From Novice to Professional, Second Edition* by Magnus Lie Hetland (Apress, 2008)

- *Dive into Python* by Mark Pilgrim (Apress, 2004; free online version also available at `http://diveintopython.org/`)

- *Python in a Nutshell: A Desktop Quick Reference* by Alex Martelli (O'Reilly, 2006)

- *Python Cookbook: Recipes from the Python Community* by Alex Martelli, Anna Martelli Ravenscroft, and David Ascher (O'Reilly, 2005)

CHAPTER 4

■■■

Data Organization
Organizing Chaos

A preliminary step to designing and programming an algorithm is gathering data and sorting it. When you first go out to test a thesis or write code to analyze network traffic, only part of the information is readily available; some of the data is still unknown. First estimations are made based on the first set of data files. As data is gathered, new insights and understandings arise, resulting in possible changes to the processing script and data gathering application, such as adding a previously unlogged parameter and graphing it over time. Some changes may include data gathering over substantial longer time periods than originally anticipated. Consequently, to accommodate for manageable data files, a reduction in the sampling rate is required, implemented by logging only every nth value. Another plausible scenario is that of parsing log files, where the generating application, for example, a web server, recently went through a software upgrade altering the file format and the file name scheme.

The situation can get more complex. Some files may have an error due to a hardware malfunction of the recording apparatus; or some portions of the file are corrupt due to hard drive issues (back up!), or the application that stored the file had a bug and generated incorrect data. By now, you realize you need to modify the erroneous data or remove it from your analysis, be it manually or automatically.

In some cases, part of the data should be used as a teacher set to help define the algorithm, while another set of data should be used as a tester set to estimate performance. In this case, you may need to feed the algorithm additional information regarding the contents of the files so that more complex tests can be carried out.

Documenting file contents is important so that the knowledge of what each file contains is not lost. A few years from now I doubt you'll remember what each and every file is; but you might be expected to reuse your previous work. So annotating, or note taking, is of value. Ideally you'd like the annotations and documentation to reside with the data, and not in an inaccessible notebook.

By now you have quite a number of different file types: varying number of parameters, different file lengths, different logging periods, various file formats, several file name schemes, clean and raw data, annotated data, and much more. Ideally, you'd like to use data from all the files, even if some of them have partial information or conform to a different file format; they still hold valuable information. Or it could be that you'd like to use historical information to ensure backward compatibility with older versions of the software.

A lot of the work has many unknowns. Data gathering is an iterative process in nature, and if you don't manage your data files properly, you'll lose control. I'm not suggesting that we stop and design an entire data management infrastructure from the get-go. On the contrary, I think data should be gathered as I've described. However, following some simple guidelines and conventions can make life a lot easier. The purpose of this chapter is to address all these issues: file names, file formats, data organization, data cleaning, and annotation and data documentation. I'll touch on each topic, suggesting guidelines and conventions to help manage data more easily for the programmer and the processing application.

File Name Conventions

Our first step in data organization is deciding on a file name convention. You'd be surprised at the odd names people choose for their files. Not because they're not inventive enough, rather because they've never given it much thought. File name conventions are also of value when more than one person accesses the data. A good convention will help all data users locate files and manage them: your administrator will find it easier to restore previously backed-up files if he knows the file name pattern. A good naming convention should also have in mind scripts, or programs, so that automation is easier to implement. For example, if the file names contain the day of the week, it's easier to have those limited to three letters, Sun, Mon, Tue, Wed, Thu, Fri, Sat, instead of full day names, allowing the script that processes them to be less complex.

Date and Time in a File Name

We remember a lot based on date. "Remember that time when we ran that test? That was when you joined the group, about a year and a half ago." One of the best ways to capture date and time information is to use it to name a file. Following this guideline allows easy file searches. Instead of going through the files one at a time, opening them, and looking at the contents, you can browse the directory contents and find data based on date. The following are benefits of using date and time in a file name:

- Date is useful information. Just looking at the file name tells you a lot about the file.

- File names are almost guaranteed to be unique. This is important when your data logging application is creating file names, because it won't overwrite existing files. If you want to further ensure uniqueness, include the time in seconds along with the date information.

- File names are retained when copying or moving even if modifying. However, if you rely on the operating system to record the file names, you will find that there are issues with that: copying files using different media and/or over a network might not always retain all the date information such as creation date. They will, however, retain the file name.

- It's easy to automate and write scripts in this manner. A script to display all the graphs from last month is straightforward to implement.

- The convention is easily followed on a wide range of systems and programming languages. The application that records the data can be written in C programming language and not necessarily Python.

We therefore would like our file names to embed the date and time, preferably up to a second resolution. That being said, there are a lot of possible ways to denote date and time. Personally, I follow the date and time format suggested in ISO 8601: YYYY-MM-DDThh:mm:ss (see the section "Final Notes and References") with some modifications, as it is not possible to have a file name with colon (:) as is required by the format. Instead of colons, I use a dash (-). Another possible modification is replacing letter T used to separate the date and time portions in the ISO standard with a dash as well. The side benefit of those two replacements (replacing both the colons and the T with a dash) is that now there's a single field separator that separates year, month, day, hour, minute, and second. This is quite valuable for automation and is easily implemented in most programming languages. Some prefer keeping the character T as it does help remind where the date ends and when the time starts, and it's not all that complex to manage either. Leaving the T or replacing it with a dash are both good options and mostly are a matter of personal preference. As you'll soon see, we have a dedicated function for parsing dates, strptime(), that can handle the T quite easily.

Python provides us with the split(substr) function, which splits a string into a list of substrings once substr is encountered. In this case, split('-') will split the date-time format:

```
>>> a_date = "2008-04-02-22-14-14"
>>> a_date.split('-')
['2008', '04', '02', '22', '14', '14']
```

The following example extracts the month as an integer:

```
>>> int("2004-04-12-11-11-11".split('-')[1])
4
```

In the latter example, I chose to operate directly on the string, not saving it in a variable. The month is the second element in the list, hence to access it I index it: [1] (counting starts at 0). The function int() converts the string value to an integer.

If you follow the scheme where T is used instead of a dash, you can use the function strptime(), which is part of the time module. I assume strptime() is short for string-parse-time; regardless if it's true, it helps to remember the function name:

```
>>> from time import strptime
>>> strptime("2003-06-28T09-29-22", "%Y-%m-%dT%H-%M-%S")
(2003, 6, 28, 9, 29, 22, 5, 179, -1)
```

Note Small and capital letters are used to distinguish between a date and time fields, mainly because the character m can mean both month and minutes. So the convention is that time is denoted by caps (HH, MM, SS) and date is denoted by small letters (yy, mm, dd). There's one exception and that's the year: when using a four-digit notation (e.g., 2008), the characters are capitalized: YYYY.

As you can see, it's quite easy to extract date and time information in Python from a file name so long as one conforms to the convention. Processing all the files from, say, April 2008 can be done using a single split() command followed by an if statement.

Useful File Name Titles

Another important aspect of a file name is a useful title. A short, descriptive title can be a time-saver. SystemY or MarsTelescopeA are good candidates. Avoid titles that describe the data such as Logfiles or TemperatureAndFlow. You want to describe the system more than the data; the data will speak for itself when you analyze it. If you do want to describe the data, do so in addition to describing the system: Sys736Logs is a good option.

The following sample titles further clarify this point:

- PumpRawData is lacking system description. What if you have several pumps you want to test for flow? One alternative is to use the pump's serial number: Pump472RawData (assuming 472 is the pump's serial number).

- VoltageSys2AMay2008 is probably not a good title either. If you append the date to this title, you might end up with a title that looks like this: VoltageSys2A-May2008-2009-01-01-01-01-01. So which one is it—year 2009 or year 2008?

- VoltageCurrentSystem2A is OK; however, I'd opt to rename it to be *less* specific, or should I say, more general: ElectricalDataSystem2A. The reason for the renaming is that it's possible you'll decide to record additional values, say, power, as well as voltage and current, and unless you want to rename your code to look for different headers, having a file name titled VoltageCurrentSystem2A that also has power values will be a bit misleading.

File Name Extensions

The last part of the file name convention is an indication of the file format, usually denoted by the file name extension. File name extensions are typically three characters long (some are less, such as .gz, and some are longer, such as .html). We'll try to follow a convention of three characters for the extension, again because it will be easier for the processing application. I suggest thinking about three distinct file name extension subcategories:

- *Known file formats*: Image formats follow very specific extensions: .jpg, .png, .bmp, .tiff, and more. These file names have a meaning, so if you're recording data in those file formats, use the known extensions. There are also known extensions for compressed file formats, video file formats, and others, so use them accordingly.

- *Text file formats*: Here I suggest using either a .txt or a .csv extension. If the text file format is not the Comma Separated Values (CSV) format, use the .txt extension, suggesting it is viewable by most text editors. Exceptions to this guideline include files that already have a known extension, for example, INI files: although they are text files, you really want to capture that they're files holding initialization values. The same would apply to batch files and shell scripts. But those typically are not data files.

- *Binary file formats*: Binary file formats are not as self-descriptive as CSV files. And unlike CSV or plain text files, they are hard to view without knowing in advance the specific file format. For this reason, binary file formats should be accompanied by a header file that describes the contents and format of the binary files. However, it's still valuable to know a bit more about the binary file format even if the exact format is unknown. The following is the suggested convention: one character denoting whether the data is signed (i), unsigned (u), or floating point (f) followed by the number of bits used to store the data, as described in Table 4-1.

Table 4-1. *Suggested Binary File Name Extensions*

Description	Precision	Extension
Signed integers	8, 16, 32, 64	.i08, .i16, .i32, .i64 (respectively)
Unsigned integers	8, 16, 32, 64	.u08, .u16, .u32, .u64 (respectively)
Floating point	32 (float)	f32
	64 (double)	f64

- *Other binary file formats*: When binary files contain several values of different precisions, the convention described in the Table 4-1 is not feasible, at least not in a three-character extension notation. In that case use .bin or .x.bin where x is a number. The reason for the x is that it's conceivable you'll have several file formats of varying precisions, and a good way to tell them apart would be to add an integer prefix. Notice that they still all end with a .bin, enabling easy file distinction.

In Conclusion

Three items are important to file naming conventions: date and time in a file name, useful and descriptive file name titles, and proper file name extensions. If you follow these conventions, you'll find that writing scripts to manipulate these files is simple.

Using these conventions, we have file names that follow the scheme Title-YYYY-mm-dd-HH-MM-SS.ext with the placeholders detailed in Table 4-2.

Table 4-2. *Convention Scheme for File Name* Title-YYYY-mm-dd-HH-MM-SS.ext

Placeholder	Description
Title	A descriptive title of your choice
YYYY	Year the file was created
mm	Month the file was created. In the case of January, mm is 01.
dd	Day file was created. In the case of the 7th, dd is 07.
HH	Hours in 24-hour notation. 11 p.m. would be represented as 23. Values are from 00 to 23.
MM	Minutes. 5 minutes past the hour is 05.
SS	Seconds. 7 seconds past the minute is 07.
ext	An extension describing the file format, three characters long (if possible).

■**Note** In case of values occupying less than the assigned number of digits, a zero is added. So if the time is 5 minutes past 1 o'clock, the value of hh will be 01 and the value of mm will be 05.

Example: Automating File Name Creation

Listing 4-1 presents an implementation, unique.py, that conforms to the file name conventions suggested previously.

Listing 4-1. *Creating a Unique File Name, unique.py*

```
from time import localtime
# a script to create unique file names based on title,
# date and time stamp and an extension
datetime_stamp  = '%4d-%02d-%02dT%02d-%02d-%02d' % localtime()[:6]
title = 'SysALogs'
ext = 'csv'
print 'Unique filename: %s-%s.%s' % (title, datetime_stamp, ext)
```

Here's the result I got from executing python unique.py:

```
Unique filename: SysALogs-2008-09-03T09-29-36.csv
```

■**Note** We're assuming that files are generated at a slower rate of one file per second and that there's only one application logging data, hence a file name based on seconds is unique. Also, in case of a system time change, there's a chance of files being nonunique. Before creating a file, we could check whether a file with the same name exists, but for clarity reasons it's left out of the script.

The function localtime() is part of the time module and provides a tuple of values representing the year, month, day of the month, hours, minutes, seconds, week day, day of the year, and daylight saving time (phew). We only require the first six arguments of localtime() to create our unique file name. To access the first six elements of the tuple, we use the slicing operator [:6]. So localtime()[:6] returns the very six elements we're interested in for creating our unique file name.

Next we use the % operator to format the string containing the timestamp: '%4d-%02d-%02dT%02d-%02d-%02d'. The substring '%4d' means up to four digits; the substring '%02d' means two digits, and in case there are less than two digits, padded with zeros. We also use the % operator to output the final unique file name, which is composed of the strings stored in variables title, datetime_stamp, and ext. In this case we use '%s' to format strings instead of integers.

Other Schemes

Unfortunately, automating file name creation and using the date and time mostly applies if you're writing the application that generates the data files. That's not always the case: you might be using an embedded system's output files and have no control of the source code. As long as the system generating the files has a real time clock, and assuming you can change the code, or later change the file names, following the preceding convention is doable.

On the occasions where a real time clock is unavailable, a different naming scheme should be employed. One of the alternatives to using a timestamp in a file name is a running index. That's a bit more complex than using the date because now we have to figure out what's the last index used. That being said, it's still a good option: it provides consistency, and unless files are randomly deleted, it also provides some sort of chronological order. Incidentally, that's the scheme used by most digital cameras.

Example: Running Index

Listing 4-2 is a suggested running index implementation. The script will look for files according to a title and extension and determine a running index (up to 999). It will then create a file accordingly. Repeatedly running the script will create files with incrementing index values.

Listing 4-2. *Running Index Implementation*

```
# a script to create unique file names using a running index
from os.path import exists

index_stamp = 1
max_index   = 999    # maximum number of files
title       = '../data/SysALogs'
ext         = 'txt'

while index_stamp < max_index:
    unique_filename = '%s-%03d.%s' % (title, index_stamp, ext)
    if exists(unique_filename):
        index_stamp += 1
        continue
    f = open(unique_filename, 'wt')
    f.write("Data")
    f.close()
    break

# report status
if index_stamp >= max_index:
    print "Could not create a unique filename"
else:
    print "Created unique file: ", unique_filename
```

The general operation of this script is as follows: first we create a file name string with the current index. Next, we check to see whether the file exists by calling the function exists(), which is part of the os.path module (more on os.path in Chapter 10). If the file exists, we increment the index and restart the loop; this is done with the statement `continue`. In case the file name we've created does not exist, we proceed with writing the data to the file and breaking out of the `while` loop. Lastly, in case a unique file name was not available (we check up to index 999, per variable `max_index`), the script reports that a unique file name could not be created.

Notice that we choose to pad the running index with zeros as denoted by the substring `'%03d'` in the line `unique_filename = '%s-%03d.%s' % (title, index_stamp, ext)`. This is generally a good idea and allows easier processing of file names, as they have identical lengths, and the strings representing the file names can be easily sliced.

■**Note** If you change the value of `max_index`, be sure to change the format string accordingly. For example, if `max_index` is `99999`, replace `%03d` with `%05d` in the format specifications for `unique_filename`. This can also be done automatically by calculating the number of digits using `int(log10(max_index)+1)` and using the result in the format specifications (see the section "Example: Searching Inside a Text File" in Chapter 5).

File Formats

Up to this point we've discussed the form of the file names. Now it is time to discuss the format of the contents, that is, file formats. As previously pointed out, you may not be able to choose the file format used to store the data. Assuming you do have influence over the file format, the question is what format to use. A good file format is portable, easily recognizable, and does not impact performance drastically, be it size or computation overhead, depending on the nature of the application.

When you select a file format, consider the amount of data you'll be dealing with. If you're looking at large amounts of data, you want to be as efficient as possible in both storing the data and accessing it, sacrificing a bit for portability and using a less self-descriptive file format. This means choosing a binary format. If the amount of data is not large and you want the data to be self-descriptive and portable as much as possible, choose text file formats, specifically CSV. By large amounts of data, consider the following:

- How much storage space do you have? If you're running a desktop PC, a reasonable size to be dealing with is less than 1 terabyte. Of course, this number is ever-changing as storage space and processing power increase. At times you will find that due to storage space limitations your only option is going with binary files. The reason for this is that text representation is not as efficient as binary representations. 8-bit integers (characters) require 1 byte of storage in binary form and from 1 to 3 bytes in text form used in CSV. Storing floating-point values, which typically require 4 or 8 bytes in binary form, will now require a considerably larger amount of bytes. The value 0.00000095367431640625 (which is 2 to the power of minus 20) will now require 22 bytes to represent properly in a CSV file. And that's not counting the separators and delimiters.

- How critical is performance to your application? The smaller the data files, the faster you can process them. There's no need to parse the data, simply read it. If performance is your major concern, opt for binary file format.

■**Note** The sentence "The smaller the data files, the faster you can process them" is not always correct. In case of compressed files, data files are smaller but require more processing power to work with, hence performance is worse, not better. However, assuming no compression, performance of binary files is usually better.

So from a high-level file format category, you want to decide whether you'll be looking at binary data or text data. Table 4-3 lists the pros and cons of using either.

Table 4-3. *Pros and Cons of Binary and Text File Formats*

	Pros	Cons
Text	Self-descriptive (usually) Does not require specific knowledge of the file format Can be viewed by any text editor	Not storage efficient Medium read/write access Requires "text" parsers
Binary	Relatively small storage space Fast read and write access	Not so self-descriptive Requires knowledge of the file format Requires a specific application to view data

Text and binary are high-level categorizations. When dealing with text files, we will mostly limit our discussion to plain text files and CSV files and touch lightly on other file formats. When dealing with binary files, we'll talk mostly about straightforward file formats such as u16 and i32 and not complex file formats such as MP3 and GZ that might support compression and/or encryption.

CSV File Format

The CSV file format is a text file format and can be viewed by any text editor. Furthermore, most spreadsheet applications are capable of reading and writing CSV files, parsing the values properly into rows and cells. In CSV files, values are separated by commas; values are strings that represent numbers, dates, titles, or any other textual fields. If the string value has a comma in it, quoting is required, that is, the string will have beginning and ending quotes. Alternatively, the comma in the field can be escaped (more on this in Chapter 5). CSV format does not require a fixed number of fields per line (also called a row), which can be quite useful: it allows easy annotation of headers or descriptions of the data, which in turn can later be read by most any spreadsheet and/or editor with all the information recorded still intact and easily accessible.

The following are the contents of a valid CSV file:

```
System A
Data generated by logger1
"Header, 1",Header 2
Value 1,1
Value 2,AA
```

Example: Stock Price Charts

Following a convention that stores a short description of the data in the beginning lines of the CSV files can be very useful for annotating a graph or a report associated with the data in the file.

To follow along with the example, ensure your directory structure is similar to that presented in Chapter 2 in the section "Example: Directory Structure for the Book." Your base directory should be Ch4; within Ch4 there should be three subdirectories named src, data, and images. If you wish to use a different scheme, be sure to change the file path variable and the call to function savefig() in the script in Listing 4-3, which appears a little later in this section.

For this example you can download data from the NASDAQ stock exchange web site (http://www.nasdaq.com). Select a stock, for instance, the NASDAQ-100 (IXNDX) or your company's stock chart, you wish to display on the intranet web site. You will be presented with a chart of the stock. When you click the chart, the NASDAQ web site presents the actual values used to create the chart. You can choose to download the file in Excel format: do so, and save the file under directory Ch4/data/charts.xls.

If you open the file Ch4/data/charts.xls in a text editor, you'll notice that there's header information describing what each column means:

Date	Open	High	Low	Close/Last	Volume
09/02/2008	1904.75	1912.72	1843.07	1850.14	0
08/29/2008	1897.56	1899.56	1866.81	1872.54	0
08/28/2008	1907.17	1921.19	1904.20	1915.12	0
08/27/2008	1886.76	1913.53	1881.54	1900.30	0

In reality, the file format is a form of CSV, the separator being a tab instead of a comma. We can easily overcome this with Python's csv module by specifying the delimiter to be tab '\t'. Listing 4-3 shows our implementation, stock_charts.py, which reads a stock chart file and presents a graph with the header information properly displayed. Be sure to save it in folder Ch4/src. The result will be a PNG image, stock_price.png, in directory Ch4/images.

Listing 4-3. *stock_charts.py, Plotting NASDAQ charts.xls File*

```
from pylab import *
import csv
from time import gmtime, mktime
```

```
# modify the following to point to your data file
filepath = '../data/charts.xls'

# read the entire CSV file and store it in an array of lists
# use tab ('\t') as a delimiter
data = []
for row in csv.reader(open(filepath), delimiter='\t'):
    data.append(row)

# split the data to header and values
header = data[0]
values = array(data[1:])

# the first column is date information in a string format
# we transform it to a day of year format
# notice that this will not work over year boundary (need to add 365)
yearday = zeros(len(values[:, 0]))
for i, day in enumerate(values[:, 0]):
    market_close_time = (int(day[6:]), int(day[:2]), int(day[3:5]), \
        16, 0, 0, 0, 0, 0)
    yearday[i] = gmtime(mktime(market_close_time)).tm_yday

# plot the data
for i in range(1, 5):
    plot(yearday, values[:, i], label=header[i], linewidth=3)

# annotate the start and end dates
text(yearday[0], values[0, 1], values[0, 0])
text(yearday[-1], values[-1, 1], values[-1, 0])

grid()
legend()
ylabel('Stock price [USD]')
xlabel('Days from start of the year '+values[0, 0][6:])
title('NASDAQ-100 (IXNDX) Stock price, period %s-%s' % (values[-1, 0], values[0,0]))
savefig('../images/stock_price.png')
```

We start by reading the CSV data file and passing a tab as a delimiter. The first line in variable data is the header information, describing what each column means: Date, Open, High, Low, Close/Last, and Volume. The remaining lines are the values to plot. We therefore split the variable data into header and values, accordingly. We also convert the values to a NumPy array using the function call array(). Using a NumPy array, the data will be easier to process and plot; more about NumPy in Chapter 7.

The following is not so much an explanation of working with CSV files but is important to fully understand the script.

Next is the so-called linearization process. Much like in the GPS example of Chapter 1, data in charts.xls is not linear. The information is stock prices on a daily basis; however, stocks are not traded every day, weekends being the prime example but also holidays. If we plot the information as is, neglecting these "holes" in the data, the picture presented will be skewed. So instead, we need to choose a different time base, one that will take into consideration nontrade days. I chose to use the day-of-the-year value: January 1 is 1, January 2 is 2, . . . December 31 is 365 or 366 (leap year dependent).

Since I don't want to get into the process of determining leap years or summing up the days in each month, I've decided to use the time module again. The idea here is to use the function gmtime() and as a side effect, retrieve the day-of-the-year value. Function gmtime() receives a value representing the number of seconds elapsed since the epoch, a fixed point in time (see more about the epoch in Chapter 5). While this sounds even more complicated than calculating the day of the year, in reality it's easier because of function mktime(). Function mktime() receives a tuple of nine values, detailed previously, and returns the number of seconds since the epoch. So we first construct a tuple of those nine values, the first three being year, month, and day, which are known to us, and arbitrarily assigning the hour to be 4 p.m. (which coincides with the end of trade). We leave the remaining fields zero. We then feed this number to gmtime() and receive a new tuple, now properly populated with the year of day, the eighth element of the tuple, accessible with tm_yday, which we save in vector yearday.

■**Note** The script does not take into account data over more than one year. To accommodate for this, you could take into consideration the number of days in a year (365 or 366, depending on a leap year) and use the lowest year as a baseline.

We then plot the data and annotate the graph. For the legend, we use the header values of the CSV file stored in variable header. We also use actual values from the variable values to annotate the start and end of period on the graph itself, the title, and the x-axis label (see Figure 4-1).

■**Note** If you look closely at the data in charts.xls, you'll notice that it's reversed, that is, backward in time. One of the side effects of using the day-of-the-year value is that values are now plotted from lower to higher values, that is, older times are on the left, and newer events are on the right. If you'd like to reverse this behavior, issue the command gca().axes.invert_xaxis().

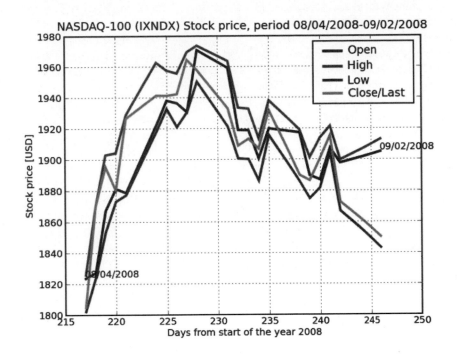

Figure 4-1. *Stock price chart output*

Example: Automatically Reading Yahoo! Financial Data

The following discussion is a bit off-topic, but as it is a direct continuation of the previous example, this is probably a logical spot for it.

There's an alternative method to manually saving the `charts.xls` file from NASDAQ. One such option is using the matplotlib.finance module. The two core functions that fetch the data and parse it are `fetch_historical_yahoo()` and `parse_yahoo_historical()` (although you could easily parse the data yourself). Another function of interest is the `candlestick()` function, which plots a candlestick graph of the stocks.

Listing 4-4 is a modification of the previous example to use the functions from the matplotlib.finance module. Notice that there are some other minor changes to the code because the data structure is a bit different from the NASDAQ `charts.xls` file. You can control the stock you wish to view and the start and end dates by changing the values `stock_name`, `t_start`, and `t_end`.

Listing 4-4. *Fetching and Plotting Yahoo! Data*

```
from pylab import *
from matplotlib.finance import *

# stock name and period
stock_name  = 'NDX'
t_start     = datetime.datetime(2008, 1, 1)
```

```
t_end       = datetime.datetime(2008, 1, 31)
year_start  = datetime.datetime(2008, 1, 1)

# retrieve and parse stock data
data    = fetch_historical_yahoo(stock_name, t_start, t_end)
y       = array(parse_yahoo_historical(data))

# dates might not be trade days, so update values
# to show actual dates retrieved
t_start = num2date(y[0, 0])
t_end   = num2date(y[-1, 0])

# normalize the x-axis to show values from the start of year
y[:, 0]  = y[:, 0]-date2num(year_start)+1

# plot a candlestick graph
figure()
candlestick(gca(), y)

# annotate the graph with additional text
start_str  = "%d-%02d-%02d" % (t_start.year, t_start.month, t_start.day)
end_str    = "%d-%02d-%02d" % (t_end.year, t_end.month, t_end.day)
title('Stock: %s, period %s to %s' % (stock_name, start_str, end_str))
xlabel('Days from start of the year %d' % t_start.year)
ylabel('%s Stock price [USD]' % stock_name)
text(y[0, 0], y[0, 1], start_str)
text(y[-1, 0], y[-1, 1], end_str)
grid()
savefig('../images/%s_candlestick_yahoo-%s-%s.png' % \
    (stock_name, start_str, end_str))
```

Some notes:

- The time base is normalized, that is, the dates are shown from the start of the year 2008 and not the epoch. This is implemented in line y[:,0] = y[:,0]-date2num(year_start)+1.

- The actual dates requested might not be trade days. Therefore, the start and end times are updated after the data is fetched and parsed. This is done in line t_start = num2date(y[0, 0]) and t_end = num2date(y[-1, 0]).

Figure 4-2 shows the results of the example in Listing 4-4.

Figure 4-2. *Automatically generated candlestick graph*

Example: Creating a CSV File

The following is an example of writing a list to a CSV file. I assign some arbitrary mixed data (strings and numbers) to a list named data and write it to file. Try it yourself, and then open the created file test.csv to view the file contents.

```
>>> L = [['Time', 'Value', 'Notes'], [0, 20, 'Start point'],\
...     [0.1, 'Middle point'], [2]]
>>> import csv
>>> f = open('../data/test.csv', 'wb')
>>> csv.writer(f).writerows(L)
>>> f.close()
```

Here are the contents of the test file, test.csv:

```
Time,Value,Notes
0,20,Start point
0.1,Middle point
2
```

Try changing the values of the list, such as adding a comma to one of the strings. Now, open the file in a spreadsheet application: did the application manage to read the comma properly? Open the file in a text editor and notice the string containing the comma is now quoted. The csv module took care of adding quotes as required. More about the csv module in Chapter 5.

USING THE CSV MODULE INSTEAD OF THE SPLIT() FUNCTION

So far we've used Python's csv module liberally. You might be wondering why we're not using the function `split(',')` instead of the `csv.reader` object. The answer is that the csv module also addresses special cases such as a string that includes a comma. Consider the following row:

`"Surname, Name", 2008, 450`

Module csv will handle this properly and return three elements. However, `split(',')` will return four elements: the quoted string will be broken in two.

CSV Limitations

All's not roses in the world of CSV. Here are some things to consider:

- *Size*: CSV files are typically not size efficient, compared with binary file formats.

- *Performance*: There's also a performance hit with CSV files because they require parsing. An application, be it a spreadsheet application or even our code in Python, calls a function to translate the CSV file into values more easily used by the application. That is, it parses fields and rows and translates from text to integer or floating point in the case of number values. Running the parser to read the CSV file takes time, so reading a large file will take considerable time. If performance is of importance and your application reads very large files, consider using a binary file format instead.

What to Store

As a general rule, store as much information as possible. Unfortunately, sometimes that's simply not possible. Consider the data rate of an uncompressed HDTV video signal at 1280×720 pixels, 30 frames per second, true colors (24 bits). That's 1280×720×30×3 bytes per second, or roughly 83 megabytes per second and on the order scale of today's hardware limitations. Which means you'll have to discard some of the information or compress it, or get better hardware.

Deciding what to store and what not to store will be very much system dependent. Some opt for decimating the data, which has its implications. Others decide on discarding a parameter they deem less important. Barring file size limitations, consider the following guidelines in deciding what to store:

- Write header file information in the beginning of the file, describing the system and the data, including units of measurement. You can use free-form text for this. Some even go a further step by adding a special character (e.g., #) at the beginning of every line, ensuring the reader understands those are remarks and not part of the data.

- Include a header for each column, explaining what each column means. It's very useful for both viewing the files using a spreadsheet and for automated scripts to visualize the data.

- Always try to store the time and date. Store the date and time values in the first column. You can follow the ISO 8601 specifications, or you might opt to use a different notation. An alternative valuable notation to ISO 8601 format is to store the number of seconds that have elapsed since the epoch: 1 January 1970 on most Linux machines. That way you have a number that is very easy to manipulate, as opposed to a date and time that requires parsing. There's also a side benefit and that is if you have several files, you can use the same time base for all of them. The seconds-since-the-epoch notation is very useful in binary formats.

Here's an example of the contents of a file that follows the preceding guidelines:

```
#Units,Celsius
#Sensor,A1
#System serial number,401
Date and Time,Temperature,Pressure
2005-09-15T01:07:08, 42.0,53.1
2005-09-15T01:07:14, 42.0,53.2
2005-09-15T01:07:19, 39.0,51.8
```

When to Use CSV

Use CSV whenever possible, with the following exceptions:

- Performance is an issue.

- File size is an issue.

- Data is already in a different format.

Binary Files

Binary files are an efficient method of storing data. The term "binary files" means files that are not represented as ASCII text; that is, if you open these files in a text editor, the data will appear to be gibberish. In reality there's no difference between binary files and text files, other than what the data in the files represent. From the computer's perspective, they're both just files. So in essence, if the file is not a text file, it's a binary file, but that's a loose definition.

As discussed previously, there are merits to using binary file formats, and those are typically size and performance. There's also another reason, and that's the nature of the data. A digital picture is not easily represented as a text file (it can be though—for example, every pixel value is an integer in a CSV file). The same applies to compressed files. Regardless of the reason, it's almost impossible to avoid using binary files.

In this book, when I refer to binary files, I typically mean one of the following file formats: an array of values, an array of structs, or other commonly used binary file formats.

An Array of Values

The most simple binary file format we'll be using is an array of values, that is, a repeating single data type. The file could be holding 16-bit signed values or unsigned bytes. The array-of-values file format lends itself nicely to storing simple binary data.

Example: Reading and Writing an Array of Binary Values

The Python array data type is an ideal candidate for this sort of binary file handling. The array data type is part of the array module, so to use it, issue the following command:

```
>>> from array import *
```

To create an array, call the array() function with the data type and optional initialization parameters, as follows:

```
>>> a = array('h') # array of signed shorts, of zero size
>>> a
array('h')
>>> b = array('L', [1000, 2000, 3000]) # array of three unsigned longs
>>> b
array('L', [1000L, 2000L, 3000L])
>>> c = array('d', range(10)) # array of doubles, from 0 to 9 including
>>> c
array('d', [0.0, 1.0, 2.0, 3.0, 4.0, 5.0, 6.0, 7.0, 8.0, 9.0])
```

The data types listed in Table 4-4 can be used in initializing array objects.

Table 4-4. *Array Data Types*

Data Type	Data Meaning and Size
'c'	Character, 1 byte.
'u'	Unicode character, 2 bytes.
'b'	Signed character, 1 byte.
'B'	Unsigned character, 1 byte.
'h'	Signed short, 2 bytes.
'H'	Unsigned short, 2 bytes.
'i'	Unsigned int, size is CPU dependent.
'I'	Unsigned int, size is CPU dependent.
'l'	Signed long, 4 bytes.
'L'	Unsigned long, 4 bytes.

Data Type	Data Meaning and Size
'f'	Floating-point value, 4 bytes.
'd'	Floating-point value, 8 bytes.

Of these data types, as a guideline, try not to use the 'i' and 'I' data types, since they're system dependent and might prove problematic when you transfer your code to another system (unless of course that functionality is exactly what you require).

Writing array values to file is done using the tofile() member function of the array data type:

```
>>> f = open('b.u32', 'wb')
>>> b.tofile(f)
>>> f.close()
```

Reading is performed using the fromfile() member function of the array data type. The function fromfile() also requires the number of values to read. If you supply a number greater than the number of elements in the file, an exception is raised; however, values will still be retrieved.

```
>>> d = array('L')
>>> f = open('b.u32', 'rb')
>>> d.fromfile(f, 3)
>>> f.close()
>>> d == b
True
```

An Array of Structs

A more complex binary data structure we'll be dealing with is an array of structs. The word "struct" is taken from the C programming language and describes a structure combined of several data types.

Suppose data is stored as follows: long, float, float, long, float, float, and so forth. This series can be viewed as an array of structures, with the structure being { long, float, float }. In this sense, an array of values, discussed previously, is also an array of structs with the struct being a single data type, for example, { char }. If you're familiar with C, the preceding structure might be described as in Listing 4-5.

Listing 4-5. *A Struct in C*

```
struct some_binary_file_format
{
    long epoch;
    float fTemperature;
    float fPressure;
};
```

Note that unlike our previous binary file formats, this one doesn't lend itself to a nice extension naming convention such as .u16 or .f32, so we simply choose the extension .bin, noting that it's a binary file.

Example: Reading and Writing an Array of Structs

In this example, we'll create a structure containing two data types (long and float), write it to file, and then read it using two different methods: a structure at a time and the entire file at once. You can follow along by entering the commands interactively at the Python shell.

First, we have to import the struct module:

```
>>> import struct
```

To illustrate the concept of an array of structs, we'll create a list of rows. Each row is a list of three values: a long and two floats, which represent a structure. We'll generate a relatively short list, only two rows long:

```
>>> L = [[ 10L, 1.0, 2.0], [20L, 0.125, 0.25]]
```

Next, we define two variables, filename and format, so we don't have to enter them every time:

```
>>> filename = '../data/structs.bin'
>>> format = 'Lff'
```

I'm assuming there's a directory named ../data; if one does not exist, either create it or change the value of the variable filename accordingly. The format 'Lff' means a long, followed by a float and a float per Table 4-4. Next, we write the list to file:

```
>>> fout = open(filename, 'wb')
>>> for row in L:
...     data = struct.pack(format, row[0], row[1], row[2])
...     fout.write(data)
...
>>> fout.close()
```

The first call to open() opens a file in binary mode. We then use a for loop and iterate over the rows in the list L. Every row is packed using the function struct.pack(). The function struct.pack() accepts a format and then the values to pack. The return value is a string that can be written to file. We then write the string to file. Finally, the last line closes the file.

So now we should have a file named ../data/structs.bin. This file contains the list of values from the list L. Let's read it a struct at a time:

First, we'll start by defining a variable equivalent to the size of the struct format:

```
>>> struct_size = struct.calcsize(format)
```

The function struct.calcsize() calculates the size in bytes of the format. Armed with the struct size, we start reading the data, a struct at a time:

```
>>> fin = open(filename, 'rb')
>>> data = fin.read(struct_size)
>>> data
'\n\x00\x00\x00\x00\x80?\x00\x00\x00@'
```

The first line opens the file for reading in binary mode. We then use the function
read(n) to read n bytes and store them in the variable data. So now the variable data holds
the first structure from the binary file, but it isn't legible yet. We'll need to unpack it, using
struct.unpack(), that is, convert it from a string to a tuple of values using the format specifier 'Lff'. But since we'll be reading and unpacking several values, it stands to reason to use
a while loop as follows:

```
>>> while data:
...     values = struct.unpack(format, data)
...     print values
...     data = fin.read(struct_size)
...
(10, 1.0, 2.0)
(20, 0.125, 0.25)
>>> fin.close()
```

The while condition evaluates to True as long as variable data is nonempty, hence data
will be processed until the end of the file. Each struct read is unpacked to a tuple of values
using the struct.unpack() function. Once a struct is unpacked, we read the next structure.
This continues until all the structs are read from the input file. Lastly, we close the file.

The second method we'll examine here is reading the entire file at once. To do so, we first
read the entire file to memory, using the read() function:

```
>>> data = open(filename, 'rb').read()
>>> len(data)
24
```

If no parameters are provided for read(), the entire file is read into memory until an end
of file (EOF) is reached. This might not be a problem with small files, but with larger files be
wary; your computer might not be able to handle all the data at once, so you will need to read
the files in chunks per the previous method. Note that I've chosen not to assign a file handle
for the data file and let Python handle the closing of the file for me.

The function struct.unpack() accepts format as a parameter and unpacks the data to a
tuple. However, we need to unpack the entire array, not just the first structure. We can take
the obvious route of using a for loop to unpack the binary data a piece at a time. An alternative approach is to change the format value to unpack() from a single 'Lff' to a repetitive
'LffLffLff...'. This allows unpacking of the entire binary data in one call to struct.unpack().
Luckily, Python provides us with a very useful tool for multiplying strings, the multiplication
operator:

```
>>> 'Lff'*5
'LffLffLffLffLff'
```

We can calculate the size of the array we want to unpack by dividing the length of the data
by the size of one struct. In our case, that's len(data)/struct_size. So to generate a format to
unpack by, we multiply the format by that value, which folds neatly into the following:

```
>>> print struct.unpack(format*(len(data)/struct_size), data)
(10, 1.0, 2.0, 20, 0.125, 0.25)
```

■**Note** (Advanced readers) This implementation assumes the file is in accordance with the native operating system's byte order. If you try to unpack data in this manner with any of the struct's byte order, size, and alignment format characters, such as @, =, <, >, and !, the function will fail.

Other Binary File Formats

Binary files can be more complex and can follow a different scheme from the repeating fixed-size structure. Some employ compression, which typically involves a non-fixed-size structure. Others might store data sequentially, that is, using the data of the preceding example, you could write all the long values, followed by the float values. In that case, a different method to read the file should be employed, but it's quite straightforward if you know the file format. In this book I'll touch lightly on this topic, specifically about known file types such as pictures and compressed files. Since the number of file formats is virtually unlimited, the topic is too vast for one book to cover.

Header Files

Unlike CSV files, with binary files you can't really tell whether the information is in integer representation, floating point, or an altogether different scheme. This means that you, the programmer, need to know in advance what file format you're dealing with. At first that might not seem such a complex task, but in reality, it's not trivial. Even with the same notation as explained previously in this chapter, say, .u16, you still don't know what the values represent: are they sampled voltage values? Is there a timestamp? And you might have several binary file formats you're dealing with.

To resolve this, we use a header file to describe each file type, or directory, in case all the files conform to the same format. A header file is a text file that describes the format of the binary file. But if we're using a text file, we might as well use CSV!

It's a good idea to have the same base file name for the header file as the binary file (excluding extension). I typically add an .hdr.csv extension for my header files; for example, for file Lava2001-03-21T08-22-23.f32 I name the header file Lava2001-03-21T08-22-23.f32.hdr.csv.

Here's an example of header file contents for an array-of-structs file format:

```
"Name", "Number of bytes", "Format", "Units"
"Time Elapsed since epoch", 4, "integer", "seconds"
"Temperature", 4, "float", "Degrees Celsius"
"Pressure", 4, "float", "Psi"
```

The nice thing about this structure is that it's quite self-explanatory. It lends itself easily to automation and scripting.

I've also added a column titled Units. This column is obvious; however, you will find later that it's quite useful. Say you know the temperature is an integer, but what exactly does it represent? Degrees? And if so, are those in Kelvin, Fahrenheit, or Celsius?

If the file format is different and does not follow the repeating fixed-size structure format, you can come up with a header that best describes that file format. In the case of sequential data, the header file might look like this:

```
"Name", "Number of bytes", "Format", "Units", "#Values"
"Time Elapsed since epoch", 4, "integer", "seconds", 100
"Temperature", 4, "float", "Degrees Celsius", 100
"Filtered values", 4, "float", "Degrees Celsius", 100
```

This format implies that the data is sequential, having 100 values for each parameter. This is a more complex file format and not at all popular due to the complexity associated with implementing a format that behaves like this; you'd have to remember all the information and then store it to file instead of gathering values and storing them one at a time. Again, at times, you're given data files to work with and can't control the file format.

Readme Files

Readme files are documentation files placed in a directory describing the contents of the files in that directory. There's no clear definition of the contents of Readme files, only that the information should be in clear text so as to be viewed by any text editor. Some Readme files have directions on what should be run and how to use the software. Others add author information and credentials. Using Readme files is an excellent way to document what you've done without the overhead of writing a user's manual. Here are occasions where I found using Readme files of value:

- They are helpful for describing the contents of data in directories: file formats, origin of data, date and time, person in charge, and so forth. See Chapter 1 for an example of a Readme file describing data.

- When directories contain both data and scripts to analyze them, there's bound to be a multitude of scripts. Describing the entry point, or what the user should run first, is a time saver—especially if a process is required before running the scripts, for example, uncompressing the data. Describe that in your Readme file.

Readme files can be as detailed or as cryptic as you'd like. Just remember that they're there to help; include detail in them according to the level of the user or developer so they understand what's going on.

The common full file name for Readme files is Readme.txt.

INI Files

As you add content and capabilities to your scripts, you'll find that you need to control the scripts' behavior using options, such as running the script but only generating a text output, without graphs or running the scripts on a different set of data points. As the number of options increase, you'll need methods for controlling the options. There are several ways to implement options. Following are the common ones:

- Interactive input from the user, for example, "Generate graphs (y/n)?"

- Command-line parameters such as the -l in the command ls -l.

- An external configuration file holding the choices and parameters. To change the behavior of the script, the user changes the values in the configuration file. The script reads the configuration file and acts accordingly.

The latter option, a configuration file, is also referred to as an INI file. The reason is that back in the days before the registry was introduced in Windows, applications used to store parameters in files having the application name and ending with an .INI extension. In Linux this is commonly referred to as a configuration files; configuration files typically reside in the directory /etc and have a .conf extension. Python supports INI files natively with the ConfigParser module.

Much like Readme files describing the data, INI files describe the parameters, options, and choices used to run a script. They provide a clean way of explaining what the options mean. The general markup of an INI file (config file) is a section, denoted by brackets, followed by a list of parameters and their assigned values and optional remarks, as outlined in Table 4-5.

Table 4-5. *INI File Format*

INI/Config Line	Format	Notes
Section	[section]	Used to group parameters logically
Parameter	param1=value1 *or* param1:value1	Used to set a parameter to a value
Remark	; remark *or* # remark	Used to document sections and parameters

Example: Reading and Writing INI Files

Listing 4-6 shows an implementation of writing an INI file using the ConfigParser module.

Listing 4-6. *Creating an INI (Config) File*

```
# creating an INI (config) file
import ConfigParser
options = ConfigParser.ConfigParser()
options.add_section('User Options')
options.set('User Options', 'all_data', True)
options.set('User Options', 'graph', 1)
options.add_section('Plot')
options.set('Plot', 'grid', True)
f = open('../data/options.ini', 'w')
options.write(f)
f.close()
```

First we import the ConfigParser module. We then set sections with the add_section() method and parameters and values with the set() method. Lastly, we create a file and output the ConfigParser object to file, generating an INI file. The following are the results from running the script in Listing 4-6:

```
[Plot]
grid = True

[User Options]
graph = 1
all_data = True
```

Reading an INI file is even easier. Assuming you have run the previous script, you should now have an INI file named `../data/options.ini`. The script in Listing 4-7 will read that file and parse its contents.

Listing 4-7. *Reading an INI (Config) File*

```
# read an INI (config) file
import ConfigParser
read_opts = ConfigParser.ConfigParser()
read_opts.read('../data/options.ini')

# print parameters and values
for section in read_opts.sections():
    print "[%s]" % section
    for param in read_opts.items(section):
        print param
```

The function `ConfigParser.read()` accepts a file name (use `readfp()` if you want to use a file object) and parses the INI file with the `ConfigParser` object. The code following the `read()` function call prints the sections, options, and values. Here are the results from running the script in Listing 4-7:

```
 [Plot]
('grid', 'True')
[User Options]
('all_data', 'True')
('graph', '1')
```

XML

XML, or Extensible Markup Language, has been growing in popularity as a data file format. XML is more descriptive than CSV and definitely more descriptive than binary, hence its popularity. XML is a very good format for data files, but it has its overhead. Mainly it requires a complex parser to read the data and check data validity. While that's true for CSV as well, CSV is much less complex.

XML, however, is left out of scope for this book, mainly because CSV provides us with the functionality we require, but also because the topic is too large to be addressed properly in this book. If you do require XML processing, rest assured that Python has extensive XML support. There's also a large selection of books available on XML, and I suggest you consult with them or the Internet should you require XML support.

Other File Formats

There are a large number of other file formats you're likely to encounter. These include image formats such as PNG, JPEG, bitmaps and GIF, or compressed file formats such as ZIP or GZ, and yes, XML too.

It is far beyond the scope of this book to detail and discuss all these file formats. One of the benefits of using Python is its popularity and an active developer base with an extensive number of freely available packages contributed by the Python community. There's a good chance there's already a module out there that's suitable for reading different file formats and converting them to programmer-friendly values. For example, a module we'll be exploring in Chapter 9, the Python Imaging Library (PIL), supports most popular image formats.

Locating Data Files

As described in the introduction to this chapter, as you gather data, you're bound to end up with files of various types: raw data files, clean data files, processed data files, files of older file formats, and the list goes on and on. The question is, how do you organize all this data, and furthermore, how do you later locate it for analysis?

This section suggests several approaches to organizing files and what's more important, maintaining well-organized data. One approach is storing files in directories and subdirectories, and we'll discuss methods to locate the files using that approach; another is to use catalog files and annotate them.

Organization into Directories

The most popular method of organizing files is in directories. If you go with this approach, try to have all your subdirectories containing data files in a parent directory named data or similar. If you intend to preprocess the data, split the directory into "raw" and "clean" data. The reason you want to do this is that you may find out later that the preprocessing algorithm has a bug or that a different method should be employed to preprocess the data. Or if you manually preprocessed the data (that is, cleaned up the data files, removed wrong files, edited others, etc.), you may later realize you accidentally erased the wrong data file or that you made some other mistake.

From here on, there are several options, for example, putting all the data files in one directory or creating subdirectories and organizing files there. Personally, I like to split the directories further for several reasons. One is that it gives me greater control over documentation: it's possible to generate Readme files for every directory. The other is that it allows greater control over what files to process, for example, I could process all files from directory systemA. Lastly, it helps provide a more aesthetic view, and that's an important part of any engineering work.

The actual breakdown into subdirectories is very problem specific. It could be based on dates, type of files, contents, and pretty much anything else you would like. However, do try to group the directories in one root directory, as it will be a lot easier to iterate through the data.

```
data
    raw
        systemA
```

```
        systemB
        systemC
    clean
        systemA
        systemB
        systemC
```

Searching for Files

One of the obvious methods for searching for a file is by recursively going through all the sub-directories and looking for files that match a given pattern.

Example: Storing Directory Contents in an Array

When you first look for a file, you don't always find it on your first search, maybe because you chose the wrong file name pattern or because of a simple typo. There's a good chance you'll require additional searches. Now if you have a significant number of data files, it can be tedious to rewalk the entire directory again. Every search is laborious, and time spent finding files will increase dramatically. Instead, it's possible to store the intermediate result in a data structure.

Try this yourself. Define the function `get_all_files()`, as shown in Listing 4-8, and call it interactively in Python by issuing `allfiles = get_all_files(some_path)`. Observe the results by issuing `print allfiles` at the Python shell.

Listing 4-8. *A Function to Retrieve All Files in a Directory and Store It in an Array*

```python
import os
def get_all_files(srchpath):
"""Get the names, paths and sizes of all the files in a directory."""
    allfiles = []

    for root, dirs, files in os.walk(srchpath):
        for file in files:
            pathname = os.path.join(root, file)
            filesize = os.path.getsize(pathname)
            allfiles.append([file, pathname, filesize])
    return allfiles
```

The function stores an entry to each file in a list (`allfiles`). Each entry in the list holds the file name, path name, and file size. A path name is the full path plus a name of a file (e.g., `/home/shai/file.txt`); a file name is the name of the file excluding the path (e.g., `file.txt`), and file size is given in bytes. The function `os.walk()` was described in Chapter 1 and should not require additional clarifications. I've made use of the function `os.path.getsize()` to retrieve the size of a file.

■Note In cases where file names contain non-English characters, I've seen the function `getsize()` raise an exception because it was unable to read the file. If you're dealing with such files, either rename them or add a `try`/`except` clause to catch the exception.

Indexing

The act of going through directories and recording file information in an organized manner is called indexing. Done properly, indexing can allow fast searches.

Example: Searching for Duplicate Files

Continuing our previous example, now that we have an array containing all the files in a directory, we can perform fast searches on the array. We can sort the array based on file size and find the ten largest files; or we can look for files matching a given pattern. In this example we'll explore a more complex search, one that checks for duplicate files. This is a true need, one that arises especially when dealing with a large number of files.

Assuming you have followed the unique file name convention suggested earlier, there shouldn't be any duplicate file names. However, that's not always the case. Consider the following: data is generated by copying pictures from a digital camera. Many digital cameras follow a simple running index scheme (see the section "Other Schemes" earlier in this chapter) whereby file names follow the pattern `Header0001.jpg`, `Header0002.jpg`, and so on, with each camera having its own `Header` string. After you copy the files to your computer, you delete the old files in the camera, clearing space for new pictures. New pictures taken by the camera will in turn start from index 1 and eventually, as they're copied to your computer, will have nonunique file names. To ensure files are not accidentally overwritten, you copy over each batch of pictures to a directory of its own, each directory named uniquely based on date and time. So you end up with several directories, but their contents could contain nonunique file names. Maybe some are the same. Can we clear some up?

Another scenario is that of backups, or that of using several storage locations, say, your laptop and your home PC. You may have copies of data lying around in several spots, and the question again is whether you have multiple copies of the same data. Of course, if you follow a central server approach and that server is backed up on a regular basis, you'll find that these occasions are rare. Still, it's nice to be able to identify duplicate files, and that's the motivation behind this example.

In the example we'll confine ourselves to the following: we assume files to be identical if they have the same file name and file size. While this isn't necessarily true, the example can be easily modified to compare contents as well.

We'll show three different implementations and discuss the best solution of the three. In all three methods we'll use a dictionary object.

■Note To be able to follow along, ensure you've defined the function `get_all_files()` from the previous example. Run it in interactive Python and store the results in an array as follows: `allfiles = get_all_files(pathname)`.

Method 1: We use the file name as the unique key in our dictionary, mydict1. The value is a list of [filepath, filesize]. At first, mydict1 is empty. For every entry, we ask whether the file name is a key to the dictionary. If it wasn't encountered, we add the list [filepath, filesize] as a value to the key, file name. If the key is in the dictionary, it means that this file name has been encountered in the past. We then retrieve the file size and compare it with the current entry file size. Listing 4-9 shows the implementation.

Listing 4-9. *Looking for Duplicate Files, Method 1*

```
def find_dupes_1(thefiles):
    """Searches for file duplicates, method 1."""
    result1 = []
    mydict1 = dict()

    for filename, pathname, filesize in thefiles:
        if filename in mydict1:
            [dup_file, dup_size] = mydict1[filename]
            if dup_size == filesize:
                result1.append(pathname)
        else:
            mydict1[filename] = [pathname, filesize]
    return result1
```

One of the obvious shortcomings of this method is that there might be several files with the same file name but different sizes; the algorithm might not catch some of them. For example, if the first file is of size A, and several other files have the same file name but are of size B, the algorithm will not identify files of size B as duplicates.

Method 2: This method uses the path name as the unique key in the dictionary mydict2 and the list [filename, filesize] as the value. Since we're using the path name as the key, it's guaranteed to be unique; there are no two files with the same file name and path name. To check whether a file name already exists in the dictionary, we iterate through all the elements in the dictionary using the iteritems() method. If the file name and the file size are identical, we announce them to be a duplicate. If not, we add the associated path name as key and the [filename, filesize] as a new value to the dictionary (see Listing 4-10).

Listing 4-10. *Looking for Duplicate Files, Method 2*

```
def find_dupes_2(thefiles):
    """Searches for file duplicates, method 2."""
    result2 = []
    mydict2 = dict()

    for filename, pathname, filesize in thefiles:
        for k, v in mydict2.iteritems():
            if v[0] == filename and v[1] == filesize:
                result2.append(pathname)
        else:
            mydict2[pathname] = [filename, filesize]
    return result2
```

While this method does resolve the shortcoming of method 1 in that if there are several files with the same file name, they will all be checked, the implementation is not a good one. The major issue is that we use a dictionary object to store values and neglect to use the inherent hashing mechanism properly: we iterate through all the items linearly. We probably could've just as well used an array.

Method 3: This method uses the file name as the key in the dictionary object mydict3. The difference from method 1 is that instead of a list holding [pathname, filesize], we now hold an *array* of [pathname, filesize] lists for every key, much like in a real dictionary where one entry (key) might have several definitions (values). The second change we introduce is that we don't ask whether the file name (key) is part of the current set of keys. Instead, we simply access the dictionary object with the file name using the method get(). If there's an entry, we go through the array of [pathname, filesize] values and check for duplicate files. If one matches, it's a duplicate. If none matches, we append our new [pathname, filesize] to the array of current values. In case there's no entry for the file name, we add it as a new entry to the dictionary object (see Listing 4-11).

Listing 4-11. *Finding Duplicate Files, Method 3*

```
def find_dupes_3(thefiles):
    """Searches for file duplicates, method 3."""
    result3 = []
    mydict3 = dict()

    for filename, pathname, filesize in thefiles:
        if mydict3.get(filename):
            for [dup_file, dup_size] in mydict3[filename]:
                if dup_size == filesize:
                    result3.append(pathname)
            mydict3[filename].append([pathname, filesize])
        else:
            mydict3[filename] = [[pathname, filesize]]
    return result3
```

Of the three methods, the third one is the best because it uses hashing properly.

To check performance for yourself, copy the function implementations per Listing 4-9, 4-10, and 4-11 to a text editor, save them under scriptname.py, and then issue execfile('scriptname.py') in an interactive Python shell. Once that's done, here's a short set of commands you can use to measure performance. Be sure to change the srchpath variable to point to a directory containing a large number of files, with some duplicates.

```
>>> srchpath = 'c:/Python25'
>>> allfiles = get_all_files(srchpath)
>>> t = []
>>> from time import clock as clk
>>> t.append(clk()); res1 = find_dupes_1(allfiles); t.append(clk())
>>> t.append(clk()); res2 = find_dupes_2(allfiles); t.append(clk())
>>> t.append(clk()); res3 = find_dupes_3(allfiles); t.append(clk())
>>> len(allfiles)   # number of data files processed
8371
```

```
>>> print "method 1: %5.5f; method 2: %5.5f; method 3: %5.5f" % \
... (t[1]-t[0], t[3]-t[2], t[5]-t[4])
method 1: 0.00761; method 2: 5.61522; method 3: 0.01945
>>> len(res1), len(res2), len(res3)
(41, 802, 802)
```

I've imported the method clock() and renamed it to clk() (to save a few characters). The function clock(), part of the time module, returns the system clock and is very useful for comparing performance. Notice how I've entered three function calls in one line. This is important: if you split those into three separate sentences, the time it actually took you to write the command is also added to the time difference, offsetting results.

■**Note** Because method 2 is quite inefficient, for a large number of files or a slow machine it might take considerable time to compute. Although method 1 seems the fastest, in reality it's inaccurate and shouldn't be used.

In the preceding implementations, we do not check the contents of the files to ensure they are indeed identical. It is quite possible to add that capability by modifying the functions and comparing the contents of two files, file1 and file2, as well:

```
>>> if open(file1, 'rb').read() == open(file2, 'rb').read():
...     print 'identical files'
```

This method reads the entire files to memory and compares them byte by byte. Note that this is a not a good option if the files are large; reading chunks or using other mechanisms may be better (see "Comparing Files" section in Chapter 10).

Catalogs

We've discussed splitting data files into directories and subdirectories and mentioned that it's a good habit to group files in that manner. While this is an excellent method of maintaining what's what, it's limited to one division. That is, if you'd like to split files into directories based on several criteria, what do you do with a data file that fits several of those criteria? This is where catalogs come in handy.

Catalogs are text files that hold data in columns: the first column contains the file names, and subsequence columns contain subcategories (other criteria). Ideally you'd like to use CSV because there's a good chance you'll be editing the catalog file manually in a spreadsheet application or automatically with Python; CSV fits that role perfectly.

Once you have a catalog file, it's easy to select only files meeting a specific criterion and run a script on those selected files.

Example: Creating a Clean Catalog File

The first step is to generate a basic catalog file, or a clean catalog file. This clean catalog file is generated automatically, using Python. For every file encountered, the full path as well as the file size is retrieved. Listing 4-12 shows an example of creating a clean catalog of files with extension .py.

Listing 4-12. *Creating a Clean Catalog*

```
import os, csv

# rename the following to a directory of your choosing
srchpath = '../src'

# the CSV header
catalog = [['Filename', 'pathname', 'size']]

# walk directory tree
for root, dirs, files in os.walk(srchpath):
    for file in files:
        # process only .py files
        if file.lower().endswith('py'):
            pathname = os.path.join(root, file)
            filesize = os.path.getsize(pathname)
            catalog.append([file, pathname, filesize])

# create the clean catalog
f = open('../data/clean_catalog.csv', 'wb')
csv.writer(f).writerows(catalog)
f.close()
```

To follow along, change the srchpath variable to point to a directory containing Python files, such as the root Python directory (c:\Python25). I chose to list the contents of my ../src directory.

The script walks the search directory looking for Python files (files ending with the extension .py, case insensitive). For every file encountered, we retrieve the file size. We then store all the information in a CSV file as shown in previous examples.

```
Filename,pathname,size
get_all_files.py,../src/get_all_files.py,385
read_ini.py,../src/read_ini.py,282
write_ini.py,../src/write_ini.py,330
cmp_fd.py,../src/cmp_fd.py,2285
unique.py,../src/unique.py,273
tips.py,../src/tips.py,151
create_catalog.py,../src/create_catalog.py,595
stock_charts.py,../src/stock_charts.py,1290
yahoo_data.py,../src/yahoo_data.py,1218
read_write_structs.py,../src/read_write_structs.py,795
running_index.py,../src/running_index.py,613
```

Next you take notes. For example, if a script is a draft, you mark it as such. So now you have an additional column: "Draft?" The contents of the catalog file will look something like this:

```
Filename,pathname,size,Draft?
get_all_files.py,../src/get_all_files.py,385,
read_ini.py,../src/read_ini.py,282,
write_ini.py,../src/write_ini.py,330,
cmp_fd.py,../src/cmp_fd.py,2285,Yes
unique.py,../src/unique.py,273,
tips.py,../src/tips.py,151,Yes
create_catalog.py,../src/create_catalog.py,595,
stock_charts.py,../src/stock_charts.py,1290,
yahoo_data.py,../src/yahoo_data.py,1218,
read_write_structs.py,../src/read_write_structs.py,795,
running_index.py,../src/running_index.py,613,
```

For the purpose of this exercise, I chose to use .py files, but you could just as well use the script on data files. In this manner, running a script on only clean data from the annotated catalog is manageable and reproducible.

■**Note** Maintaining catalog files is a delicate job. Ensure your catalog files are always under version control, or better yet, a software configuration management system (for example, CVS, Subversion, or Mercurial—see Chapter 2). You will constantly need to re-create clean (unannotated) catalogs if data is added. Consider investing time in maintaining your catalogs to keep them clean and up to date. If you find that the number of columns in your catalog files has increased and is unmanageable, consider using a database instead of a CSV file.

Files vs. a Database

There are a lot of pros for using databases over the management of files in directories. If your data becomes too complex to manage, rethinking and redesigning your data infrastructure is not a bad idea. That being said, I personally have found that databases do not add to my productivity. In my mind, the reasons are as follows:

- *The nature of the work*: When you design a database, it's important to know a lot of the information up front. A good database relies on a good database design. And good database design relies on knowing the information and structure beforehand. The work described here does not follow that path. As presented in the beginning of the chapter, it's an iterative process; you do not know all the information before you start. And your application is mostly for your usage, not for end users (at least at first). It's not "production-level" code yet. When it does get to production level, that is, it's an application to be used by end users, rethinking the data organization is a good idea, at which point you should consider using a database as well.

- *The nature of the data*: The nature of the data described here is somewhat flat. There are not a lot of connections and interconnections and hierarchy and logic. There's simply a lot of data. There's a need to analyze it, fast. Some of the files are quite large, and while it's possible store large files in a database, it's probably not the most efficient way.

- *Overhead*: Databases introduce overhead. Some may argue that it's not significant, and they may be right. However, there's another piece of code, a database engine, that needs interfacing. Yes, Python provides good database support, but it's not the same as opening a file natively in your operating system. The overhead is in several layers: backup is more complex, code writing requires additional libraries, designing databases requires some experience (which you might not have), transferring the work to another computer is not easy, and maintenance is also required.

■**Note** It's worth mentioning that the SQLite database module (sqlite), which is part of the Python Standard Library, has very little overhead and is an excellent package for working with databases should you require one.

- *Immediate interaction*: Say you'd like to browse for data and view files. With a database you'd have to write an application just to extract data, and then to view it. The interaction is less immediate in my mind.

I know I'm not being fair in my analysis; I'm mostly showing the cons of databases. So to offset that, I'll say that databases do have their role. If you feel that you'd like to store your data in a database, you should at least know that Python provides a great number of tools for you to choose from, so even then, Python is the right programming language for you.

Final Notes and References

Data organization is an important part of any serious data analysis and visualization project. If you follow through with the guidelines suggested in this chapter, I believe you will find that the overhead associated with maintaining data coherently is minimal, and furthermore that it's easy to write scripts to process large sets of data.

I have found the following of great value, when deciding on the file name format or the date and time format in a log file:

- "Numeric representation of Dates and Time: The ISO solution to a long-standing source of confusion," `http://www.iso.org/iso/support/faqs/faqs_widely_used_standards/widely_used_standards_other/date_and_time_format.htm`

CHAPTER 5

■ ■ ■

Processing Text Files
Text Is Everywhere

A considerable amount of data we process is text based. From a simplistic approach, text files are files that contain characters. The Python scripts we write are text files, the HTML files our web browser receives are text files, the e-mail messages we read are text files. They're simply everywhere. Because of the abundance of text files, you're likely to analyze data that comes in some form of a text file.

But in reality, there's no difference between a text file and another file, say, a binary file. They're both just files that occupy space on your hard drive. The important difference is what text files represent. If you look at data in a text file, a byte at a time, and convert every value using the ASCII table, you will be able to find (usually) intelligible text.

■**Note** ASCII, short for American Standard Code for Information Interchange, is a 7-bit character encoding. Each character has a number (0–127) associated with it. Characters can also include digits and symbols. To view the ASCII table in Python, issue the following: `for i in range(128): print i, repr(chr(i))`. Note that nonprintable characters (usually values 32 and below) will be displayed with their hexadecimal notation.

In a sense, text files are regular files that have information encoded in accordance with a known code. Nontext files, that is, binary files, will have values that don't necessarily correspond to the ASCII table, and if you use the ASCII table to decode a binary file, you'll probably end up with gibberish, not with text.

Text files can conform to yet another set of rules, say, the CSV format or the XML markup language. Text files that don't necessarily conform to any mapping other than the ASCII table are called *plain text files*. You'll mostly encounter plain text files and CSV files in this chapter.

The goal of this chapter is to present tools to work with text. First, we'll talk about strings and how to process them, and then continue with a discussion of reading and writing files, complementing the discussion with a considerable number of examples. We then turn to some topics that are likely to pop up when dealing with text files: handling CSV files, reading date and time information and parsing it, and working with regular expressions, a powerful tool for processing text. Lastly, since date and time are denoted differently around the world, we turn to a discussion about reading data that originated in a different locale.

Text and Strings

Text is composed of strings of characters, usually separated by spaces or other separators, such as commas, dots, and punctuation marks. Processing text is therefore based on processing strings.

You've already seen a discussion of strings in Chapter 3, one that deals with strings as sequences of characters: slicing, indexing, and concatenating. But in essence, we didn't deal with the string as a text object. You could've just as well thought of the string as a sequence of numbers, and the discussion would still be valid.

While that approach is correct, it's too simplistic. When we view strings that way, we lose important information. Consider this book: it's made of text. But as you read it, there's more information than just a sequence of characters. There are words, lines, and punctuation marks. And even then, there's still yet more information: for example, words that begin with a capital letter have a different meaning. Those distinctions are important to us when we're reading text.

The following section deals with functions and ideas that help us write code to process higher-level textual concepts; "string" is no longer merely a sequence of characters.

Splitting Text

The first tool at our disposal is the `split()` function, which is a string method:

```
>>> "split second".split()
['split', 'second']
```

The `split()` function splits a string into a list of strings once a separator is encountered. The default separator is a whitespace string and is one of the following: carriage return `'\r'`, line feed `'\n'`, tab `'\t'`, vertical tab `'\v'`, form feed `'\f'`, and a space. Vertical tabs and form feeds are less frequently used.

The `split()` function does not include the separators in the list, nor does it care how long the separator string is. This is especially useful if you're splitting text that's made of columns, with a varying number of spaces between fields:

```
>>> grocery_list = """Milk    2
... Eggs   12"""
>>> print grocery_list
Milk    2
Eggs   12
>>> grocery_list.split()
['Milk', '2', 'Eggs', '12']
```

Much like it's useful to split text on words, it's also useful to split text on lines. The function `splitlines([keepends])` splits a string based on line endings and removes the line endings, that is, removes the characters `'\n'` or `'\r\n'` if they exist. In case the optional value keepends is True, end-of-line characters are retained:

```
>>> grocery_list = """Milk    2
... Eggs   12"""
>>> grocery_list.splitlines()
['Milk    2', 'Eggs   12']
>>> grocery_list.splitlines(1)
['Milk    2\n', 'Eggs   12']
```

Example: Counting the Number of Words and Number of Lines in a String

At times you'd like to count the number of words, or the number of lines in a string. This can be done by using the function `len()` to count the number of elements in the lists generated from the calls to functions `split()` and `splitlines()`, as demonstrated in Listing 5-1.

Listing 5-1. *Counting the Number of Words and Lines in a String*

```
def word_line_count(s):
    """Returns the number of words and the numbers of lines in a string."""

    return (len(s.split()), len(s.splitlines()))
```

The function returns a tuple: the first element is the number of words in the string, and the second element is the number of lines in the string.

Once you define the function, use it as follows:

```
>>> grocery_list = """Milk    2
... Eggs   12"""
>>> word_line_count(grocery_list)
(4, 2)
```

Joining Strings

Much like you can split a string into a list of strings, you can join a list of strings into a new string using the `join()` member function. Remember, though, that `join()` is a string method; therefore you must have a string to operate on to begin with. So if you'd just like to combine a list of strings with no spaces in between, you should write the following:

```
>>> SOS = ['...', '---', '...']
>>> "".join(SOS)
'...---...'
```

Converting Strings to Numbers

Common use of the `split()` function is to parse the text and then extract numeric data, which usually comes in the form of a string of digits. Once extracted, the strings representing numbers can be converted to an actual Python numeric representation instead of a sequence of digits.

Converting strings to numbers can be done with either `float()`, `int()`, or `long()` function calls:

```
>>> float('3.25')
3.25
>>> int('100')
100
```

If you try to convert a string that doesn't represent a number to a number, an exception is raised:

```
>>> float('split')
Traceback (most recent call last):
  File "<stdin>", line 1, in <module>
ValueError: invalid literal for float(): split
```

This can be used to your advantage: say you're looking to print only the number of items from the grocery list in previous examples. Simply employ the EAFP principle to convert every string to a number and print it.

```
>>> grocery_list = """Milk    2
... Eggs   12"""
>>> for item in grocery_list.split():
...     try:
...         print int(item),
...     except ValueError:
...         pass
...
2 12
```

In this example, I took special care to discard only ValueError exceptions, which occur in case of a conversion problem.

Example: Base Conversion—Binary, Octal, Decimal, and Hexadecimal

At times, it's useful to convert a number from one base representation to another. In case you're dealing with octal, decimal, and hexadecimal bases, this is easily achieved using the functions int(), hex(), and oct().

Since we're dealing with representations of numbers, it stands to reason we use strings. I've therefore chosen to define several functions, all of which accept a string as an argument. As shown in Listing 5-2, these functions are hex2dec(), hex2oct(), dec2hex(), dec2oct(), oct2dec(), and oct2hex(). The names of these functions are self-explanatory.

Listing 5-2. *Base Conversion Helper Functions*

```
def oct2dec(s):
    return str(int(s, 8))
def hex2dec(s):
    return str(int(s, 16))
def dec2oct(s):
    return oct(int(s))
def dec2hex(s):
    return hex(int(s))
```

```
def hex2oct(s):
    return dec2oct(hex2dec(s))
def oct2hex(s):
    return dec2hex(oct2dec(s))
```

I've left out the docstrings: I think the function names are documentation enough. I also chose to use int(); the function long() would've worked just as well. The functions do not perform any sort of error checking (e.g., ensuring that they received a string as an input).

Here's a possible use of these functions:

```
>>> hex2dec('ffff')
'65535'
>>> oct2hex('777')
'0x1ff'
```

■**Note** In Python 2.6, the notation of the octal base accepts a zero and the o character: 0o or 0O. This change is accompanied with the introduction of binary numbers in Python 2.6 and above. Binary numbers are denoted with a leading 0B or 0b (zero and the character b).

BINARY CONVERSION IN PYTHON 2.5

At the time of the writing of this book, the external packages used to create much of the code did not yet catch up to Python version 2.6, and so I resorted to using version 2.5. In case you're in the same boat and would like to use the binary base-conversion helper functions, here's a short implementation of the dec2bin() function that works in Python 2.5 as well. Combine this function with the function int() or long() to implement all other base conversions.

```
def dec2bin(s):
    bin_list, num = [], int(s)
    if num < 0:          # we don't convert negative numbers
        raise ValueError, "value must be positive"
    if not num:     # special case, number is zero
        return '0'
    # regular case
    while num:
        bin_list.append('1' if (num & 1) else '0')
        num >>= 1
    return "".join(reversed(bin_list))
```

The way the function works is as follows. The string representing a decimal value is converted into a number. The number is then checked for special cases (negative, zero) and proceeds to the conversion in the while loop.

> Within the `while` loop, if the number's least significant bit is equal to 1 (condition `num & '1'`), a 1 is added to the list of digits, `bin_list`; otherwise, a `'0'` is added to the list. I've used a conditional expression similar to the `?:` expression in C (go to `http://docs.python.org/whatsnew/2.5.html` and scroll down to PEP 308). The number is then right-shifted 1 bit, and the whole cycle repeats itself. The `while` loop ends when the shifted number reaches zero, effectively meaning all its binary digits were converted. Finally, the function returns a string from the list of digits, only the string has to be reversed since we've converted from the least significant bit first to the most significant bit last. I've used the iterator `reversed()` to present the binary digits in the proper sequence.
>
> The function does not accept negative values. It shouldn't be too hard to support negative numbers as well, but I've never used negative binary numbers, and so the need has never arisen.

Let's complete the preceding helper function by implementing the functions `bin2oct()`, `bin2dec()`, `bin2hex()`, `oct2bin()`, and `hex2bin()` using `dec2bin()`, as shown in Listing 5-3. If you're running version 2.6, I would suggest implementing the function `dec2bin()` as a simple `return(bin(int(s)))`; if you're using version 2.5, use the implementation suggested in the sidebar "Binary Conversion in Python 2.5."

Listing 5-3. *Binary Conversion Helper Functions*

```
def bin2oct(s):
    return dec2oct(bin2dec(s))
def bin2dec(s):
    return str(int(s, 2))
def bin2hex(s):
    return dec2hex(bin2dec(s))
def oct2bin(s):
    return dec2bin(oct2dec(s))
def hex2bin(s):
    return dec2bin(hex2dec(s))
```

Testing Your Implementation: exec and assert

This is a bit of an off-track discussion and somewhat advanced, but I thought it appropriate in the context of the preceding discussion.

As you implement the base-conversion helper functions, you'll find that it's quite possible that you've made a mistake. Those are implementations of nested function calls and are prone to human error.

Python provides several testing modules: `doctest` and `unittest` (see the Python Standard Library, `http://docs.python.org/library/test.html`). However, I chose a different approach, one that does not make use of these modules, in hopes of shedding light on two new statements: `exec` and `assert`.

The first statement, `assert`, will return an `AssertionError` in case a condition isn't met. This is quite useful for testing purposes:

```
>>> assert 1 == 2
Traceback (most recent call last):
  File "<stdin>", line 1, in <module>
AssertionError
```

Adding assert statements in your code is a good way to ensure things behave the way you expect them to, for example, making certain an argument passed to a function is of a specific type.

■**Tip** assert statements are not executed when you run Python with the optimization switch turned on (-O).

The statement exec executes a string as if you typed it in the interpreter:

```
>>> exec "print 1+2"
3
```

The exec statement can be used for automating command execution.

At first, exec might not seem such a big deal. But consider those functions in the previous example: there are 12 functions corresponding to all combinations of base conversions, bin2oct(), bin2dec(), bin2hex(), oct2bin(), and so forth. Testing all these functions is tedious. If you watch closely though, you'll find there's a pattern. And when there's a pattern, it stands to reason to write a computer program to perform the task for us. This is exactly where exec comes to life. The idea is to create a list of strings, each string detailing a function to be executed, and then executing each and every string (see Listing 5-4).

Listing 5-4. *Testing Base-Conversion Function Implementations*

```
def testbases():
    """Tests implementation of base conversion functions"""

    v0 = {'bin':'0', 'oct':'0', 'dec':'0', 'hex':'0x0'}
    v1 = {'bin':'1111', 'oct':'017', 'dec':'15', 'hex':'0xf'}

    for v in [v0, v1]:
        perms = [(a, b) for b in v for a in v if a != b]
        for (s1, s2) in perms:
            tc = "assert %s2%s(v['%s']) == v['%s']" % (s1, s2, s1, s2)
            exec tc
```

I created two test vectors: v1 and v2. Variables v1 and v2 are dictionaries containing a string representing the base as the key and a string representing the number as the value. I took care in ensuring that the string representing the base names follows the three-letter notations I've used for the function names. I then iterate through my test vector list and execute each test case (tc). Let's break this down into smaller chunks.

I first create a list comprehension named perms that generates all permutations of bases as long as they're not identical (hence the condition a != b):

```
>>> v = {'bin':'0', 'oct':'0', 'dec':'0', 'hex':'0x0'}
>>> perms = [(a, b) for b in v for a in v if a != b]
>>> from pprint import pprint
>>> pprint(perms)
[('dec', 'bin'),
 ('hex', 'bin'),
 ('oct', 'bin'),
 ('bin', 'dec'),
 ('hex', 'dec'),
 ('oct', 'dec'),
 ('bin', 'hex'),
 ('dec', 'hex'),
 ('oct', 'hex'),
 ('bin', 'oct'),
 ('dec', 'oct'),
 ('hex', 'oct')]
```

To modify this list comprehension to generate actual assertion calls requires some string manipulation, but you already know how to use format specifiers, so here it is:

```
>>> for (s1, s2) in perms:
...     tc = "assert %s2%s(v['%s']) == v['%s']" % \
...         (s1, s2, s1, s2)
...     print tc
...
assert dec2bin(v['dec']) == v['bin']
assert hex2bin(v['hex']) == v['bin']
assert oct2bin(v['oct']) == v['bin']
assert bin2dec(v['bin']) == v['dec']
assert hex2dec(v['hex']) == v['dec']
assert oct2dec(v['oct']) == v['dec']
assert bin2hex(v['bin']) == v['hex']
assert dec2hex(v['dec']) == v['hex']
assert oct2hex(v['oct']) == v['hex']
assert bin2oct(v['bin']) == v['oct']
assert dec2oct(v['dec']) == v['oct']
assert hex2oct(v['hex']) == v['oct']
```

I've printed a string associated with the command to be executed. The strings represent commands that check the functionality of the base helper functions. Now all that's needed is exec tc.

■**Note** If you're using the built-in function `bin()` available in Python 2.6 and not the implementation of `dec2bin()` in the sidebar "Binary Conversion in Python 2.5," be sure to change the notation to include a leading `0b` in case of binary values. The octal notation `0o` is optional in version 2.6, and the default behavior is just a leading zero without an `o`, so there's no need to change those. Vector `v0` would then be `v0 = {'bin': '0b0', 'oct': '0', 'dec': '0', 'hex': '0x0'}`.

The nice thing about this implementation is that you can easily add other bases, say, the functions that convert base 5: `qui2bin()`, `qui2oct()`, `qui2dec()`, and so on (I've used the notation `qui`, which is short for quinary, base 5).

Find and Replace

The next set of interesting functions are `find()` and `replace()`. The method `find()` locates the first occurrence of a substring in a string and takes the general form `find(substring[, start[, end]])`. The parameters `start` and `end` are optional and are used to limit the search to indices that are greater than or equal to `start` and are less than `end`, if those arguments are provided:

```
>>> grocery_list = "Milk   2\nEggs   12"
>>> grocery_list.find('2')
7
>>> grocery_list.find('2', 10)
16
>>> grocery_list.find('2', 10, 16)
-1
```

In case a substring isn't found, the return value is `-1`.

■**Caution** Be sure to compare the value of `find()` with `-1`, and not with `True`, as `-1` (substring not found) is considered `True`. That is, instead of writing `if str.find(substr)`, write `if str.find(substr) != -1`.

The function `replace()` doesn't really replace items in a string, as strings are immutable. Instead, it creates a new string, with every occurrence of the old substring replaced with the new substring:

```
>>> grocery_list = "Milk   2\nEggs   12"
>>> grocery_list.replace('Eggs', 'Organic Eggs')
'Milk   2\nOrganic Eggs   12'
```

The `replace()` method will replace as many occurrences as are possible unless the `count` argument is provided, as follows: `replace(old, new[, count])`—in which case only the number of values up to and including `count` will be replaced.

In case you'd like to know in advance how many substitutions will occur, you can use the count(substr) method, which counts the number of occurrences of a substring in a string:

```
>>> grocery_list = "Milk    2\nEggs   12"
>>> grocery_list.count('2')
2
>>> grocery_list.count('Eggs')
1
```

The method count() also accepts an optional start-of-search and end-of-search indices: count(substr[, start[, end]]); the behavior is similar to that of function find().

Stripping Strings

Stripping strings is the process of removing extra whitespace characters or other set of characters from a string. The method strip([chars]) removes whitespace characters from both the right side and the left side of a string. If chars is provided, characters from the string chars are used as separators instead of whitespace characters, each character acting as a separator. Methods rstrip([chars]) and lstrip([chars]) do so on the right or left sides only, respectively:

```
>>> "Hello    ".rstrip()
'Hello'
>>> '*-*-* SECTION BREAK *-*-*'.strip('*-')
' SECTION BREAK '
```

Example: Removing Extra Spaces

In this example, we'd like to remove extra spaces from some text. We could try to use the replace() method, replacing two spaces with one:

```
>>> grocery_list = "Milk    2\nEggs   12"
>>> new_grocery_list = grocery_list.replace("  ", " ")
>>> print new_grocery_list
Milk  2
Eggs 12
```

That didn't work well: there are two spaces between Milk and 2 after the call to replace(). The reason for this is that replace() is not a recursive search and replace. After a replace has been made, the function keeps on looking for other occurrences, but the ones that have already been replaced add up together to form extra spaces again: those are not replaced. For example, four spaces become two, and not one. Of course, you could keep on replacing until there are no more changes to the string, but that's a bit cumbersome.

Another approach is to use split(), splitlines(), strip(), and join():

```
>>> grocery_list = "Milk    2\nEggs   12"
>>> for line in grocery_list.splitlines():
...     clear_line = [s.strip() for s in line.split()]
...     print " ".join(clear_line)
...
```

```
Milk 2
Eggs 12
```

I've used a for loop to iterate through the split lines. For every line, I've created the list clear_line, which is each word stripped of separators (in our case extra spaces). I then joined the list of words with a space.

If all this seems considerable effort for a simple task, you're absolutely right. There are other, better ways to perform this: regular expressions. More about these in the section "Regular Expressions" toward the end of this chapter.

String Formatting

Using format specifiers, presented in Chapter 3, you can control string format very accurately. But format specifiers do not take into consideration that we're dealing with text and words; they treat strings mostly as a sequence of characters.

The functions presented in this section add string formatting options that are more suited for working with words and text.

The methods upper() and lower() return strings with all characters in uppercase or lowercase, respectively:

```
>>> " Middle of Town ".upper()
' MIDDLE OF TOWN '
>>> " Middle of Town ".lower()
' middle of town '
```

The function swapcase() returns a string with the characters' case inverted:

```
>>> " Middle of Town ".swapcase()
' mIDDLE OF tOWN '
```

The method capitalize() returns a string with the first letter in uppercase and the remaining letters in lowercase. Note that this affects only the first character of the string, disregarding English grammar rules or whether there are punctuation marks or line breaks:

```
>>> "first sentence.\nSecond sentence.  Third Sentence".capitalize()
'First sentence.\nsecond sentence.  third sentence'
```

The method title() capitalizes every first letter of a sentence. Again, not in accordance with the English grammar rules, as some words in titles should not be capitalized (e.g., "the"):

```
>>> "first sentence.\nSecond sentence.  Third Sentence".title()
'First Sentence.\nSecond Sentence.  Third Sentence'
```

The method center(n[, char]) returns a string of length n with left and right padding of the string with char (default is space) so as to have the string centered in the middle:

```
>>> " Middle of Town ".center(26, '*')
'***** Middle of Town *****'
```

The methods ljust(n[, char]) and rjust(n[, char]) perform left and right justification, respectively, with the optional fill character being char:

```
>>> "East side".rjust(20)
'           East side'
>>> "West side".ljust(20, '-')
'West side-----------'
```

String Conditionals

The following is a set of string conditionals: methods that ask questions about strings.

The method endswith(substr[, start[, end]]) returns True if a string ends with substr. The start and end arguments limit the search indices similarly to previously discussed string functions; from now on I'll refrain from explaining their effect. The endswith() function is useful for checking file name extensions, for example:

```
>>> "a20.jpg".endswith('jpg')
True
>>> "a20.jpg".endswith('JPG')
False
```

The second expression evaluates to False because endswith() is case sensitive. However, substr can be a tuple as well, accommodating several condition tests:

```
>>> "a20.JPG".endswith(('jpg', 'JPG'))
True
```

The method startswith(substr[, start[, end]]) is similar to endswith() only in that it checks the beginning of a string.

The methods isalpha(), isdigit(), and isalnum() return True if all the characters in the string are alphabetic, digits, or both, respectively:

```
>>> "a20.jpg".isalnum()
False
```

The reason the method isalnum() returns False in the preceding example is that the character '.' (dot) is not alphabetic nor a digit.

Similarly, the methods islower(), isspace(), istitle(), and isupper() return True if the string is all lowercase, all whitespace, of the title form (first letter in every word capitalized), or all uppercase, respectively:

```
>>> "a20.jpg".islower()
True
```

Note The conditionals starting with is, such as islower(), will return False if the string is empty.

More on Strings

The preceding isn't a full account of strings and string methods. For example, in Python 2.6 a new formatting function, str.format(), is provided (see http://docs.python.org/library/ string.html). If your work is text-heavy, have a look at the online documentation for additional information. The discussion that follows relies on the preceding string methods but not on ones that were not discussed.

Files

Text files are files that contain textual data, that is, text strings. We've talked about strings and text extensively; now it's time to talk about files.

In Python, you access files using the file data type. Working with files is quite similar to doing so in other programming languages: open a file and receive a file object, read from the file or write to the file using the file object, and lastly close the file, again using the file object. You can open a file either for reading, writing, or appending, and you can open it in binary mode or text mode.

Opening a File

To open a file, use the open(filename[, mode [, buffering]]) built-in function. The function open() returns a file object that is used for subsequent file operations. The first argument, filename, is required. The second argument, mode, is optional and can take the values listed in Table 5-1.

Table 5-1. *File Open Modes*

Mode	Description
r	Opens a file for reading. This is the default value if mode isn't specified.
w	Opens a file for writing, overwriting an existing file.
a	Opens a file for writing in append mode; all write operations are performed at the end. If the file doesn't exist, it is created.
r+	Opens a file for reading and updating. If the file doesn't exist, an exception is raised.
w+	Creates a new file for writing and updating, overwriting an existing one.
a+	Opens a file for reading and writing in append mode. All write operations are performed at the end. If the file doesn't exist, it is created.

Adding the character 'b' to the mode ensures the file is open in binary mode (e.g., 'rb'). Adding the character 't' to the mode ensures the file is opened in text mode (e.g., 'wt'). A file can be opened either in text mode or in binary mode, but not both (default is text mode).

The difference between binary mode and text mode is whether Python tries to convert line-ending characters it encounters to '\n'. In Windows, the characters '\r\n' are used to denote the end of the line; in Linux, it's just '\n'. To have a consistent method to access *text* files, use text mode. When dealing with binary files, or when it's important for you to have end-of-line characters unmodified, use the binary mode.

■**Note** In append mode, write operations are performed at the end of the file, effectively guarding existing data, whereas in write mode, you're allowed to write anywhere in the file, possibly overwriting data.

The third parameter, buffer, is optional as well and determines the file buffering mode. See http://docs.python.org/library/functions.html for information about buffering.

Closing a File

Contrary to the open() function, which is a built-in function, the close() function is a member function of the file object and not a built-in function. To close files, use the file method f.close() (assuming f is a file object). It's generally good practice to close a file once you're done with it. But in case you don't, Python closes the file for you automatically once the file object is no longer in use. The following sample shows how to open and close a file:

```
>>> f = open('somefile.txt')
>>> f
<open file 'somefile.txt', mode 'r' at 0x00BD03C8>
>>> f.close()
>>> f
<closed file ' somefile.txt', mode 'r' at 0x00BD03C8>
>>> type(f)
<type 'file'>
```

Writing Text

Once a file is open for writing (or appending) and before it's closed, you can write strings to it using the methods write(str) and writelines(strseq).

The method write() writes a string to the file:

```
>>> grocery_str = "Milk    2\nEggs    12"
>>> f = open('../data/tobuy.txt', 'wt')
>>> f.write(grocery_str)
>>> f.close()
```

The contents of the file tobuy.txt are

```
Milk    2
Eggs    12
```

The method writelines(strseq) writes a sequence of strings to a file:

```
>>> grocery_list = ["Milk", "2", "Eggs", "12"]
>>> f = open('../data/tobuylist.txt', 'wt')
>>> f.writelines(grocery_list)
>>> f.close()
```

The contents of file `tobuylist.txt` are

```
Milk2Eggs12
```

Notice how `writelines()` does not add spaces nor line breaks.

■Note I've assumed you are following the book convention of having your source code reside in directory `Ch5/src` and your data directory in `Ch5/data`. If that's not the case, change the path to your data files in the preceding examples.

Reading Text

Once a file is open for reading, you can make use of the methods `read()`, `readline()`, or `readlines()` to read the file contents. You can also iterate over the file object to read a line at a time. I found that when dealing with text files, my code typically falls into one of three categories:

1. Reading the entire file at once using the methods `read()` or `readlines()`. This option is preferable if the files are not too large.

2. Iterating over the file object, reading a line at a time. This option is preferable for larger text files.

3. Using a `while` loop with the method `read(n)`. This option is a good candidate in case you don't necessarily want to treat the file as lines of text.

Reading the Entire File at Once

Assuming you're dealing with not-too-large files, using method `read()` or `readlines()` to read the entire file at once should be your first choice.

The method `read([n])` reads n bytes from the file, returning them as a string. If n is not specified or negative, the entire file is read. For this example, we'll use the file `tobuy.txt` generated in the previous section, "Writing Text" (first snippet of code):

```
>>> f = open('../data/tobuy.txt')
>>> text = f.read()
>>> f.close()
>>> print text
Milk    2
Eggs    12
```

or more compactly:

```
>>> print open('../data/tobuy.txt').read()
Milk    2
Eggs    12
```

The method readlines() reads the file at once, returning a list of strings:

```
>>> open('../data/tobuy.txt').readlines()
['Milk   2\n', 'Eggs   12']
```

Iterating Over the File Object

This option is suited for cases when you want to process your file a line at a time, but you don't want to read the entire file at once, due to, say, memory constraints. Here's an example:

```
>>> for i, line in enumerate(open('../data/tobuy.txt')):
...     print "%d: %s" % (i, line.rstrip())
...
0: Milk   2
1: Eggs   12
```

Using a while Loop

Use this method in conjunction with read() to process chunks of the file at a time. Again, this is best suited for larger files and in cases where you don't want to treat a file as a list of lines:

```
>>> f = open('../data/tobuy.txt')
>>> ch = f.read(1)
>>> while ch != 'k' and ch:
...     print ch,
...     ch = f.read(1)
...
M i l
>>> f.close()
```

This example reads the file a byte at a time and stops upon encountering the character 'k' or an end-of-file where ch would then evaluate to False.

Working with Text Files

Now that we have the basics covered, that is, reading and writing files and processing strings, it's time to combine the two new skills.

This section is presented as a list of examples. The examples can be used for educational purposes, but they can also be used to form the basis of helper functions for text-based data processing. With time, I hope you modify the code presented here to best fit your needs.

It is important that you treat these examples for what they are, that is, examples and not production code. Most of the functions do not perform any sort of error checking or handle exceptions and should not be used as-is but only for educational purposes. When possible, I've added a discussion on how these examples can be improved upon.

For the purpose of working with larger files than the contrived grocery list used previously, I've selected to use the electronic version of the book *Flatland*, by Edwin A. Abbott, available for download from Project Gutenberg, located at http://www.gutenberg.org. A direct link to the e-book at the time of the writing of this book is `http://www.gutenberg.org/files/97/97.txt`. Once you download the file, save it in folder `data` under the original file name `97.txt`. Your directory structure should look similar to that presented near the end of Chapter 2 in the section "Example: Directory Structure for the Book":

```
Ch5
    src
    data
```

In this directory structure, `src` is where you code is, as well as your current working directory, and `data` indicates the location of data files (namely `97.txt`—the *Flatland* e-book).

Example: Character, Word, and Line Count

Similar to the example presented in the beginning of the chapter, now you're confronted with the task of counting the characters, words, and lines in a file, and not just a string.

The solution is an immediate extension of the example provided before, using `split()`, `splitlines()`, and `len()`. I've named the function `wc()`, which is a popular command name on Linux shells `wc filename` (see Listing 5-5).

Listing 5-5. *Counting the Number of Characters, Words, and Lines in a File*

```
def wc(filename):
    """Returns the number of characters, words and lines in a file.

The result is a tuple of the form (#characters, #words, #lines)."""

    data = open(filename, 'rb').read()
    return (len(data), len(data.split()), len(data.splitlines()))
```

The function returns a tuple of three elements: the first element is the number of characters in the file, the second element is the number of words, and the third element is the number of lines. I've also selected to open the file in binary mode and not in text mode. This is so that the number of characters will be counted properly, without any conversions of `'\r\n'` to `'\n'` that would throw numbers off count.

■**Note** Notice how I've indented the docstring; it's standard practice that in case more than one line is needed to document the function, a blank line is added immediately after the short function description. Subsequent documentation is left justified with no indentation.

It's possible that you're dealing with truly large files, in which case a different approach should be employed: iterating over the file object (see Listing 5-6).

Listing 5-6. *Counting the Number of Characters, Words, and Lines in a Very Large File*

```
def wc_large(filename):
    """Returns the number of characters, words and lines in a large file.

The result is a tuple of the form (#characters, #words, #lines)."""

    num_chars, num_words, num_lines = 0, 0, 0
    for line in open(filename, 'rb'):
        num_chars += len(line)
        num_words += len(line.split())
        num_lines += 1
    return (num_chars, num_words, num_lines)
```

Here are the results from running both functions:

```
>>> wc('../data/97.txt')
(216562, 36553, 3920)
>>> wc_large('../data/97.txt')
(216562, 36553, 3920)
```

Example: head and tail

Most Linux system administrators know and love the head and tail command-line utilities. It's a fast check on how an installation is coming along, it's great for probing message logs, and it's good to see whether any errors occurred during boot time.

The way the head and tail command-line utilities work is that they print n lines from the beginning or end of a file, respectively. You'd typically use these commands to look at log files because most log files are plain text files with data written sequentially: a recent event is logged at the end of a file.

The following command will print the last 20 lines from the dmesg log file (a common Linux log file):

```
$ tail -20 /var/log/dmesg
```

Using the method readlines(), both head() and tail() functions are easily implemented, as shown in Listing 5-7.

Listing 5-7. *head() and tail() Functions*

```
def head(filename, n=10):
    """Prints the first n lines of the file."""

    for line in open(filename).readlines()[:n]:
        print line.rstrip()

def tail(filename, n=10):
    """Returns the last n lines of the file."""
```

```
for line in open(filename).readlines()[-n:]:
    print line.rstrip()
```

Note It's also possible to replace the line `print line.rstrip()` with `print line,` (notice the comma) to suppress the extra line breaks.

In case your files are too large to be read entirely into memory, things get trickier. Implementing the `head()` function is possible by iterating over the file object, as shown in Listing 5-8.

Listing 5-8. *head() Function for Very Large Files*

```
def head_large(filename, n=10):
    """Returns the last n lines of a very large file."""

    for i, line in enumerate(open(filename)):
        print line.rstrip()
        if i == n-1: break
```

You can convince yourself both functions return proper results by modifying the code to return a list and then comparing the returned values from the two functions.

Unfortunately, implementing the function `tail()` in a similar manner, iterating over the file object, is much more complex. First, you'd have to go through the entire file, reading every line. Remember, this is a large file, therefore doing so will take considerable time. And even then, the second problem you encounter is that you don't know in advance which line is the last line, so you'd either have to perform two passes on the file, on the first one counting the number of lines and on the second one printing the last n lines, or you'd have to continually store the last n lines read. In both cases, yikes. A third approach is to use random access functions to start reading files at the end and work your way backward. This requires use of the function `seek()`, which will be covered in Chapter 10.

Example: Splitting and Combining Files

Back in the day, computer users used to transfer files on 360K diskettes. Since this was rather painful, they opted to use a file compression utility that did both splitting and compressing. Alas, one of the disks always seemed to be misplaced, rendering the data totally useless.

Which brings up a common task when dealing with large files: you may need to split them into smaller, more manageable files. By that, I don't mean that each chunk contains legible information, merely that now you can use size-limited media (e-mail, flash drive) to transfer the split files. The receiving end will then need to reconstruct the original file from the split files.

The function `splitfile()` splits a file into n smaller files, each with a modified file name that is composed of the original file name plus the split file index (e.g., `97.txt.1`). The function `combinefiles()` combines several files of the preceding pattern into one, as demonstrated in Listing 5-9.

Listing 5-9. *Splitting and Combining Files*

```python
def splitfile(filename, size=1024**2):
    """Splits a file into n smaller files.

Files are created with a running index."""

    fin, index = open(filename, 'rb'), 0
    data = fin.read(size)
    while data:
        index += 1
        outfilename = filename+'.'+str(index)
        fout = open(outfilename, 'wb')
        fout.write(data)
        fout.close()
        print "Created file %s, size %d" % (outfilename, len(data))
        data = fin.read(size)
    return


def combinefiles(filename):
    """Combines a previously split file.

Filename extensions are assumed a running index.
Important note: if a file named 'filename' exists it will be overwritten."""

    fout, index = open(filename, 'wb'), 0
    while True:
        index += 1
        try:
            data = open(filename+'.'+str(index), 'rb').read()
            fout.write(data)
        except IOError:
            break
    fout.close()
    print "Created file %s from %d file(s)\n" % (filename, index-1)
```

The functions themselves are self-explanatory and should prove easy enough to follow. Here's how you would use them:

```python
>>> splitfile('97.txt', 100000)
Created file 97.txt.1, size 100000
Created file 97.txt.2, size 100000
Created file 97.txt.3, size 16562
```

Now copy the files 97.txt.* to a temporary folder, say, /tmp and issue

```python
>>> combinefiles('/tmp/97.txt')
Created file 97.txt from 3 files
```

To satisfy yourself that indeed the files are identical, issue the following:

```
>>> data1 = open('../data/97.txt', 'rb').read()
>>> data2 = open('/tmp/97.txt', 'rb').read()
>>> data1 == data2
True
```

In the implementation of the function `combinefiles()` I've chosen to again use the EAFP approach. Alternatively, I could've listed the directory contents using `os.listdir()` or used the glob module to achieve the same; the glob module will be discussed in Chapter 10.

While the topic of this section is text files, the functions `splitfile()` and `combinefiles()` should work on binary files just as well, since we've opened the files in binary mode.

■**Caution** The function `combinefiles()` will overwrite an existing file if it already exists.

Lastly, the function `combinefiles()` will overwrite a file if it exists; if you'd prefer a different functionality, you can use the function `os.path.exists()` to first ensure the file does not exist and act accordingly (ask for user preference or return without overwriting the file).

Example: Searching Inside a Text File

The examples up to this point dealt with the files themselves, not really with the information they hold. The examples going forward will look at the contents as well, that is, read the file and process text.

A common programming task involves searching for a string inside a file. A yet even more common task is the searching of a string in multiple files, but we leave that to future discussions (see Chapter 10). In Linux, a handy utility achieves this: grep. grep also provides more complex searches, ones that include regular expressions, but in this example we limit our discussion to simple string searches.

Searching inside a text file is easily implemented in Python, as you can see in Listing 5-10.

Listing 5-10. *Searching Inside a Text File*

```
def srchfile(filename, substr):
    """Searches for a substring in a file."""

    for i, line in enumerate(open(filename, 'rt')):
        if line.find(substr) != -1:
            print "%5d: %s" % (i, line.rstrip())
```

I've used the iterator `enumerate()` to retrieve both the line and the line number, as the line number is displayed in the `print` statement later on. I've also used the method `rstrip()` to remove the extra new-line character. Here's the output from running the command `srchfile('../data/97.txt', 'Guide')`:

```
2645: Prostrating myself mentally before my Guide, I cried, "How is it, O
2685: about your Wife," said my Guide: "she will not be long left in anxiety;
2732: "Here we descend," said my Guide.  It was now morning, the first hour
2762: yet," said my Guide, "the time will come for that.  Meantime I must
2803: of my own.  I absolutely depended on the volition of my Guide, who said
3091: "Look yonder," said my Guide, "in Flatland thou hast lived; of Lineland
```

There's room for improvement of the function srchfile(). First, the function is case-sensitive. To allow for case-insensitive searches, I would suggest adding a parameter to the function that controls whether searches are case sensitive or not. In case of a case-insensitive search, srchfile() would make use of the function upper() (or lower()) and convert both the line to be searched and the search string itself prior to calling find().

Another improvement would be to fix the line number indentation. Currently the line number is right-aligned five spaces. In case the number of lines is 100,000 or greater, this will create an indentation problem. Changing the implementation to read the entire file at once gives us a total line count, allowing the calculation of the maximum number of digits using the function log10(), which is part of the math module (see Chapter 7) as follows:

```
>>> numlines = 1234
>>> from math import log10
>>> maxdigits = int(log10(numlines))+1
>>> maxdigits
4
```

This will only work if you know the line number in advance, hence the change to the function to read the entire file at once. Listing 5-11 shows a possible implementation of fixing the indentation problem.

Listing 5-11. *Searching Inside a Text File (Proper Indentation)*

```
def srchfile_ex(filename, substr):
    """Searches for a substring in a file."""

    lines = open(filename).readlines()
    fmt = r'%' + str(int(log10(len(lines)))+1) + r'd: %s'
    for index, line in enumerate(lines):
        if line.find(substr) != -1:
            print fmt % (index, line.rstrip())
```

Notice how I've first created a format specifier, fmt, using a raw string and then used it to print the line number and the string.

Example: Working with Comments

I find that I repeatedly turn back to code I once wrote. And what's funny, I seem to remember mostly the comments. An interesting approach to viewing comments is to think of the comment symbol (#) as a separator. With this in mind, you can implement some interesting searches, as shown in Listing 5-12. For example, you can search inside comments only, or perform the complement search, that is, one that ensures you're *not* searching comments.

Listing 5-12. *Working with Comments*

```
def srchcomments(filename, substr):
    """Searches inside Python source comments."""

    for index, line in enumerate(open(filename, 'rt')):
        L = line.split('#')
        if len(L) == 2:
            if L[1].find(substr) != -1:
                print "%5d: %s" % (index, line.rstrip())
```

This code is hardly foolproof. It assumes that the # symbol appears only once, text before the # is always code, and text after # is a comment. This is not always true; for example, in the preceding code, in the fourth line, L = line.split('#'), # is hardly a comment separator. Nevertheless, in many occasions the function works fine.

Using the function in Listing 5-12 as a starting point, you could for example, write a function to convert comments that are not on a line of their own to be single-line comments. That is, convert

```
print x,    # prints x and suppress a line break
```

to

```
# prints x and suppress a line break
print x,
```

C++ STYLE COMMENTS

I originally encountered this problem with C/C++. A compiler I was using to write code accepted the C++ style comments, whose behavior is similar to Python's comments (only with the symbols // instead of #). However, another older compiler was used that didn't accept the C++ style comment. I had to convert all my single-line comments of the form // comment to C-style comments of the form /* comment */. I used a script similar to the preceding script. Luckily for me, the symbols // didn't appear anywhere in the code other than as part of the comments themselves.

Example: Extracting Numbers from a Text File

At times, it's useful to be able to extract only the numbers in a text file. This could be for the purpose of creating files based on existing ones, say, for testing purposes. Another scenario might be you have a system that maintains the number of users in a text file, and you'd like to write a script to increment that number.

The function presented in Listing 5-13 reads a text file and creates a modified version of the file with all the numbers incremented. For the purpose of this example, numbers are separated by whitespace characters.

Listing 5-13. *Incrementing File Contents*

```
def increment_contents(filename):
    """Increments values in a file, creating a new file."""

    data = open(filename, 'rt').readlines()
    for i, line in enumerate(data):
        for word in line.split():
            try:
                data[i] = line.replace(word, str(int(word)+1))
            except ValueError:
                # uncomment the following if you'd like feedback
                # print word, "is not a number"
                pass
    open(filename+'.inc', 'wt').writelines(data)
```

The function reads the entire file into memory and then processes the data a line at a time (it's also possible to achieve the same functionality by iterating over a file object). Every line is split into words. The code then tries to convert every word to a number, and upon success, replaces the number with an incremented value. I've used the replace() method to do that, and that's the reason you see another str() function call after the increment: replace() method requires a string, not a number.

In implementing the function, I've chosen to use the EAFP approach, that is, I've tried to convert every single word I've encountered into an int, and then increment it. On success, the data is modified. If a ValueError occurs because the conversion didn't succeed, it means that the string cannot be converted to an int, in which case I've ignored the word.

A different approach might have been to check whether the word is composed of digits using the isdigit() method, but that approach will fail on other characters such as the plus symbol. I think that EAFP here is a clear winner.

To test the function, I again resort to the grocery list. Assume the contents of file ../data/ grocery_list.txt are as follows:

```
Milk 12
Eggs 12.0
Olives 1e2
Voodoo dolls 1+1j
```

After executing increment_contents('../data/grocery_list.txt'), a new file, ../data/ grocery_list.txt.inc, is created with the following contents:

```
Milk 13
Eggs 12.0
Olives 1e2
Voodoo dolls 1+1j
```

The function only increments the value 12 because I've used the function int(). Had I used the function float(), all first three values would have been properly incremented. However, the first number would then be converted into a float value, and I wanted to leave it as an int.

Handling both float and int values is possible with nested exception handling. First, the function tries to use int(), and if int() fails, it tries to use float() (see Listing 5-14).

Listing 5-14. *Incrementing File Contents Using float() and int()*

```
def increment_contents_both(filename):
    """Increments values in a file, creating a new file.

Works with both ints and floats."""

    data = open(filename, 'rt').readlines()
    for i, line in enumerate(data):
        for word in line.split():
            try:
                data[i] = line.replace(word, str(int(word)+1))
            except ValueError:
                try:
                    data[i] = line.replace(word, str(float(word)+1))
                except ValueError:
                    # uncomment the following if you'd like feedback
                    # print word, "is not a number"
                    pass
    open(filename+'.inc', 'wt').writelines(data)
```

Lastly, the functions assume that numbers are always separated by spaces, which might not always be correct. An alternative approach would be to split based on punctuation marks as well as spaces (see "Example: Words Used Only Once" later in this chapter for splitting on punctuation marks as well).

CSV Files

Up to this point we've been working with plain text files. Plain text files typically do not follow any format other than their contents are text based. But in reality, when you're dealing with data files, they're more structured than plain text files. As discussed previously in Chapter 4, the CSV file format is a good format for structured text-based data files. The purpose of this section is to provide tools for more advanced log file processing that will be presented in the next section.

The csv Module

The csv module, which is part of the Python Standard Library, provides simple methods to read and write CSV files. To use the csv module, issue import csv; the remaining discussion assumes you've imported the csv module properly.

There are two basic objects you'll be working with: the csv.reader and the csv.writer. As their names suggest, one is used for reading, while the other is used for writing.

The csv.reader object splits a line of text into a list of words (also referred to as *fields*). While you might think it's simpler to split the line of text using the split() string method, some caveats make this a bit more complex than is apparent.

Consider a CSV file with contents as follows (assume it is stored in the file ../data/sometext.csv):

```
1/1/2000,"Some text, and a comma"
1/1/2000, "Some text, and a comma"
```

If I were to use the split() function, I'd get

```
>>> L = open('../data/sometext.csv').read().split(',')
>>> from pprint import pprint
>>> pprint(L)
['1/1/2000',
 '"Some text',
 ' and a comma"\n1/1/2000',
 ' "Some text',
 ' and a comma"\n']
```

Not really what I wanted, plus fields and rows aren't separated properly.

Using the csv.reader object, I get a better result:

```
>>> f = open('../data/sometext.csv')
>>> for line in csv.reader(f, skipinitialspace=True):
...     print line
...
['1/1/2000', 'Some text, and a comma']
['1/1/2000', 'Some text, and a comma']
```

The csv.reader Object

To create a csv.reader object, use the following syntax: csv.reader(f[, dialect='excel'] [, params]). The first parameter, f, is the CSV file, but it can also be any iterable object. The second parameter is the dialect. Since there are no clear definitions of what a CSV file constitutes (and there are quite a bit of nuances), you can specify a dialect, which is a set of rules instructing the csv.reader parser how to handle those differences. Furthermore, you can use an existing dialect and override some parameters of its behavior using the params field.

In the previous example, I didn't specify a dialect, which defaulted to the 'excel' dialect. I did provide a format parameter, instructing the csv.reader to ignore the space at the beginning of the field (there's an extra space after the comma in the second line of text in my input file). You can view the list of dialects in your system by issuing csv.list_dialects().

Once you have a csv.reader object, you can iterate through the object and retrieve a list of fields.

The csv.writer Object

The csv.writer object complements the csv.reader in that it allows writing of CSV files. Creating a csv.writer object is similar to creating the csv.reader object: csv.writer(f[, dialect='excel'][, params]). The difference (aside from the write vs. read operation) is that the csv.writer object strictly requires a file, and not an iterable object. Once you have a csv. writer object, you can use the writerow() or writerows() methods:

```
>>> lines = [["1/1/2000", "Some text, and a comma"]]
>>> csv.writer(open('../data/outtext.csv', 'w')).writerows(lines)
```

■**Note** I've created a list of rows (notice the double brackets), even though there is but one row. This is to match the input expected by the csv.writer object. If you pass the csv.writer object a list, and not a list of rows, the results might not match what you expect.

More csv Functionality

The csv module allows considerable customization including the use and creation of user-defined dialects. I won't be covering this topic; however, I will be covering some parameters and their meaning.

The *delimiter* specifies the field separator. That is, the row is split on an occurrence of the delimiter, provided it is not escaped or quoted. To change the delimiter, add delimiter=char as an argument to the csv object; char must be a character:

```
>>> for line in csv.reader(open('../data/sometext.csv'), delimiter='/'):
...     print line
...
['1', '1', '2000,"Some text, and a comma"']
['1', '1', '2000, "Some text, and a comma"']
```

The parameter quotechar specifies the quoting character used to denote a string in a CSV file.

```
>>> lines = [["1/1/2000", "Some text, and a comma"]]
>>> f = open('../data/outtext.csv', 'w')
>>> csv.writer(f, quotechar='|').writerows(lines)
>>> f.close()
```

The preceding example results in the following:

```
1/1/2000,|Some text, and a comma|
```

In this example, the date wasn't quoted, while the text was—the reason being that the text contained the delimiter. To override quoting behavior, change the value of quoting to csv. QUOTE_MINIMAL, csv.QUOTE_ALL, csv.QUOTE_NONNUMERIC, or csv.QUOTE_NONE. The names quite obviously indicate their functionality. In case you select a csv.QUOTE_NONE and a field contains the delimiter, you'd have to supply an escapechar as well:

```
>>> lines = [["1/1/2000", "Some text, and a comma"]]
>>> f = open('../data/outtext.csv', 'w')
>>> cw = csv.writer(f, quoting=csv.QUOTE_NONE, escapechar='~')
>>> cw.writerows(lines)
>>> f.close()
```

The preceding example results in the following:

```
1/1/2000,Some text~, and a comma
```

DictReader and DictWriter Objects

The csv module provides us with additional useful objects: the DictReader and DictWriter objects, which are similar to the csv.reader and csv.writer objects.

If you follow the convention that places a header at the beginning of a CSV file, that is, that each column in the CSV file starts with a *field name* (see Chapter 4 for a discussion of this), accessing values can be done by accessing the dictionary with the field name as key.

Let's turn to an example. To follow along, create the file ../data/tobuy.csv with the following content:

```
Item,Count
Milk,2
Eggs,12
Tomatoes,5
```

Now let's create a DictReader object:

```
>>> import csv
>>> fcsv = open('../data/tobuy.csv')
>>> for row in csv.DictReader(fcsv):
...     print "Please buy ", row['Count'], row['Item']
...
Please buy  2 Milk
Please buy  12 Eggs
Please buy  5 Tomatoes
```

I've accessed the values in the CSV file using 'Count' and 'Item' as keys to the dictionary object, row: row['Count'] and row['Item']. If columns were switched, the code would still work as expected.

Similarly, you can create a DictWriter object as follows:

```
>>> header = ['Item', 'Count']
>>> rows = [['Organic Eggs', 5], ['Cucumbers', 12]]
>>> fcsv = open('../data/tobuy_more.csv', 'wb')
>>> dict_wr = csv.DictWriter(fcsv, header)
```

```
>>> dict_wr.writerow(dict(zip(header, header)))
>>> for row in rows:
...     dict_wr.writerow(dict(zip(header, row)))
...
>>> fcsv.close()
```

I first created the header, a list of strings, and the data, a list of rows. I then opened a file named ../data/tobuy_more.csv for writing and attached it to a csv.DictWriter object named dict_wr. As you can see, csv.DictWriter requires the header information as well.

Now this is where it gets a little tricky. First, I'd like to write the header information to the CSV file. To do so, I create the following dictionary:

```
>>> dict(zip(header, header))
{'Count': 'Count', 'Item': 'Item'}
```

I then pass this dictionary as a parameter to the function writerrow(), a method of DictWriter, in essence creating the header field.

Now, all that's required is to do the same for the data, that is:

```
>>> for row in rows:
...     dict_wr.writerow(dict(zip(header, row)))
```

And here are the results:

```
Item,Count
Organic Eggs,5
Cucumbers,12
```

As you can see, the DictWriter object is not as simple to work with. That's why I rarely use it, although I use DictReader quite a bit. For a full account of DictReader and DictWriter, please consult with the Python Library Reference.

Date and Time

While text files are important, text isn't really the object of this book; it has to do more with numbers. The most universal form of data you're bound to see when processing data files is date and time. Text files that record information based on date and time, especially recording the events that transpired, are commonly referred to as *log files*.

I recently performed a search for file names containing the word "log" in my C:\Windows directory. I came up with dozens of files that are indeed log files. I opened some of them in my favorite editor, and of those that did record date and time, the date and time information was in varying forms.

One file had timestamps that looked like this:

```
06/21/2008 21:57:20: Some text
06/21/2008 21:57:25: Some text
```

Unfortunately, not every line started with a timestamp. Another file looked like this:

```
2008-10-21    20:37:26 Some text
2008-10-21    20:37:26 Some text
```

And yet another one looked like this:

```
=== Logging stopped: 6/26/2008  15:53:09 ===
Some text [15:53:09:109]: Some text
Some text [15:53:09:109]: Some text
=== Verbose logging stopped: 6/26/2008  15:53:09 ===
```

and this:

```
[Thu Aug 12 22:36:49 2004] Some text
[Sat Aug 14 12:54:01 2004] Some text
[Sat Aug 14 13:25:21 2004] Some text
[Sat Aug 14 14:41:48 2004] Some text
```

Of those log files, the ones I particularly like are those that don't save hard disk space and always dump a timestamp in every entry. The reason for this is that parsing the data later can be done without state machines, simplifying the code considerably. (For a discussion of state machines, refer to *Text Processing in Python* by David Mertz [Addison-Wesley, 2003], also available online at http://gnosis.cx/TPiP.) Log files that sporadically write date and time information are even harder to swallow. Clearly, the person writing those did not think of the parsing application—did he assume that a person will actually read this and not a computer?

So here's a tip for you, when you implement log files:

■Tip When writing log files, start a line of text with full date and time information.

The time module, available as part of the Python Standard Library, allows easy handling of date and time information.

Time Module

The time module provides a set of helper functions and structures that facilitate handling of date and time in a simple manner. A point in time, that is, both date and time, can be represented in one of two ways in the module:

- *A nine-elements tuple*: This tuple includes year, month, day, hours, minutes, seconds, weekday, Julian day, and DST (DST stands for daylight savings time). Of this tuple, the values weekday and Julian day are redundant: you can calculate these values based on other values—year, month, and date. We'll refer to this tuple as the struct_time tuple.

- *Number of seconds since the epoch*: The epoch is a fixed time reference point and is system dependent. On my system, the epoch is Thu Jan 01 00:00:00 1970. At times people use the word "epoch" to mean the number of seconds elapsed since the epoch and not the fixed time reference; this is usually done in context and should be easy enough to discern.

Some time functions accept the struct_time tuple, while others accept the epoch. It's not complex to switch representations. With those two notations covered, let's explore the time module. But first, to use the module, be sure to issue import time.

The struct_time Tuple

It's possible to access a specific struct_time tuple element by indexing it; for example, if t is a struct_time tuple, t[0] is the year value. However, using indices is quite hard to follow, and you'll constantly have to look up the documentation to figure out which index is the correct index to the specific value you're looking for. Instead, you can use the member variables tm_year, tm_month, tm_day, tm_hour, tm_min, tm_sec, tm_wday, tm_yday, and tm_isdst to retrieve these values:

```
>>> from time import localtime
>>> localtime()
(2008, 10, 26, 9, 37, 35, 6, 300, 0)
>>> localtime().tm_year
2008
>>> localtime().tm_yday
300
```

In this example, I've introduced the function localtime(), which returns the current time as a struct_time tuple.

Parsing and Formatting Date and Time

The functions strftime() and strptime() are the two functions you're most likely to use when dealing with log files. The function strptime(), which was introduced in Chapter 4, accepts a template parse string and the string to parse, and returns a struct_time representation of the time. The function strftime() does the opposite: transforms a tuple into a string based on a supplied pattern. Both functions use a similar notation to indicate the values in the struct_time tuple, as listed in Table 5-2.

Table 5-2. *Selected Identifiers for* strftime() *and* strptime()

Identifier	Description	Values Range
%Y	Year with century as a decimal number.	
%m	Month as a decimal number.	1–12
%d	Day of the month as a decimal number.	1–31
%H	Hour as a decimal number.	0–23

Continued

Table 5-2. *Continued*

Identifier	Description	Values Range
%M	Minutes as a decimal number.	0-59
%S	Seconds as a decimal number.	00–61 (61 for leap seconds)
%w	Weekday as a decimal number.	0–6 (where 0 is Sunday)
%j	Day of the year as a decimal number.	001–366 (366 for leap years)
%z	Time zone field. DST doesn't have an identifier of its own and is part of this field.	
%a, %A	Locale's weekday name, abbreviated and full.	
%b, %B	Locale's month name, abbreviated and full.	

The full table includes additional identifiers and is available online at `http://docs.python.org/library/time.html`.

In the section "Example: Extracting Date and Time Information from File Contents" later in this chapter, we'll extract the date and time using the `strptime()` function from some of the samples I've provided at the beginning of the section.

Example: Logging Information with a Date and Timestamp

The purpose of this example is to create a log file in accordance with the tip presented previously in the "Date and Time" section and the ISO time format recommendation (see Chapter 4).

We'll use the function `localtime()`, which returns a `struct_time` tuple containing the current time. We then format the current time using the `strftime()` function:

```
>>> from time import localtime, strftime
>>> strftime("%Y-%m-%dT%H-%M-%S", localtime())
'2008-10-23T12-16-41'
```

(From now on, I'll assume you either imported the functions by name or imported the entire time module so I don't have to write that `import` statement every time.) While this notation is handy for file names, maybe in log files you'd like to have something a little more self-explanatory. In such cases, you can use the `asctime()` function:

```
>>> asctime(localtime())
'Thu Oct 23 12:18:42 2008'
```

However, I'll use the following format:

```
>>> strftime('%d-%b-%Y %H:%M:%S', gmtime())
'23-Oct-2008 12:23:48'
```

This is to show formats other than the ISO format and because there's little room to mis-understand it. However, I recommend following the ISO time format whenever possible.

■**Tip** The ISO date and time format, in my mind, is the preferred method of writing date and time information. It might be a little more cryptic at first and might take some getting used to, but it's consistent and very
easy to work with. For example, to sort date in ISO time format, you can sort the actual string without converting it to numerical values.

The output from `asctime()` adds, in my mind, an unnecessary value, redundant information if you will: the day of the week. The format I've selected is problematic as well in case of
a different locale (see the section "Locale" later in this chapter), but it's pretty hard to get it
wrong; it's probably the most self-explanatory of the formats presented. But it's more a matter
of personal taste.

So now that we have the date and time as a string, time to write it to a log file. Listing 5-15
presents an example script you can run that generates a log file that adheres to the guidelines
I've given in this chapter and previous ones.

Listing 5-15. *Creating Log Files*

```
from time import strftime, gmtime, sleep
time_str = strftime("%Y-%m-%dT%H-%M-%S", gmtime())
flog = open("../data/LogExample%s.txt" % time_str, 'wt')
for i in range(5):
    sleep(1.7)
    logline = "%s | Some data %d\n" % \
        (strftime('%d-%b-%Y %H:%M:%S', localtime()), i)
    flog.write(logline)
flog.close()
```

I've introduced another function from the time module: `sleep()`. The `sleep()` function
accepts as an argument the amount of time in seconds it should sleep and returns once that
time period has elapsed. I chose to use a fractional value so the log file might appear more
"real," that is, not in fixed time increments:

```
23-Oct-2008 12:59:25 | Some data 0
23-Oct-2008 12:59:27 | Some data 1
23-Oct-2008 12:59:29 | Some data 2
23-Oct-2008 12:59:30 | Some data 3
23-Oct-2008 12:59:32 | Some data 4
```

Another benefit of the `strftime()` function is that it adds a leading zero for values that
do not require the full length of the field, thus 1 a.m. will show as 01 in the hour fields. This is
extremely useful when parsing, as the time format has a fixed length and can be string sliced.

One of the problems associated with logging is that your program crashes, and you might
lose important information. To overcome this, you can open and close the log file every time
you log data (or once in a while) to protect data in case of a crash—your file is still updated.

Another alternative is to use the logging module from the Python Standard Library, which I won't be covering here. Refer to http://docs.python.org/library/logging.html for information about the logging module.

Example: Extracting Date and Time Information from File Contents

We've already seen an example of using strptime() in Chapter 4. Let's cover it in more detail here. This time, we'd like to parse some of the date and time formats presented in the beginning of the section "Date and Time."

For the purpose of this example, I'll assign a string to each different time format and parse every string. By now you should be able to write the wrapper functions to implement reading and writing from a file using either the regular file operation or the csv module. To show that the format was read properly, I'll print the asctime() version of the time.

```
>>> log1 = '06/21/2008 21:57:20: Some text'
>>> time1 = strptime(log1[:19], '%m/%d/%Y %H:%M:%S')
>>> asctime(time1)
'Sat Jun 21 21:57:20 2008'
```

If you look at the time information in the string log1, it appears that it follows a fixed length. That's especially evident because of the leading zero in the month field (06). Therefore, to extract just the date and time information, I've sliced the string in the beginning. From there, I used the strptime() function to do the rest of the work. However, had the day been a value less than or equal to 12 (it's currently 21), I wouldn't know in advance whether the format is %m/%d or %d/%m. Furthermore, in case the timestamp isn't a fixed-size string, I would need to resort to other methods such as splitting the string and working with substrings.

On to the next string.

```
>>> log2 = '2008-10-21\t20:37:26 Some text'
>>> print log2
2008-10-21        20:37:26 Some text
>>> time2 = strptime(log2[:19], '%Y-%m-%d\t%H:%M:%S')
>>> asctime(time2)
'Tue Oct 21 20:37:26 2008'
```

This example includes a string with the date and time separated by a tab and a slightly different format. But again, hardly a problem for strptime().

Parsing the date and time information of the remaining strings shouldn't be too complex.

The Epoch: "Linearizing" the Time Base

Up to this point we've been using the struct_time tuple exclusively. It's time to talk about the epoch representation. As I mentioned, seconds elapsed since the epoch is another time representation supported by the time module. At times, it's more beneficial to use an epoch representation than a struct_time representation.

The first reason that springs to my mind is that of visualization. If you want to plot data as a function of time, and your time base is in the form of a struct_time, it's pretty hard to do. You'd have to come up with ways to "linearize" the time base so that the time base won't be skewed.

You've seen two examples of linearizing the data. One was in Chapter 1, where I manually linearized the data by multiplying the hours value by 3600, adding the minutes value multiplied by 60, and then adding the seconds. The second example was given in Chapter 4 where I used mktime() and gmtime() to calculate the day of the year value as my linear time base.

While these are good options, there's a more standardized way, and that is using the epoch notation. As I mentioned previously, the epoch is system dependent and serves as a reference point in time against which time is measured by the total amount of seconds elapsed (fractional values are allowed as well).

To figure out the epoch in your system, issue asctime(gmtime(0)). From here on out, you already have a linear time base, the epoch representation!

Let's modify the GPS example from Chapter 1. As you recall, the time information was as follows: hhmmss.ss, where the second set of ss values, after the decimal point, represent fractions of a second. Let's consider the values '140055.00' and '140156.00', which are one minute and one second apart. The original calculation used multiplications and additions:

```
>>> vals = ['140055.00', '140156.00']
>>> [float(x[0:2])*3600+float(x[2:4])*60+float(x[4:6]) for x in vals]
[50455.0, 50516.0]
>>> _[1]-_[0]
61.0
```

The difference between the two values (and what we're really after, as you recall we set the start of the time base at zero) is 61 seconds, as should be expected. We can alternatively calculate the epoch representation using the function mktime() from the time module and use that to calculate the time difference:

```
>>> [mktime((0, 0, 0, int(x[0:2]), int(x[2:4]), int(x[4:6]), 0, 0, 0)) \
... for x in vals]
[943963255.0, 943963316.0]
>>> _[1]-_[0]
61.0
```

I've used filler values for other unknown fields such as day and month. (Module datetime of the Python Standard Library provides functionality that deals with time differences as well but is beyond the scope of this discussion.)

We get the same result. So what's the benefit of using the epoch-based functions from the time module? There are several:

- The preceding example was pretty simple and did not contain date information as well. Suppose your data recorder also records the date. What happens at midnight? You'll get a rollover if you don't take into account the date, which makes things considerably more complex. You can of course add the day into calculations. But what happens when a month changes? That's a bit more complex: months don't have the same number of days in them, so you'd need a lookup table. And what about leap years? You see, it gets complicated. Instead, use mktime(), which takes all of these issues into consideration.

- Using the epoch enables sharing a time base across files. This means that you can pull in information from all sorts of data sources and treat them as one.

- If you're dealing with timestamped binary data files, writing the time base can be challenging as well. Instead of coming up with complex representations for the time base, use the epoch representation (see Chapter 10 for a general discussion of binary files and an example of time-based binary files).

Example: End-of-Day Report

The end-of-day report is a summary report of a log file presenting data at the end of the day. Here are two scenarios where this report is useful:

- *Ending quote for a stock*: Suppose you have a log file with the stock prices over a long period of time, say, a month. The end-of-day report prints the stock price at the end of trade days.

- *Patient discharge*: A patient is being treated at the hospital and during his treatment all information is logged. You'd like to know the patient discharge state, that is, you want to receive an end-of-day report with patient's status.

To illustrate the problem, we'll create a log file , `../data/SystemALogs.txt`, that will be composed of timestamps and a log message, as follows:

```
Sat Oct 25 08:15:01 2008, Message 1
Sat Oct 25 09:30:31 2008, Message 2
Sun Oct 26 09:19:32 2008, Message 3
Mon Oct 27 08:05:31 2008, Message 4
Wed Oct 29 07:17:40 2008, Message 5
Wed Oct 29 08:44:04 2008, Message 6
Wed Oct 29 09:44:05 2008, Message 7
Wed Oct 29 12:30:50 2008, Message 8
Thu Oct 30 11:22:03 2008, Message 9
```

In this case, the log file is sorted, which is to be expected. But even if that's not the case, the algorithm we employ should still work properly.

To print an end-of-day report, I'll use the following algorithm. A dictionary object stores an end-of-day report per day. The key of the dictionary should uniquely identify a day. I chose to use the tuple (year, day of the year) for that purpose. For the dictionary value, I'll be using a tuple containing the epoch and the message. The reason I'm using the epoch is that first, I can easily compute it using `mktime()`, and second, it's a simple value to check against. A larger epoch value means a more recent event.

We process the file line by line and extract the information to create the key and value to access the dictionary. In case the key is already in the dictionary, we check whether the information in the current line is from a later time, and if it is, we update the value accordingly. If the key doesn't exist in the dictionary, we add the computed key and value pair to the dictionary. Once we're done processing the file, we print the dictionary object. As you can see, the algorithm doesn't rely on the log file to be sorted to produce correct results.

I've chosen to use the csv module to show usage of the module in a full script, presented in Listing 5-16. In this specific case, a simple split, or string slicing, would've worked just as well.

Listing 5-16. *End-of-Day Report Implementation*

```
# end-of-day report
from time import mktime, strptime, ctime
import csv

d = {}

for row in csv.reader(open('../data/SystemALogs.txt')):
    # t is a struct_time tuple
    t = strptime(row[0], '%a %b %d %H:%M:%S %Y')

    # calculate seconds since the epoch
    t_epoch = mktime(t)

    # construct a key and value
    key = (t.tm_year, t.tm_yday)
    val = (t_epoch, row[1])

    try:
        # do we have a more recent entry?
        if d[key][0] < t_epoch:
            d[key] = val
    except KeyError:
        # current date is not in dictionary
        d[key] = val

for epoch, line in d.itervalues():
    print ctime(epoch), line
```

I've also introduced a new function from the time module in Listing 5-16, ctime(). The function ctime() accepts the number of seconds since the epoch and prints out a date string representation.

Here are the results from running the script on the preceding log file:

```
Sat Oct 25 09:30:31 2008  Message 2
Thu Oct 30 11:22:03 2008  Message 9
Mon Oct 27 08:05:31 2008  Message 4
Wed Oct 29 12:30:50 2008  Message 8
Sun Oct 26 09:19:32 2008  Message 3
```

The results are correct, but they aren't sorted by date. This can be easily remedied if instead of printing the files you'd store them to a list and then call the function sort() to sort the list.

Example: Combining Data from Several Sources Based on the Epoch

One of the benefits of using the epoch is that it is a standard time base to work with. The intention of this example is to combine data from several sources, in this case two log files, and present a coherent report. For the purpose of this example, we'll split the file SystemALogs.txt from the previous example into two files: SystemBLogs.txt and SystemsCLogs.txt. Our script should combine them back into a sorted log file.

Following are the contents of SystemBLogs.txt:

```
Sun Oct 26 09:19:32 2008, Message 3
Wed Oct 29 07:17:40 2008, Message 5
Thu Oct 30 11:22:03 2008, Message 9
```

And the contents of SystemCLogs.txt:

```
Sat Oct 25 08:15:01 2008, Message 1
Sat Oct 25 09:30:31 2008, Message 2
Mon Oct 27 08:05:31 2008, Message 4
Wed Oct 29 08:44:04 2008, Message 6
Wed Oct 29 09:44:05 2008, Message 7
Wed Oct 29 12:30:50 2008, Message 8
```

Trying to sort these lists based on text will generate the wrong results. So the idea is to convert every timestamp string into an epoch representation and sort based on that value. For this purpose we'll create a list of rows. Each row will be composed of [t_epoch, line], where t_epoch is the converted time representation and line is the entire line of text. We then use the sorted() function to sort the lists and dump the data back to file, removing the epoch information (see Listing 5-17).

Listing 5-17. *Script to Combine Two Time-Based Log Files*

```python
from time import mktime, strptime
data = []
data1 = open('../data/SystemBLogs.txt').readlines()
data2 = open('../data/SystemCLogs.txt').readlines()
fmt = '%b %d %H:%M:%S %Y'
for line in data1+data2:
    # t is a struct_time tuple
    t = strptime(line[4:24], fmt)

    # calculate seconds since the epoch
    t_epoch = mktime(t)

    # append data
    data.append([t_epoch, line])

data = [line[1] for line in sorted(data)]
open('../data/SystemsBCLogs.txt', 'wt').writelines(data)
```

This script assumes you're combining two files. More often than not, if you need to combine log files, you'll need to combine more than two files. Refer to Chapter 10 for discussion on working with several input files.

Additional Time and Date Functions

We've covered most of the functionality available in the time module. For most of your log file processing needs and other time-based processing requirements, the module is comprehensive and complete. There are additional time- and date-related modules available in Python. The datetime module provides functionality that includes operations on dates using a more object-oriented approach. The calendar module provides general calendar-related operations. Refer to the Python Standard Library for additional information.

Regular Expressions

Regular expressions are pattern-matching expressions used for searching and replacing text. At times, they are more flexible than the string operations presented previously. To use regular expressions, you'll have to import the regular expression module (named re), which is part of the standard library. The module re is similar to Perl's built-in support of regular expressions.

Your next step is to design a pattern to match against and decide what function to use on that pattern. The most notable functions are findall(pat, str), which finds all occurrences of a regular expression pattern pat in the string str; split(pat, str), which splits the string str whenever a regular expression pattern pat is encountered; and sub(pat, repl, str), which substitutes the occurrence of a pattern pat in a string str with a supplied substitute repl.

There are additional functions in the module, including match(), search(), and compile() to name a few, but I will not be covering those here: the preceding three functions should take care of most our data processing needs.

Regular Expression Patterns

A regular expression pattern is basically a string. The pattern can contain both regular characters and special characters. A regular character matches itself. So the pattern 'a' matches the character 'a' whenever encountered, and the pattern 'txt' matches the string 'txt' whenever encountered:

```
>>> import re
>>> re.split(r'a', 'Flatland')
['Fl', 'tl', 'nd']
>>> re.split(r'txt', '97.txt')
['97.', '']
```

So far, re.split() is similar to the split() function introduced previously in the chapter. However, the strength of regular expressions lies in the special characters. These characters provide additional functionality to the pattern itself. Let's take a look at some. The first one is the dot character ('.'). The dot character matches any single character except for a new line:

```
>>> re.findall(r'a.', 'Flatland')
['at', 'an']
```

The character '+' means one or more occurrences of the pattern, the character '?' means zero or one occurrences of the pattern, and the character '*' means zero or more repetitions of the pattern. Note that these are modifiers of the pattern, that is, they change the behavior of the pattern, whereas the dot symbol is not a modifier of the pattern, it's part of the pattern. Here are some examples:

```
>>> re.findall(r'.?a', 'Flatland')
['la', 'la']
>>> re.findall(r'a.*', 'Flatland')
['atland']
```

The first example finds the pattern composed of zero or one characters, followed by the character 'a'. The second example matches the character 'a' followed by any number of characters.

One might question why is it that the first pattern matched one character before the character 'a', since obviously zero characters would've worked as well? Or why did the second pattern matched the string 'atland' where 'a' would've worked just as well? The answer is that regular expressions are greedy by default, that is, they try to match as many characters as possible. You can turn off the greedy behavior by adding a '?' character after the modifiers presented previously, that is, '??', '+?', and '*?'.

The next special characters are the '^' and '$' characters, which match the start and end of a string, respectively. Here are some examples that demonstrate these special characters:

```
>>> re.findall(r'^.*a', 'Flatland')
['Flatla']
>>> re.findall(r'^.*?a', 'Flatland')
['Fla']
>>> re.findall(r'a.*$', 'Flatland')
['atland']
```

These searches can be expressed in English as follows. The first line matches as many characters as possible between the start of the string and the character 'a'. The second line finds as few characters as possible between the start of the string and the character 'a' (notice the nongreediness modifier, '*?'). The third line matches the character 'a' and the remaining characters until the end of the line.

I think we're ready for an example now.

Example: Removing Extra Spaces with Regular Expressions

Previously in this chapter, I've shown how to remove extra spaces in a string. We've used split() to split the words on spaces and then strip() to remove the excess spaces. We then used join() to combine the list back into a string.

With regular expressions, the same can be achieved more easily:

```
>>> grocery_list = "Milk    2\nEggs  12"
>>> re.sub(r' +', ' ', grocery_list)
'Milk 2\nEggs 12'
```

I've used the function sub() with the pattern ' +' (a space followed by the plus sign) to replace one or more spaces with one space.

Special Sequences

Special sequences are used to match some interesting combinations. Here's a short list: '\d' matches a decimal digit, '\s' matches a whitespace, and '\w' matches an alphanumeric character. If you use uppercase, the opposite is achieved, that is, '\D' matches anything but a decimal digit, '\S' matches anything but a whitespace, and '\W' matches anything but an alphanumeric character. Since the '\' character is a modifier, it's a good idea to use the raw string format, r' ', as you've seen previously, so as not to escape characters on several levels (i.e., on the string level and on the regular expression level).

```
>>> grocery_list = "Milk   2\nEggs  12"
>>> re.findall(r'\d+', grocery_list)
['2', '12']
```

Alternatives

The special character '|' is used to match either pat1 or pat2 in the regular expression r'pat1|pat2':

```
>>> grocery_list = "Milk   2\nEggs  12"
>>> re.sub(r'Milk|Eggs', 'Chocolate', grocery_list)
'Chocolate   2\nChocolate  12'
```

Ranges

You can also match a range of values using brackets. The pattern '[12]' will match both the character '1' and the character '2':

```
>>> grocery_list = "Milk   2\nEggs  12"
>>> re.sub('[12]', '0', grocery_list)
'Milk   0\nEggs  00'
```

You can also denote a range of characters using the '-' character. The pattern '[1-5]' matches any character from 1 to 5, inclusive.

Lastly, follow up with a '^' after the left bracket to negate the range:

```
>>> grocery_list = "Milk   2\nEggs  12"
>>> re.sub('[^0-5]', '*', grocery_list)
'*******2*******12'
```

When to Use Regular Expressions

It's hard to decide whether to use a regular expression or just plain string operations. Regular expressions are hard to master, but practice makes perfect as the saying goes. Try solving the same problem with string functions and with regular expressions to get a feel for what's the better approach.

If using string operations makes things more complicated to follow, resolve to regular expressions. At times, a simple regular expression makes the code more readable and elegant.

Such a case was presented previously in the example of removing extra spaces. At other times, it's the other way around. Opt for simplicity and clarity of your code whenever possible.

That being said, there is a special case where I've found that using regular expressions is far better than using string methods, and that is when I'd like to split or replace a string based on several options. The main reason is that string method `split()` requires a separator and does not accept several options, whereas with regular expressions you can provide a range of separators.

Example: Words Used Only Once

We finalize this discussion of regular expressions with an example that uses a dictionary in conjunction with text. The idea is to find words used only once in a file. The motivation behind this example is that words used only once might be typographical errors in source code.

To implement the solution, we'll use a dictionary to count the number of occurrences of each and every word in a file (see Listing 5-18).

Listing 5-18. *Finding Words Used Only Once*

```
from string import punctuation, whitespace
import re
def nonce(filename):
    """Returns words used only once in a file."""

    data = open(filename, 'rt').read()
    d, result = dict(), []
    for word in re.split('['+punctuation+whitespace+']', data):
        d[word.lower()] = d.get(word.lower(), 0)+1
    for word, occur in d.iteritems():
        if occur == 1:
            result.append(word)
    return result
```

The function `nonce()` should prove quite readable. The heart of the script lies in the `for` loop, which splits the text using a regular expression. This is a prime example where a regular expression is better than the string method `split()`: the split happens on either a punctuation character or a whitespace character by means of the regular expression range specifier, `'[]'`.

Bear in mind that this script is good for mostly source code and not plain-text English. The reason is that it doesn't take into consideration such things as plural forms (e.g., "girls" and "girl" are considered two different words) and other spoken language characteristics.

Internationalization and Localization

At times you're faced with working with data files that originated in a different locale. This could pose some problems: date and time notations can be different from what your code expects, or the text characters can be of another language.

The purpose of this section is to introduce the topic of internationalization (i18n) and localization (l10n). I'll touch on two topics: the locale and its impact on date notations, and

Unicode, which is a convenient method to support different languages, at least when it comes to text files.

Locale

In the context of software, *locale* is a set of rules governing the behavior of some functions that are either country or language oriented. From a data analysis perspective, if a log file containing a timestamp of both date and time is used, and the locale is not identical to the one in use, the function strptime() might fail. For example, some countries use day/month/year notation while others use the month/day/year notation.

To accommodate for different locales, Python provides support via the locale module, which is part of the Python Standard Library. To use it, issue the command import locale. To set a locale, issue the command locale.setlocale(category, locale). You can either enable the entire set of rules using the category locale.LC_ALL or set specific ones. In our case, we'll be using LC_ALL, which also controls the behavior of the functions strftime() and strptime().

Generally speaking, you should set your locale upon program entry.

```
>>> import locale
>>> locale.setlocale(locale.LC_ALL, 'fr')
'French_France.1252'
# if the above doesn't work, try replacing 'fr' with 'fr_FR.ISO-8859-1' or 'french'
>>> from time import gmtime, strftime, strptime
>>> fmt = '%d-%B-%Y'
>>> strftime(fmt, localtime())
'26-octobre-2008'
>>> strptime(_, fmt)
(2008, 10, 26, 0, 0, 0, 6, 300, -1)
```

The first line imports the locale module. I then set the locale to be 'French_France.1252', which basically means the language French, the country France. It's possible to mix language and country, for example, passing the string 'French_Canada' to set the language to French but the country to Canada. In Windows, I've found that the notation `'Language_Country'` works well, whereas I've had some issues with abbreviations (e.g., `'fr_CA'` didn't work well for me). In Linux, I've found that the notation in the form `'en_US.ISO-8859-1'` works well, so for French Canada, on Linux, I've set the locale to `'fr_CA.ISO-8859-1'`.

For additional information regarding the locale module, refer to the Python Standard Library: `http://docs.python.org/library/locale.html`.

We're not done with locale yet; I'll present another example after talking a bit about Unicode.

Unicode Strings

The original ASCII table is based on the English language and does not account for a lot of other languages and symbols. Several designs were introduced to try to resolve this, and lately it appears that Unicode (`http://www.unicode.org`) is the industry standard.

The Unicode standard addresses such topics as *character encoding*, *character properties*, *visual representation*, and more. From a very simplistic approach, Unicode tries to support characters and symbols from other languages by assigning every character (and there are tens of thousands of those, if not more) a unique integer number while maintaining compatibility with the ASCII table. This means that some Unicode characters are represented by 4 bytes, not 1 byte.

The problem starts when you want to write your Unicode string to file. Writing 4 bytes instead of 1 every time is space consuming. If the characters you use are simple English characters, they are all well within the ASCII table and thus contain less than 8 bits. To write them, you don't need 4 bytes—1 byte will suffice. In this case, you can choose to *encode* your Unicode string as an 8-bit value, known as UTF-8. UTF stands for Unicode Transformation Format.

If the characters you use are not all from the English alphabet, you might need more bytes to represent your Unicode string. In most cases, 2 bytes is more than enough, which means you can encode your Unicode string using UTF-16 encoding. However, you're also likely to use characters from the English alphabet (or other ASCII symbols), in which case some characters may be encoded with 8 bits. And so some encoding supports those variable size schemes as well.

From our perspective, it is sufficient to know that Python natively supports Unicode strings. And furthermore, we can encode and decode Unicode strings using a host of encoding schemes, including UTF-8 and UTF-16. Unicode strings follow the notation `u''`.

Working with Unicode

Unicode strings behave similarly to regular strings. As mentioned previously, if a character in the Unicode string matches the ASCII value, that value is used. So to construct a Unicode string made of ASCII characters, simply call the `unicode()` function with the string:

```
>>> unicode('a string')
u'a string'
```

However, if that is the case, and you are using ASCII characters, what's the point of Unicode? Fair enough, let's add nonstandard characters, that is, characters with ordinal value above 128.

The value 0xa9 corresponds to © and is pretty hard to type on most keyboards. So instead, I've used its ordinal value in Unicode. Python retains the value as an ordinal value and does not print the symbol associated with it. If we dump the Unicode string to file, it will be possible to view the special characters in most editors or web browsers. In this case, the generated file is ../data/special.txt.

```
>>> u = 'a string'+u'\u00a9'
>>> u
u'a string\xa9'
>>> open('../data/special.txt', 'wb').write(u.encode('utf-8'))
```

The write() method accepts only strings, not Unicode strings. So for us to be able to use the write() function and write the Unicode strings to file, we'll have to use the encode() method, which accepts the encoding to be used. In this case I've selected the UTF-8 encoding, which is widely popular.

The function decode() complements encode() and returns the decoded Unicode string:

```
>>> u.encode('utf-8')
'a string\xc2\xa9'
>>> u.encode('utf-16')
'\xff\xfe\x00 \x00s\x00t\x00r\x00i\x00n\x00g\x00\xa9\x00'
>>> u.encode('utf-16').decode('utf-16')
u'a string\xa9'
```

For example, to read an entire text file encoded in UTF-16, issue the following: open('../data/somefile.txt').read().decode('utf-16').

Example: The Hebrew Alphabet

The purpose of this example is to generate a file with the Hebrew alphabet. If you don't have Hebrew installed on your system (which I suppose is the case for most folks out there), you can try other, more popular characters, as I'll show shortly.

■**Note** Alphabet is a Hebrew word. It is composed of the first two letters of the Hebrew language: Aleph and Bet.

The Hebrew alphabet, shown in Figure 5-1, starts with the letter Aleph mapping to the value 0x5D0 and ends at the letter Tav, mapped to value 0x5EA in Unicode. Unless you have the Hebrew keyboard installed on your system, manually typing Hebrew letters is not a trivial task. Therefore, you'll have to construct the alphabet using a Unicode string. Since we don't want (or can't) manually type the values, we'll construct a list of Unicode letters and then generate a string from the list. The function unichr() will be used to construct the characters from their ordinal value, similar to the function chr():

```
>>> letters = [unichr(letter) for letter in range(0x5d0, 0x5eb)]
>>> alephbet = ''.join(letters)
>>> open('../data/alephbet.txt', 'w').write(alephbet.encode('utf-16'))
```

אבגדהוזחטיךכלמםןנסעףפץצקרשת

Figure 5-1. *The Hebrew alphabet*

Once we have the Unicode string, all that's required is to write it to file. Since the write() function only accepts strings, and not Unicode strings, we have to encode the string. In our case, the Hebrew Unicode values require 16 bits, so we therefore encode with UTF-16.

The Latin alphabet has special characters, as shown in Figure 5-2: the accented letters, starting at value 0xC0 and ending at 0xFF. Therefore, you could modify the preceding script to generate the Latin special characters as follows:

```
>>> letters = [unichr(letter) for letter in range(0xc0, 0x100)]
>>> latin = ''.join(letters)
>>> open('../data/latin.txt', 'w').write(latin.encode('utf-16'))
```

ÀÁÂÃÄÅÆÇÈÉÊËÌÍÎÏÐÑÒÓÔÕÖ×ØÙÚÛÜÝÞßàáâãäåæçèéêëìíîïðñòóôõö÷øùúûüýþÿ

Figure 5-2. *Some interesting Latin characters*

Example: Writing Today's Date in the Current Locale

The purpose of this example is to print the current date and time, in a specific locale, to file. If you're using the English_United States locale, this will be rather boring. So instead, I've decided to use the Hebrew locale again, since we're all familiar with it by now (see Listing 5-19). Since Python doesn't always print other character sets in the interpreter, it's best to write the results to file and view them in a text viewer, editor, or web browser.

Listing 5-19. *Today's Date in the Current Locale*

```
import locale
from time import strftime, strptime, localtime
from sys import platform

if platform == 'linux2':
    locale.setlocale(locale.LC_ALL, 'hebrew')
elif platform == 'win32':
    locale.setlocale(locale.LC_ALL, 'Hebrew_Israel')
elif platform == 'cygwin':
    raise Exception('Cygwin not supported')
else:
    print "Untested platform: ", sys.platform
today = strftime('%B %d, %Y', localtime())
todayU = unicode(today, 'cp1255')
open('../data/today.txt', 'w').write(todayU.encode('utf-16'))
```

At first, I try to guess the encoding for Hebrew based on the current platform using the `sys.platform` value. As I've mentioned earlier, Linux, Windows, and Cygwin all have different locale abbreviations.

After I set the locale, I can query the preferred locale encoding with the function `locale.getpreferredencoding()`, which is quite useful in determining how to encode the Unicode string. Unfortunately, I have found that the preferred encoding in the case of Hebrew should be `cp1255` and not the one returned by the `getpreferredencoding()` function. Lastly, I encode the string and write it to file using UTF-16.

Figure 5-3 shows the results.

```
נובמבר 18, 2008
```

Figure 5-3. *A date in Hebrew*

More on Unicode

The topic of Unicode is vast, and numerous books are available that discuss it. As for online information, I have found the Python library reference a valuable resource. If you're looking for information regarding i18n and l10n in general, including code pages and locale information, the following might prove useful:

- *The Unicode Consortium*: `http://www.unicode.org`.

- *Wikipedia*: `http://en.wikipedia.org/wiki/Locale`. Be sure to follow the links to topics such as character encoding and Unicode.

- *International Components for Unicode*: `http://www.icu-project.org/`.

Final Notes and References

String and text processing is a very large field, especially with the popularity of the Internet and search engines; most of the data available online is in some form of text. This chapter has covered a considerable number of the topics associated with text processing in the context of data analysis.

However, there's a lot more to learn. Two topics presented here were but briefly discussed: regular expressions and i18n and l10n. Considerable documentation is available on the Internet on these two topics, so by all means refer to online resources. I hope that I've covered the basics properly to allow you to proceed without much trouble.

The following book is of great value for the topics discussed in the chapter:

- *Text Processing in Python* by David Mertz (Addison-Wesley, 2003; also available online at `http://gnosis.cx/TPiP`)

CHAPTER 6

■■■

Graphs and Plots
Visualizing Data

Graphs and plots are efficient methods to present data. Done properly, a graph can convey an idea better than an entire article.

What a graph should portray is a function of your target audience, so when you plot a graph, bear that in mind. If your target audience is technical people, they might require additional technical information. If your target audience is investors, another approach is required. In this chapter we won't be discussing what to present and what not; instead, assuming you know what you want to present, I'll show you how to do so. Examples include how to plot bar charts and pie charts, how to add markers and control line ticks, how to annotate the graphs with text and arrows, and more.

Regardless of your target audience, some ideas and methodologies always hold true. Sources for data should be accurate and verified. Graphs should be easily reproducible by running the code that generated them. (How many times did your boss ask you to modify the report? If the graph was generated with a documented script, doing so should prove easy enough.) And lastly, your graphs should be aesthetically pleasing. Consulting with colleagues could be beneficial as well: What do they understand from the graph? Was the key idea captured? Is the output professional?

In this chapter we'll discuss the basics of creating and annotating graphs. We'll start by exploring the plot() function, continue with text and grid annotation, explore some other types of graphs, and lastly introduce patches, a method to attach graphical objects to a figure.

The Matplotlib Package

The matplotlib package, available at http://matplotlib.sourceforge.net/, is the main graphing and plotting tool used throughout this book. The package is versatile and highly configurable, supporting several graphing interfaces. Matplotlib, together with NumPy and SciPy (see Chapters 7 and 8), provides MATLAB-like graphing capabilities, with perhaps the limitation of 3-D plots, which matplotlib does not support.

The benefits of using matplotlib in the context of data analysis and visualization are as follows:

- Plotting data is simple and intuitive.

- Performance is great; output is professional.

- Integration with NumPy and SciPy (used for signal processing and numerical analysis) is seamless.

- The package is highly customizable and configurable, catering to most people's needs.

The package is quite extensive and allows, for example, embedding plots in a graphical user interface. Currently, the package supports several graphical interfaces including wxPython (`http://www.wxpython.org/`) and PyGTK (`http://www.pygtk.org/`), to name a few. However, GUI topics are beyond the scope of the book. We will focus on plotting graphs rather than discussing the GUI engine itself. For a full account of matplotlib, try the online documentation, available as a PDF document, at `http://matplotlib.sourceforge.net/Matplotlib.pdf`.

Going forward, you should ensure that you have matplotlib installed and working properly. Refer to Chapter 2 if you require additional information on installing the package or visit the package's web site.

Interactive Graphs vs. Image Files

There are several ways you can use matplotlib:

- Create dynamic content to be served on a web server: for example, generating stock price images on the fly or displaying traffic information on top of a map.

- Embed it in a graphical user interface, allowing users to interact with an application to visualize data.

- Automatically process data and generate output in a variety of file formats, including JPG, PNG (Portable Network Graphics, see `http://www.libpng.org/pub/png/`), PDF, and PostScript (PS). This option is best suited for batch processing of a large number of files.

- Run it interactively, with the Python shell in X or Windows. This option is good during the development phases of the code.

Of the preceding options, and in view of the book topics, we'll explore two: 1) generating plots of varying file formats and 2) using matplotlib interactively. I typically use both options depending on the stage of my code. In the early stages of development, I work interactively with a small sample of the data: plot, zoom in, change graph parameters, annotate, rinse and repeat. Once my code is ready, I let it loose so to speak on the full set of data files. Since that might mean tens if not hundreds of graph windows, I prefer to write them as files instead, and then use an image viewer to view the results one at a time.

So let's start. First and foremost, import PyLab as follows:

```
>>> from pylab import *
```

WHERE DOES THIS FUNCTION COME FROM?

A frustration to some, especially those experienced with Python, is that issuing the command `from pylab import *` will import several packages. Some feel they'd like to know whether a specific function is a part of NumPy or matplotlib. The solution is simple—use `help`! For example, here's the output from `help(diff)`:

```
>>> help(diff)
Help on function diff in module numpy.lib.function_base:

diff(a, n=1, axis=-1)
    Calculate the nth order discrete difference along given axis.
```

As you can see in the first line, `diff()` is a function from the NumPy package, or more specifically, `numpy.lib.function_base`.

As previously mentioned, this imports matplotlib, NumPy, and SciPy. Although generally speaking you shouldn't import everything quite so liberally, in the case of PyLab, make an exception: it's considerably easier to work with the entire package loaded into memory, and unless memory is a constraint, the usability is great. Going forward, I'll assume you've imported PyLab as just described.

Our next step is to plot a graph. We'll plot the list `[0, 1, 2]`:

```
>>> plot(range(3))
[<matplotlib.lines.Line2D object at 0x018680F0>]
```

There's no visible output yet (other than matplotlib's response), and the reason for this is we haven't specified how exactly we want the graph drawn: interactive figures or hard copy files.

Interactive Graphs

Interactive graphs, like the one shown in Figure 6-1, plot the graph in a separate window in X or Windows. If you'd like this option, enter `show()` at the Python shell or call the function `show()` in a script.

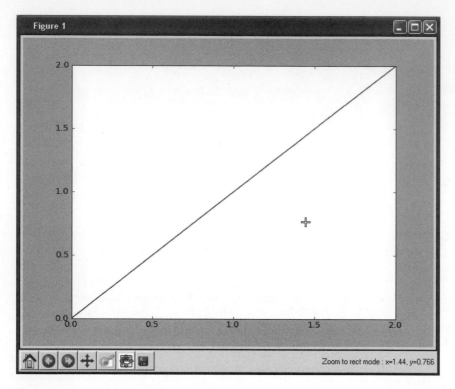

Figure 6-1. *Interactive graph*

The function show() opens up an interactive window. Several notes about this window:

- The window is numbered, as you can see by the label "Figure 1." This is useful if you have several windows and would like subsequent plots to either override or appear on a specific figure. To switch between figures, use the figure(n) function, where n stands for the figure index. If you'd like a new figure, and don't particularly care about the figure index, issue the command figure(), which will create an empty figure with the next available index.

- The x-axis and y-axis were created automatically to fit the data. In a lot of the cases, matplotlib does an excellent job of automatically selecting the right axis (as in this example). However, if you want a different range of values to be displayed, that's doable with the axis() command, more on which appears later in the chapter in the section "Axis."

- The location of the mouse is printed on the right corner of the figure. This is very useful if you're trying to zoom in on data and find a specific data point. This functionality is not available when you plot graphs to file (i.e., noninteractive mode).

- You have several buttons on the lower-left side of the figure to allow interaction with the graph. The five leftmost buttons are used for zooming and zooming history. The first button from the left (with the house icon) is used to change axes to the original plot axes. The left and right arrow buttons cycle backward and forward through previous axes changes. The fourth button allows changing of the axes origin, and the fifth button from the left enables zooming. The sixth button from the left controls the margins of the plot in respect to the containing window, and lastly the seventh button allows saving the image to disk.

■**Note** If you're not using matplotlib interactively in Python, be sure to call the function `show()` *after* all graphs have been generated, as it enters a user interface main loop that will stop execution of the rest of your code. The reason behind this behavior is that matplotlib is designed to be embedded in a GUI as well. In Windows, if you're working from interactive Python, you need only issue `show()` once; close the figures (or figures) to return to the shell. Subsequent plots will be drawn automatically without issuing `show()`, and you'll be able to plot graphs interactively.

Saving Graphs to Files

The function `savefig()` enables writing images of varying formats to a file. Out of the box, matplotlib supports several file formats including PDF, PNG, and PS. The simplest way to generate a file containing a graph is to issue `savefig(filename)`, where `filename` has the extension associated with your selected image format:

```
>>> figure()
>>> plot(arange(3))
[<matplotlib.lines.Line2D object at 0x0186A2D0>]
>>> savefig('line.png')
>>> import os
>>> [file for file in os.listdir('.') if file.endswith('png')]
['line.png']
```

You should be able to view the figure in most image viewers or your web browser.

■**Note** Matplotlib returns objects as they're created. In the preceding example, the returned object is noted by the line [`<matplotlib.lines.Line2D object at 0x0186A2D0>`]. Going forward I'll omit these responses in the interest of making the interactive code easier to follow.

I called the function `savefig()` with the file name extension as part of the string holding the file name, instructing `savefig()` to create a PNG file. Similarly, I could've created a PostScript file by issuing `savefig('line.ps')`.

The dictionary object `FigureCanvasBase.filetypes` holds a list of supported file types in your system:

```
>>> from pprint import pprint
>>> pprint(FigureCanvasBase.filetypes)
{'emf': 'Enhanced Metafile',
```

```
'eps': 'Encapsulated Postscript',
'pdf': 'Portable Document Format',
'png': 'Portable Network Graphics',
'ps': 'Postscript',
'raw': 'Raw RGBA bitmap',
'rgba': 'Raw RGBA bitmap',
'svg': 'Scalable Vector Graphics',
'svgz': 'Scalable Vector Graphics'}
```

FINDING WHAT YOU'RE LOOKING FOR IN COMPLEX MODULES

So how did I figure out `FigureCanvasBase.filetypes` holds the supported file types? Did I read the entire manual? Hardly. Some of the packages we work with are really large, and mastering all the intricacies of variables and objects that control their behavior is not a trivial task. So I use some quick-and-dirty tricks, and although they might not be the "proper" way to do things, they help me get the job done, and that's what really counts. So let me show you what I've done to figure out the available file types.

To figure out the base file types, I issued `savefig()` with a bogus file format: `savefig('a.ext')`. The result was, of course, an exception (`ValueError`) but I also received some useful information: `"Supported formats: emf, eps, pdf, png, ps, raw, rgba, svg, svgz."` But that's not exactly what I wanted; I wanted an enumeration of the file formats so I can index them rather than parse a string returned by an exception. So I traced back the source of the error from the exception output: the error originated in file `C:\Python25\lib\site-packages\matplotlib\backend_bases.py` line 1290. Next, I opened up the file `backend_bases.py`, jumped to line 1290, and started reading the code. Python is a very readable language, and it didn't take me long to figure out that the formats are stored in variable `self.filetypes.keys`. Since `self` points to the container object, I scrolled up some more and found that the calling method is named `print_figure` and is part of the class `FigureCanvasBase`, hence `FigureCanvasBase.filetypes`.

Reading the exceptions generated by matplotlib, along with exploring modules and their names, also helped me find the objects `matplotlib.colors.cnames` and `matplotlib.colors.ColorConverter.colors`, both listing possible colors (see the section "Colors" later in the chapter). That being said, reading the manual is also a very viable option.

You can pass a `format` argument to `savefig()` to control the output file generated instead of specifying it in the file name string. You can also control other parameters such as dots per inch (dpi) and face color for the color of the figure. A more general form of `savefig()` is `savefig(fname[, param1=value1][, param2=value2])`. Table 6-1 lists some parameters. In the examples, assume `fn` is a string containing a file name.

Table 6-1. *savefig() Parameters*

Parameter	Description	Default Value	Example
dpi	Resolution in dots per inch	None (On my system the actual dpi is 100.)	savefig(fn, dpi=150)
facecolor*	The figure's face color	'w' for white background	savefig(fn, facecolor='b')
format	File format	'png'	savefig('image', format='pdf')

* Refer to Table 6-4 for a list of color values.

You can combine several parameters: savefig('file', dpi=150, format='png'). The function savefig() supports additional options; see help(savefig) for a full account.

Plotting Graphs

This section details the building blocks of plotting graphs: the plot() function and how to control it to generate the output we require. We've used the plot() command extensively throughout the book. It's now time to examine it more closely.

The plot() function is highly customizable, accommodating various options, including plotting lines and/or markers, line widths, marker types and sizes, colors, and legend to associate with each plot. The functionality of plot() is similar to that of MATLAB (http://www.mathworks.com) and GNU-Octave (http://www.gnu.org/software/octave/) with some minor differences, mostly due to the fact that Python has a different syntax from MATLAB and GNU-Octave.

Lines and Markers

First, we'll create a vector to plot using NumPy (see Chapter 7 for a full account of the NumPy package):

```
>>> figure()
>>> y = array([1, 2, -1, 1])
>>> plot(y)
>>> show()
```

If you don't have a GUI installed with matplotlib, replace show() with savefig('filename') and open the generated image file in an image viewer.

■**Note** Going forward, I'll omit the show() call from listings. Be sure to issue show() or savefig() if you'd like to follow along.

I've passed the vector y as an input to plot(). As a result, plot() drew a graph of the vector y using auto-incrementing integers for an x-axis. Which is to say that if you don't sup-ply x-axis values, plot() will automatically generate one for you: plot(y) is equivalent to plot(range(len(y)), y). So let's supply x-axis values (denoted by variable t):

```
>>> figure()
>>> t = array([10, 11, 12, 13])
>>> plot(t, y)
```

The call to function figure() generates a new figure to plot on so we don't overwrite the previous figure.

On to more options. Next we want to plot y as a function of t but display only markers, not lines. This is easily done:

```
>>> figure()
>>> plot(t, y, 'o')
```

To select a different marker, replace the character 'o' with any of the markers in Table 6-2. For a full account of available markers, issue help(plot).

Table 6-2. *Some Plot Markers*

Character	Marker Symbol
'o'	Circle
'^'	Upward-pointing triangle
's'	Square
'+'	Plus
'x'	Cross (multiplication)
'D'	Diamond

Much like there are different markers, there are also different line styles, a few of which are listed in Table 6-3.

Table 6-3. *Some Plot Line Styles*

Character(s)	Line Style
'-'	Solid line
'--'	Dashed line
'-.'	Dash-dot line
':'	Dotted line

If you'd like both markers and lines, concatenate the symbols for line styles and markers. To plot a dash-dot line and diamond symbols as markers, issue the following:

```
>>> plot(t, y, 'D-.')
```

Figure 6-2 shows the output of the examples in this section.

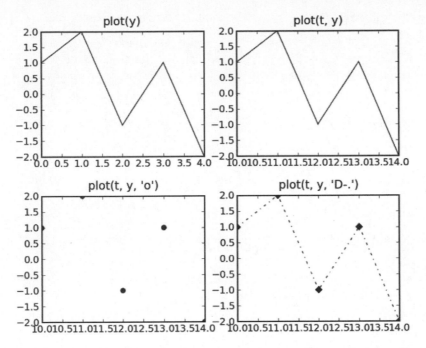

Figure 6-2. *Output of previous examples. Order is from left to right, top to bottom.*

Plotting Several Graphs on One Figure

We use graphs to visualize data and compare it. What's more natural than displaying several graphs in one plot so we can compare results? There are two ways to do that in matplotlib. The first one is by adding more vectors to the `plot()` function:

```
>>> plot(t, y, t, 2*y)
```

or

```
>>> plot(t, y, '+', t, 2*y, 's-')
```

The second method is by calling `plot()` repeatedly. Sometimes you might have only partial data to plot. Say you have vector y, but then you modify it and want to print both the original vector and the newly modified vector. What do you do? One option would be to store the intermediate value, but what if you have 20 of those? That means calling `plot()` with some 20+ arguments.

When you call `plot()` with an already existing figure, there are two possible outcomes. One is that the figure is erased, and the new plot is drawn. The other is that the figure is not erased, and the new plot is added to the figure. This behavior is determined by the hold status of the figure. You can control the hold status with the `hold()` function: calling `hold(True)` will ensure new plots don't erase the figure, whereas `hold(False)` will do the opposite. Issuing the command `hold()` with no arguments will toggle the hold status. As a general rule, it's best to specify the hold behavior you require and not rely on the default behavior, that is, `hold(True)` or `hold(False)`.

Line Widths and Marker Sizes

Next in this discussion of customization is controlling line widths and marker sizes. This is done by passing linewidth (or lw for short) and markersize (or ms for short) arguments to plot(), as shown in Listing 6-1. Both arguments accept a floating-point value; the default value is 1.

Listing 6-1. *Plotting Several Lines in One Graph with Different Line Styles and Markers*

```
I = arange(6)
plot(I, sin(I), 'o', I, cos(I), '-', lw=3, ms=8)
title("plot(I, sin(I), 'o', I, cos(I), '-', lw=3, ms=8)")
```

Figure 6-3 shows the results of this example.

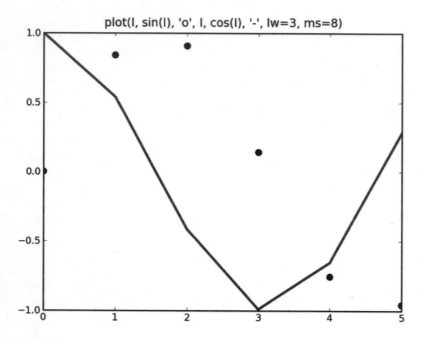

Figure 6-3. *Plotting several graphs in one figure*

When you plot multiple lines in one plot() function call, the parameters linewidth and markersize control *all* the lines in the same plot() command. If you'd like different lines with different line styles or different marker sizes in the same figure, draw each plot with an individual call to the plot() function and use the hold() function, as shown in Listing 6-2.

Listing 6-2. *Different Line Widths in One Graph*

```
figure(); hold(True)
I = arange(6)
plot(I, sin(I), lw=4)
plot(I, cos(I) , lw=2)
```

Colors

Finally, on our list of plotting basics is controlling color. Just like marker style and line style, you can control color with one character, according to the list in Table 6-4.

Table 6-4. *Color-Character Lookup Table*

Character	Color
'b'	Blue
'c'	Cyan
'g'	Green
'k'	Black
'm'	Magenta
'r'	Red
'w'	White
'y'	Yellow

As you might have noticed, matplotlib automatically chooses a different color for subsequent line plots if a color is not specified. You can select your preferred color by supplying a color character:

```
>>> figure()
>>> I = arange(6)
>>> plot(I, sin(I), 'k+-', I, cos(I), 'm:')
```

This will plot two lines: the first is a black line with plus markers and a connecting solid line, and the second is a magenta dotted line.

If you'd like a color that does not appear in Table 6-4, you can choose one from the dictionary object matplotlib.colors.cnames. The dictionary contains a better color selection and has over a hundred values. And lastly, if that dictionary is not enough, you can provide an explicit Red-Green-Blue (RGB) value. In case you're using the dictionary values or an explicit RBG value, you have to provide the color argument as a parameter to a plot() call:

```
>>> plot(randn(5), 'y', lw=5)   # 'y' from the color table
>>> plot(randn(5), color='yellowgreen', lw=5)   # using matplotlib.colors.cname
>>> plot(randn(5), color='#ffff00', lw=5) # explicit yellow RGB
```

See help(matplotlib.colors) for additional color information.

Note The function randn(n) in the preceding example generates a random vector of size n.

Controlling the Graph

For a graph to convey an idea aesthetically, the data, although highly important, is not everything. The grid and grid lines, combined with a proper selection of axis and labels, present additional layers of information that add clarity and contribute to overall graph presentation.

Now that we have the basics of plotting lines and markers covered, we turn to controlling the figure: controlling the x-axis and y-axis behavior and setting grid lines.

Axis

The axis() function controls the behavior of the x-axis and y-axis ranges. If you do not supply a parameter to axis(), the return value is a tuple in the form (xmin, xmax, ymin, ymax). You can use axis() to set the new axis ranges by specifying new values: axis([xmin, xmax, ymin, ymax]). In the special case you'd like to set or retrieve only the x-axis values or y-axis values, use the functions xlim(xmin, xmax) or ylim(ymin, ymax), respectively.

Other than the range limits, the function axis() also accepts the following values: 'auto', 'equal', 'tight', 'scaled', and 'off'. The value 'auto', the default behavior, allows plot() to select what it thinks are the best values. The value 'equal' forces each x value to be the same *length* as each y value, which is important if you're trying to convey physical distances, say, in a GPS plot. The value 'tight' causes the axis to change so that the maximum and minimum values of x and y both touch the edges of the graph. The value 'scaled' changes the x-axis and y-axis ranges so that x and y have both the same length (i.e., aspect ratio of 1). Lastly, calling axis('off') removes the axis and labels.

To illustrate these axis behaviors, I've plot a circle, as demonstrated in Listing 6-3.

Listing 6-3. *Plotting a Circle*

```
R = 1.2
I = arange(0, 2*pi, 0.01)
plot(sin(I)*R, cos(I)*R)
```

Note The reason I chose a circle of radius 1.2 is that in the case of a radius of "nicer" numbers (say 1.0 or 2.0), the automatic axis solution works very well, and it's hard to show the effects of the different axis options.

Figure 6-4 shows the results of applying different axis values to this circle.

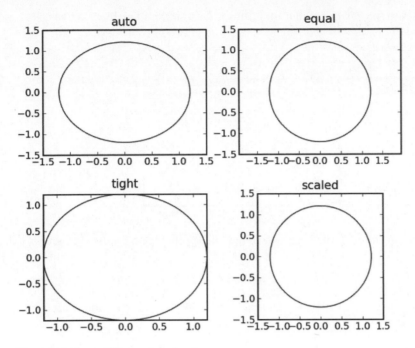

Figure 6-4. *Controlling axis behavior*

Grid and Ticks

The function grid() draws a grid in the current figure. The grid is composed of a set of horizontal and vertical dashed lines coinciding with the x ticks and y ticks. You can toggle the grid by calling grid() or set it to be either visible or hidden by using grid(True) or grid(False), respectively.

To control the ticks (and effectively change the grid lines as well), use the functions xticks() and yticks(), as shown in Listing 6-4. The functions behave similarly to axis() in that they return the current ticks in case no parameters are passed and are used to set ticks once parameters are provided. The functions take an array holding the tick values as numbers and an optional tuple containing text labels. In case the tuple of labels is not provided, the tick numbers are used as labels.

Listing 6-4. *Grid and Tick Example*

```
R = 1.2
I = arange(0, 4*pi, 0.01)
plot(sin(I)*R, cos(0.5*I)*R)
axhline(color='gray')
axvline(color='gray')
grid()
xticks([-1, 0, 1], ('Negative','Neutral','Positive'))
yticks(arange(-1.5, 2.0, 1))
```

Figure 6-5 shows the output generated from Listing 6-4 without issuing the last two calls to xticks() and yticks() (left graph) and with xticks() and yticks() calls (right graph). Notice the labels on the x-axis.

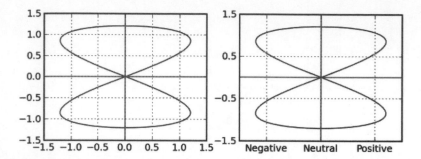

Figure 6-5. *Controlling grid and axis: the left graph shows the default xticks(), the right graph displays labels.*

I've also made use of the functions axhline() and axvline(), which plot a line across the x-axis and y-axis, respectively. The axhline() and axvline() functions accept many parameters, including color, linewidth, and linestyle, to name a few.

Subplots

In some of the previous figures in this chapter, I've displayed several smaller graphs in one figure; these are known as *subplots*. The subplot() function splits the figure into subplots and selects the current subplot. The subplots are numbered from left to right, top to bottom, so the upper-left subplot is 1, and the lower-right subplot is equivalent to the number of subplots. Notice that this is different from the default counting behavior used in Python: numbers start at 1 and not at 0.

To split the figure into 2-by-2 subplots and select the upper-left subplot for plotting, issue subplot(2, 2, 1). Alternatively, you can pass the string '221', which does the same thing: subplot('221'). It's also possible to combine subplots of different sizes in one figure. This is a bit tricky and requires subplotting with different subplot sizes. Listing 6-5 gives an example that generates a subplot on the upper half of the figure and two subplots on the lower part of the figure, the results of which you can see in Figure 6-6.

Listing 6-5. *Subplots of Varying Sizes*

```
figure()
subplot(2, 1, 1)
title('Upper half')
subplot(2, 2, 3)
title('Lower half, left side')
subplot(2, 2, 4)
title('Lower half, right side')
```

Figure 6-6. *Subplots of varying sizes*

Tip Subplots are especially useful in visualizing several aspects of the same data. For example, the GPS example in Chapter 1 shows x and y coordinates in one subplot and velocity in another subplot. Events (e.g., speeding) are marked in both, providing a visual link between the two subplots.

Erasing the Graph

The functions cla() and clf() clear the axes and the figure, respectively. These functions are useful when you're working with an interactive environment and would like to clear the current axes (i.e., setting the axes to default values and clearing the plotted lines). It's also possible to clear the figure altogether, erasing also the axes and subplots, using the clf() function.

Lastly, you can choose to close the figure window; this is done by calling the function close(). If you provide a number to close(), the figure associated with the number is closed. So close(1) will close Figure 1, leaving other figures open. If you'd like to close all the figures, issue close('all').

Adding Text

There are several options to annotate your graph with text. You've already seen some: using the xticks() and yticks() function. The following functions will give you more control over text in a graph.

Title

The function title(str) sets str as a title for the graph and appears above the plot area. The function accepts the arguments listed in Table 6-5.

Table 6-5. *Text Arguments*

Argument	Description	Values
fontsize	Controls the font size	'large', 'medium', 'small', or an actual size (i.e., 50)
verticalalignment or va	Controls the vertical alignment	'top', 'baseline', 'bottom', 'center'
horizontalalignment or ha	Controls the horizontal alignment	'center', 'left', 'right'

All alignments are based on the default location, which is above the graph, centered. So setting ha='right' will print the title starting at the middle (horizontally) and extending to the right. Similarly, setting ha='left' will print the title ending in the middle of the graph (horizontally). The same applies for vertical alignment. Here's an example of using the title() function:

```
>>> title('Left aligned, large title', fontsize=24, va='baseline')
```

Axis Labels and Legend

The functions xlabel() and ylabel() are similar to title() only they're used to set the x-axis and y-axis labels, respectively. Both these functions accept the text arguments from Table 6-5:

```
>>> xlabel('time [seconds]')
```

Next on our list of text functions is legend(). The legend() function adds a legend box, associating a plot with text:

```
>>> I = arange(0, 2*pi, 0.1)
>>> plot(I, sin(I), '+-', I, cos(I), 'o-')
>>> legend(['sin(I)', 'cos(I)'])
```

The legend order associates the text with the plot. Had I called legend() with the inverted list, the result would be a wrong legend.

An alternative approach is to specify the label argument with the plot() function call, and then issue a call to legend() with no parameters:

```
>>> I = arange(0, 2*pi, 0.1)
>>> plot(I, sin(I), '+-', label='sin(I)')
>>> plot(I, cos(I), 'o-', label='cos(I)')
>>> legend()
```

Figure 6-7 shows the addition of an x-axis label and legend.

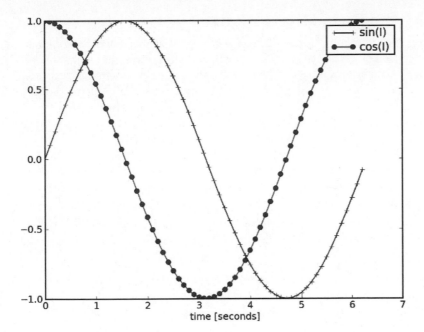

Figure 6-7. *Adding an x-axis label and legend*

You can also control the location of the legend box via the loc parameter. This is important if you don't want the legend text to hide the graph line. loc can take one of the following values: 'best', 'upper right', 'upper left', 'lower left', 'lower right', 'right', 'center left', 'center right', 'lower center', 'upper center', and 'center'. Instead of using strings, you can use numbers: 'best' corresponds to 0, 'upper left' corresponds to 1, and 'center' corresponds to 10. Using the value 'best' moves the legend to a spot less likely to hide data; however, performance-wise there may be some impact.

The function legend() has additional options that let you add a drop shadow and control the spacing between the text within the legend, among other things. Consult with the interactive help for additional information.

Text Rendering

The text(x, y, str) function accepts the coordinates in graph units x, y and the string to print, str, and renders the string on the figure. You can modify the text alignment using the arguments in Table 6-5. The following will print text at location (0, 0):

```
>>> figure()
>>> plot([-1, 1], [-1, 1])
>>> text(0, 0, 'origin', va='center', ha='center')
```

The function text() has many other arguments such as rotation (which was used in Chapter 1) and fontsize. See help(text) for a complete list of arguments.

Mathematical Symbols and Expressions

Last on our list of text-related functions is one that renders mathematical symbols and expressions. The syntax to use mathematical symbols provided by matplotlib is similar to that of TeX. To render mathematical expressions, use a raw string and enclose your mathematical expression with $ signs. For Greek letters, start with a slash followed by the name of the letter. So to print Alpha (α), your string should be r'α'. Fractions can be created using the \frac{num}{den} notation; for example, r'$\frac{\pi}{4}$' is the symbol π divided by four. Subscripts are denoted with an underscore, so to render the text a_i, write r'a_i'.

It is beyond the scope of the book to cover the entire TeX syntax supported by matplotlib. For additional information, refer to the online matplotlib web site (at the time of the writing of this book, the following link was available: http://matplotlib.sourceforge.net/users/mathtext.html). That being said, whenever you encounter a mathematical expression in this book, you're more than likely be able to figure out how it works with the small subset of commands presented in this section.

Example: A Summary Graph

The script in Listing 6-6 is an example summarizing the functions we've discussed up to this point: plot() for plotting; title(), xlabel(), ylabel(), and text() for text annotations; and xticks(), ylim(), and grid() for grid control.

Listing 6-6. *Plot Summary Example*

```
I = arange(0, 2*pi+0.1, 0.1)
plot(I, sin(I), label='sin(I)')
title('y = sin(x)')
xlabel('x [rad]')
ylabel('Function y = sin(x)')
text(pi/2, 1, 'Max value', ha='center', va='bottom')
text(3*pi/2, -1, 'Min value', ha='center', va='top')
xticks(arange(0, 2*pi, pi/2), \
    ('0', r'$\frac{\pi}{2}$', r'$\pi$', r'$\frac{3\pi}{2}$'))
xlim([0, 2*pi])
ylim([-1.2, 1.2])
grid()
```

The result of this example appears in Figure 6-8.

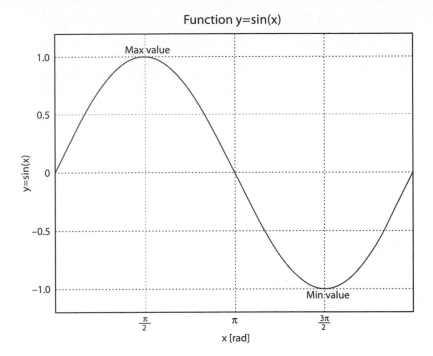

Figure 6-8. *Plot summary example*

More Graph Types

While the regular line and marker plots are excellent visualization tools, they're hardly the only ones. This section provides a quick overview of some other 2-D graph options.

Bar Charts

A favorite of many, bar charts allow quantitative comparison of several values. To use a bar chart, call the function bar(left, height), where left is the x coordinates of the bar and height is the bar height. The function bar() allows for considerable customization; issuing help(bar) will provide most of the details.

Example: GDP, N Top Countries

For this example, which plots the purchasing power parity (GDP) of various countries, you'll need the CIA GDP Rank Order file, available from the CIA World Factbook (https://www.cia.gov/library/publications/the-world-factbook/rankorder/2001rank.txt); this is a tab-delimited file, perfect for easy data processing. I'll assume that you've downloaded the file and saved it in folder Ch6/data; the source code resides in Ch6/src, and the output files are located in Ch6/images.

First, we'll define a function to read the data, as we will use it in several examples in the chapter. The code in Listing 6-7 should be saved under file src/read_world_data.py.

Listing 6-7. *Function read_world_data()*

```
import csv, re

def read_world_data(N=10, fn='../data/2001rank.txt'):
    """A function to read CIA World Factbook file.

N is the number of countries to process.
See https://www.cia.gov/library/publications/the-world-factbook/
    rankorder/2001rank.txt."""

    # initialize return lists
    gdp, labels = [], []

    # read the data and process it
    for i, row in enumerate(csv.reader(open(fn), delimiter='\t')):
        # skip first several lines
        if i > 3:
            # remove the dollar, comma and space characters
            gdp_value = re.sub(r'[\$, ]', '', row[2])

            # store data in billions of dollars
            gdp.append(float(gdp_value)/1e9)
            labels.append(row[1].strip())
        # stop analyzing the data after N countries have been processed
        if i > N+2:
            break
    return (gdp, labels)
```

The function reads data from the first N countries and returns their GDP alongside the country names. I've made use of two modules. The first, the csv module, reads the data, which is tab delimited. The second, the re module, gets rid of the dollar sign, comma, and space characters in the GDP value field.

Armed with read_world_data() function, we turn to plot the bar chart (see Listing 6-8).

Listing 6-8. *Plotting the GDP Bar Chart*

```
# a script to plot GDP bar chart
from pylab import *

# initialize variables, N is the number of countries
N = 5

execfile('read_world_data.py')
gdp, labels = read_world_data(N)
```

```
# plot the bar chart
bar(arange(N), gdp, align='center')

# annotate with text
xticks(arange(N), labels)
for i, val in enumerate(gdp):
    text(i, val/2, str(val), va='center', ha='center', color='yellow')
ylabel('$ (Billions)')
title('GDP rank, data from CIA World Factbook')
```

The script by now should be quite readable. Notice that I've decided to put the read_world_data() function in a separate file, and so to be able to use the function, I've called the function execfile('read_world_data.py').

If you scroll down to the end of CIA GDP rank order file, you'll find a note similar to this:

This file was last updated on 23 October, 2008

It's a good idea to extract the date information and add it to the title (or some other spot of your choice):

```
>>> last_line = open('../data/2001rank.txt').readlines()[-1]
>>> title('GDP rank, data from CIA World Factbook, '+last_line[31:-1])
```

Alternatively, you can modify the function read_world_data() to return this string as well. Figure 6-9 shows our bar chart.

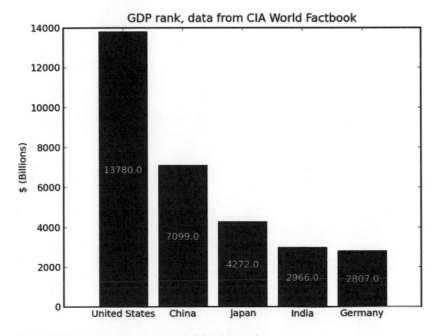

Figure 6-9. *Bar chart showing World GDP rank*

It's also possible to add error bars. To add an error bar equivalent to ±1000 billion dollars (talk about an error, eh?), add this line to the script shown in Listing 6-8, just after the bar() function call:

```
errorbar(arange(N), gdp, 1000*ones(N), color='k')
```

Finally, the function barh() plots a horizontal bar chart instead of a vertical one should you require one.

Histograms

Histograms are charts that show the frequency, or occurrence, of values. In matplotlib, the function hist() is used to calculate and draw the histogram chart. At a minimum, you must supply an array of values. You can control the number of cells in a histogram by specifying them as follows: hist(values, numcells). Alternatively, you can specify the histogram bins hist(values, bins), where bins is a list holding histogram bin values. The return value from hist() is a tuple of probabilities, bins, and patches. Patches are used to create the bars; I'll go into more detail in the "Patches" section later in the chapter.

The function hist() has other customization options, including the histogram orientation (vertical or horizontal), the alignment of bars, and more. Again, refer to the interactive help: help(hist).

Example: GDP, Histogram

We turn again to the GDP ranks from the CIA World Factbook; this time we plot a histogram of the N largest economies. Again, we use the read_world_data() function implemented in the previous example (see Listing 6-9).

Listing 6-9. *Plotting GDP Histogram*

```
# a script to plot GDP histogram
from pylab import *

# initialize variables; N is the number of countries, B is the bin size
N, B = 50, 1000

execfile('read_world_data.py')
gdp, labels = read_world_data(N)

# plot the histogram
prob, bins, patches = hist(gdp, arange(0, max(gdp)+B, B), align='center')

# annotate with text
for i, p in enumerate(prob):
    percent = int(float(p)/N*100)
    # only annotate non-zero values
    if percent:
        text(bins[i], p, str(percent)+'%',
            rotation=45, va='bottom', ha='center')
```

```
ylabel('Number of countries')
xlabel('Income, billions of dollars')
title('GDP histogram, %d largest economies' % N)

# some axis manipulations
xlim(-B/2, xlim()[1]-B/2)
```

Figure 6-10 shows the resulting graph.

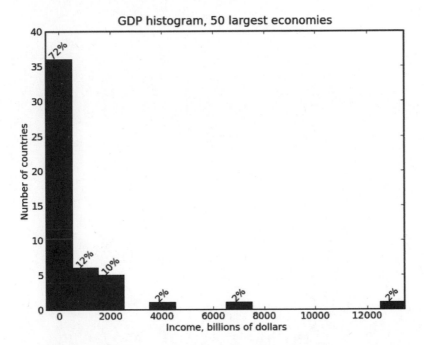

Figure 6-10. *GDP histogram, N largest economies*

Again, the script should prove quite readable. I'd like to turn your attention to what might appear to be an odd modification I've made to the x-axis using the call to function xlim(). The purpose of this call is to modify the default behavior of the x-axis ranges. The motivation behind this modification is that since I've chosen 'center' for the histogram bins, the automatic x-axis range includes negative values, because the leftmost bin is centered at zero but has a width, part of it in the negative x-axis. I didn't like this behavior and chose to override it by manually setting the axis. Instead of setting a fixed number, I've first retrieved the current axis by calling xlim(), and then modified the x-axis by subtracting and adding half the bin width, B/2, to the axis.

As a general rule, when you modify default behavior like this, try to use parameters as much as possible (in the preceding example, using the parameter B, not the value 1000, and retrieving current values with xlim()); this will allow for more flexible scripts that cater to a wider range of input values.

Pie Charts

Pie charts are as simple to use as bar charts. The function that implements pie charts is pie(x), where x holds the values to be charted.

Example: GDP, Pie Chart

Listing 6-10 presents a script to generate a pie chart, shown in Figure 6-11, again making use of the function read_world_data().

Listing 6-10. *Plotting a GDP Pie Chart*

```
# a script to plot GDP pie chart
from pylab import *

# initialize variables, N is the number of countries
N = 10

execfile('read_world_data.py')
gdp, tags = read_world_data(N)

# plot the bar chart
pie(gdp, labels=tags, shadow=True)
title('GDP rank, data from CIA World Factbook')
```

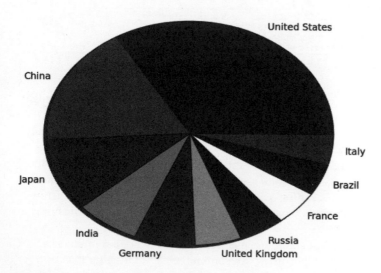

Figure 6-11. *GDP pie chart, N largest economies*

■**Note** I've decided to use the variable `tags` instead of `labels` so that the call to `pie()` would be a little less confusing. Had I stuck with the original name, `labels`, the call to pie would've been `pie(gdp,` `labels=labels, shadow=True)`, which still would've worked, but would seem a bit confusing in my opinion.

Logarithmic Plots

The functions `semilgox()` and `semilogy()` are used to plot the x-axis and y-axis in a logarithmic scale, respectively. Logarithmic plots of type `semilogy()` are common when plotting power or intensity values, for example, those of the Richter magnitude scale, which measures seismic energy. Likewise, measurements of quantities used with frequencies, for example, are commonly plotted on a logarithmic x-scale denoting octaves and decades. There's also the option of using a `loglog()` plot, which means both x-axis and y-axis are logarithmic. This is the case in Bode plots, common in engineering fields.

All three functions, `semilogx()`, `semilogy()`, and `loglog()`, can be modified with arguments similar to those presented with the `plot()` function.

The function `logspace(start, stop, numpoints=50, endpoint=True, base=10.0)` can be useful in creating a range of values to be plot with the preceding functions. The `start` and `stop` values are the exponent values. `logspace()` generates logarithmically spaced values between `10**start` and `10**stop`. You can decide whether the end value, `10**end`, is returned by specifying `endpoint=True`. If you'd like a base other than 10, set `base` to the value you require.

```
>>> figure()
>>> I = 2*logspace(1, 5, 5)
>>> I
array([  2.00000000e+01,   2.00000000e+02,   2.00000000e+03,
         2.00000000e+04,   2.00000000e+05])
>>> semilogx(I, [20, 19, 8, 2, 2], '+-')
>>> grid()
>>> title('Logarithmic plot, semilogx()')
>>> xlabel('Frequency [Hz]')
>>> ylabel('Amplitude [dB]')
```

Figure 6-12 shows the results of the preceding example.

Figure 6-12. *Logarithmic plot*

Notice that when plotting with semilogx(), semilogy(), and loglog(), the labels are the original values, not the logarithms of the values. If you'd like to print the logarithmic values, you should probably use a regular plot() function with log() or log10() of the values. This is useful, for example, in estimating the energy in decibels (dB):

```
>>> def db(x):
...     """Returns the value of x, in decibels."""
...     return 20*log10(abs(x))
>>> plot(db(array([1000, 980, 970, 400, 30, 2, 1, 1])))
```

Polar Plots

Polar plots draw polar coordinate values: a radius at a given angle. Polar plots are commonly used to draw antenna radiation patterns, as they depict the energy the antenna transmits at any given angle. Polar plots are implemented using the polar(theta, r) function.

To set the labels along the radius, use the rgrids(radii, labels) function, which works similarly to xticks() and yticks(). If you don't provide the labels value, the radii values are used as labels. You can also set the angle at which the labels are plotted (the default is 22.5 degrees). Similarly, the function thetagrids() plots the angle ticks and labels, as demonstrated in Listing 6-11.

Listing 6-11. *A Polar Plot*

```
theta = arange(0, 2*pi, 0.01)
polar(theta, cos(theta), theta, -cos(theta))
rgrids([0.5, 1.0], ['Half', 'Full'])
theta_labels = ['0', r'$\frac{\pi}{2}$', r'$\pi$', r'$\frac{3*\pi}{2}$']
thetagrids(arange(0, 360, 90), theta_labels)
title(r'A polar plot of $\pm cos(\theta)$')
```

Figure 6-13 shows the resulting polar plot.

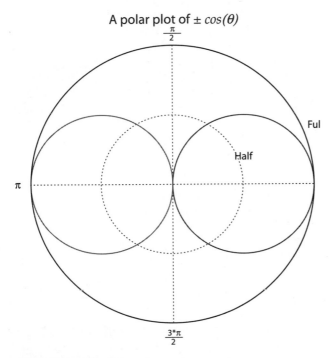

Figure 6-13. *Polar plot*

In the title, I've used the ± symbol denoted by '$\pm$'.

Stem Plots

Stem plots draw a vertical line from (x, 0) to (x, y) for every (x, y) value as well as a marker at (x, y). Stem plots are used to denote discrete data and are popular for plotting filtering windows (see Listing 6-12).

Listing 6-12. *A Stem Plot of Filter Windows*

```
from pylab import *
N = [4, 8, 16, 64]
for i, n in enumerate(N):
    subplot(2, 2, i+1)
```

```
stem(arange(n), hamming(n))
xticks(arange(0, n+1, n/4))
yticks([0, 0.5, 1])
xlim(-0.5, n+0.5)
legend(['N=%d' % n])
```

Figure 6-14 shows the results of this listing.

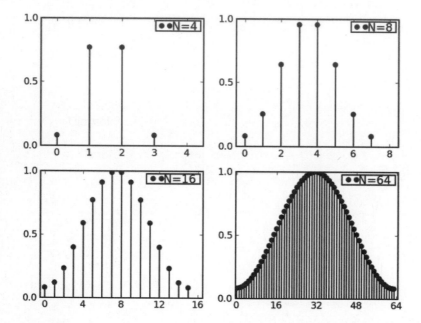

Figure 6-14. *Stem plots of a Hamming window with different N values*

In the preceding example, I've made use of the legend() function to denote the number of elements used in the plot, as I think it's clearer than a title. Notice that I had to supply a list to legend(['N=%d' % n]) (notice the brackets). Had I not supplied a list, the string 'N = %d' would have been split because legend() assumes a sequence of elements and assigns each one a plot line. I've also made use of the hamming() function to create a Hamming window, commonly used in filtering values.

Additional Graphs

Matplotlib also supports a great number of graphs used to depict more complex data. Here's a short list of some of the graphs available:

- Functions contour() and contourf() are used for contour plots. Contour plots draw a line connecting equal (x, y) value pairs. They're used in weather maps, detailing lines of equal pressure or temperature; in topographical maps, detailing the terrain; in physics graphs, to describe fields; and more.

- Function specgram() displays the frequency contents of data over time. specgram() can be used, for example, to plot the frequencies of a sound wave as a function of time.

- Both the contour() and specgram() functions rely on a color map to depict the data. Color maps are a relation between a value and a color. Matplotlib provides a set of color maps that include such names as autumn() and hot() to ease the selection of a color map.

- Function quiver() implements quiver plots, which are typically used to describe force fields in physics. The quiver plot is a set of arrows depicting the force at each point (direction and magnitude).

Example: Plotting Frequency Content of a Signal

At times it's of value to plot the frequencies a signal is composed of as a function of time. For example, in an audio signal, a different frequency means a different note, so plotting frequencies as a function of time is a possible "musical visualization."

In this example, shown in Listing 6-13, we create a signal composed of several discrete frequencies and display those frequencies as a function of time using a specgram().

Listing 6-13. *Specgram of a Signal*

```
from pylab import *
Fs = 256
times = [3, 7, 5]
frequencies = [100, 20, 80]

y = array([])
for t, f in zip(times, frequencies):
    x = cos(2*pi*arange(t*Fs)/Fs*f)
    y = append(y, x)

specgram(y, 256, Fs)
xlabel('Time [sec]')
ylabel('Frequency [Hz]')
```

I've set the frequency of sampling at 256 samples per second and created a signal composed of 100 Hertz (Hz) for 3 seconds, 20 Hz for 7 seconds, and then 80 Hz for 5 seconds. I then plot the signal using specgram(), with the results shown in Figure 6-15.

Figure 6-15. *A specgram*

Figure 6-15 clearly shows that in the first 2 seconds the frequency is 100 Hz, in the next 8 seconds the frequency is 20 Hz, and in the last 5 seconds the signal's frequency is 80 Hz.

■**Note** If you look closely at the figure, you'll notice there's a half-a-second shift in the specgram. This is due to an overlapping window of size 128 samples. See `help(specgram)` for information on the overlapping window.

You can change the colors used to display the specgram using a color map function. Simply issue `hot()` or `autumn()` at the end of the script, and observe the results. See `help(colormaps)` for a full account of available colormaps.

Example: A Repelling Force Field

The following example illustrates the use of `quiver()` to depict a force field. At each point in the figure, an arrow points at the direction of the acting force as well as its magnitude, denoted by the size of the arrow.

```
from pylab import *

x = arange(-5, 6, 1)
y = arange(-5, 6, 1)
```

```
u, v = meshgrid(x, y)
quiver(u, v)

xticks(range(len(x)), x)
yticks(range(len(y)), y)

axis([-1, 11, -1, 11])
axis('scaled')
title('A repelling force field!')
```

I've made use of the function meshgrid(x, y), which generates two matrices: the first is a matrix of repeating values of x, and the second is a matrix of repeating values of y. The output is used to plot the quiver, shown in Figure 6-16. I then update the axis to reflect the proper ranges.

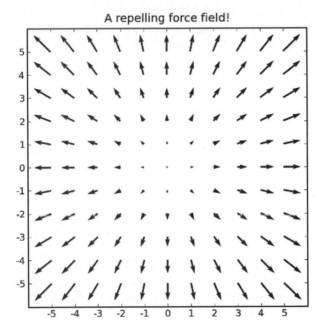

Figure 6-16. *A quiver plot depicting a force field*

Getting and Setting Values

As you start plotting and generating visual output, you'll find that you're using more and more of the "helper" functions, functions that don't necessarily plot the data, rather control the graph behavior and arrange labels just the way you want them.

So far we've used two methods to modify a plot behavior. One was using dedicated functions such as axis(), xlim(), and ylim() to control the plot ranges. The other method you've seen was passing arguments to functions, for example, the rotation argument in the text() function.

A third method is available, one that makes use of the object-oriented design of matplotlib. It involves two functions, setp() and getp(), which retrieve and set a matplotlib object's parameters. The benefit of using setp() and getp() is that automation is easily achieved.

Up to this point we've suppressed the output from matplotlib so that the interactive scripts are easier to follow. We now turn to looking at those outputs. Whenever you issue a plot() command, matplotlib returns a *list* of matplotlib objects. This is important; the return value from calling plot() is a list of objects, not the matplotlib object itself, even if you only have one line to plot.

```
>>> from pylab import *
>>> p = plot(arange(5))
>>> type(p)
<type 'list'>
>>> type(p[0])
<class 'matplotlib.lines.Line2D'>
```

The function setp(matobj) prints a list of properties you can set for matobj, where matobj is a matplotlib object. The function accepts either a list of matplotlib objects or just one object:

```
>>> setp(p[0])
<output suppressed>
```

If you're not sure of what values a parameter can take, issue setp(p, 'param'):

```
>>> setp(p[0], 'visible')
  visible: [True | False]
```

So to hide the plot, you could issue

```
>>> setp(p[0], visible=False)
```

or to set the label associated with a line, issue

```
>>> setp(p[0], label='Line1')
>>> legend()
```

The function setp() also accepts lists of matplotlib objects, in which case all the matplotlib objects in the list will be set.

■**Note** To query acceptable parameters, enclose the parameter to be queried in quotes: setp(p, 'linewidth'). To set a parameter value, do not include the quotes, but do use an assignment: setp(p, linewidth=4).

Similarly, to retrieve values, use the getp() function. The function getp() is a little less forgiving in that it requires one matplotlib object, not a list of objects.

```
>>> getp(p[0], 'linewidth')
1.0
```

Setting Figure and Axis Parameters

In the preceding examples we stored the return value from the call to the function plot(), which is a matplotlib object of a line, specifically the line we drew (actually, a list containing one line). But how do we modify the behavior of the figure or the axis?

The function gcf() returns a handle to the current figure. The function gca() returns a handle to the current axis. Armed with these, we can now modify the axis and figure parameters.

To set the y label, instead of calling ylabel('Y value'), we could issue the command

```
>>> setp(gca(), ylabel='Y value')
```

But what are the benefits of using setp() in this manner over simply calling ylabel()? The answer is automation. Let's turn to an example.

Example: Modifying Subplot Parameters

Suppose you'd like to write a function that receives a figure number and then modifies all the subplot titles in the figure (if they exist) to numbered titles. For example, for a figure of 2-by-2 subplots in use, you'd like the subplot titles to be from 1 to 4 (if they all exist). You don't know in advance how many subplots are in a figure.

This is an ideal case for using setp() and getp(), as demonstrated in Listing 6-14.

Listing 6-14. *Numbering Subplots*

```
from pylab import *
def number_subplots(fignum):
    """Numbers the subplots in a figure."""

    # switch to the requested figure
    figure(fignum)

    fig = gcf()

    for i, fig_axe in enumerate(getp(fig, 'axes')):
        fig_axe.set_title(str(i+1))

    axis()
```

Some notes regarding the function number_subplots(). First, we set the focus to the figure we'd like to work on by calling figure(fignum). Next, we retrieve a handle to the figure with gcf(). The following step assumes some knowledge of the matplotlib object structure. But even if you're not familiar with the structure, it's pretty simple to figure out what's going on by exploring the objects. To illustrate this, create a simple figure with two empty subplots:

```
>>> figure()
>>> ax1 = subplot(2, 1, 1)
>>> ax2 = subplot(2, 1, 2)
```

Now retrieve the current figure properties with getp(gcf()):

```
>>> getp(gcf())
    alpha = 1.0
    animated = False
    axes = [<matplotlib.axes.AxesSubplot object at 0x035B4350>, <matplotlib.axes
.AxesSubplot object at 0x035B7AF0>]
    children = [<matplotlib.patches.Rectangle object at 0x03594FB0>, <matplotlib
.axes.AxesSubplot object at 0x035B4350>, <matplotlib.axes.AxesSubplot object at
0x035B7AF0>]
```

(I've removed the extra output lines as they're not important for the discussion.) Look closely at two properties: axes and children. The parameter axes holds a list of two values, and the parameter children holds a list of three values. Further examination shows that the axes objects are all contained within the children values. In reality, these are the two axes for the two subplots. So to get a list of these, we can simply call getp(gcf(), 'axes'), as the code indeed does. We then set the titles and call the axis() function to force a redraw.

There's a caveat in the implementation of the function number_subplots(): numbering is performed in accordance with the creation of the subplots. That is, if the bottom-left subplot was created before the top-left subplot, it will have the smaller title value associated with it and not the regular subplot numbering (left to right, top to bottom). If you'd like to change this, you'll have to look at the positions of the subplots and assign numbers accordingly. This is somewhat more complex and not all that educational, so I've opted to leave it out of the discussion.

A lot of the parameters that are accessible via setp() and getp() are also accessible by means of dedicated functions. Instead of setting the y-axis label parameter with setp(), you can call the ylabel() function. When possible, I prefer using the function version over setp() and getp() because I think it's easier to follow.

Exploring the matplotlib object by use of the dir statement is also a very good method to probe the capabilities of a matplotlib object. Most of the functions are self-explanatory and let you set and retrieve values associated with a matplotlib object. In case you're not sure, use the help() function in an interactive Python session. From a partial comparison I've made, matplotlib object methods are equivalent to the properties available with getp() and setp(), so you can use either:

```
>>> matobj = gcf()
>>> [func for func in dir(matobj) if func.startswith('get')]
['get_alpha', 'get_animated', 'get_axes', 'get_children', 'get_clip_box', 'get_c
lip_on', 'get_clip_path', 'get_contains', 'get_dpi', 'get_edgecolor', 'get_facec
olor', 'get_figheight', 'get_figure', 'get_figwidth', 'get_frameon', 'get_label'
, 'get_picker', 'get_size_inches', 'get_transform', 'get_transformed_clip_path_a
nd_affine', 'get_visible', 'get_window_extent', 'get_zorder']
```

Final note: working with setp() and getp() or the set and get methods of the matplotlib object is an advanced topic. These functions allow closer control of the behavior of plots and graphs and are not easy to master. They require a good understanding of the matplotlib object hierarchy. Regardless of the complexity, I believe this is an important concept. As you draw more graphs and deal with more data, you'll find that the default functionality, although great, isn't *exactly* what you want. And in these cases, turning to setp() and getp() is a good option. I hope that I've exposed you enough to the topic to let you experiment on your own.

Patches

So far we've worked with text and lines, which are both implemented as matplotlib objects. But those two objects at times are not enough. A third object, the patch, allows drawing other types of shapes that don't necessarily fall under the category of a line or text.

The way you work with patches is that you assign them to an already existing graph, because in a sense patches are "patched" on top of a figure. Table 6-6 gives a partial listing of available patches. In this table, the notation xy indicates a list or tuple of (x, y) values.

Table 6-6. *Available Patches*

Patch	Description
Arrow(x, y, dx, dy)	An arrow, starting at location (x, y) and ending at location (x+dx, y+dy)
Circle(xy, r)	A circle centered at xy and radius r
Ellipse(xy, w, h, angle)	An ellipse centered at xy, of width w, height h, and rotated angle degrees
Polygon([xy1, xy2, xy3,...])	A polygon made of vertices specified by xy points
Wedge(xy, r, theta1, theta2)	A wedge (part of a circle) centered at xy, of radius r, starting at angle theta1 and ending at angle theta2
Rectangle(xy, w, h)	A rectangle, starting at xy, of width w and height h

To use patches, follow these steps:

1. Draw a graph.

2. Create a patch object.

3. Attach the patch object to the figure, using the add_patch() function.

■**Note** Although this might seem like a considerable effort to add, say an arrow patch, in reality these three steps can be folded into one line. To draw an arrow from (0, 0) to (1, 1), issue gca().add_patch(Arrow(0, 0, 1, 1)).

Example: Adding Arrows to a Graph

In this example we'll draw a graph and connect every two points on the graph with an arrow.

First draw a simple graph:

```
>>> x = arange(10)
>>> y = x**2
>>> plot(x, y)
```

Now create a list of all the arrows:

```
>>> ars = [(x0, y0, dx, dy) for (x0, y0, dx, dy) in zip(x, y, diff(x), diff(y))]
```

This is a bit tricky. First, the function `diff()` creates a difference of every two elements in a vector, for example, `diff([1, 2, 3, 30])` is `[1, 1, 27]`. This is exactly what we need for our dx and dy values for the `Arrow()` function. Second, we combine x, y, dx, and dy using the `zip()` function and return a list of tuples by using a list comprehension. Luckily for us, `zip()` uses the shortest vector, so even though `diff()` vectors are shorter by 1, it's not an issue.

Now, all that's left is to iterate through the list comprehension and attach an arrow to the graph:

```
>>> cur_axes = gca()
>>> for x0, y0, dx, dy in ars:
...     cur_axes.add_patch(Arrow(x0, y0, dx, dy))
>>> title('Arrows!')
```

Figure 6-17 shows the added arrows.

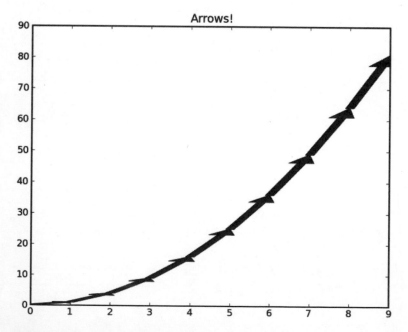

Figure 6-17. *Patching arrows*

Needless to say, Arrow(), as well as other patches, can be customized considerably; you can adjust color, length, width, and more.

Example: Some Other Patches

The code in Listing 6-15 generates a list of patch objects and attaches them to a figure. The figure is originally empty.

Listing 6-15. *Some Patches*

```
from pylab import *

# Import Ellipse and Wedge to current namespace
from matplotlib.patches import Ellipse, Wedge

# a list of some patches
my_patches = [
    Arrow(0, 4, 0, -4, facecolor='g'),
    Circle([-2, 2], 1.5, linewidth=4, fc='orange'),
    Ellipse([2, 3], 4, 1, 45.0, edgecolor='r'),
    Polygon([[4, 2], [3, 3], [1, -1], [3, -1]], ls='dashed', fill=False),
    Wedge([-1, 0], 3, 200, 300, fc='m', ec='m'),
    Rectangle([1, -2], 3, -2, fill=False, lw=5, ec='r')
    ]

# draw a figure
figure()
axis([-5, 5, -5, 5])

# add the patches
cur_ax = gca()
for p in my_patches:
    cur_ax.add_patch(p)

title('Patches')
```

Figure 6-18 shows the results of the code in Listing 6-15.

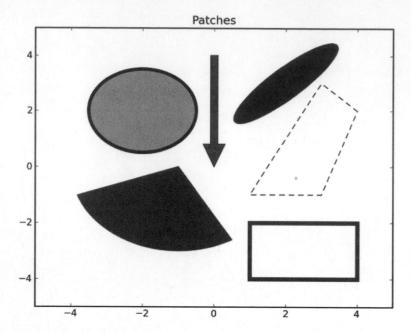

Figure 6-18. *Some patches*

The patch objects `Ellipse` and `Wedge` are not automatically imported to the current namespace when you issue `from pylab import *` (unlike `Arrow`, `Circle`, `Polygon`, and `Rectangle`), so I've manually imported them to the namespace with the statement `from matplotlib.patches import Ellipse, Wedge`.

I've also passed arguments to the patches to show how to use them: `facecolor` (or `fc`), `edgecolor` (or `ec`), `linestyle` (or `ls`), `linewidth` (or `lw`), and `fill`.

Final Notes and References

We've explored the matplotlib package, a rich package that supports plotting in Python. The strong suit of matplotlib is easy plotting of simple and complex graphs with a high-number of customization options. If you're not familiar with the package, exploring it with IPython's tab completion, complemented by `help()`, trial and error, and the manual, should yield excellent results in no time.

For the purposes of the book and the examples provided, this chapter covers all topics. However, your needs may be different, and I hope that you now have the tools to explore this package on your own.

The matplotlib web site is an excellent source of information, and I encourage you to explore it and learn more about the package.

- The matplotlib web site, `http://matplotlib.sourceforge.net/`

## CHAPTER 7

Math Games
Preprocessing Data Prior to Visualization

Math is a fundamental tool in data visualization. Python provides outstanding math support and as such is an ideal development environment for analysis prior to visualization. There are several reasons I find using Python for this purpose so appealing. First is Python's interactive nature: it's easy to manipulate data and observe intermediate results, as well as modify and quickly plot them. The second reason, and probably the factor contributing the most, is the wide range and popularity of freely available, mature numerical packages. Lastly, Python is also structured, allowing the development of production-level code used to generate quality reports.

In this chapter we'll explore Python's math capabilities, the built-in modules math, cmath, and random, and the excellent package we'll use extensively (and have used in previous chapters), NumPy.

Modules math and cmath

Python provides two flavors of math modules: math and cmath. The math module has functions that are common to most programming languages and in essence is using the C math function calls. Functions from module math return floating-point numbers. In case of improper arguments an error will be raised:

```
>>> import math
>>> math.sqrt(-1)
Traceback (most recent call last):
  File "<stdin>", line 1, in <module>
ValueError: math domain error
```

Module cmath returns complex results:

```
>>> import cmath
>>> cmath.sqrt(-1)
1j
```

■**Note** If you see -1.#IND in response to sqrt(-1), it means that NumPy is already imported but without complex math. This is probably due to a previously issued from numpy import * or from pylab import * command, or you have a Python distribution that loads NumPy automatically, which automatically issues these commands for you.

Complex numbers are supported natively in Python with the complex built-in data type. This is probably a contributing factor to Python's popularity as a platform for numerical computation. The imaginary part of complex number has a trailing j as shown in the preceding example. Most arithmetic operations and function calls can be performed on complex numbers.

If you do not require complex number support, opt for using module math over cmath. First, it will provide you with valuable exception information if the parameter to a function is out of the domain, as shown previously. Second, cmath always returns complex results, even if results can be represented as noncomplex numbers, in which case the imaginary value will be zero. Lastly, some functions are only available in the math module, as listed in Table 7-1.

Table 7-1. *Functions Available Only in the math Module*

Function	Description	Example
ceil(x)	Returns the smallest integer greater than or equal to x	ceil(2.5) returns 3.0. ceil(-2.5) returns -2.0.
floor(x)	Returns the largest integer less than or equal to x	floor(2.5) returns 2.0. floor(-2.5) returns -3.0.
fabs(x)	Returns the absolute value of x	fabs(-2.5) returns 2.5.
fmod(x, y)	Returns the remainder of x divided by y	fmod(2.5, 2) returns 0.5. fmod(-2.5, 2) returns -0.5. fmod(2.5, -2) returns 0.5. fmod(-2.5, -2) returns -0.5.
modf(x)	Returns the integer and fractional parts of x	modf(2.5) returns (0.5, 2.0). modf(-2.5) returns (-0.5, -2.0).
frexp(x)	Returns the exponent, e, and mantissa, m, such that $x = m \times 2^e$	frexp(2.5) returns (0.625, 2). frexp(-2.5) returns (-0.625, 2).
ldexp(m, e)	Returns $m \times 2^e$	ldexp(0.625, 2) returns 2.5. ldexp(-0.625, 2) returns -2.5.

Power, logarithmic, trigonometric, and hyperbolic functions are available in both math and cmath modules, as listed in Table 7-2, with the exception of the functions pow(x, y), atan2(x, y), and hypot(x, y).

Table 7-2. *Power, Logarithmic, Trigonometric, and Hyperbolic Functions in the math and cmath Modules*

Function	Description	Example (math)	Example (cmath)
Power			
exp(x)	e^x	exp(1) returns 2.7182818284590451 (e).	exp(pi*1j) returns -1.
pow(x, y)	x^y	pow(-2, 2) returns 4.	N/A, use operator **.
sqrt(x)	Square root of x	sqrt(4) returns 2.	sqrt(2j) returns 1+1j.
Logarithmic			
log(x[, base])	Logarithms of x—if base is not specified, defaults to natural logarithms	log(16, 2) returns 4.	log(-1) returns 3.1415926535897931j (jπ).
log10(x)	Logarithms of x, base 10	log10(3) returns 0.47712125471966244.	log10(-1) returns 1.3643763538418414j.
Trigonometric			
sin(x), cos(x), tan(x)	Sine, cosine, and tangent of x	sin(pi/2) returns 1.0.	cos(1j) returns (1.5430806348152437+0j).
asin(x), acos(x), atan(x)	Arc sine, arc cosine, and arc tangent of x	asin(1) returns 1.5707963267948966 (π/2).	acos(2) returns 1.3169578969248164j.
atan2(y, x)	Arc tangent of y/x, preserves quadrant information and avoids division by zero	atan2(-1, 1) returns -0.78539816339744828 (-π/2).	N/A
hypot(x, y)	$\sqrt{(x^2+y^2)}$	hypot(3, 4) returns 5.0.	N/A
Hyperbolic			
sinh(x), cosh(x), tanh(x)	Hyperbolic sine, cosine, and tangent of x	cosh(0) returns 1.0.	sinh(1j*pi) returns 1.2246063538223773e-016j (0).
Constants			
e, pi	2.7182818284590451, 3.1415926535897931		

FUNCTION ATAN2

Function `atan2(y, x)` is very useful in that it maintains angle values of a point in a plane, as shown previously in Chapter 1. That is, if x and y represent coordinates in a plane, `atan2(y, x)` returns the angle from the origin. Consider the point located at (1,1): its angle is 45 degrees ($\pi/4$); point (−1,−1) has an angle of −135 degrees (or 225 degrees). If you were to use `atan(y/x)`, both points (1,1) and (−1,−1) would yield 45 degrees, losing quadrant information. However, using `atan2(y, x)` the correct values are returned.

There's also a side benefit that if x is zero, the angle is calculated properly, whereas `atan(y/x)` would raise an exception. Function `atan2()` is not particularly useful in complex math as values already represent Cartesian points.

Example: A Newton Fractal

In this example we use complex math to create a fractal based on the Newton-Raphson method (or simply Newton's method). Fractals are used by scientists to investigate chaotic systems: systems whose state over time is highly dependent on initial conditions. The purpose of this example is to show the capabilities of Python's complex math and explore some ways to visualize data other than a regular plot; fractals are a perfect match.

Newton's method is an iterative procedure to find numerical solutions, or roots, to an equation of the form f(z) = 0 using an initial guess. One of the characteristics of the method is that in case of several solutions, we cannot tell in advance, based on the initial guess, what the converged solution will be (usually). If you were to map out the initial guesses based on the solution, you would find they converge to results in an image known as Newton's fractal, which is geometrically interesting.

If you'd like to read more about Newton's method, have a look at http://en.wikipedia.org/wiki/Newton%27s_method; there's a lot of additional information available on the Internet.

The function we'll map is f(z) = z^4 + 1. This function has four roots:

```
>>> from cmath import pi, cos, sin
>>> solutions = [cos((2*n+1)*pi/4)+1j*sin((2*n+1)*pi/4) for n in range(4)]
```

To verify that these are indeed solutions to the equation:

```
>>> [z**4 for z in solutions]
[(-1+4.4408920985006262e-016j), (-1+4.4408920985006262e-016j), (-1.0000000000000
004+6.6613381477509412e-016j), (-1+8.8817841970012523e-016j)]
```

The imaginary parts are on the order of scale of 10^{-16} and are due to inaccuracies of the trigonometric functions, π, and the floating-point representation; the imaginary parts are actually zero.

Newton's method takes an initial guess and calculates the next guess by applying the equation $z_{n+1} = z_n - f(z_n) / f'(z_n)$, where f'(z) is the derivative of f(z), or in our case z = z-(z**4+1)/(4*z**3). To check whether the new value is a "good" solution, we reapply it to the original equation, f(z), and check how close it is to zero. In reality, we check whether the absolute value is less than `delta`, a predefined small value. The number of iterations is an indication of how fast the solution was reached. We'll use this to select the color depth of each solution: solutions that converged fast will be brighter. Once our guess converges, we check what solution it converged to and color it accordingly. Since there are four solutions, there will be four colors (at varying color depths) in the fractal. Listing 7-1 generates said Newton's fractal in the region $(0, 0)$–$(1, 1)$.

Listing 7-1. *fractal.py*

```python
from PIL import Image
from cmath import *

# creates a z**4+1 = 0 fractal using the Newton-Raphson
# root finding method
delta      = 0.000001  # convergence criteria
res        = 800       # image size
iters      = 30        # number of iterations

# create an image to draw on, paint it black
img = Image.new("RGB", (res, res), (0, 0, 0))

# these are the solutions to the equation z**4+1 = 0 (Euler's formula)
solutions = [cos((2*n+1)*pi/4)+1j*sin((2*n+1)*pi/4) for n in range(4)]
colors = [(1, 0, 0), (0, 1, 0), (0, 0, 1), (1, 1, 0)]

for re in range(0, res):
    for im in range(0, res):
        z = (re+1j*im)/res
        for i in range(iters):
            try:
                z -= (z**4+1)/(4*z**3)
            except ZeroDivisionError:
                # possibly divide by zero exception
                continue
            if(abs(z**4+1) < delta):
                break

        # color depth is a function of the number of iterations
        color_depth = int((iters-i)*255.0/iters)

        # find to which solution this guess converged to
        err = [abs(z-root) for root in solutions]
        distances = zip(err, range(len(colors)))

        # select the color associated with the solution
        color = [i*color_depth for i in colors[min(distances)[1]]]
        img.putpixel((re, im), tuple(color))

img.save('../images/fractal_z4s_%03d_%03d_%03d.png' % \
    (iters, res, abs(log10(delta))), dpi=(150, 150))
```

We use the Python Imaging Library (PIL) to draw the fractal. We start by creating an RGB image of size res specifying the fractal's resolution. We then implement Newton's method with a for loop, and an if statement to check for convergence.

While the iteration is straightforward, deciding which of the four solutions a specific guess converges to and then mapping to the right color and color depth requires some clarifications.

The colors list is composed of the colors red, green, blue, and yellow, each represented by a tuple of Red-Green-Blue (RGB) values:

```
colors = [(1, 0, 0), (0, 1, 0), (0, 0, 1), (1, 1, 0)]
```

Variable color_depth is directly responsible for the color depth (or shade) of the displayed color. For a small number of iterations, color_depth is closer to 255, and for a greater number of iterations, this number is closer to 0, resulting in a brighter color for faster converging points (smaller number of iterations).

Once color_depth is calculated, we find the solution closest to our converging value. Since we're using complex numbers, the value closest is the one with the minimum distance, or in complex math, the one with the smallest value of err = abs(guess-solution).

To implement this, we generate a list of values corresponding to the distances using a list comprehension. Here's an example using an arbitrary point:

```
>>> z
(0.70710678118883818+0.70710678118883818j)
>>> err = [abs(z-root) for root in solutions]
>>> err
[3.23949326e-012, 1.41421356, 2.00000000, 1.41421356]
```

Next, we combine these values with the numbers 0–3, which represent the indices to the colors list, using the zip() function:

```
>>> zip(err, range(len(colors)))
[(3.23949326e-012, 0), (1.41421356, 1), (2.0000000, 2), (1.4142135, 3)]
```

We then find the minimum error by calling the function min(). To find the correct color, we index the color associated with min(distances)[1], which is the second element in the zipped tuple. Maybe it's easier to show interactively than explain:

```
>>> distances = zip(err, range(len(colors)))
>>> min(distances)
(3.23949326e-012, 0)
>>> min(distances)[1]
0
>>> colors[min(distances)[1]]
(1, 0, 0)
```

Finally, we use a list comprehension to multiply the RGB values by the color depth. This is because the putpixel() method requires a tuple detailing the RGB values:

```
color = [i*color_depth for i in colors[min(distances)[1]]]
img.putpixel((re, im), tuple(color))
```

■Tip As you experiment with parameters, you may wish to save some of the outputs. These runs can take a considerable time to complete, so it's a good idea to have different file names for the outputs as opposed to a single file name, ensuring files are not accidentally overwritten. Unlike data files, the outputs of these runs are dependent on input parameters and the code (e.g., version of the script) that generated them and are not date or time dependent. It doesn't matter whether the run was performed last week or last year; the results should be the same. The notation I've used is one that details all the parameters used to create the output within the file name: `'../images/fractal_z4s_%03d_%03d_%03d.png' % (iters, res, abs(log10(delta)))`. Names of the output files detail the inputs that generated them. An even better approach (one that in this case will somewhat disturb the pleasing output) is annotating the images with text describing the parameters used. And lastly, if you use a version control system (see Chapter 2), the version number of the script that generated the output is a very welcomed addition either in the file name or in an annotation.

Figure 7-1 is a collage of outputs generated by the script with `resolution=200` and values of `iters` ranging from 1 to 9 (top left is `i = 1`; bottom right is `i = 9`). We'll touch on collages in Chapter 9. Figure 7-2 is the result of a longer run with `resolution=800` and `iters=30`.

Figure 7-1. *Collage of Newton's fractals with iterations from 1 (top left) to 9 (bottom right)*

Figure 7-2. *Newton's fractal, max number of iterations equaling 30*

■**Tip** The preceding example explores the region (0, 0)–(1, 1). If you wish to explore around the origin, that is, around (0, 0), change the line `z = (re+1j*im)/res` to `z = ((re-res/2)+1j*(im-res/2))/res`.

Module random

Other than mathematical functions, Python also provides a rich library for random numbers. Random numbers are important in a variety of software applications. In game programming, random numbers are used to change the behavior of elements in the game to make it more interesting or unpredictable. When writing simulations, random numbers are used to generate data that simulates the real world. Random numbers can also be used to answer probability questions, as you'll soon see.

The random module provides random values based on a wide variety of distribution functions including uniform distribution, Gaussian distribution, and more. Module random also supports Python's lists naturally, with random functions operating on sequences.

Table 7-3 gives a partial list of some useful random functions.

Table 7-3. *Functions of the random Module*

Function	Description	Example/Note
Integers		
randint(a, b)	Returns a random number between a and b (including a and b)	randint(0, 1) returns 0 or 1 (randomly).
randrange([start,] stop[, step])	Same as randint() except it allows a step value	randrange(3, 7, 2) returns 3, 5, or 7 (randomly).
Floating-Point Numbers		
random()	Returns a real value between 0.0 and 1.0 (excluding 1.0)	random()
uniform(a, b)	Returns a real value between a and b (excluding b)	uniform(120, 220) returns a random number between 120 and 220 (excluding 220).
gauss(u, sigma)	Returns a Gaussian distributed value with u as mean and sigma as standard deviation	gauss(1, 2)

Module random provides an additional number of other distributions: Log normal and Weibul, to name a couple. Refer to the Python Standard Library documentation for a full account.

Using random to Solve Probability Questions

The following examples use the random module to solve probability-based questions numerically.

Example: Hard Disk Head

Return to zero: Consider the following: a hard disk head is normally resting at location 0, representing the start of the disk. Files (of size zero) are evenly distributed between location 0 and 1, where 1 represents the end of the disk. The head is required to access files randomly. After each read, the head returns to location zero. The question is, what is the average distance the head moves?

The answer is not hard: on average, the head moves a distance of 1.0 (don't forget it has to go back to location 0). You can easily verify this using a simple script:

```
>>> from random import random
>>> N = 1000 # number of files the head seeks
>>> tot_dist = 0
```

```
>>> for i in range(N):
...     tot_dist += random()*2
...
>>> tot_dist/N
1.0253061728681021
```

The larger the value of N, (and assuming a good random() implementation), the more accurate the result.

Not returning to zero: Now consider the scenario where the head does not go back to location 0, but stays where it was before. Finding the average distance the head moves is a bit harder analytically, but numerically, with a simple script, the solution emerges quickly.

```
>>> from random import random
>>> N = 1000 # number of files the head seeks
>>> tot_dist, cur_loc = 0, 0
>>> for i in range(N):
...     new_loc = random()
...     tot_dist += abs(cur_loc-new_loc)
...     cur_loc = new_loc
...
>>> tot_dist/N
0.33576448266202374
```

This number turns out to be 1/3.

Example: Friends Meeting

We turn to another example, one that makes use of a visual output as well.

Two friends decide to meet between 8 p.m. and 9 p.m. Once one of the friends arrives at the designated meeting spot, he waits for 10 minutes for his friend to show up. So if for example Friend 1 arrives at 8:40, he'll wait until 8:50 for Friend 2 to show up. Friend 1 doesn't know if Friend 2 already showed up earlier (the same is true for Friend 2, he doesn't know if Friend 1 showed up). But both friends are smart enough to know that if they arrive at 8:55, for example, they only need wait until 9:00 and not 9:05. The question: what's the probability that these two friends meet?

We again turn to the random module to help us solve this problem (see Listing 7-2). Only this time, we also visualize the result, hopefully gaining some insight as to how to solve the question analytically.

Listing 7-2. *Friends Meeting*

```
from random import random
from pylab import *

N   = 40000 # number of events

# generate N events of friends times
friend1, friend2 = [], []
```

```
for i in range(N):
    friend1.append(random())
    friend2.append(random())

# find all occurrences of friends meeting
met = array([(x, y) for (x, y) in zip(friend1, friend2) \
    if abs(y-x) < 1.0/6 ])
not_met = array([(x, y) for (x, y) in zip(friend1, friend2) \
    if abs(y-x) >= 1.0/6 ])

# plot the result, this might shed some light on the problem!
plot(met[:, 0], met[:, 1],'+m')
plot(not_met[:, 0], not_met[:, 1],'og')
title("Probability of meeting: %1.3f" % (float(len(met))/N))
xlabel('Time of arrival of Friend 1')
ylabel('Time of arrival of Friend 2')
axis('scaled')
```

The first step is to generate a considerable number of events, in this case 40,000. An event is composed of two numbers: one associated with Friend 1's time of arrival and one associated with Friend 2's time of arrival. We store both their times in lists. The process of generating the events is performed in the first for loop. The function random() returns a value between 0 and 1, which maps out to the time of arrival: 0 is 8 p.m., 1 is 9 p.m.

Now that we have a considerable number of events, we ask at what times the friends meet. The friends meet if the difference between their times of arrival is less than 10 minutes, or 10 minutes / 60 minutes * 1.0 = 1/6 (1.0 is the range of random values). But it's also possible that Friend 1 arrives after Friend 2 and not the other way around. So we should be asking whether friend1–friend2 is less than 1/6, as well as whether friend2–friend1 is less than 1/6. This can be elegantly coded as abs(friend1-friend2) < 1.0/6.

The actual implementation makes use of a list comprehension, returning a tuple of (x, y) values that match the condition abs(x-y) < 1.0/6., which means the friends have met. We then construct an array of these values (a NumPy array, more on this shortly) so we can easily access the x and y vectors, without any for loops. We also build a list of times the friends did not meet because we want to plot both, in different colors and markers.

Next we plot the results and calculate the probability of the friends meeting, numerically, as shown in Figure 7-3.

This visualization really helps. The corridor in the middle describes the events corresponding to the two friends meeting. The probability is the area of this corridor and can be calculated by the area of the entire square minus the area of the top-left triangle and the bottom-right triangle. Each triangle has an area of $0.5 \times (5/6)^2$, and the total probability of meeting is $1 - (5/6)^2 = 11/36 = 0.3055\ldots$ which is pretty close to the estimated numerical value (displayed in the figure title).

Figure 7-3. *Visualizing friends meeting*

Random Sequences

Another set of functions available under the random module operates on sequences. These include the functions listed in Table 7-4.

Table 7-4. *Functions from the random Module for Operating on Sequences*

Function	Description
choice(s)	Returns a random element from the sequence s
shuffle(s)	Shuffles the sequence s
sample(s, n)	Returns a subsequence of size n from s

For the examples in this section, we create a deck-of-cards sequence using the zip() built-in function. Each card is represented as a tuple holding a number 1–13 and a character, 'S', 'H', 'D', 'C', corresponding to spades, hearts, diamonds, and clubs.

```
>>> from random import *
>>> cards = zip(range(1, 14)*4, 'S'*13+'H'*13+'D'*13+'C'*13)
>>> cards[0:5]
[(1, 'S'), (2, 'S'), (3, 'S'), (4, 'S'), (5, 'S')]
>>> choice(cards)
(7, 'C')
>>> shuffle(cards)
>>> cards[:5]
```

```
[(4, 'C'), (10, 'D'), (1, 'C'), (7, 'C'), (12, 'D')]
>>> sample(cards, 5)
[(12, 'S'), (12, 'H'), (8, 'C'), (8, 'D'), (5, 'S')]
```

A DECK OF CARDS

There are lots of ways to implement a deck of cards, and the method described here is a bit tricky. The reason I chose it is that it shows another way of creating a deck of cards other than a double `for` loop (see *Beginning Python: From Novice to Professional* for an implementation using a double `for` loop in a list comprehension). There are benefits to using `for` loops: they're straightforward to implement and read, and in this specific case, we can use full names for the sign of the card (e.g., `'Spade'` instead of `'S'`).

If I were to use NumPy's `ndarray` object (discussed in the next section), I'd opt to use the line `zip(arange(52)/4+1, 'SHDC'*13)`, but this is tricky too because the division by 4 might yield noninteger values in future versions. Maybe a more prudent approach would be to add a `floor()` function call.

In any case, what should concern you more is the readability of your code. Don't forget that there's a good chance you'll be the person maintaining it as well. If you're more comfortable with a double `for` loop, use the `for` loop approach. If you're more comfortable zipping flat arrays, the options shown here are viable approaches. It's a matter of personal preference, as performance is hardly an issue. This brings up another point: performance. Opt for readability over performance if possible. After all, Python is a high-level programming language: if you *really* need code performance, other programming languages might prove a better choice. Even better, you can extend Python with other programming languages.

Module NumPy

NumPy's `ndarray` object has been the basic building block for a lot of the data processing and visualization scripts presented throughout the book. We now turn to exploring this package and discussing its usage.

■Note Although used in previous chapters, we have not explicitly seen calls to import NumPy. Nevertheless, we did use NumPy's `ndarray` object extensively. The reason we have not seen NumPy imports is that we have been using the `from pylab import *` command instead, which imports, among other packages, the NumPy package as well.

The `ndarray` object provides substantial added functionality to Python's `array` object and has a lot in common with Matlab's matrix data structure. Such functionality includes matrix operations, linear algebra, and more. It also provides the basic building blocks for more complex numerical methods as will be explored in future chapters. The name "ndarray" stands for N-dimensional array, and as it implies, this object supports N-dimensional arrays.

NumPy is a full and rich package. I will only cover topics that are important for the ideas discussed in the book, and as such, this chapter should be considered a quick introduction. If you'd like to learn more about NumPy, consult with the references at the end of the chapter.

■Note I'll use the terms "array" and "ndarray" interchangeably. In both cases I am referring to NumPy's ndarray object—there's little use for Python's array object once NumPy is imported.

Array Creation

Chapter 3 covered Python's built-in data structures including tuples, lists, and dictionaries. If you recall, there were several methods to create most of these data structures: we've used brackets for lists as well as the list() function, we've used curly braces for dictionaries as well as the dict() function, and so on. Unfortunately, there's no specific symbol set aside for NumPy arrays, so the options are to use either the array() function or functions that return an array, the array creation functions.

The most straightforward method to create and initialize an array is from a list:

```
>>> from numpy import *
>>> v = array([1, 2])        # Here and below array means ndarray.
>>> v
array([1, 2])
>>> m = array([[1, 0], [0, 4]])
>>> m
array([[1, 0],
       [0, 4]])
```

Other methods to create arrays are available, ones that are more useful when dealing with larger amounts of data points, as described in Table 7-5.

Table 7-5. *Array Creation Functions*

Function	Description	Example
N-Dimensional Arrays		
array(s)	Creates an array based on the sequence s.	array(((1, 2), (3, 4))) returns array([[1, 2], [3, 4]]).
ones(t)	Creates an N-dimensional array initialized with 1s based on the tuple t.	ones(2) returns array([1., 1.]).
zeros(t)	Similar to ones(t), only initialized with zeros.	zeros((2, 2)) returns array([[0., 0.], [0., 0.]]).

Function	Description	Example
Two-Dimensional Arrays (Matrices)		
eye(n[, m])	Creates a 2-D array of size n × m, the major diagonal filled with ones and the remaining matrix zeros. If m is not provided, it is assumed equal to n.	eye(2, 3) returns array([[1., 0., 0.], [0., 1., 0.]]).
One-Dimensional Arrays (Vectors)		
arange([start,]stop[, step])	Creates an array of values starting at start, ending at (but excluding) stop with an increment step. This is similar to array(range(start, stop, step)), only that arange() can return noninteger values as well.	arange(1, 2, .5) returns array([1. , 1.5]).
linspace(start, stop, num=50)	Creates a linearly spaced vector of size num from start to stop; refer to the interactive help for additional options.	linspace(1, 10, 3) returns array([1. , 5.5, 10.]).
logspace(start, stop, num=50)	Similar to linspace, only values are spaced evenly from 10^{start} to 10^{stop} on a logarithmic scale; refer to the online help for additional options.	logspace(0, 1, 3) returns array([1., 3.16227766, 10.]).

Some additional array creation functions (fromfile(), empty()) exist, but in most cases, you'll find the ones in Table 7-5 sufficient. There's some redundancy in those as well: ones(10) results in the same array as zeros(10)+1.

Slicing, Indexing, and Reshaping

Arrays can be resized using the reshape() and resize() functions and indexed and sliced using Python's slicing and indexing operators, [ ] and [:]. The difference between the two functions is that resize() resizes an existing array, whereas reshape() returns a new array based upon the data in the original array.

```
>>> a = arange(12).reshape(4, 3)
>>> a
array([[ 0,  1,  2],
       [ 3,  4,  5],
       [ 6,  7,  8],
       [ 9, 10, 11]])
>>> a[1]
array([3, 4, 5])
>>> a[-1]
array([ 9, 10, 11])
>>> a[1, 1]
```

```
4
>>> a[:, 1]
array([ 1,  4,  7, 10])
>>> a[1, :2]
array([3, 4])
```

N-Dimensional Arrays

NumPy arrays are N-dimensional arrays and can be created in the same manner as 1-D and 2-D arrays:

```
>>> ones((2, 3, 4))
array([[[ 1.,  1.,  1.,  1.],
        [ 1.,  1.,  1.,  1.],
        [ 1.,  1.,  1.,  1.]],

       [[ 1.,  1.,  1.,  1.],
        [ 1.,  1.,  1.,  1.],
        [ 1.,  1.,  1.,  1.]]])
```

A useful operator for N-dimensional arrays is ..., which means, "all the remaining dimensions."

```
>>> a = ones((2, 3, 4))
>>> a
array([[[ 1.,  1.,  1.,  1.],
        [ 1.,  1.,  1.,  1.],
        [ 1.,  1.,  1.,  1.]],

       [[ 1.,  1.,  1.,  1.],
        [ 1.,  1.,  1.,  1.],
        [ 1.,  1.,  1.,  1.]]])
>>> a[0, ...]
array([[ 1.,  1.,  1.,  1.],
       [ 1.,  1.,  1.,  1.],        }  ie, other in a: instance of ones (3,4)
       [ 1.,  1.,  1.,  1.]])                                     h  w
>>> a[0, 1, ...]
array([ 1.,  1.,  1.,  1.])
```

One of the common questions is how useful N-dimensional arrays are. Some people feel that they do pretty well with one or two dimensions and have little use for N-dimensions. My experience with N-dimensional arrays is that they provide an excellent data storage when dealing with a combination of several parameters. Consider a simulation with four parameters, each parameter having a range of values. Suppose you want to map out the simulation, that is, calculate the results for every given combination of parameters and also store the results, because the running time is long. How would you store the results? One method is to write them to a list, flattening the data. An alternative method is using an N-dimensional array.

Example: Comparing Mortgages

The following example discusses how to store data as a function of several parameters (typically more than two) using both N-dimensional arrays and flat data structures.

Since at the time of writing this book the subprime mortgage crisis has hit the world markets, I thought it appropriate to give an example comparing mortgages. By all means I'm not financially savvy, so please don't use this as advice in selecting a mortgage! Now to define the problem.

Fixed mortgage payments are a function of three parameters: the loan amount (which is also called the *present value*), the interest rate, and the number of payments. Banks typically have different interest rates as a function of the number of payments, a person's record, and possibly also the loan value.

So based on these three parameters (present value, interest rate, and number of payments), we'd like to map out monthly payments—that is, what the expected monthly payment is for every value in the range of parameters.

For this example, we'll assume that we're considering loans in the amounts of $100,000 to $140,000 in increments of $20,000, mortgage interest rates range from 3 percent to 5 percent in increments of 0.5 percent, and number of payments is 60 to 300 in increments of 60 (representing 5 to 25 years in increments of 5 years). We'll use the function pmt(), which is part of the NumPy package. The function returns a fixed monthly payment for a fixed-rate mortgage (see http://en.wikipedia.org/wiki/Fixed_rate_mortgage).

We construct lists representing the range of values we'd like to map out. We implement these lists using the arange() function described previously in this chapter.

THE CONVENIENCE OF USING ARANGE() AND LINSPACE()

Here's another example of why NumPy provides convenience over non-math-oriented data structures. To implement a list of values with noninteger increments, we can use a list comprehension. For example:

```
>>> interests = [x/2.0+3 for x in range(5)]
```

While this is perfectly OK, it's less readable than something like this:

```
>>> interests = arange(3.0, 5.5, 0.5)
```

In the former method (using a list comprehension), you'd have to do some math to realize exactly what values are being used. In the second method, they're clearly spelled out: from 3 to 5.5 (excluding 5.5) in increments of 0.5.

I'm assuming the decision not to include the edge value (i.e., 5.5) in the function arange() is to have it behave in a similar manner to range() and xrange(). My personal preference would've been to include the edge value.

Alternatively, you could use the linspace() function:

```
>>> interests = linspace(3.0, 5.0, 5)
```

which in this specific example is awkward: the number 5 (the last argument) has to be precalculated to reach an increment of 0.5.

A final note: Those values are annual values, and to use them properly you'd have to divide them by 12 (months) and by 100 (percentage values). Regardless, this is required in both a list comprehension implementation and an `arange()` implementation. I've left it out so that the example would be clearer to follow. The ability to multiply (or divide) an array by a value will be shown in the next section.

Next we iterate over the range of loans, the number of payments, and the interest rates and construct a data structure to hold the results: monthly payments. We examine two data structures:

- A flattened list of rows, with each row being a list containing loan size, number of payments, interest rate, and monthly payment. This is a native Python list.

- An N-dimensional array where each dimension corresponds to a different parameter: interest rate, number of payments, and loan size. This is a 3-D NumPy array.

Listing 7-3 compares these two structures.

Listing 7-3. *Flattening Data vs. N-Dimensional Data*

```
from numpy import *
loans          = arange(100000, 160000, 20000)
num_payments   = arange(5, 30, 5)*12
interests      = arange(3, 5.5, 0.5)/100.0/12.0

# method 1, storing results in a list
res1 = []

# method 2, storing results in an array
res2 = zeros([len(loans), len(num_payments), len(interests)])

for i, loan in enumerate(loans):
    for j, num_pay in enumerate(num_payments):
        for k, interest in enumerate(interests):
            res1.append([loan, num_pay, interest, \
                -pmt(interest, num_pay, loan)])
            res2[i][j][k] = -pmt(interest, num_pay, loan)
```

The benefit of using an N-dimensional array is that indexing is a lot easier and faster. For example, assuming param1 is fixed and set at 0, the results can be accessed with res2[0, ...]. Achieving the same in a list will probably require iterating over the entire list res1 and comparing the value of the first parameter. There's overhead both in code in actual performance:

```
>>> for row in res1:
...     if(row[0] == 120000 and row[1] == 120):
...         print row
...
[120000, 120, 0.0025000000000000001, 1158.7289363806954]
[120000, 120, 0.0029166666666666668, 1186.6304095428363]
```

```
[120000, 120, 0.0033333333333333335, 1214.941657978555]
[120000, 120, 0.0037499999999999999, 1243.6609050842044]
[120000, 120, 0.0041666666666666666, 1272.7861828689065]
>>> res2[1, 1, ...]
array([ 1158.72893638,  1186.63040954,  1214.94165798,  1243.66090508,
        1272.78618287])
```

However, the results of the list are much more readable: they list all combinations of parameters in human readable form. You could do the same with res2 but that requires a for loop:

```
>>> values = res2[1, 1, :]
>>> for i, v in enumerate(values):
...     row = [loans[1], num_payments[1], interests[i], v]
...     print row
...
[120000, 120, 0.0025000000000000001, 1158.7289363806954]
[120000, 120, 0.0029166666666666668, 1186.6304095428363]
[120000, 120, 0.0033333333333333335, 1214.941657978555]
[120000, 120, 0.0037499999999999999, 1243.6609050842044]
[120000, 120, 0.0041666666666666666, 1272.7861828689065]
```

In the for loops, I've used enumerate() on the list of values we're iterating over. The reason for this is that NumPy arrays require indices, and those are integers, whereas Python lists do not. So in a sense, lists here could be more elegant code-wise (no need to use enumerate()).

Lastly, the list implementation can lend itself very nicely to storage in a CSV file, which in itself is also a flattened data structure. That being said, you could also flatten the array and do the same.

Although N-dimensional arrays are interesting data structures, most examples in this book are based on 1-D arrays (vectors) and 2-D arrays (matrices), as they cover most anything we do. Even 3-D plots are really represented by 2-D matrices: the indices represent x and y, and the cell value represents z.

Choosing either N-dimensional arrays or flattened data structures is dependent on the exact problem you're trying to solve.

Math Functions

Simple arithmetic operations are possible on arrays: addition, subtraction, division, multiplication, and exponentiation as well as most math functions available in math and cmath modules (albeit now they're implemented as part of NumPy).

Example: Visualizing Fourier Expansion of a Rectangular Wave

The following is an example showing a Fourier expansion of a rectangular wave using a sum of sine waves. Fourier expansion is used in numerous applications ranging from solving differential equations to signal processing. This example will show how we could treat a NumPy array as a vector of values and operate on that vector as if it were a function. We use a Fourier expansion of sine waves (NumPy arrays) to generate a rectangular wave (another NumPy array). We implement the equation $f(t) = 4/(\pi*n)*\sin(2*\pi*n*t*num\_cycles)$, which is a Fourier series expansion of a rectangular wave (see Listing 7-4). The parameter num_cycles determines the number of cycles we're expanding. In this example we'll set the number to 2 to view two cycles.

Listing 7-4. *Visualizing a Fourier Expansion*

```
# plots a Fourier expansion of a rectangular wave
from pylab import *

# prepare the plot
figure()
hold(True)

# number of points to display the wave
N = 2**8
t = linspace(0, 1, N)
y = zeros(N)

for n in range(1, 8, 2):
    # the sine waves, added
    y += 4/(pi*n)*sin(2*pi*n*t*2)

    # plot the graph
    plot(t, y)

# annotate the graph
axis([0, 1, -1.4, 1.4])
grid()
xlabel('Time [seconds]')
ylabel('Value []')
title('Fourier expansion of a rectangular wave')
legend()
```

We import the entire PyLab module, which also includes NumPy and the plotting commands: both are required in this example. We then prepare an empty plot: each new calculation of the expansion will be plotted on top of the previous one, so we issue the command hold(True) to ensure subsequent plots do not erase existing ones.

The first array object is created with the command t = linspace(0, 1, N) (we could've also used an arange() function call instead). Array object t is a 1-D array, a vector. All our subsequent operations and math functions will operate on this vector. We then initialize the series expansion variable, y, using the zeros() function. The heart of the computation lies in the for loop. Each sine wave is added to the previous one, and the result is stored in y. The simple line y += 4/(pi*n)*sin(2*pi*n*t*2) is in reality operating on entire arrays, showing the strength of the array object.

We then plot y as it is being calculated and annotate the graph once the expansion is complete, as shown in Figure 7-4.

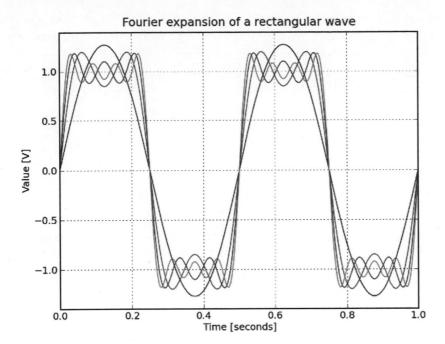

Figure 7-4. *Fourier expansion of a rectangular wave*

Array Methods and Properties

Arrays are objects and as such have functions called *methods* and variables called *properties*. Using IPython (see Chapter 2), you can list an object's methods and properties by using character completion, accessible via the Tab key. Alternatively, you can issue the following:

```
>>> import numpy
>>> [m for m in dir(numpy.ndarray) if not(m.startswith('__'))]
['T', 'all', 'any', 'argmax', 'argmin', 'argsort', 'astype', 'base', 'byteswap',
 'choose', 'clip', 'compress', 'conj', 'conjugate', 'copy', 'ctypes', 'cumprod',
 'cumsum', 'data', 'diagonal', 'dtype', 'dump', 'dumps', 'fill', 'flags', 'flat'
, 'flatten', 'getfield', 'imag', 'item', 'itemset', 'itemsize', 'max', 'mean', '
min', 'nbytes', 'ndim', 'newbyteorder', 'nonzero', 'prod', 'ptp', 'put', 'ravel'
, 'real', 'repeat', 'reshape', 'resize', 'round', 'searchsorted', 'setfield', 's
etflags', 'shape', 'size', 'sort', 'squeeze', 'std', 'strides', 'sum', 'swapaxes
', 'take', 'tofile', 'tolist', 'tostring', 'trace', 'transpose', 'var', 'view']
```

I've used the preceding list to create Table 7-6; it's only a subset of the methods and attributes, and I chose to describe those I feel are the most useful for data processing and visualization. I've also split the methods into categories for easier viewing. Methods are denoted with (), while properties do not have a trailing parenthesis. In this table, a refers to an array variable.

Table 7-6. *Array Methods and Attributes (Partial)*

Function	Description	Examples
Logical		
all()	True if all elements of a are true (nonzero).	arange(10).all() returns False (the first element is zero). arange(-5, -2).all() returns True.
any()	True if at least one element of a is true (nonzero).	arange(10).any() returns True.
nonzero()	A tuple of indices to nonzero elements of a.	arange(3).nonzero() returns (array([1, 2]),).
Indexing		
sort()	Sorts elements in a.	a = arange(3, 0, -1) sets a to array([3, 2, 1]). a.sort() changes a to array([1, 2, 3]).
searchsorted(x)	Returns indices to insert x such that the array's order is preserved. Assumes a is already sorted.	arange(4).searchsorted(1.5) returns 2.
Modifying		
clip(min, max)	If an element of a is less than min, returns min; if an element of a is greater than max, returns max; otherwise, returns the element.	arange(5).clip(1, 3) returns array([1, 1, 2, 3, 3]).
compress(cond)	Returns an array whose elements match the condition specified in cond; equivalent to a[cond].	a = arange(10) a.compress(a > 5) returns array([6, 7, 8, 9]). a[a > 5] returns array([6, 7, 8, 9]).
fill(x)	Sets all values of an array to x; equivalent to a[:] = x.	a = zeros([2, 2]) a[:] = -1 sets a to array([[-1., -1.], [-1., -1.]]). a.fill(-2) sets a to array([[-2., -2.], [-2., -2.]]).

Math

For math examples, assume a = array([1, 1j, -1]), which can also be expressed as a = exp(1j*pi*arange(3)/2).

cumprod()	Cumulative product. Each element is the product of the previous elements in the array.	a.cumprod() returns array([1.+0.j, 0.+1.j, 0.-1.j]).
cumsum()	Cumulative sum. Each element is the sum of the previous elements in the array.	a.cumsum() returns array([1.+0.j, 1.+1.j, 0.+1.j]).

Function	Description	Examples
real and imag	Real and imaginary values of elements in a.	a.imag returns array([0., 1., 0.]). a.real returns array([1., 0., -1.]).
conj()	Complex conjugate of a (negation of the imaginary part; rows and columns transposed).	a[1].conj() returns -1j.
max(), min()	Maximum and minimum values of a (performed on real part only).	a.max() returns (1+0j). a.min() returns (-1+0j).
mean()	Mean value of a.	a.mean() returns 0.333333333333333331j (1j/3).
prod()	Product of all the values in a.	a.prod() returns -1j. Note that a.prod() is equal to a.cumprod()[-1].
ptp()	Peak-to-peak value of a; equivalent to a.max()-a.min().	a.ptp() returns (2+0j).
round()	Rounded values of a.	exp(a).round() returns array([3.+0.j, 1.+1.j, 0.+0.j]).
std()	Standard deviation of elements in a.	arange(2).std() returns 0.5.
sum()	Sum of all the values in a.	a.sum() returns 1j. Note that a.sum() is equal to a.cumsum()[-1].
trace([n])	Sum of the diagonal of a 2-D array. If n is provided, sums the offset diagonal.	eye(N).trace() returns N.
var()	Variance of elements in a.	arange(2).var() returns 0.25.
Shape Related		
flatten()	The values in a as a 1-D array.	eye(2).flatten() returns array([1., 0., 0., 1.]).
ndim	Number of dimensions of a.	eye(4, 5).ndim returns 2.
repeat(n)	Copies a over n times, flattened.	eye(2).repeat(2) returns array([1., 1., 0., 0., 0., 0., 1., 1.]).
reshape(d1, d2, ...)	Generates a new array of size (d1, d2, ...).	arange(4).reshape(2, 2) returns array([[0, 1], [2, 3]]).
resize(d1, d2,...)	Resizes the current array to size (d1, d2,...).	a = arange(4) a.resize(2, 2) sets a to array([[0, 1], [2, 3]]).
shape	A tuple representing shape of a.	eye(3, 4).shape returns (3, 4).
transpose()	Transposes a matrix. This is equivalent to conjugate but without negating the imaginary parts.	eye(2, 3).transpose() returns array([[1., 0.], [0., 1.], [0., 0.]]).

Continued

Table 7-6. *Continued*

Function	Description	Examples
Conversion		
tofile(fname)	Writes an array to file (binary).	eye(2).tofile('eye2.bin')
fromfile(fid)	Reads an array from file (binary).	a = fromfile(open('eye2.bin'))
tolist()	Converts an array to a list	eye(2).tolist() returns [[1.0, 0.0], [0.0, 1.0]].

Example: A Magic Square

A *magic square* is a square with the sum of each row and column equal and the same. Typically, magic squares do not allow numbers to repeat twice. In this example, we'll generate magic squares, populating the values from 1 to N^2 in a square of size N by N.

A modern variation on the magic square idea is the Sudoku puzzle game. The ideas presented in this example can be modified to provide solutions to Sudoku puzzles (see http://en.wikipedia.org/wiki/Sudoku for possible strategies for implementing a computer solution).

Back to our example. We'll create a magic square implementing the De la Loubère method (also known as the Siamese method), which works for squares of odd values of N only. Constructing a magic square is performed by placing the first value, 1, in the middle column at the top. Incremented values are placed diagonally up and to the right. If the spot up and to the right is outside the square, it is wrapped around to the bottom row (if exceeded at the top) or to the first column (if exceeded to the right) or both. If a cell is already occupied, the value moves a row below (again, wrapping if needed). Figure 7-5 illustrates the algorithm with example magic squares of sizes 3 and 5.

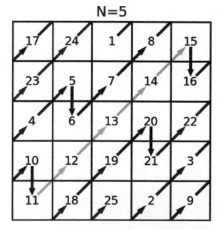

Figure 7-5. *De la Loubère method*

An implementation of the algorithm using an array is presented in Listing 7-5.

Listing 7-5. *Creating a Magic Square*

```python
from numpy import *
def magicsq(n=3):
    """Returns a magic square of size n; n must be odd"""

    if n % 2 != 1:
        raise ValueError, "Magic(n) requires n to be odd"
    m, row, col = zeros([n, n]), 0, n/2
    for num in xrange(1, n**2+1):
        m[row, col] = num       # fill the cell
        col = (col+1) % n
        row = (row-1) % n
        if m[row, col]:
            col = (col-1) % n
            row = (row+2) % n
    return m


def testmagicsq(m):
    """Returns True if m is a magic square."""
    msum = sum(m[0, :])
    return all(m.sum(0) == msum) and all(m.sum(1) == msum)
```

The main `for` loop is quite straightforward and follows the algorithm strictly. However, calculation of the column and row values using the modulo (%) operator is tricky and requires some explanation. Consider the way the algorithm is specified: increment the column value and check whether the new value is within the size of the matrix. If it is not, wrap it around to the beginning. A similar approach is taken with the row: decrement and wrap if required. Instead of implementing these two steps, an increment/decrement followed by an `if` statement, we could use the modulo operation, which captures the idea quite elegantly: `col = (col+1) % n`.

I've chosen to initialize the variables `m`, `row`, and `col` with a multiple assignment. Multiple assignments can also be used inside the `for` loop: `col, row = (col+1) % n, (row-1) % n`; however, in my mind it's less clear, and there's no impact performance-wise. My personal preference is to use multiple assignments in initializations and not calculations.

I've defined another function here, `testmagicsq()`, which checks whether a square is indeed a magic square. The function also works on even values (which is a plus) and makes use of the `sum()` member function of the array object.

■**Tip** Python supports testing via several built-in packages, including `doctest` and `unittest`. However, for the purpose of this example, I've chosen to write a dedicated test function, which will further show the properties of NumPy arrays.

The function sum(0) returns an array of the sums of columns (i.e., along axis 0); sum(1) returns an array summing rows (along axis 1). Here's a listing demonstrating summing along the 0 axis and the 1 axis:

```
>>> a = eye(2, 3)
>>> a
array([[ 1.,   0.,   0.],
       [ 0.,   1.,   0.]])
>>> a.sum(0)
array([ 1.,   1.,   0.])
>>> a.sum(1)
array([ 1.,   1.])
>>> m = magicsq(5)
>>> m.sum(0)
array([ 65.,   65.,   65.,   65.,   65.])
>>> m.sum(1)
array([ 65.,   65.,   65.,   65.,   65.])
```

As can be seen, the matrix eye(2, 3) has two rows and three columns. Summing along axis 0 via sum(0) returns a 1-D array (a vector) holding the sums of all three columns. Consequently, sum(1) returns a vector holding the sum of the rows. The next lines show how this can be used to check for "magic-ness" of a square—both vectors, sum(0) and sum(1), should be equal element-wise to the sum along an arbitrary axis.

In the testmagicsq() function I've chosen to compare both sums of columns and of rows with the sum of the first column: sum(m[0, :]). If you compare a vector (1-D array) with a scalar (a single value), the result is a vector with each element compared with the scalar. To ensure all are indeed equal to the required sum, you could use the all() member function. I've opted to use the notation all(m.sum(0) == msum) over (m.sum(0) == msum).all() because I think it's more readable, but that again is personal preference; both do the job.

■Note In the function testmagicsq(), it's not enough to check that m.sum(0) is equal to m.sum(1) because this only checks that the sums of rows is equal to the sums of columns. However, that's not a sufficient condition. Consider the array m = array([[1, 0], [0, 2]]): it satisfies the condition m.sum(0) == m.sum(1), but it's not a magic square. You might raise the question whether the array eye(N) is a magic square—the function testmagicsq() will return True, but maybe this is a trivial case of a magic square.

One other interesting aspect of the Siamese method is that the sum along the diagonal is also identical to the sum of each row and each column; that's true for both diagonals. The function trace() calculates the sum along the diagonal (top left to bottom right). To calculate the sum of the second diagonal (bottom left to top right), you could use the fliplr() function.

```
>>> m = magicsq(5)
>>> m.trace()
65.0
>>> fliplr(m).trace()
65.0
```

Other Useful Array Functions

Other than ndarray properties and methods, the NumPy package also provides functions that operate on arrays but are not part of the ndarray object class. For a full account, issue the following:

```
>>> import numpy
>>> dir(numpy)
```

As you can see, many functions are available from various fields of interest:

- *Vector operations*: convolve(), cross(), correlate(), and vdot()

- *Matrix operations*: diag() and trace()

- *Statistical functions*: cov(), var(), std(), mean(), and histogram()

- *Financial functions*: fv(), pv(), and pmt()

- *Polynomial operations*: polyadd(), polymul(), polydiv(), polyfit(), polyder(), polyint(), and roots()

- *Operations that change vector and matrix sizes and orientations*: flipud(), fliplr(), and rot90()

- *Functions that generate windows for filtering*: hamming(), hanning(), bartlett(), blackman(), and kaiser()

We'll explore some of these functions in Chapter 8. If you'd like to know more about these functions, issue help(numpy.function). For example, here's a function I particularly like using:

```
>>> help(numpy.diff)
Help on function diff in module numpy.lib.function_base:
diff(a, n=1, axis=-1)
    Calculate the nth order discrete difference along given axis.
```

I use diff() to calculate the difference between two consecutive elements in an array. I've used it several times already in the book, including in the section "Example: Adding Arrows to a Graph" in Chapter 6. You could also modify the friends meeting example in this chapter to use diff() instead of a list comprehension.

Final Notes and References

The range of applications for which NumPy is of value is large. And as evidence, you'll find that a considerable number of packages rely on NumPy, and for a good reason: NumPy provides a solid base for mathematical arrays.

An interesting module that comes with the Python Standard Library is the decimal module. This module provides support for decimal floating-point values and allows, for example, arbitrary percision. The decimal module is a bit less intuitive than regular numbers in Python, but should you require higher percision, and provided you're willing to accept some performance loss, this module is a good option. Another module, introduced with Python version 2.6, is the fractions module, which supports rational number arithmetic.

Should you require additional information on NumPy or the other topics discussed in this chapter, I hope you find the following references of value:

- NumPy home page, `http://numpy.scipy.org/`
- Guide to NumPy by Travis E. Oliphant, the lead developer of NumPy, `http://www.tramy.us/numpybook.pdf`
- "De la Loubère Method," Wikipedia, `http://en.wikipedia.org/wiki/Siamese_method`
- "Fourier Series," Wikipedia, `http://en.wikipedia.org/wiki/Fourier_series`
- "Newton Fractals," Wikipedia, `http://en.wikipedia.org/wiki/Newton%27s_method`
- The Python Standard Library, `http://docs.python.org/library/index.html`
- Decimal module, `http://docs.python.org/library/decimal.html`
- Fractions module, `http://docs.python.org/library/fractions.html`

CHAPTER 8

■ ■ ■

Science and Visualization
Numerical Analysis and Signal Processing

I've covered a great deal of the topics associated with data analysis and visualization: reading and writing files, text processing and converting text to numerical data, plotting and graphing, writing scripts, and implementing algorithms. It's time to take a deeper dive and analyze numerical data.

This chapter deals with two important topics: numerical analysis and signal processing. These two topics appear in many sciences: mathematics, computing, engineering, and more. From a simplistic point of view, *numerical analysis* is concerned with algorithms that yield numerical values: a solution to a nonlinear equation, the decimal representation of π, and more. *Signal processing* deals with processing signals, that is, values that change over time. Signal processing includes such topics as detection and filtering.

Most universities and colleges offer undergraduate courses that teach these topics. But you don't have to be an engineer or a computer scientist to use the methods and ideas discussed in the chapter. Most of the topics are easy to follow, as I've tried to keep the math to a minimum.

If you have a strong numerical analysis and signal processing background, this chapter should prove a good starting point for these topics in Python. If you're new to the ideas of numerical analysis and signal processing, I hope to shed some light so that you can pick it up from here with relevant scientific literature. In particular, I'd like to point out one of the books that made a great deal of impact on me (and many others), *Numerical Recipes: The Art of Scientific Computing, Third Edition* by William H. Press, Saul A. Teukolsky, William T. Vetterling, and Brian P. Flannery (Cambridge University Press, 2007; for more information, see http://www.nr.com). Although the book implements algorithms using C/C++ (my original copy was in the Pascal programming language), it provides a wealth of information on numerical algorithms and should prove easy enough to port to Python.

In my view, the field of numerical analysis is a cookbook of algorithms to numerically solve mathematical problems. And so in a sense, that's how the chapter is organized as well: as a list of problems and solutions. Each topic will be explored with examples in hopes that you'll modify the examples to fit your needs. And that's also how I suggest you refer to the chapter:

as a cookbook of algorithms. While it's quite possible to read through and learn the algorithms one at a time, it's probably easier to read specific sections as you engage problems associated with them in real life. So my suggestion is this: skim through the table of contents to acquaint yourself with what's available, and then try to solve a specific problem by reading the relevant section.

In this chapter, I've used SciPy, matplotlib, and NumPy extensively. These three packages are rich and complex, and as a result, I was only able to cover some of the functionality, not all of it. I therefore chose to cover topics and show examples of problems I personally encountered. I hope you'll find the examples of value.

Finding Your Way: Variables and Functions

The NumPy package provides us with two useful helper functions. I call them helper functions because they don't fall into any specific numerical analysis or signal processing category.

When one works in an interactive environment, one constantly defines variables. It's hard to remember what variables are defined and what they mean. The function who() prints a list of all ndarray variables (NumPy arrays):

```
>>> who()
```

```
Upper bound on total bytes  =       0
>>> up, down = arange(10), arange(10, 0, -1)
>>> who()
Name            Shape           Bytes           Type
===============================================================================
down            10              40              int32
up              10              40              int32

Upper bound on total bytes  =       80
```

The function lookfor() is great for searching inside docstrings. So to look for functions that perform numerical integration, issue

```
>>> lookfor('integrate')
Search results for 'integrate'
-------------------------------
numpy.trapz
    Integrate y(x) using samples along the given axis and the composite
```

SciPy

SciPy (http://www.scipy.org/) is an open source scientific library for Python. The idea of SciPy is similar to that of Octave-Forge (http://octave.sourceforge.net/), which provides extra packages for GNU-Octave (http://www.octave.org) and toolboxes that enhance MATLAB (http://www.mathworks.com). SciPy is built on top of NumPy and so requires NumPy to work properly.

SciPy is organized into several modules, some of which are detailed in Table 8-1.

Table 8-1. *SciPy Packages*

Package	Description
Fftpack	Fast Fourier Transform
Integrate	Integration functions, including ordinary differential equations
Interpolate	Interpolation of functions
Linalg	Linear algebra
Optimize	Optimization functions, including root-solving algorithms
Signal	Signal processing
Special	Special functions (Airy, Bessel, etc.)

We'll be exploring most of SciPy modules that deal with numerical analysis and signal processing. Additional SciPy modules include sparse matrices (module sparse), statistics (module stats), and more; they will not be covered in this book.

To import a SciPy module, issue `import scipy.modulename`:

```
>>> import scipy.linalg
```

or

```
>>> from scipy import linalg
```

Personally, I prefer the latter option: `linalg.eig()` is shorter to code than `scipy.linalg.eig()` (plus I think it's easier to read).

Linear Algebra

Linear algebra is a branch in mathematics that deals with matrices, vectors, and solving systems of linear equations. SciPy and NumPy provide us with many functions to deal with these topics: solving systems of linear equations, matrix and vector operations, and matrix decompositions.

Solving a System of Linear Equations

To solve a system of linear equations, we first write the problem in matrix notation.

```
2 * x + 3 * y = 10
3 * x -     y = -1.5
```

We start by defining a matrix, `M`, and a vector, `V`. The matrix is composed of the coefficients of x and y, which are 2 and 3 on the first row, hence [2, 3], and 3 and –1 on the second row, hence [3, -1]:

```
>>> from pylab import *
>>> M = array([[ 2, 3], [3, -1]])
```

Next we define the vector of the results, [10, -1.5]:

```
>>> V = array([10, -1.5])
```

Now all that's required is to use the function solve():

```
>>> solve(M, V)
array([ 0.5,  3. ])
```

meaning that x is equal to 0.5 and y is equal to 3.

It's also possible to reach the solution by calculating the inverse of the matrix M and multiplying it by vector V:

```
>>> dot(inv(M), V)
array([ 0.5,  3. ])
```

I've introduced two functions here: inv() and dot(). The function inv() calculates the inverse of a matrix, and the function dot() performs a dot product. Had I multiplied inv(M) with V, I would've received an *element-by-element* multiplication, and not the result we're interested in:

```
>>> inv(M)*V
array([[ 0.90909091, -0.40909091],
       [ 2.72727273,  0.27272727]])
```

Generally speaking, you should use solve() instead of inv(). The function solve() can handle what mathematicians call "less-behaved" matrices.

Vector and Matrix Operations

Much like dot(), the function vdot() returns the dot product of two vectors. So if you're only interested in the value of x in the previous example, you can write

```
>>> dot(inv(M)[0], V)
0.50000000000000022
```

The function inner(v1, v2) will perform an inner product, that is, multiply every element in v1 with the corresponding element in v2 and then sum them together:

```
>>> V1 = array([10, -1.5])
>>> V2 = array([1, 2])
>>> sum = 0
>>> for i in range(len(V1)):
...     sum + = V1[i]*V2[i]
...
>>> sum
7.0
>>> inner(V1, V2)
7.0
```

I've implemented an inner product operation with a for loop and compared the results with the results of the function inner(). As can be expected, the results are the same. Note that the function `inner()` does not multiply an element with its conjugate (negative imaginary part).

The function `inner()` works on matrices as well:

```
>>> M = array([[2, 3], [3, -1]])
>>> M
array([[ 2,  3],
       [ 3, -1]])
>>> inner(M, inv(M))
array([[  1.00000000e+00,   1.11022302e-16],
       [  5.55111512e-17,   1.00000000e+00]])
```

Similarly, `outer()` performs an outer product of two vectors or matrices:

```
>>> V1 = array([10, -1.5])
>>> V2 = array([1, 2])
>>> outer(V1, V2)
array([[ 10. ,   20. ],
       [ -1.5,   -3. ]])
```

The function `transpose()` will permute axes, and `conjugate()` will permute axes and negate the imaginary part of a matrix or vector:

```
>>> V1 = array([10, -1.5])
>>> V2 = array([1, 2])
>>> outer(V1, V2)
array([[ 10. ,   20. ],
       [ -1.5,   -3. ]])
>>> outer(V2, V1)
array([[ 10. ,   -1.5],
       [ 20. ,   -3. ]])
>>> all(outer(V1, V2) == transpose(outer(V2, V1)))
True
>>> conjugate(V1+1j*V2)
array([ 10.0-1.j,   -1.5-2.j])
```

The function `det(m)` will return the determinant of matrix `m`:

```
>>> det(array([[2, 3], [3, -1]]))
-11.0
```

Matrix Decomposition

Matrix decomposition is the rewriting of a matrix to a specific form. There are many decompositions including LU decomposition, singular value decomposition, and QR decomposition. NumPy's linear algebra module supports some matrix decompositions via the functions in Table 8-2.

Table 8-2. *Some Matrix Decomposition Functions*

Function	Description
cholesky(m)	Cholesky decomposition
eig(m)	Eigenvalue decomposition
qr(m)	QR decomposition
svd(m)	Singular value decomposition

The following code performs eigenvalue decomposition with verification of the results:

```
>>> A = array([[1, 2], [0, 1]])
>>> L, v = eig(A)  # calculate eigenvalues and eigenvectors
>>> det(A - eye(2)*L)   # verify eigenvalues (should be zero)
0.0
>>> dot(A, v[:, 0]) - L[0]*v[:, 0]  # verify eigenvector (should be 0)
array([ 0.,   0.])
>>> dot(A, v[:, 1]) - L[1]*v[:, 1]  # verify eigenvector (should be 0)
array([  2.22044605e-16,   0.00000000e+00])
```

I've created a matrix A and calculated its eigenvalues $\lambda_{1,2}$ (stored in vector L) and eigenvectors $v_{1,2}$ (stored in matrix v). Once the eigenvalues are evaluated, they can be verified by calculating $\det(A - \lambda * I)$, which should be zero; this is done in the second line. Also, for every eigenvector $\lambda v = A * v$, this is verified in the last two lines.

We will not be covering other matrix decompositions here; if you require additional information, help() is quite informative.

Additional Linear Algebra Functionality

Additional linear algebra functionality is available with the scipy.linalg module. To access SciPy's linear algebra functions, issue import scipy.linalg or from scipy import linalg. SciPy's added functionality includes

- Matrix decomposition functions: lu() for LU decomposition and qr() for QR matrix decomposition, as well as functions for other decompositions.

- Matrix and vector operators such as norm() to calculate a matrix or vector norm.

- Matrix functions, for example, expm() and tanm(). Matrix function names are similar to regular function names but with an added character m.

Numerical Integration

Numerical integration is the process of numerically computing a definite integral. There are many occasions where numerical integration is important. Examples include calculating the area of a shape or the area under a graph, and solving differential equations.

For the purpose of this discussion we'll calculate the area of half a circle of radius 1. We already know this area to be $\pi/2$. So in a sense, calculating the area of half a circle is equivalent to calculating the numerical value of π.

First, we create two vectors: x and y. These two vectors satisfy the circle equation $x^2 + y^2 = 1$:

```
>>> N = 7
>>> x = linspace(-1, 1, N)
>>> y = sqrt(1-x**2)
>>> x**2 + y**2
array([ 1.,   1.,   1.,   1.,   1.,   1.,   1.])
```

I chose the variable N arbitrarily; N is the number of points in the vectors x and y.

To visualize the numerical integration, I plot rectangles that approximate the area of the circle:

```
>>> figure()
>>> dx = x[1]-x[0]
>>> for i in range(len(x)-1):
...     rect = Rectangle((x[i], 0), dx, 0.5*(y[i]+y[i+1]))
...     gca().add_patch(rect)
...
>>> title('Approximating the area of half a circle')
>>> axis('equal')
```

The area under the curve, that is, the integral, is approximately the sum of these squares. Each square's area is 0.5*(y[i]+y[i+1])*dx, so the total sum can be written as follows:

```
>>> dx*(sum(y[0:-1]+y[1:]))
2.9175533787759904
```

I've multiplied the result by 2 so we can compare with π instead of $\pi/2$. Obviously, the bigger N is, the closer this number will be to π:

```
>>> for N in [5, 10, 20, 100]:
...     x = linspace(-1, 1, N)
...     dx = x[1]-x[0]
...     y = sqrt(1-x**2)
...     est_pi = dx*sum(y[0:-1]+y[1:])
...     print "N=%d, estimated pi is %f" % (N, est_pi)
...
N=5, estimated pi is 2.732051
N=10, estimated pi is 3.019232
N=20, estimated pi is 3.101560
N=100, estimated pi is 3.138218
```

As you can see, for N = 100, the accuracy is about 1 percent. Figure 8-1 captures this visually.

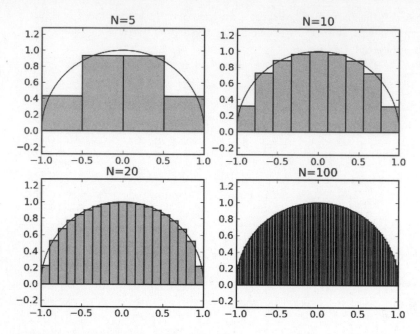

Figure 8-1. *Calculating the area of a circle*

In calculating the area of the circle, I chose values that are evenly spaced. In case you'd like to use non-evenly spaced values, the implementation is more complex. Also, the method uses rectangles to approximate the area under the curve, but in this particular example (and many others), trapezoidals are probably better suited, which brings us to the function trapz(y, x). The function accepts vectors y and x and returns the numerical integral. The following performs numerical integration of non-evenly spaced x values using the function trapz():

```
>>> x = array([-1, -0.9, -0.4, 0.0, 0.4, 0.9, 1])
>>> y = sqrt(1-x**2)
>>> trapz(y, x)*2
2.9727951234089831
```

Figure 8-2 shows a visual representation of the trapezoidal integration.

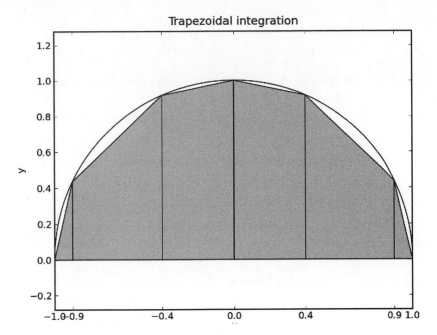

Figure 8-2. *Calculating the area of a circle using the trapezoidal method and non-evenly spaced values*

More Integration Methods

Additional integration algorithms are available with the module scipy.integrate. To use this module, issue from scipy import integrate.

We'll limit our discussion to the algorithm quad(), which uses a Gaussian quadrature to numerically integrate a *mathematical* function. Unlike previous methods such as trapz(), using quad() requires supplying a mathematical function and not the x and y vectors.

■**Note** I've used the term "mathematical function" to differentiate this type of function from a general-purpose Python function. A mathmatical function is one that returns a numerical value given an input numerical value, for example, y = f(x). In reality, we implement a mathematical function as a Python function.

```
>>> from scipy.integrate import quad
>>> def half_circle(x):
...     return sqrt(1-x**2)
...
>>> pi_half, err = quad(half_circle, -1, 1)
>>> (pi_half*2, err)
(3.1415926535897967, 1.0002354500215915e-009)
```

I defined a mathematical function half_circle() that returns the y coordinate value of the upper half circle of radius 1, given an x coordinate value. I then called quad() with the arguments half_circle, the function to integrate, and -1 and 1, the range of values to integrate. The function quad() returns a value and an error.

The module scipy.integrate also supports solving of ordinary differential equations using functions ode() and odeint(). We will not be discussing these functions. If you're interested in solving differential equations, refer to the SciPy home page: http://www.scipy.org/SciPy.

Interpolation and Curve Fitting

Interpolation and *curve fitting* deal with fitting functions to discrete known values. There are several reasons you would want to fit functions to points of data, among which are

- Fitting a known function to gathered experimental data. This can be helpful in determining other parameters of the experiment.

- Evaluating the numerical values of functions at additional points (other than the given ones).

Interpolation allows efficient implementations that are tailor-made to a specific problem. Instead of writing a lookup table for all the possible values, you could come up with an interpolation polynomial that is more efficient, albeit with possible loss of performance and accuracy. At other times, you might choose to implement a known function such as sqrt() instead of using a library-supplied algorithm to *increase* performance (again, at the possible cost of accuracy).

INVERSE SQUARE ROOT AND QUAKE III

If you're interested in efficient algorithms to calculate numerical functions, you may find the article "Fast Inverse Square Root" by Chris Lomont, http://www.lomont.org/Math/Papers/2003/InvSqrt.pdf, interesting. The article describes a very efficient algorithm to implement the inverse square root of a number that appeared in the source code of the computer game Quake III. The implementation makes use of the Newton-Raphson method (and not interpolation). The article assumes knowledge of C.

Piecewise Linear Interpolation

Let's turn back to our half-a-circle example. This time, we'll limit ourselves to a quarter of a circle, that is, positive values of x and y. We start by calculating the y values for x equal to 0, 0.2, . . . , 1. We'll store the results in vectors xp and yp:

```
>>> xp = linspace(0, 1, 6)
>>> xp
array([ 0. ,  0.2,  0.4,  0.6,  0.8,  1. ])
>>> yp = sqrt(1-xp**2)
```

We'd like to calculate the values of y for x values equal to 0.1, 0.3, . . . , 0.9 given xp and yp. We'll use the function interp(x, xp, yp) for this. The function returns the value of the piecewise linear function defined by xp, yp at a requested point x. What this means is interp() returns the value of a point on a line connecting two adjacent (xp, yp) points:

```
>>> xi = arange(0.1, 1.0, 0.2)
>>> yi = interp(xi, xp, yp)
```

The vector yi holds the interpolated values at points 0.1, 0.3, . . ., 0.9.

The following visualizes a piecewise linear interpolation for the quarter of a circle:

```
>>> figure()
>>> hold(True)
>>> x = linspace(0, 1, 500)
>>> y = sqrt(1-x**2)
>>> plot(x, y, 'b', label='ideal')
>>> plot(xp, yp, 'or', label='interpolation points')
>>> plot(xp, yp, '--r', label='piecewise linear function')
>>> plot(xi, yi, 'sg', label='interpolated values')
>>> legend(loc='best')
>>> grid()
>>> axis('scaled')
>>> axis([0, 1.1, 0, 1.1])
>>> title('Piecewise linear interpolation')
```

Figure 8-3 shows the results of this visualization.

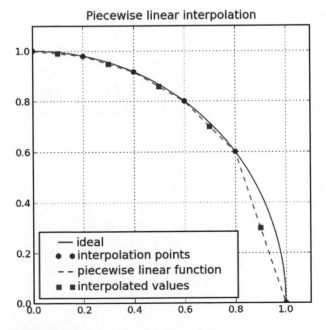

Figure 8-3. *Piecewise linear interpolation*

For the purpose of the example, the values xp and yp are computed, but in reality, these values can originate from sampled data. As you can see from the graph, the interpolated value at 0.9 is considerably less accurate than other interpolated values. Typically, the more points you add, the more accurate the result.

Polynomials

Polynomials are mathematical expressions that involve a sum of integer powers of a variable multiplied by a coefficient. Examples include $2x^2 + x - 1$ as well as x. However, sin(x) is not a polynomial. The reason polynomials are so important is that they involve only basic operations: addition, subtraction, and multiplication (integer powers can be implemented with several multiplications), and this property makes them very easy to implement in computing. Taylor series expansion (http://en.wikipedia.org/wiki/Taylor_series) is a prime example of transforming a function to a polynomial, easily computed.

To be able to operate on polynomials with NumPy and SciPy, we represent a polynomial as a vector. The first element in the vector is the coefficient to the highest power, and the last element in the array is the coefficient to the lowest power, 0. So to express the polynomial $x^2 + 3x + 2$, issue the following:

```
>>> p = array([1, 3, 2])
```

To solve the equation $x^2 + 3x + 2 = 0$, use the function roots(p):

```
>>> roots(p)
array([-2.+0.j, -1.+0.j])
```

Notice that the imaginary parts are zero, and so the roots are –2 and –1.

If you'd like to construct a polynomial from its roots instead of its coefficients, use the function poly():

```
>>> p = poly([-2, -1])
>>> p
array([1, 3, 2])
```

Adding and subtracting polynomials is done using polyadd() and polysub():

```
>>> p1 = poly([-2, -1])
>>> p2 = array([1, 0, 0, 0])
>>> polyadd(p1, p2)
array([1, 1, 3, 2])
```

I've added $x^2 + 3x + 2$ to x^3 and got $x^3 + x^2 + 3x + 2$ as a result.

Multiplying and dividing polynomials is done using polymul() and polydiv(). The return value from polydiv() is a quotient and a remainder:

```
>>> p = polymul(array([1, 2]), array([1, 3]))
>>> p
array([1, 5, 6])
>>> polydiv(p, array([1, 3]))
(array([ 1.,   2.]), array([0]))
```

Performing integration and differentiation on polynomials is done using the functions `polyint()` and `polyder()`, respectively:

```
>>> p = poly([-1j, 1j])
>>> p
array([ 1.,  0.,  1.])
>>> polyder(p)
array([ 2.,  0.])
>>> polyint(p)
array([ 0.33333333,  0. ,  1. ,  0. ])
```

In the first line I created a polynomial from complex numbers; the polynomial created is stored in p and is $x^2 + 1$. Using `polyder()` I calculated the derivative of p and got 2x. Using `polyint()` I calculate the integral of p and got $\frac{1}{3}x^2 + x$.

Uses of Polynomials

So why is all this polystuff important? The main reason is that you can use polynomials to approximate functions both from gathered data and from analytical functions. And since polynomials only require multiplications and additions, implementing polynomials in an embedded system, for example, is straightforward.

Fitting polynomials to data is done using the function `polyfit(x, y, n)`. Given a vector of x points and a vector of y points, `polyfit(x, y, n)` will return a polynomial of degree n (highest power of x) that best fits the set of data points. Another function that is of use is `polyval(p, x)`; this function returns the value of the polynomial at x (x can be a vector).

Example: Linear Regression

A known curve-fitting algorithm is linear regression. The idea is to draw a straight line in such a way that the total distance of all the points from the line is minimal.

For the purpose of this example, we'll create a straight line and then add "measurement noise" to the values. Confronted with the new "noisy" data, we'll try to evaluate the first order polynomial that fits the data. We'll compare the results with the known true values (see Listing 8-1).

Listing 8-1. *Linear Regression with polyfit()*

```
from pylab import *

# number of data points
N     = 100
start = 0
end   = 1

A = rand()
B = rand()

# our linear line will be y = A*x + B
```

```
x = linspace(start, end, N)
y = A*x + B
y += randn(N)/10

# linear regression
p = polyfit(x, y, 1)

figure()
title('Linear regression with polyfit()')
plot(x, y, 'o',
    label='Measured data; A=%.2f, B=%.2f' % (A, B))
plot(x, polyval(p, x), '-',
    label='Linear regression; A=%.2f, B=%.2f' % tuple(p))
legend(loc='best')
```

I've randomly selected two values for A and B, and constructed a linear line with noise using randn(). Then, I used polyfit() to fit the data to a first degree polynomial, a straight line. Lastly, I plot the data along with the newly constructed linear line. Figure 8-4 shows the results of this linear regression.

Figure 8-4. *Linear regression with* polyfit()

Example: Linear Regression of Nonlinear Functions

In cases where the function you're trying to fit isn't linear, at times it's still possible to perform linear regression.

The following is an example of fitting exponential data:

```
from pylab import *

# number of data points
N     = 100
start = 0
end   = 2

A = rand()
B = rand()

x = linspace(start, end, N)
y = exp(A*x+B)
y += randn(N)/5

# linear regression
p = polyfit(x, log(y), 1)

figure()
title(r'Linear regression with polyfit(), $y=Be^{Ax}$')
plot(x, y, 'o',
    label='Measured data; A=%.2f, B=%.2f' % (A, exp(B)))
plot(x, exp(polyval(p, x)), '-',
    label='Linear regression; A=%.2f, B=%.2f' % (p[0], exp(p[1])))
legend(loc='best')
```

The regression is performed in the call to the function polyfit(). This time, I've passed x and log(y) as values allowing a linear regression on log(y) or an exponential regression on y. You can see the results of this regression in Figure 8-5.

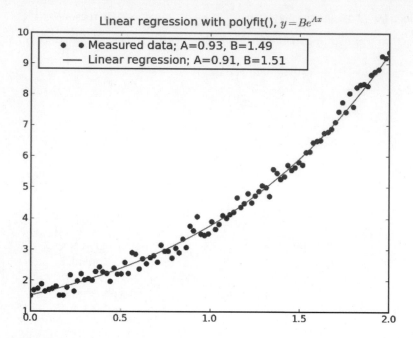

Figure 8-5. *Fitting exponential data*

Example: Approximating Functions with Polynomials

Another set of problems solvable with `polyfit()` is approximation of functions using inter-polation. The motivation behind this is a simple implementation of known functions. For the purpose of this example, we'll approximate the function sin(x).

The idea is to create a polynomial that passes through known interpolation points—that is, calculate the value of sin(x) for known n values of x, and then create a polynomial of degree n − 1 that passes through all these points.

We start by selecting a set of points from 0 to π/2; these will be our interpolation points. Values outside this range can be computed using trigonometry identities and the interpolation function. We select five points for interpolation, thus deciding the degree of the interpolation polynomial to be 4. Once the points are selected, we calculate the sine of these points.

For the purpose of this example, I've chosen sine values that can be easily computed using the `sqrt()` function. You might argue that I'm cheating here, because I'm using a nonlinear function (square root) to calculate sin(x) and not purely polynomials. But you've already seen how to calculate the square root of a number using Newton's method in Chapter 7.

■**Tip** The selection of interpolation points is an interesting topic, and work by the mathematician Pafnuty Chebyshev has contributed much to the topic. See `http://en.wikipedia.org/wiki/Pafnuty_Chebyshev` and `http://en.wikipedia.org/wiki/Chebyshev_nodes`.

The values I'll select for interpolation are 0, 30, 45, 60, and 90 degrees. The reason I chose these values is that I know their exact sine values: 0, ½, √2/2, √3/2, and 1, respectively. Or, in vector form:

```
>>> values = [0, pi/6, pi/4, pi/3, pi/2]
>>> sines = sqrt(arange(5))/2
>>> sines
array([ 0. , 0.5, 0.70710678, 0.8660254, 1. ])
```

Given these, interpolation is straightforward:

```
>>> p = polyfit(values, sines, len(values)-1)
>>> p
array([  2.87971125e-02,  -2.04340696e-01,   2.13730075e-02,
         9.95626184e-01,   2.22044605e-16])
```

So if you were to implement sin(x), all you need is to store the values of p given previously and then write a simple routine to calculate the value of sin(x) using the polynomial. If you're using NumPy, simply call `polyfit()`.

Let's plot the difference between our implementation of sin(x) and Python's built-in sin(x) function:

```
>>> figure()
>>> x = linspace(0, pi/2, 100)
>>> plot(x, polyval(p, x)-sin(x), label='error', lw=3)
>>> grid()
>>> ylabel('polyval(p, x)-sin(x)')
>>> xlabel('x')
>>> title('Error approximating sin(x) using polyfit()')
>>> xlim(0, pi/2)
```

Figure 8-6 illustrates this difference.

Figure 8-6. *Interpolation accuracy*

The results are quite accurate, less than 0.003 at worst.

Spline Interpolation

The scipy.interpolate module adds additional interpolation functions. One of these is the spline(xp, yp, x) interpolation function. Notice that the arguments to the function spline() are ordered differently from those of the function interp(). Spline interpolation is a piecewise polynomial interpolation that adheres to specific rules to yield smooth results.

Let's turn to the previous circle example:

```
from scipy.interpolate import spline
from pylab import *
xp = linspace(0, 1, 6)
yp = sqrt(1-xp**2)
xi = linspace(0, 1, 100)
yi = interp(xi, xp, yp)
ys = spline(xp, yp, xi)
figure()
hold(True)
plot(xi, yi, '--', label='piecewise linear', lw=2)
plot(xi, ys, '-', label='spline', lw=2)
legend(loc='best')
grid()
title(r'Spline interpolation of $y=\sqrt{1-x^2}$')
xlabel('x')
```

```
ylabel('y')
axis('scaled')
axis([0, 1.2, 0, 1.2])
```

In Figure 8-7, I've compared a piecewise linear interpolation with a spline interpolation. The spline interpolation appears "smoother."

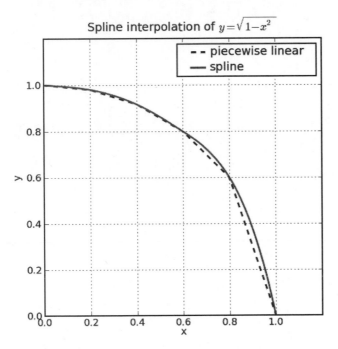

Figure 8-7. *Spline interpolation*

Solving Nonlinear Equations

In Chapter 7 we've talked about Newton's method and used it to draw fractals. Newton's method was used to solve a nonlinear equation.

The module scipy.optimize provides us with additional tools to solve nonlinear equations, as well as other optimization routines that will not be discussed here. Of those routines, I'd like to highlight three: fsolve(f, x0), bisect(f, a, b), and newton(f, x0). All these functions try to solve the equation f = 0, where f is a mathematical function implemented in Python.

Suppose we'd like to calculate $\sqrt{3}$ for the previous example. The idea is to construct a function such that the solution will be $\sqrt{3}$. This is easily done by setting $f = x^2 - 3 = 0$:

```
>>> def f(x):
...     """Returns x**2-3"""
...     return x**2-3
...
>>> f(10)
```

Let's use the functions `fsolve()`, `bisect()`, and `newton()` to calculate the roots. For `fsolve()` and `newton()`, we'll use x0 = 1, which is called the initial guess. The initial guess is a value that is close to the desired result. For `bisect()`, we need to provide a region for the search. We'll set the region to (1, 2) because we know the square root of 3 is less than 2 but greater than 1:

```
>>> from scipy import optimize
>>> optimize.fsolve(f, 1)
1.7320508075688772
>>> optimize.newton(f, 1)
1.7320508075688772
>>> optimize.bisect(f, 1, 2)
1.7320508075690668
>>> _**2
3.0000000000006564
```

Although in the simple case of square root of 3, all these functions provide accurate results, the algorithms are computationally intensive. In most these functions you can control how accurate you'd like your result to be by passing proper arguments to the functions. Of course, for a simple question as the one presented here, it's best to use `sqrt(3)`.

Special Functions

The scipy.special module provides a host of special functions that surface usually in higher mathematics and physics. These include

- Bessel functions, integrals, derivatives, and zeros of Bessel functions
- Airy functions
- Gamma functions and error functions
- Special polynomials: Legendre, Chebyshev

and many more. To use the functions, issue the following:

```
>>> from scipy import special
>>> special.chebyt(2)
poly1d([  2.00000000e+00,  -4.44089210e-16,  -1.00000000e+00])
```

For a full account, issue `help(special)`.

Signal Processing

Up to this point in the chapter, we've dealt with numerical analysis. Going forward, the topics are related to signal processing. Signal processing is a vast field that deals with signals: values that change over time. Popular signal processing algorithms include the processing of sound, such as an equalizer; others include algorithms for radars, CAT scanning, and many more.

This part of the chapter will cover some of the functionality available with the module scipy.signal and complement the discussion with examples. You'll learn about some basic algorithms to detect signals in the presence of noise and functions to design filters. However, this section is but only a taste of the topic, and I encourage you to consult with the references at the end of the chapter and professional literature for efficient signal processing algorithms.

Functions where, select, and find

The first set of functions we'll cover is where(), select(), and find().

The function find(cond) finds the indices to an array for which a condition is met:

```
>>> from pylab import *
>>> squares = arange(10)**2
>>> squares
array([ 0,  1,  4,  9, 16, 25, 36, 49, 64, 81])
>>> I = find(squares < 50)
>>> I
array([0, 1, 2, 3, 4, 5, 6, 7])
>>> squares[I]
array([ 0,  1,  4,  9, 16, 25, 36, 49])
```

We created a vector holding the squares of the numbers 0–9 and found all the indices to the vector that satisfy the condition that the squares are less than 50. Notice that the return value is a vector of indices, and if you require the values and not the indices, you have to access the original array, which is squares[I] in the preceding example.

The function where(cond, x, y) accepts three arrays of the same size: cond, x, and y, and then evaluates every element in cond. If the element evaluates to True, the return value is the corresponding element from x; if the return element evaluates to False, the return value is the corresponding element from y:

```
>>> up = arange(10)
>>> up
array([0, 1, 2, 3, 4, 5, 6, 7, 8, 9])
>>> down = arange(10, 0, -1)
>>> down
array([10,  9,  8,  7,  6,  5,  4,  3,  2,  1])
>>> highest = where(up > down, up, down)
>>> highest
array([10,  9,  8,  7,  6,  5,  6,  7,  8,  9])
```

The function select(cond, vals, default=0) adds functionality to the function where() by allowing for several conditions. The function accepts a list of conditions specified in cond and returns the corresponding element associated with vals if a condition is met; if none of the conditions are met, the default value is selected.

```
>>> up = arange(10)
>>> ramp = select([up < 4, up > 7], [4, 7], up)
>>> ramp
array([4, 4, 4, 4, 4, 5, 6, 7, 7, 7])
```

The first three elements of up are less than 4, so the condition up < 4 is met, causing the selection of value 4. The last three elements are greater than 7, causing the selection of the value 7, and values greater than or equal to 4 yet less than 7 are retained as is because the default is set to be equal to up. As a matter of fact, this functionality is called *clipping* and is available as both a method of the NumPy ndarray object and as a stand-alone function, clip().

So now that you know of the functions find(), where(), and select(), what can you do with them? The answer is simple: they're great for picking up values, what we call *detection* in signal processing.

Example: Simple Detection of Signal in Noise, Part 1

The detection of signals in the presence of noise plays an integral role in a great number of applications. For example, it is used in communication systems in the detection of signals such as radio or television broadcasts and differentiating them from noise, in medicine with the detection of an ECG signal, and more.

For the purpose of this example, we'll first construct a clean signal. By a signal, I mean a one-dimensional array (vector), where values are stored as a function of time. Our purpose will be to detect "events," which will be represented by narrow triangles placed randomly in time. There can be several events in a signal.

To generated a triangular pulse, I'll use the signal.triang() function (which is really a window function, more on that later in the chapter in the section "Window Functions"). The function generates a triangular window of a specified size. We randomly place triangular pulses in the signal vector, as shown in Listing 8-2.

Listing 8-2. *Randomly Placing Triangular Spikes*

```
from pylab import *
from scipy import signal

# parameters controlling the signal
n = 100
t = arange(n)
y = zeros(n)
num_pulses = 3
pw = 11
amp = 20

for i in range(num_pulses):
    loc = floor(rand()*(n-pw+1))
    y[loc:loc+pw] = signal.triang(pw)*amp

# add some noise
y += randn(n)

figure()
title('Signal and noise')
xlabel('t')
ylabel('y')
plot(t, y)
```

First I defined some parameters I'll be using. The number of points in the signal is n and is equal to 100. The number of triangular pulses I'll place is 3, denoted by num_pulses. Each triangular pulse will be generated using pw=11 points. The maximum value for the triangular spike will be amp, denoting amplitude.

Once I have all the parameters defined, I create two vectors: the time vector, t, and the values vector, y. The vector t is some arbitrary timestamp, in this example incrementing values starting at zero and ending at n – 1. The vector y is initially set at zero.

Next I randomly place triangular spikes. The location, loc, where the triangular spike will be placed is randomly generated with the call to the function rand() that generates a value between 0 and 1, and so I randomly pick a value between 0 and n – pw + 1 to ensure spikes aren't placed outside the vector y. Once I have all the spikes placed, I add noise by use of the function randn() that generates a normally distributed noise, also known as Gaussian distribution, or "white noise." I've chosen to use a normal distribution with variance 1 and mean 0. Notice that randn() is different from rand().

Figure 8-8 shows a randomly generated signal.

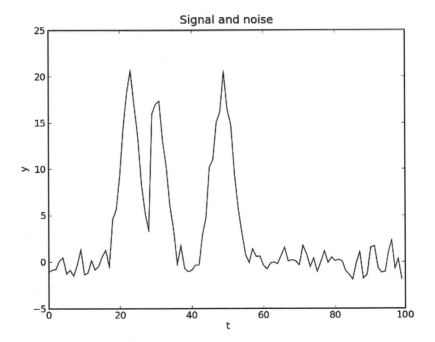

Figure 8-8. *Three triangular spikes with noise*

I did not check to see that spikes do not overlap, so as you run the script at times you'll view one or two spikes instead of three. This is fine, since we want to add some randomness to the example.

So far we've just created the signal. Now let's detect it. For detection, we'll use a simple algorithm: whenever a value is above a set threshold, we'll declare this as an event, or detection. We'll set the threshold at amp/2 and make use of the function find(), as shown in Listing 8-3.

Listing 8-3. *Detecting Signals*

```
# detect signals
thr = amp/2
I = find(y > thr)

# plot signal with noise plus detection
figure()
hold(True)
plot(t, y, 'b', label='signal with noise')
plot(t[I], y[I], 'ro', label='detections')
plot([0, n], [thr, thr], 'g--')

# annotate the threshold
text(2, thr+.2, 'Threshold', va='bottom')

title('Simple signal detection in noise')
legend(loc='best')
```

Figure 8-9 shows the result.

Figure 8-9. *Simple signal detection in the presence of noise*

Functions diff and split

Another set of functions that's of use in signal detection is `diff()` and `split()`. The function `diff(v)`, which was introduced in previous chapters, returns a vector composed of differences of elements in v. The function `split(v, indices)` splits a vector on `indices`.

```
>>> v = arange(10)
>>> split(v, [4, 8])
[array([0, 1, 2, 3]), array([4, 5, 6, 7]), array([8, 9])]
```

Example: Simple Detection of Signal in Noise, Part 2

In the previous example, you saw how to perform simple detection using `find()`. We've displayed all points that were above a specific threshold. In many occasions, we're less interested with points above a threshold because the threshold is arbitrarily chosen; we're more interested with the highest points above a threshold.

Here we pick up from the previous example. This time, we'd like to spot the peak in each detection. Listing 8-4 presents the code to do that.

Listing 8-4. *Peak Detections*

```
# peak detections
J = find(diff(I) > 1)
for K in split(I, J+1):
    ytag = y[K]
    peak = find(ytag == max(ytag))
    plot(peak+K[0], ytag[peak], 'sg', ms=7)
```

The implementation is a bit tricky, so let's walk through it. The idea is this: we split the detections into separate groups, and in each group, we find the peak and plot it.

The first problem of splitting detections makes use of the indices of detected values. A group is considered one detection if the indices are consecutive. Whenever there's a jump in indices, it means a new group:

```
>>> I = find(y > thr)
>>> I
array([ 9, 10, 11, 12, 13, 14, 42, 43, 44, 45, 46, 47, 66, 67, 68, 69, 70, 71])
```

So the group [9, 10, 11, 12, 13, 14] is one group, the group [42, 43, 44, 45, 46, 47] is the second group, and the group [66, 67, 68, 69, 70, 71] is the last group.

The function `diff(I)` will return values other than 1 whenever there's a new group. Whenever the difference is greater than 1, it means the start of a new group:

```
>>> diff(I)
array([ 1, 1, 1, 1, 1, 28, 1, 1, 1, 1, 1, 19, 1, 1, 1, 1, 1])
>>> J = find(diff(I) > 1)
>>> J
array([ 5, 11])
```

So we'd like to split on the sixth element (denoted by 5) and the twelfth element (denoted by 11). This is done with the split() function:

```
>>> split(I, J+1)
[array([ 9, 10, 11, 12, 13, 14]), array([42, 43, 44, 45, 46, 47]), array([66, 67, 68,
69, 70, 71])]
```

All that's needed now is finding the peak, which is coded as find(ytag == max(ytag)). In Figure 8-10, peak detections are marked by squares.

Figure 8-10. *Peak detections*

Waveforms

Additional SciPy functionality includes several waveforms that can be used when you're designing a signal processing algorithm or testing it. These include sawtooth(), square(), gausspulse(), and chirp():

```
from pylab import *
from scipy import signal

cycles = 10
t = arange(0, 2*pi*cycles, pi/10)

waveforms = ['sawtooth', 'square']
```

```
for i, waveform in enumerate(waveforms):
    subplot(2, 2, i+1)
    exec 'y = signal.' + waveform + '(t)'
    plot(t, y)
    title(waveform)
    axis([0, 2*pi*cycles, -1.1, 1.1])
```

Figure 8-11 shows the resulting waveforms.

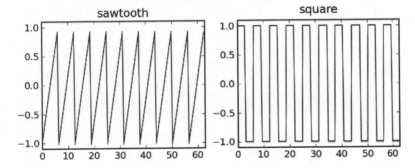

Figure 8-11. *Some waveforms*

The difference between waveforms and the triangular window used earlier is that they're repetitive, whereas triang() generates a single window.

The functions gausspulse() and chirp() are a bit more specialized; refer to the interactive help for information on using them.

Fourier Transform

Fourier transform is a linear operation that transforms a function from the *time domain* to the *frequency domain*. Much like the sound you hear can be viewed as an amplitude as a function of time, it can also be viewed by its frequency components: basses are the low frequencies of audio, for example.

The topic of Fourier transforms is quite large and requires some mathematical rigor. I will not be trying to address the topic in depth here; instead, I will show how you can use PyLab to perform Fourier transforms on sampled data.

To convert a signal from time domain to frequency domain, use fft(x). FFT, which stands for Fast Fourier Transform, is an efficient implementation of the transformation. Generally speaking, if the number of elements in x is a power of 2, the results are quite fast:

```
>>> from time import time as t
>>> t1 = t(); sum(fft(arange(2**20))); print t()-t1
(-0.013107186881825328-0.00555419921875j)
0.233999967575
>>> t1 = t(); sum(fft(arange(2**20-1))); print t()-t1
(-0.0054081712733022869+0.048980712890625j)
0.547000169754
```

The first fft() was performed on a vector the size of 2^{20}, which is a power of 2; the second one was performed on a *shorter* vector but the took longer to compute, more than twice as long, because its size is not a power of 2.

To transform data from the frequency domain to the time domain, use ifft(x).

Example: FFT of a Sampled Cosine Wave

A cosine wave is made of one frequency (actually, two frequencies if you include the negative frequency). Let's generate a cosine wave and calculate its frequency using fft(), as shown in Listing 8-5.

Listing 8-5. *Fourier Transform of a Cosine Wave*

```
N = 2**9    # we prefer powers of 2
F = 25      # a wave at 25 Hz
t = arange(N)/float(N)  # sampled over 1 second
x = cos(2*pi*t*F)   # the signal
subplot(2, 1, 1)
plot(t, x)
ylabel('x []')
xlabel('t [seconds]')
title('A cosine wave')
grid()

subplot(2, 1, 2)
f = t*N
xf = fft(x)
plot(f, abs(xf))
title('Fourier transform of a cosine wave')
xlabel('f [Hz]')
ylabel('xf []')
xlim([0, N])
grid()
```

I first defined a few parameters: N is the number of points in the signal, and f is the frequency of the cosine wave. I then created a time vector, t, which is made of evenly spaced samples between 0 and 1, representing 1 second. I then calculated the sampled cosine wave and plotted it along with its Fourier transform. I've chosen to plot the absolute of the transformed signal, seeing as Fourier transforms return complex values (albeit in this case those complex values are zero). Figure 8-12 shows the results.

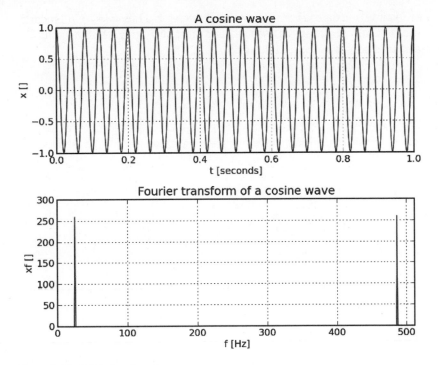

Figure 8-12. *FFT of a signal*

■**Note**   There's a frequency content at 25 Hz (the left spike), but there's also another one at 487 Hz. That's really the value corresponding to –25 Hz, that is, 512 – 25. If you'd like to view the frequency domain centered around 0 Hz, use the function `fftshift()`.

Window Functions

In the FFT example I carefully chose a cosine wave that will have a full number of cycles in 1 second, which is basically any integer number for the frequency value. The reason for this was had I chosen a noninteger value, I would've ended up with a signal that does not have full wave cycles. The problem with this signal is when you perform the FFT of the signal, you'll start seeing other frequencies and not just the frequency of your original signal. The reason for this is, in essence, FFT assumes the signal is repetitive; that is, it's not just from 0 to 1 second, it's from minus infinity to infinity. And so it treats the signal as if it's copied left and right an infinite number of times. If the signal has an integer number of cycles, it will nicely fit when copied left and right. But in reality, you can't guarantee an integer number of waves in your sampled signal, so you'll start seeing these sampling effects. To minimize the effect, we can use a window function.

Several window functions such as hamming(), hanning(), bartlett(), and kaiser() help minimize this effect but with a cost: the signal itself is also distorted. To use a window, multiply it by the time-domain vector, as shown in Listing 8-6.

Listing 8-6. *Hamming Window*

```
N = 2**9   # we prefer powers of 2
F = 25.5   # wave frequency
t = arange(N)/float(N)  # sampled over 1 second
f = t*N    # frequency domain
x = cos(2*pi*t*F)   # the signal
xh = x*hamming(512) # multiply with a hamming window
plot(f, abs(fft(x)), 's-', label='original')
plot(f, abs(fft(xh)), 'o-', label='with Hamming')
xlim([0, 50])
xticks(arange(0, 55, 5))
legend()
grid()
title('Signal with Hamming window')
xlabel('Frequency [Hz]')
ylabel('Amplitude []')
```

I've plot the FFT of two vectors: the original and the one with a Hamming window. In Figure 8-13, you can see I've zoomed on the 25.5 Hz frequency to show the effects of the window function.

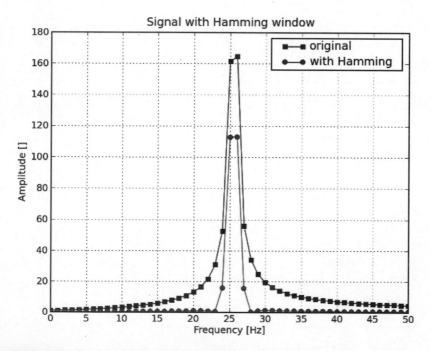

Figure 8-13. *Signal with Hamming window*

The scipy.signal module provides additional window functions. To access these, issue

```
>>> from scipy import signal
>>> help(signal)
```

and scroll down to the window functions section.

Filtering

One of the reasons to transform a time-domain signal to a frequency-domain signal is for the purpose of filtering. A *filter* is an operation that changes a signal. Much like filters in your kitchen sink, filters let some frequencies pass (water), while stopping other frequencies (large food remains). Filters are used in a variety of applications, ranging from audio to radar systems.

Filters are categorized by their behavior. A filter that lets through low frequencies and stops high frequencies is called a low-pass filter (LPF). Similarly, a high-pass filter (HPF) will allow only high frequencies to pass. There are also other categorizations such as band-pass filters (allows only a specific band of frequencies), band-stop filters (allows anything but a specific band of frequencies), and notch filters (suppresses very few frequencies).

Filters are further categorized by their behavior to an impulse input—that is, the output of the filter as a function of time assuming you were to input a short spike to the filter. Filters that eventually will forget the impulse are known as finite-impulse-response (FIR) filters, and filters that never forget are known as infinite-impulse-response (IIR) filters. From a very simplistic approach, if a filter does not rely on previous outputs (no feedback), it is considered an FIR; otherwise, it's an IIR.

Filter Design

Assuming you know what filter you wish to design, this section will help you do so. Filter design is an advanced topic, and as such this section is meant for those who require a few pointers on designing filters in Python with SciPy.

The scipy.signal module includes several functions to help design a filter. The function iirdesign() is used for designing an IIR filter. It is quite complete, and it's best to read the online help and follow it through. Other useful IIR design filters include butter(), cheby1(), cheby2(), and ellip(). FIR filter design functionality is provided with functions remez() and firwin(). I won't be covering those, but should you need to use them, the online help is quite informative. Finally, if you'd like to view the frequency response of a filter, use the functions freqz() and freqs().

The code in Listing 8-7 will design a low-pass Butterworth filter (an IIR filter) and plot its frequency response.

Listing 8-7. *Frequency Response of a Filter*

```
N = 256      # number of points for freqz
Wc = 0.2     # 3dB point
Order = 3    # filter order

# design a Butterworth filter
[b, a] = signal.butter(Order, Wc)

# calculate the frequency response
[w, h] = signal.freqz(b, a, N)

# plot the results
figure()

subplot(2, 1, 1)
plot(arange(N)/float(N), 20*log10(abs(h)), lw=2)
title('Frequency response')
xlabel('Frequency (normalized)')
ylabel('dB')
ylim(ylim()[0], ylim()[1]+5)
grid()

subplot(2, 1, 2)
plot(arange(N)/float(N), 20*log10(abs(h)), lw=2)
title('Frequency response (3dB point)')
xlabel('Frequency (normalized)')
ylabel('dB')
text(Wc+.02, -3, '3dB point', va='bottom')
ylim([-3, 0.1])
grid()
```

I've made use of two functions: `butter()` and `freqz()`. The function `butter()` designs an IIR filter with specified parameters (order and cutoff frequency), and the function `freqz()` returns a frequency response. Note that the frequency response is a complex number, and so I've plot the amplitude in dB of the absolute value: `20*log10(abs(h))`, as shown in Figure 8-14.

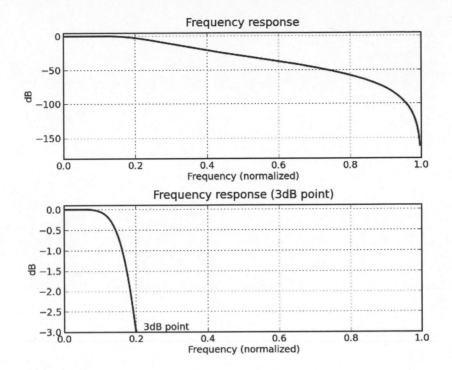

Figure 8-14. *Frequency response of a low-pass filter*

To filter data given a specific filter, use the function scipy.lfilter(b, a, x). Let's turn to an example.

Example: Heart-Rate Monitor

For the purpose of this example, I'll generate a signal that *simulates* the data generated from a heart-rate monitor connected to a patient. Please do not use this in any sort of production system; it's merely for educational purposes (and not meant to truly represent heart signals!).

The patient walks around, and as a result, two signals are picked up: 1) the heart signal and 2) a signal associated with the patient's movement, or what is typically referred to as a *movement artifact*. Listing 8-8 shows these signals in my simulation.

Listing 8-8. *Heart Rate Simulation*

```
# heart signal simulation
N = 256     # number of samples per second
T = 2       # number of seconds
hr = 1.67   # 100 beats per minutes
F1 = 0.5    # movement frequency

t = arange(T*N)/float(N)
y1 = 5*sin(2*pi*t*F1)      # movement artifact
```

```
# add heart signals
y2 = zeros(size(y1))
for i in range(int(T*hr)):
    y2[i*N/hr:i*N/hr+10] = signal.triang(10)

# combine movement with beats
y = y1+y2

# create a high-pass filter
[b, a] = signal.butter(3, 0.05, 'high')

# filter the signal
yn = signal.lfilter(b, a, y)

# plot the graphs
figure()

subplot(2, 1, 1)
title('Heart signal with movement artifact (simulation)')
plot(t, y, lw=2)
xlabel('t [seconds]')
ylabel('Amplitude []')

subplot(2, 1, 2)
title('Filtered signal')
plot(t, yn, lw=2)
xlabel('t [seconds]')
ylabel('Amplitude []')
```

I've defined several parameters that control the script. The value N is equal to the number of samples per second (some are used to name this value Fs, which stands for frequency of sampling). The value T is the total number of seconds, in this case 2 whole seconds. The value hr is the patient's heart rate, 100 beats per minute: 100 / 60 = 1.67 Hz. Lastly, I defined the movement artifact frequency at 0.5 Hz. I then construct a time vector, t, and a movement artifact vector, v1, and add "beats" with triangular waveforms using the signal.triang() function.

Now that I have a heart signal with a movement artifact, I turn to filter out the movement artifact. I design a second-order Butterworth HPF to do so via the call to signal.butter() and use the filter parameters to filter the signal using signal.lfilter(). Figure 8-15 shows the resulting plot.

Figure 8-15. *Filtering a signal*

Example: Moving Average

On many occasions, filtering is used to "smooth" a signal. A simple algorithm is that of a moving average. For every two consecutive points, we calculate the average and use that value instead. The points are overlapping, so a result of using the algorithm on the vector [1, 2, 0, 2] would be [1.5, 1, 1]. But why stop at two samples? Moving average can be performed on several points, returning the average of those points. In Python, you could write

```
>>> from pylab import *
>>> N = 512
>>> t = linspace(0, 10, N)
>>> x = 1-exp(-t) +randn(N)/10
>>> W = 32  # num points in moving average
>>> xf = zeros(len(x)-W+1)
>>> for i in range(len(x)-W+1):
...     xf[i] = mean(x[i:i+W])
...
>>> plot(t, x)
>>> hold(True)
>>> plot(t[W-1:], xf, lw=3)
>>> title('Moving average')
>>> legend(['signal with noise', 'filtered signal'])
>>> xlabel('t [seconds]')
>>> ylabel('x []')
```

This is a straightforward implementation using a for loop. The input to the filter is arbitrarily chosen as 1 − exp(−t) plus noise.

There is an easier approach. A moving average is an FIR filter with all its elements equal to 1/W, where W is the length of the moving average window. In this case, a quick-and-simple way to implement a moving average filter instead of the for loop is by calling the signal. lfilter() function and passing ones(W)/W as the filter values:

```
>>> from scipy import signal
>>> xf = signal.lfilter(ones(W)/W, 1, x)
```

Figure 8-16 shows the results of plotting a moving average.

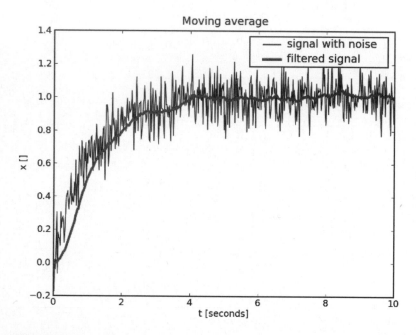

Figure 8-16. *Moving average*

Final Notes and References

The purpose of this chapter is to serve as a cookbook of algorithms in numerical analysis and signal processing. I took great care to limit the amount of math used in the examples and yet still be informative.

The topics covered in the chapter are far too great to be explored in one book, let alone one chapter. If you find these topics of interest, the following may provide additional information:

- *Numerical Recipes: The Art of Scientific Computing, Third Edition* by William H. Press, Saul A. Teukolsky, William T. Vetterling, and Brian P. Flannery (Cambridge University Press, 2007; for more information, see http://www.nr.com)

- SciPy, http://www.scipy.org/

CHAPTER 9

■■■

Image Processing
Two-Dimensional Data

Up to this point we've mostly dealt with one-dimensional data, that is, graphs and data made of essentially a series of values. We've plotted the data, analyzed it, and created an image that was later saved to file or displayed to screen.

However, image data files, or the image on your screen, is two dimensional. It is made of pixels (which is short for picture elements), each pixel having a location in two dimensions, x and y, and a value corresponding to the color. In this chapter we turn to manipulating images on the pixel level, that is, operating on the two-dimensional matrix of pixels.

Operations on images are similar to operations performed on one-dimensional data. Slicing a 1-D array of values and adding those values to another array is equivalent to copying and pasting images. Saving an array to file is equivalent to writing images in TIFF or JPEG format. So in a sense, image processing is equivalent to signal processing, only that the signals now have two dimensions.

Copying and pasting, resizing, and cropping are all simple operations supported by most GUI-based graphics applications. But with a GUI application, it's harder to perform these operations in a systematic and automated manner, for example, resizing several images and then combining them together to form a collage of images. It's doable in GUI applications, but it's typically not as easy and requires some user skills. Other simple image operations include converting file formats, rotating images, and cropping them. I'll cover these image operations, as well as how to automate them, so results are consistent.

We'll also deal with data on a numerical level, that is, reading the image, transforming it into a NumPy matrix, and then operating on the matrix itself. I'll show how you can implement some interesting algorithms that involve image processing. Lastly, I'll touch on some more complex topics such as filtering, which is the act of modifying a picture to enhance the visual output.

The basic package we'll use for all these operations is the Python Imaging Library, or PIL for short. Be sure to install PIL per the guidelines in Chapter 2. We'll also be relying on NumPy and matplotlib.

It is assumed you have read Chapter 6 and Chapter 7; the text here will rely on the material covered in those chapters to discuss topics related to image processing.

Reading, Writing, and Displaying Images

The Python Imaging Library provides us with several classes that enable image processing. The basic class, Image, supports image operations such as reading an image from file, writing an image to file, copying and pasting, resizing, and rotating.

Reading Images from File

Let's get started. To use the Image class, import it as follows:

```
>>> from PIL import Image
```

■**Note** Going forward, I'll assume you've issued from PIL import Image and will refrain from mention-ing the import statement. It's also possible to simply to write import Image instead of from PIL import Image.

Our first operation is reading an image file. Since we currently don't have any images, let's generate an image and read it from file. We'll use matplotlib patches for this, as shown in Listing 9-1. (If you're not familiar with matplotlib patches, refer to Chapter 6.)

Listing 9-1. *Creating an Image*

```
>>> from pylab import *
>>> figure()
>>> gca().add_patch(Circle((0, 0), 1))
>>> axis('off')
>>> axis('scaled')
>>> savefig('../images/circle.png')
```

The code in Listing 9-1 draws a filled circle and saves it to file ../images/circle.png.

■**Tip** I've used matplotlib to create an image file to work with, but you just as well could use any image file, for example, a JPEG picture you took with your digital camera.

Our first operation is to read the file and attach it to an Image object:

```
>>> im = Image.open('../images/circle.png')
```

■**Note** In accordance with the directory structure presented in Chapter 2, I assume that you're currently running from directory Ch9/src and that directory Ch9/images holds image files. If that is not the case, be sure to change the path to the images in the examples provided in this chapter.

Image Attributes

Now that we have an `Image` object associated with an image file, we can query the object's attributes:

```
>>> im.size
(815, 615)        (w, h)
>>> im.info
{'dpi': (100, 100)}
>>> im.mode
'RGBA'
>>> im.format
'PNG'
>>> im.filename
'../images/circle.png'
```

This is quite a bit of information. We know that the image size is 815×615 pixels wide, the resolution is 100 dpi, the mode is RGBA (we'll get to modes a little later in the chapter in the section "Creating New Images"), the image format is PNG, and the file associated with the object we've created is `../images/circle.png`.

Example: Image Catalog

My experience with analyzing image data is that images are not always taken in a consistent manner. This means that you, the programmer, have to manually crop, resize, enhance, or even delete images. This also translates into maintaining a catalog file of some sorts. An approach I found helpful is creating an automated catalog file and then annotating information as I work with data (see Chapter 4 for discussion of catalog files).

The purpose of this example is to create a basic image catalog file. The script makes use of the `Image` attributes presented in the previous section and creates a CSV catalog file in the parent directory of the searched directory. The catalog file has an extension `.cat.csv`. That is, if you're searching `/home/user`, a catalog file will be created named `/home/user.cat.csv`. The catalog file includes the name, size, format, and resolution of each image (see Listing 9-2).

Listing 9-2. *Creating an Image Catalog*

```python
from PIL import Image
import os, csv

def image_catalog(srchpath):
    """Creates a catalog file named srchpath.cat.csv."""

    # the CSV header
    catalog = [['Filename', 'Pathname', 'Format', 'Size', 'Resolution' ]]

    # walk directory tree
    for root, dirs, files in os.walk(srchpath):
        for file in files:
            pathname = os.path.join(root, file)
```

```
    try:
        img = Image.open(pathname)
        filesize = os.path.getsize(pathname)
        catalog.append([file, pathname, img.format,
            img.size, img.info])
    except IOError:      # not an image
        pass
```

```
# create the clean catalog
f = open(srchpath+'.cat.csv','wb')
csv.writer(f).writerows(catalog)
f.close()
```

The script defines a function named image_catalog(), which accepts the directory to search and produces an image catalog file in CSV format. The variable catalog is a list of rows containing image information. We iterate through the directory and look for images with the Easier to Ask Forgiveness than Permission (EAFP) approach: try to open a file as if it were an image file. In case of success, the catalog is updated. If the file is not an image, exception IOError is raised, and we pass this file.

■**Note** If your directory is supposed to contain strictly images, you might want to add a print statement before the pass notifying the user that a nonimage file was encountered.

Here are the results I got from running the script in directory images (contents of file images.cat.csv):

img.format
img.size   *img.info*

```
Filename,Pathname,Format,Size,Resolution
nightsky1.png,../images/nightsky1.png,PNG,"(815, 615)","{'dpi': (100, 100)}"
nightsky2.png,../images/nightsky2.png,PNG,"(815, 615)","{'dpi': (100, 100)}"
circle.png,../images/circle.png,PNG,"(815, 615)","{'dpi': (100, 100)}"
nightsky.png,../images/nightsky.png,PNG,"(815, 615)","{'dpi': (100, 100)}"
collage.png,../images/collage.png,PNG,"(600, 600)",{}
```

Displaying Images

You can view an image by calling the Image method show(). The method in turn calls the operating system's *default* image viewer, which is usually provided by the OS. To use a different viewer from the one supplied by the OS, associate the image with an image viewer you desire. The following will display the image ../images/circle.png created previously:

```
>>> Image.open('../images/circle.png').show()
```

Converting File Formats

One of the common operations we perform on images is converting the image file format. It's important for a couple of reasons: because we want to store images in a more efficient format using compression, or because the application that accepts the image requires a different format.

The Image method save() enables saving an image to file in a specified image format. There are two methods to specify a format: with a file name extension and by explicitly specifying the format argument.

Assuming you've created an image file ../images/circle.png per the previous listing, you can read the image and convert the file format to a JPEG file format, as shown in Listing 9-3.

Listing 9-3. *Converting PNG to JPEG*

```
>>> im = Image.open('../images/circle.png')
>>> im.save('../images/circle.jpg')                  # convert to jpeg        ①
>>> import os
>>> [fn for fn in os.listdir('../images') if fn.startswith('circle')]
['circle.jpg', 'circle.png']
```

In this particular example, you're not really converting the file, rather creating another file with a different image format (converting would mean that you also delete the original file).

Or, you could create a function to convert an image to JPEG format, as shown in Listing 9-4.

Listing 9-4. *A Function to Convert an Image to JPEG Format*

```
from PIL import Image
from os.path import splitext

def ConvertToJpeg(filename):
    """Convert an image file to a Jpeg file."""

    jpegname = splitext(filename)[0]+'.jpg'
    Image.open(filename).save(jpegname)
```

I've made use of the splitext() function, which is part of the os module to replace the original extension with a .jpg extension. The .jpg extension instructs the save() function to create a JPEG file.

As mentioned, you can also explicitly specify a format:

```
>>> im = Image.open('../images/circle.png')
>>> im.save('../images/circle', format='Jpeg')        # convert        ②
>>> [fn for fn in os.listdir('../images') if fn.startswith('circle')]
['circle.png', 'circle']
```

In this case, save() does not add an extension to the file name (that is, the file created is circle, not circle.jpg).

PIL supports a large number of file formats. Most popular image formats can be read by the Image class. Furthermore, most images can be saved using known file formats including JPEG, TIFF, and PNG. However, some image formats can only be read. Other formats such as MPEG (video files) are supported in identify mode only. For a full account, refer to the PIL handbook: http://www.pythonware.com/library/pil/handbook/index.htm.

Example: A Function to Convert All Images in a Directory to JPEG Format

A direct continuation of the idea presented previously is to write a function that iterates through a directory and converts all images to JPEG format, as shown in Listing 9-5. We'll keep the original image as well because JPEG uses a lossy compression algorithm, which might lower the original image quality. However, you can easily modify the example to remove the original images.

Listing 9-5. *Converting All Images in a Directory to JPEG*

```
import os, csv
from PIL import Image

def ConvertDirToJpeg(srchdir):
    """Converts all images in a directory to a jpeg file."""

    # walk directory tree
    for root, dirs, files in os.walk(srchdir):
        for file in files:
            # pathname holds the image file name
            pathname = os.path.join(root, file)
            try:
                # convert the file to a JPEG file
                img = Image.open(pathname)
                jpegname = os.path.splitext(pathname)[0]+'.jpg'
                if os.path.exists(jpegname):
                    print "Did not create %s; file already exists." % jpegname
                else:
                    img.save(jpegname)
                    print "Created file "+jpegname
            except IOError:      # oops, not an image
                pass
```

The script again makes use of the EAFP approach: try to open a file as an image and if all goes well, convert it to a JPEG image. To run the function, enter ConvertDirToJpeg(dirname).

■**Note** In case the function ConvertDirToJpeg() is called with a nonexisting directory, no output is generated, not even a warning message. If you require such functionality, be sure to modify the function and include it.

Image Manipulation

So now we can read images, display them, and convert file formats. But in converting file formats, we haven't really changed the image, we merely saved it in a different format.

In this section we turn to perform basic image manipulations, that is, modifying the contents of an image: cutting and pasting, cropping, and rotating.

Creating New Images

PIL provides us with the ability to create images, not just read them from file. This is especially useful when you want to copy and paste images from other sources to a new image. The syntax for creating a new image is Image.new(mode, size, color=0). The mode argument can take one of the values listed in Table 9-1.

Table 9-1. *Image Modes*

Mode	Description
'1'	1 bit per pixel; useful for black-and-white images
'L'	1 byte per pixel (values from 0 to 255), black and white; useful for working with one color band (see the discussion about color later in the chapter).
'RGB'	Red, green, and blue, 1 byte per color, also known as true color. RGB is common when the image background is black such as on a screen monitor.
'RGBA'	Red, green, blue, and a transparency mask, 1 byte per color; common in several file formats including PNG.
'CMYK'	Cyan, magenta, yellow, and black, 1 byte per color. CMYK is common in print.

There are additional image modes, but I won't be covering them in this chapter. To view the list of available modes, issue

```
>>> from PIL import Image
>>> Image.MODES
['1', 'CMYK', 'F', 'I', 'L', 'P', 'RGB', 'RGBA', 'RGBX', 'YCbCr']
```

Refer to the PIL web site for additional information: http://www.pythonware.com/products/pil/index.htm.

The size argument in the Image.new() function is a two-element tuple detailing the width and height of the image. The color argument is a function of the mode. For example, in the case of an RGB image, the color is a tuple in the form (red, green, blue); in case of CMYK, the color takes the form (cyan, magenta, yellow, black).

```
>>> im1 = Image.new('L', (800, 600)) # black, one-band image
>>> im2 = Image.new('CMYK', (800, 600), (0, 255, 0, 0)) # magenta image
>>> im3 = Image.new('RGB', (800, 600), (255, 0, 0)) # red image
```

Copy and Paste

The methods copy() and paste() allow copying images and pasting images into other images, respectively. The method copy() requires no parameters and creates a copy of the current image. The method paste(im, xy) pastes the image im into the current image; the xy argument is a tuple indicating the (x, y) location to paste (top left). Let's turn to an example that uses the paste() method.

Example: Fractal Collage

In this example we make use of the functions new(), open(), paste(), and save() to create a collage of images. To follow along, you'll need to modify the fractal script presented in Chapter 7 in Listing 7-1 so that it's a function instead of a script. The function should be named fractal(delta, res, iter) and return an Image object representing the fractal. Refer to the Appendix for a listing of the function. Once you create the function, save it under Ch9/src/fractal_func.py.

Armed with the function fractal(delta, res, iter), we create a fractal collage, as shown in Listing 9-6.

Listing 9-6. *A Collage of Fractals*

```
from PIL import Image

# define the function fractal; assuming it's in file 'fractal_func.py'
execfile('fractal_func.py')

fsize = 200      # small fractal image width and height
nx = 3           # number of images, width
ny = 3           # number of images, height
collage = Image.new("RGB", (fsize*nx, fsize*ny))
for i in range(ny):
    for j in range(nx):
        im = fractal(0.000001, fsize, i*nx+j+1)
        print "Processing image %d of %d" % (i*nx+j+1, nx*ny)
        collage.paste(im, (fsize*j, fsize*i))
collage.save('../images/collage.png')
```

The script generates fractals with increasing numbers of iterations and pastes them into an image that serves as the image collage. The arguments to the paste() method are chosen so that the images are pasted from top left to bottom right. I've saved the image to file ../images/collage.png.

The result from running this script is shown in Figure 7-1 in Chapter 7.

Crop and Resize

Cropping and resizing modify an existing image. The function crop() selects part of the original image, and the function resize() resizes an existing image, that is, scales it so it fits the new size.

Assuming you have run the previous collage example, you should now have a file named collage.png. The function crop() accepts a tuple of four values, detailing the box to crop: (x0, y0, x1, y1). Let's read the collage.png file and crop it to show only 2 by 2 images from the fractal collage:

```
>>> img = Image.open('../images/collage.png')
>>> img.size
(600, 600)
>>> cropped_img = img.crop((0, 0, 400, 400))
>>> cropped_img.show()
```

[handwritten: x₀ y₀ , x₁ y₁]

Suppose you want to show the entire image, but scaled to size (400, 400); in this case you'd use the resize(xy) function, where xy is a two-element tuple detailing the width and height of the resized image:

```
>>> img = Image.open('../images/collage.png')
>>> img.size
(600, 600)
>>> resized_img = img.resize((400, 400))
>>> resized_img.show()
>>> resized_img.size
(400, 400)
```

[handwritten: # a resized copy is produced]

You can also use the method thumbnail(), which is similar to resize(). The difference is that resize() returns a modified image copy, whereas thumbnail() modifies the image itself.

```
>>> img.thumbnail((400, 400))
>>> img.size
(400, 400)
```

In both resize() and thumbnail() methods you can provide a filter argument that determines the method of resampling. The acceptable values are Image.NEAREST (default), Image.BILINEAR, Image.BICUBIC, and Image.ANTIALIAS (best quality). Antialiasing has the best results but might take longer to compute:

```
>>> img.thumbnail((400, 400), Image.ANTIALIAS)
```

Rotate

Lastly on our list of basic operations is the rotate() function. The function rotate(theta) rotates an image theta degrees.

From a user's perspective, rotating is a basic operation, for example, rotating a scanned document by a few degrees so it's properly displayed. But in reality, rotation isn't such a basic operation; it requires changing the width and height of the image. In the case of rotating by 90 degrees (or multiples), the rotate() function knows to swap the x-axis and the y-axis, but in case of other rotation values, both axes change, so the total area of the image changes. You can control whether you want rotate() to expand the image so it includes the entire rotated image or not by passing expand=True or expand=False, respectively.

```
                                    w   h
>>> img = Image.new('RGB', (200, 300), (0, 0, 255))      # blue rectangle
>>> img30 = img.rotate(30)
>>> img30.show()
>>> img30.size
(200, 300)
>>> img30e = img.rotate(30, expand=True)
>>> img30e.show()
>>> img30e.size
(324, 360)
```

In the first line I've created a simple blue image that is 200 pixels wide and 300 pixels high. I've then rotated the image 30 degrees with and without expanding. The results are shown in Figure 9-1. *Before rotation, the (blue) image coincided with the black*

Figure 9-1. *Rotated images: the left is not expanded, the right is expanded.*

Image Annotation

Annotating images is just as important as annotating graphs. However, in some cases, annotating an image with text disrupts the pleasing visual result. That's probably why it's less common in pictures. There's also the issue of what color to choose. In cases where the picture is mostly white, you probably want to choose nonwhite annotation.

In this section we'll cover text annotation as well as geometrical shapes to highlight specific image features.

Annotating with Geometrical Shapes

PIL provides us with the ImageDraw object, which allows annotations of an existing image. To import the ImageDraw object, issue from PIL import ImageDraw. To use the ImageDraw object, attach it to an existing image:

```
>>> from PIL import Image, ImageDraw
>>> img = Image.new('RGB', (200, 300), (0, 0, 255))
>>> draw = ImageDraw.Draw(img)
```

I've created an `ImageDraw` object named `draw` and attached it to the image `img`. Going forward, operations performed with the `ImageDraw` object will be performed on the `Image` object:

```
>>> draw.line((100, 100, 200, 200))
>>> img.show()
```

This will draw a line from (100, 100) to (200, 200).

You can use the functions in Table 9-2 to annotate an image. In the table, assume draw = ImageDraw.Draw(Image).   *[after … image is like the canvas ?]*

Table 9-2. *Some ImageDraw Functions*

Function	Description	Example
arc(xybox, start, end)	Draws an arc, a part of the circle bound by the rectangle xybox (tuple of four elements), starting at angle start and ending at angle end.	draw.arc((100, 100, 200, 200), 90, 180) will draw a quarter of a circle.
chord(xybox, start, end)	Similar to arc(), also draws a line connecting the arc edges.	draw.chord((0, 0, 100, 100), 90, 180)
ellipse(xybox)	Draws an ellipse bound by the four-element tuple xybox. If you'd like a circle, use a square for the xybox values.	draw.ellipse((50, 50, 150, 100))
line(xyseq)	Draws lines connecting elements in the sequence xyseq.	draw.line([0, 0, 10, 10, 20, 10, 20, 20])
point(xy)	Draws a point at location xy.	draw.point((40, 40))
polygon(xyseq)	Draws a polygon connecting elements in the sequence xyseq. The difference from the line() function is that the polygon is always a closed shape, allowing the use of the fill argument.	draw.polygon([10, 20, 40, 40, 50, 30, 70, 80])
rectangle(xybox)	Draws a rectangle specified by the four-element tuple xybox.	draw.rectangle((20, 60, 80, 140), fill=128)

The `ImageDraw` annotation functions accept the following optional arguments: `fill`, which determines the color of the annotation or the fill object (similar to the `facecolor` argument in matplotlib); `outline`, which determines the line to draw the object (similar to the matplotlib `edgecolor` argument); and `font`, in case of text annotations.

Text Annotations

Other than geometrical shapes, `ImageDraw` also provides text annotation with the function `text(xy, string)`:

```
>>> from PIL import Image, ImageDraw
>>> img = Image.new('L', (160, 160), 255)
>>> draw = ImageDraw.Draw(img)
>>> draw.ellipse((0, 0, 160, 160), fill=128)     # grey circle
>>> draw.text((80, 80), 'A long string')
>>> img.show()
```

Originally, I had intended on having the text centered horizontally. However, the text string has width, so I require a method to calculate the width and height of the text in pixels. Once I have the width and height, I can draw the text at location (80 – width/2, 80 – height/2). This is done using the function textsize():

```
>>> from PIL import Image, ImageDraw
>>> img = Image.new('L', (160, 160), 255)
>>> draw = ImageDraw.Draw(img)
>>> draw.ellipse((0, 0, 160, 160), fill=128)
>>> s = 'A long string'
>>> width, height = draw.textsize(s)
>>> width, height
(78, 11)
>>> draw.text((80-width/2, 80-height/2), s)     # or use (160-width)/2, (160-height)/2
>>> img.show()
```

Figure 9-2 shows the results with and without taking into consideration the string width and height.

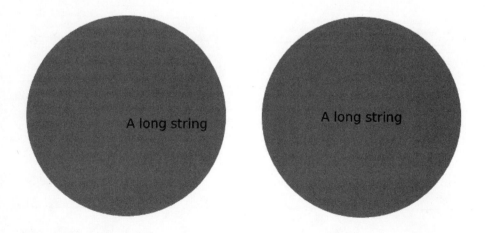

Figure 9-2. *Text annotation using text() and textsize()*

Fonts

It's also possible to use other fonts with the text() function. To do so, first create an ImageFont object. The ImageFont object is part of PIL, and to import it, issue from PIL import ImageFont. Once ImageFont is imported, you can use a font with a call to ImageFont.truetype(fontname, size). The returned ImageFont object can be passed as an argument to the text() function by means of the font argument.

Of course, to be able to use fonts, they must first be installed in your system. Windows typically comes with built-in fonts; and on Linux fonts are usually installed with X (as well as other applications). You can also use fonts from the GNU FreeFont project (http://www.gnu.org/software/freefont/).

However, font and font names are different on varying systems, and not just different operating systems: my Windows system might have different fonts than your Windows system. This means calling ImageFont.truetype(fontname, size) might work on one system and not on another. To overcome this problem, I use the function findfont(), which is part of the matplotlib.font_manager module. The function findfont() returns a string with the location of a font that best matches the requested font.

The following script annotates text with the Vera font using the findfont() function:

```
>>> from matplotlib import font_manager
>>> from PIL import Image, ImageDraw, ImageFont
>>> img = Image.new('L', (250, 100), 192)
>>> draw = ImageDraw.Draw(img)
>>> font_str = font_manager.findfont('Vera')
>>> font_str
'/usr/lib/python2.5/site-packages/matplotlib/mpl-data/fonts/ttf/Vera.ttf'
>>> ttf = ImageFont.truetype(font_str, 54)
>>> s = 'ABCabc'
>>> (w, h) = draw.textsize(s, font = ttf)
>>> draw.text((((250-w)/2, (100-h)/2), 'ABCabc', font = ttf)
>>> img.show()
```

The first two statements import the proper objects from PIL as well as matplotlib's font manager. I then create a one-band image of size (250, 100) followed by the instantiation of an ImageDraw object attached to the image.

Next I use matplotlib's findfont() function to find a font that's closest to the font Vera. The path to the font is stored in the string font_str. Following that I create an ImageFont object named ttf and use that font object to render the text. I then calculate the size of the text and render it in the middle of a gray background, as shown in Figure 9-3.

Figure 9-3. *Font rendering*

■**Note** To use a font, you must supply the font argument in calls to both functions text() and textsize().

Example: Thumbnail Index Image

In a previous example we've created a catalog of images. While that catalog is quite useful, it doesn't show the contents of those images. A more useful catalog perhaps would be a collage of the images annotated with text showing each image's file name (see Listing 9-7).

Listing 9-7. *Thumbnail Index Image*

```
# thumbnail index
import os
from PIL import Image, ImageDraw

def thumbnail_index(dirpath):
    """Create a thumbnail index from images in dirpath."""

    num_images = 5                    # no, of images in row, col
    thumb_size = (128, 96)
    cat_size = (num_images*thumb_size[0], num_images*thumb_size[1])

    fn_index = 0              # file name index
    img_index = 0            # image index

    # go through all the pictures in a directory
    for file in os.listdir(dirpath):
        # get the pathname for the file
        pathname = os.path.join(dirpath, file)

        try:    # is this an image file?

            # open the image file
            img = Image.open(pathname)

        except IOError:
            print file, "is not an image file"
            continue

        # create a thumbnail
        img.thumbnail((thumb_size), Image.ANTIALIAS)
        draw = ImageDraw.Draw(img)
        draw.text((2, 2), file)

        # do we need to create a new catalog image?
        if img_index == 0:
            thumbs_img = Image.new('RGB', cat_size)

        # calculate the location for this image
        x = img_index % num_images
        y = img_index // num_images
```

```
    # paste the thumbnail
    thumbs_img.paste(img, (x*thumb_size[0], y*thumb_size[1]))

    # increment the image index
    img_index += 1

    # have we reached the end of the catalog image?
    if img_index == num_images**2:
        img_index = 0
        thumbs_img.save('%s-%03d.cat.jpg' % (dirpath, fn_index))
        fn_index += 1

# save the last catalog file
if img_index:
    thumbs_img.save('%s-%03d.cat.jpg' % (dirpath, fn_index))
```

The function thumnail_index() accepts a directory and produces a thumbnail index image. Figure 9-4 shows the result from running the function on a collection of images my daughter particularly likes.

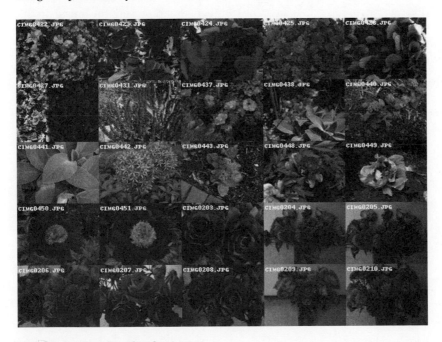

Figure 9-4. *Thumbnail index image*

For the purpose of this example, I decided not to use os.walk() and iterate through the directory listing, instead using os.listdir(). I've defined two parameters: num_images, which holds the number of images on either x- or y-axis, and thumb_size, which holds the thumbnail width and height. Next I composed a list of all the files in the requested directory. For every file, the script tries to open the file as if it were an image file. If indeed a file is an image file, a thumbnail of the image is created and pasted to the index image. Additionally, the thumbnail is annotated with the file name in the top-left corner. There's some indexing used to determine the exact location of an image in the thumbnail index image as well as creating a new thumbnail index image once the current one has filled up.

Tip An alternative approach to displaying the text directly on the thumbnail image is to display it below the image. This can be done by adding a black (or white) stripe between rows of images.

Image Processing

So far we've performed tasks that can also be performed by most GUI-based image editing applications such as GIMP, the GNU Image Manipulation Program (http://www.gimp.org/). However, GUI-based applications have a GUI user in mind and are not easily automated. We now turn to explore possibilities of writing scripts to automatically perform operations on images.

Furthermore, as you start thinking about higher-level image processing algorithms, you may realize you require access to the actual data, the numbers that represent the image. In this section, we'll also show how this can be achieved.

A word of caution: image processing is a vast field. I won't be covering even the basics here, rather showing that if you do have an image processing algorithm, it's quite likely you can implement it in Python.

Matrix Representation and Colors

An image can be represented by a matrix, each (x, y) point corresponding to a column and row in the matrix, and the value corresponding to the color.   291

The color value is a function of the mode (see Table 9-1 earlier for details). For example, in the case of an RGB image, each value of the matrix is a tuple of 3 bytes, each byte representing a different color. So in a sense, you can think of the entire image as three matrices, each matrix corresponding to the colors red, green, and blue, also known as color bands or channels.

Furthermore, each image can be split into these colors (depending on the mode, of course—there's no splitting of a 1-bit image into individual colors). This is done with the Image method split():

```
>>> im = Image.open('../images/circle.png')
>>> im.mode
'RGBA'
>>> R, G, B, A = im.split()
>>> R.mode, G.mode, B.mode, A.mode
('L', 'L', 'L', 'L')
```

Note I've assumed you have followed along with the chapter and created a file named ../images/circle.png; if not, follow Listing 9-1 to create a circle.png image.

Each split image is an image by itself, but it now contains only one-color information, hence its mode is 'L', not 'RGBA'.

To retrieve the *data* associated with the color, that is, the actual values, call the function getdata(). We can then transform the values to a NumPy array for some interesting numerical processing. Continuing our previous listing:

```
>>> from pylab import *
>>> data = array(R.getdata())
>>> type(data)
<type 'numpy.ndarray'>
>>> data.size
501225
>>> data.shape
(501225,)
```

The image data is stored as a list of all the values in the image, not a matrix representation of the image. To change it to a matrix, we use the NumPy method reshape():

```
>>> im.size
(815, 615)
>>> data = data.reshape(815, 615)
>>> data.size    # size should be the same
501225
>>> data.shape    # reshaped as a matrix
(815, 615)
```

Now that we have the data as a matrix, we can operate on the matrix instead of the image. This gives us great flexibility. Say we want to arbitrarily draw a magenta stripe in the middle of the circle; all that we need to do is modify the matrix associated with the red channel and then merge it to form a new, modified image.

■**Note** Why does changing the red channel generate a magenta output? The way I'm going to modify the matrix is by setting the red channel to 255. This means that my previously blue circle will now be a combination of blue and red, which is magenta, while the rest of the background, which is white, will remain white.

Let's do this a step at a time, from the top:

```
>>> from pylab import *
>>> from PIL import Image
>>> im = Image.open('../images/circle.png')
>>> im.mode
'RGBA'
>>> im.size
(815, 615)
>>> R, G, B, A = im.split()
>>> data = array(R.getdata()).reshape(im.size)
```

cols   *rows*

```
>>> (w, h) = data.shape
>>> data[w/2-100:w/2+100, :] = 255*ones((200, h))
>>> R.putdata(data.reshape(h*w))
>>> new_img = Image.merge('RGB', (R, G, B))
>>> new_img.show()
```

(handwritten annotation: should be h)

(handwritten: 234 : cols)

(handwritten: 200)

(handwritten: h)

(handwritten: rows)

The first line reads the image from file and displays some image information. I then split the image into four channels: red, green, blue, and the transparency mask. From here on, I'll restrict myself to dealing with the red channel only. First, I retrieve the actual numerical values associated with the red channel. This is done with a call to getdata(). In the same line, I also transform the data into a NumPy array and reshape the list to a matrix form.

Next I change the data values associated with 200 rows in the middle and set their value to 255. This in effect creates the magenta stripe. I then update the red channel with the modified data by calling the function putdata(). The function putdata() complements getdata() and expects a list, not a matrix, so I reshape the data back to a 1-D array.

Lastly, I create a new image, this time in RGB mode (I don't require transparency) by combining the original green and blue channels with the modified red channel. This is done by calling the merge() function, which is the opposite of the split() function. Figure 9-5 shows the results.

■**Note** It's also possible to perform this task using the ImageDraw object.

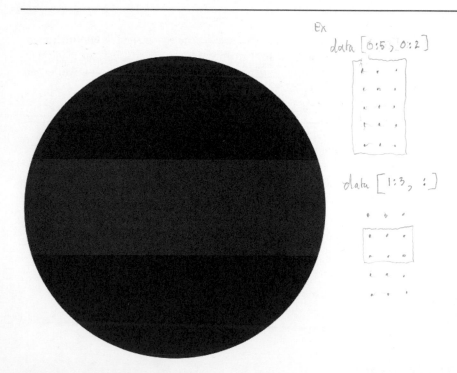

(handwritten: Ex)

(handwritten: data [0:5, 0:2])

(handwritten: data [1:3, :])

Figure 9-5. *Circle with a stripe*

So far we've covered an interesting number of functions that enable working on images with numerical values: `split()`, `merge()`, `getdata()`, and `putdata()`. We'll use some of them in a more complex example.

Example: Counting Objects (Five Parts)

The following example is rather long and deals with an interesting aspect of image processing: counting objects in an image. The idea is to write a script that counts the number of elements in a picture. Counting elements is a complex task, even for the human mind: What objects should I count? What constitutes an object? And so on.

The task of counting objects is very useful in a wide variety of applications, as indicated by just a few examples:

- *Biology*: Estimating the number of bacteria in an image from a microscope
- *Medicine*: Counting the number of axons in a tissue cross-section
- *Electronics board manufacturing*: Counting the number of imperfections in a printed circuit board or counting the number of resistors
- *Astronomy*: Counting the number of stars

For the purpose of this example, we'll create an image of the sky at night, with stars placed randomly. We'll then write a script to count the number of stars. We'll have a very sterile image, one that has a very clean background (black, night sky) and most information in one channel. However, we'll add a bit of complexity by varying shapes and sizes of stars.

Once we have an image of the sky at night, I'll talk a bit about recursion, a topic I have been avoiding thus far. Recursion will be used to implement an algorithm to fill an image. Lastly, I'll discuss some ideas and methods you could use to expand upon this example and add more capabilities to the algorithm.

Part 1: Twinkle, Twinkle, Little Star

First, we create the stars for our image of the sky at night. The night sky will be composed of white stars and a black background. Since we want the stars to be of varying sizes and shapes, we'll define a function named `star()` that creates a matplotlib patch object (see Listing 9-8).

Listing 9-8. *A Star Patch, Source of star_patch.py*

```
# create a star patch object
from pylab import *

def star(R, x0, y0, color='w', N=5, thin=0.5):
    """Returns an N-pointed star of size R at (x0, y0) (matplotlib patch)."""

    polystar = zeros((2*N, 2))
    for i in range(2*N):
        angle = i*pi/N
        r = R*(1-thin*(i%2))
        polystar[i] = [r*cos(angle)+x0, r*sin(angle)+y0]
    return Polygon(polystar, fc=color, ec=color)
```

The values that control the star patch are R, which determines the star's radius; x0 and y0, which control the star's location; color, which determines both the fill and edge color; N, which controls the number of pointy edges a star has; and thin, which controls how thin or thick a star is (on the range of 0 to 1, 1 being very thin).

■Tip The default star patch is white because we'll be using it for the night sky. Be sure to change it to a different color if you're using a white background.

I've used the Polygon object to create the star patch, with some mathematical trickery. The idea is this: I place N pointy edges on a circle of radius R with the center at (x0, y0) at fixed angle increments. I then place another set of points at a smaller radius to serve as the inner edges of the star, again at fixed angle increments but shifted so that each inner point resides exactly in the middle of the outer edge's points. The thin parameter determines the radius of the inner circle: the larger the value, the smaller the radius, and the "thinner" the star is. Lastly, I draw a line connecting all these points using the Polygon patch object.

■Note Be sure to save the star patch listing as file star_patch.py; we'll use it in future scripts.

USING A LIST COMPREHENSION

It's also possible to implement the star patch with list comprehensions. The idea is to zip together the elements in the polygon list:

```
def another_star(R, x0, y0, color='w', N=5, thin=0.5):
    """Returns an N-pointed star of size R at (x0, y0) (matplotlib patch)."""

    a = arange(0, 2*pi, 2*pi/N)
    r = thin*R
    polystar = array(zip(R*cos(a)+x0, R*sin(a)+y0, \
        r*cos(a+pi/N)+x0, r*sin(a+pi/N)+y0))
    return Polygon(polystar.reshape(N*2, 2), fc=color, ec=color)
```

Some would prefer this implementation over the previous implementation. Personally, I think both are fine; choose whichever is easier for you to follow.

It's also possible to code the entire function as a single return statement, but I strongly recommend against it, as the code would be hard to understand.

The script in Listing 9-9 generates some interesting stars.

Listing 9-9. *Generating Some Interesting Stars*

```
# show some star examples
from pylab import *

# ensure the star patch is defined properly
execfile('star_patch.py')

examples = [
    "star(10, 0, 0, 'k')",
    "star(10, 0, 0, 'k', 10)",
    "star(10, 0, 0, 'k', 5, 0.2)",
    "star(10, 0, 0, 'k', 3, 0.9)" ]

for i, example in enumerate(examples):
    subplot(2, 2, i+1)
    exec "new_star="+example
    gca().add_patch(new_star)
    title(example)
    axis('scaled')
    axis([-10, 10, -10, 10])
```

In this script I've decided to iterate over a list of strings and use the exec statement. The same string used for the exec statement is also used to create the title for the subplots (see Figure 9-6).

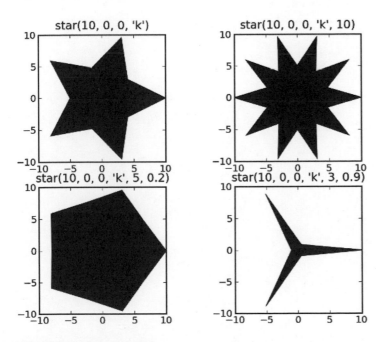

Figure 9-6. *Some star patches*

Tip To ensure a patch is displayed, issue a call to `axis('normal')` (or similar) to force a refresh of the figure.

There's room for additional work on the `star()` patch object; for example, you could add a `rotation` parameter, rotating the entire star by `rotation` degrees. This can be done by changing the argument to the functions `sin()` and `cos()` in the `star()` function. Another modification could include a hollow star, implemented by splitting the `edgecolor` and `facecolor` functionality.

Armed with the star patch, we turn to part 2 of this example: creating an image of the sky at night.

Part 2: The Sky at Night

To create a simulated image of the night sky, we use the script in Listing 9-10.

Listing 9-10. *Creating an Image of the Sky at Night, nightsky.py*

```python
# create a fictitious night sky
from random import randrange as rr

execfile('star_patch.py')

# parameters for the simulated night sky image
img_size = 800
num_stars = 25

# star parameters: number of pointy edges and radius
min_num_points = 5
max_num_points = 11
min_star_radius = 2
max_star_radius = 10

# star parameter 'thinness' is on a scale of 1 to 10
min_thin = 5
max_thin = 9

# draw the night sky
figure(facecolor='k')
cur_axes = gca()

# patch stars
for i in range(num_stars):
    new_star = star(rr(min_star_radius, max_star_radius),
        rr(0, img_size) , rr(0, img_size), 'w', \
```

```
        rr(min_num_points, max_num_points), \
        rr(min_thin, max_thin)/10.0)
    cur_axes.add_patch(new_star)

# modify axis behavior
axis([0, img_size, 0, img_size])
axis('scaled')
axis('off')

savefig('../images/nightsky', facecolor='k', edgecolor='k')
```

I've imported the function `randrange()` from the module random and decided to rename it to `rr()`, which I think is clearer to read. I then define a set of values you can tweak and observe the results. The values are self-explanatory and include such values as the image size and number of stars in the image.

The patching of stars is done in the `for` loop, which creates a new star with random values and adds it to the current figure. I then follow up by updating the image size and removing the axes. Finally, I save the image to file. Figure 9-7 shows random output from the simulated night sky.

Figure 9-7. *Simulated (random) night sky*

Part 3: Flood Fill and Recursion

We now turn to something completely different: recursion. *Recursion* describes a scenario where a function calls itself. Some known recursion algorithms implement the factorial operation and Fibonacci sequences. We'll use recursion for image processing, specifically to fill an image using a flood-fill algorithm.

Flood fill, sometimes also referred to as *bucket fill*, is an algorithm to fill a closed area of a specific color with a different color. This is a quite common operation in most image processing applications. Kids love to use it to paint digital coloring images.

To implement flood fill, we'll use recursion. In the implementation, we'll assume that the image to fill is given to us as a NumPy array, more specifically as a 2-D array (i.e., a matrix). It's also possible to manipulate a PIL Image object, but I prefer using a matrix for two reasons:

- It's more generic. I can port the flood-fill algorithm to other objects as long as I can convert the objects to a NumPy array (matrix).

- It's easier to view the code by indexing over matrix elements than to use the getpixel() and setpixel() methods provided by the Image object.

So how does flood fill work? Flood fill starts by receiving a point to start filling from. If the point is the color to be converted, flood fill will change the color to the desired color. It then moves to a point adjacent to it, say to the right, and calls itself. As the process continues, points to the right will start filling up with the new color. If the point to the right is not in the desired color (that is, shouldn't be painted), the point to the top is checked, and the process resumes. This process is repeated for left and bottom points surrounding each point. The end process is a filled, closed object.

FLOOD FILL AND MINESWEEPER

The flood-fill algorithm can also be used in the coding of the game Minesweeper (shipped with Windows). You can use the algorithm to expand an area and reveal points adjacent to mines. The algorithm will follow a similar path, and one option would be to create a matrix of values corresponding to whether a square is empty (value 0) or adjacent to a mine (value equal to the number of mines it is adjacent to), with a different value indicating a mine (say, value −1). When the user clicks on a square, the flood-fill algorithm kicks in and decides how many squares to reveal. If you're not familiar with Minesweeper, I suggest you refrain from trying it; the game is addictive.

Listing 9-11 presents a simple flood-fill implementation.

Listing 9-11. *Flood-Fill Implementation Using Recursion,* flood_fill.py

```python
from numpy import *
from sys import getrecursionlimit

def flood_fill(x, y, m, total):
    """A function to flood fill an image (matrix)."""

    if total > getrecursionlimit():
        return total

    # nothing to fill
    if m[x, y] != 255:
        return total

    m[x, y] = 128
    if(x-1 >= 0):
        total = flood_fill(x-1, y, m, total+1)
    if(x+1 <= m.shape[0]-1):
        total = flood_fill(x+1, y, m, total+1)
    if(y-1 >= 0):
        total = flood_fill(x, y-1, m, total+1)
    if(y+1 <= m.shape[1]-1):
        total = flood_fill(x, y+1, m, total+1)
    return total+1
```

The function flood_fill() is an implementation of the flood-fill algorithm described previously. I've bolded the code where recursion actually happens (the function calling itself).

The function accepts the values x and y, denoting the point to fill; m, which is the NumPy matrix; and total, which is a variable used to keep track of the recursion depth (i.e., how many times a function calls itself repeatedly).

I've chosen to fill all values corresponding to 255 with 128. In essence this means that if the object is fully red (or green or blue, depending on the band selected), it will be changed to "half" red. You can modify the function flood_fill() to accept an original color and a new color as parameters; I chose not to do so, as I think the code looks clearer that way.

Every time a function is called in a recursion, additional memory is consumed. Python limits the recursion depth with the value sys.getrecursionlimit(). If the running code exceeds this limit, a recursion exception is raised. It's possible to increase this number by calling sys.setrecursionlimit(), but that's only a small fix; inevitably, you'll reach a memory limit, which might cause a system crash.

Therefore, it's best if your code can detect these events beforehand and alert the user if such an event transpired. I have chosen to do so by returning the value total. In case total is greater than the maximum recursion depth, I can notify the user of the event.

It's also important to note that if your night sky image gets larger or the size of stars get larger (e.g., a larger radius), or if you save the image at a higher resolution (more points per star), inevitably you will hit a recursion limit because the areas to fill get larger and larger. So while this is a viable option to fill objects, maybe a different algorithm should be employed for production-level code, such as using ImageDraw's floodfill() method.

USING IMAGEDRAW FOR FLOOD FILL

The ImageDraw object also provides a floodfill() function, which may be used for the algorithm presented here. There are several reasons I chose to implement flood_fill() instead of using the ImageDraw function:

- I wanted to talk about recursion.

- ImageDraw's floodfill() doesn't return information such as the size of the filled region, which can be used to enhance the algorithm. That being said, it's quite possible to use other methods to complement this such as comparing the image before and after flood filling it.

- I wanted to show you how to tweak flood fill, for example, to include diagonals cells as adjacent cells (and not just up, down, left, and right).

So now that we have the flood_fill() function, how does that help us count the number of stars at night?

Part 4: Counting Objects

Counting objects is really easy, once you have an implementation of flood fill (see Listing 9-12). The idea is simple: go through every point in your image and fill it. The return value from flood fill is the actual number of points filled. In case there was nothing to fill, the value will be zero, but in case flood fill fills an object, the return value will be nonzero, which indicates that flood fill found and filled an object. Future calls to flood_fill() for that pixel will not fill the object, as it is already filled. Now all that's required is to count the number of times flood fill returns a nonzero value, and you have the number of objects!

Listing 9-12. *Counting Objects in a Picture*

```
from pylab import *
from PIL import Image
from sys import getrecursionlimit

execfile('flood_fill.py')

# read the image
im = Image.open('../images/nightsky.png')

# split the image into individual bands
cols, rows = im.size
R, G, B, A = im.split()

# retrieve the data from the red band as a matrix array
data = array(R.getdata())
```

```
# set all values that are nonzero to 255
# (could be due to antialiasing)
data[find(data != 0)] = 255
data = data.reshape(rows, cols)

# count the stars
count, recursion_limit_reached = 0, 0
for i in range(rows):
    for j in range(cols):
        tot = flood_fill(i, j, data, 0)
        if tot > getrecursionlimit():
            recursion_limit_reached += 1
        elif tot > 0:
            count += 1

if recursion_limit_reached:
    print "Recursion limit reached %d times" % recursion_limit_reached
print "I counted %d stars!" % count

R.putdata(data.reshape(cols*rows))
Image.merge('RGB', (R, G, B)).show()
```

The script is an implementation of the preceding algorithm. We start by importing the proper modules and calling the script flood_fill.py, which contains the flood_fill() function implementation. Next we open the image of the sky at night and split it into individual color bands. I decided to work strictly on the red band, but in reality, because we are dealing with black-and-white pictures, I could just as well have chosen any other channel (other than the transparency). I then access the data and convert it to a NumPy matrix. This is done in the call data = array(R.getdata()).

Next I implement a simple threshold. What I do is change all nonblack values to white by setting all nonzero values to 255. Other algorithms use a different approach such as setting all values above and including 128 to 255 and all values below 128 to 0. In this particular case, the results would be very similar. Notice that I run the threshold before I reshape the matrix, the reason being that I can use the find() function quite easily that way. I then reshape the image into a matrix.

Up to this point I've been dealing with reading the image, splitting it, and applying a threshold to the image. Now, I turn to using the flood_fill() function. I go through every pixel in the matrix and call the function flood_fill(). If the return value is greater than the recursion limit, I increment the number of times a recursion limit has been reached. If the return has not reached the recursion limit and is nonzero, I increment the count of objects.

Lastly, I report my results: the number of recursions that exceeded the maximum allowed value (for debugging purposes more than anything) and the number of stars counted. Here's a result from running the script on the night sky image presented earlier:

```
I counted 23 stars!
```

(We'll get to why that number is not 25 in the next section.)

To be sure I've counted all the stars in the night sky picture, and furthermore, that I did not accidentally count objects that are not stars, I decided on some sort of visual feedback of the result. I do this in the last two lines of the script: I convert the matrix data back to the red channel and construct a new image with the newly modified red channel.

If you look closely at the newly constructed image (zoom in if you'd like), you'll see that at times the edges around stars are not filled properly. I believe that the reason for this is the quantization effect we've used (threshold) that modifies all half-values to black.

Part 5: Optimizing the Algorithm

So why did the algorithm return 23 stars and not 25? (See `num_stars` value in Listing 9-10.) A plausible reason is that several stars overlapped. This would cause the algorithm to combine several objects into one. In real pictures (nonsterile, unlike those presented in the example), there could be other reasons, and this is where you can start tweaking your image processing algorithm.

But as you start working with "real" data, you'll find that sometimes the opposite happens, that is, the algorithm counts more objects than there really are. The reason for this could be because the images are not ideal, and even small specks, or noise, could throw off the number count. In that case, a possible solution would be to count only elements whose size is greater than a fixed value, that is, reading the value returned by `flood_fill()` and discarding objects whose size is too small. Another option would be to preprocess the image using a filter (see the section "Image Filtering" later in this chapter).

Another improvement to the algorithm could be giving it the capability to find the largest object. Again, this is quite possible by reading the value returned from the function `flood_fill()` and then sorting the results or finding the maximum.

And you can also try to evaluate the luminosity of the night sky, by counting the areas of all the stars. This might be used to estimate how clear the skies are or, in the case of a microscopic image, help determine whether the size of a bacteria colony has changed.

Some real images might have objects so small that you'll need to think about flood filling diagonals as well. That is, consider the character "x" drawn on a 3×3 pixel grid: there's no pixel that's adjacent to another unless you count diagonals. Modifying flood fill to include diagonals will combine the pixels that make up this "x" into one object.

The point of the matter, now that data is accessible as a NumPy matrix, is that you can implement whatever algorithm or image processing idea you might have. But in many occasions, you don't have to resort to the matrix level; PIL provides a good number of support functions.

Image Arithmetic

PIL provides a set of arithmetic operations via the module ImageChops (Chops is short for channel operations). In the night sky example, some people would prefer working on a white background (which could save quite a bit of ink if you're printing the images). Per the previous section, you could transfer the image to a NumPy array and then convert it, but in such a simple case, it makes more sense to use the ImageChops `invert()` function:

```
# display an image and its inverse
from PIL import Image, ImageChops
im = Image.open('../images/nightsky.png')
```

```
new_img = Image.new('RGB', (im.size[0]*2, im.size[1]))
new_img.paste(im, (0, 0))
new_img.paste(ImageChops.invert(im), (im.size[0], 0))
new_img.show()
```

In Figure 9-8, I've used the image generated by the script nightsky.py (Listing 9-6) with num_stars=10, min_star_radius=10, and max_star_radius=30 to show a more pronounced effect of the image inversion.

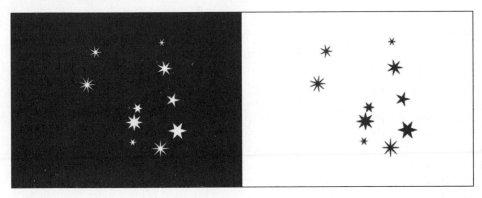

Figure 9-8. *Inverting an image: the original is on the left, and the inverted image is on the right.*

Table 9-3 lists some additional ImageChops operations. Notice that ImageChops operations operate only one channel (L) or RGB images.

Table 9-3. *Some ImageChops Operations*

Function	Description
add(img1, img2, scale=1.0, offset=0)	Adds two images as follows: (img1+img2)/scale+offset. The default values of scale and offset mean a simple addition.
constant(img1, value)	Returns an image of size img1 filled with color value.
darker(img1, img2)	Returns an image with the darker pixel from both images. This a minimum of the two images, on a pixel-by-pixel level.
difference(img1, img2)	Returns the absolute difference of two images. This is abs(img1-img2), on a pixel-by-pixel level.
lighter(img1, img2)	Returns an image with the lighter pixel from both images. This a maximum of the two images, on a pixel-by-pixel level.
subtract(img1, img2, scale=1.0, offset=0)	Subtracts two images as follows: (img1-img2)/scale+offset. The default values of scale and offset mean a simple subtraction.

There are additional functions available in ImageChops; check out either help(ImageChops) or the PIL web site (http://www.pythonware.com/library/pil/handbook/imagechops.htm).

You can create some interesting effects using these simple operations. And these effects can in turn be used for some fast image processing algorithms. Listing 9-13 presents a script that makes use of the lighter() method on two night sky images. To follow along, run the nightsky.py script and rename the generated file images/nightsky.png to images/nightsky1.png; do it again, this time renaming the generated image to images/nightsky2.png.

Listing 9-13. *Using* lighter() *on Two Images*

```
from PIL import Image, ImageDraw, ImageFont, ImageChops
from matplotlib import font_manager

# read the images
img1 = Image.open('../images/nightsky1.png')
img2 = Image.open('../images/nightsky2.png')

# create a new image, made of the lighter of the two
img3 = ImageChops.lighter(img1, img2)

# create a collage of three images
width, height = img1.size
delta = 10
img = Image.new('RGB', (width*2+delta, height*2+delta), (255, 255, 255))
img.paste(img1, (0, 0))
img.paste(img2, (width+delta, 0))
img.paste(img3, ((width+delta)/2, height+delta))

# annotate the images with text
font_str = font_manager.findfont('Vera')
ttf = ImageFont.truetype(font_str, 54)

draw = ImageDraw.Draw(img)
draw.text((delta, delta), 'Night Sky (1)', fill='white', font=ttf)
draw.text((delta*2+width, delta), 'Night Sky (2)', fill='white', font=ttf)
draw.text(((width+delta)/2+delta, height+delta*2), \
    'Combined', fill='white', font=ttf)

# display the final image
img.show()
```

I've made a collage and separated the images with a white band. Figure 9-9 shows the result.

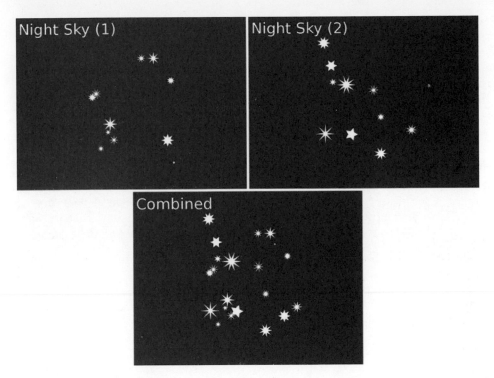

Figure 9-9. *Using* `lighter()`

It's interesting to note that in this specific case, using the function add() would have resulted in a similar image.

Image Filtering

Most GUI-based image processing applications come with a bundle of image filters. There's a wide variety of filters available, and different applications group them into different categories. Some of the common filtering categories are blur, enhancement, edge detection, and more.

From an image processing standpoint, *image filters* are known operations that help us achieve a specific effect. For example, I once used the counting objects algorithm presented as an example in this book to try to count the number of bubbles in a printed circuit board soaked in water. As you probably realize, pictures obtained from a real-life image are not as sterile as those presented in the sky at night example. And so prior to using the algorithm, I had to clean up the images. By "clean up" I mean filtering the image using known filters. I ended up using a threshold combined with a median filter, and then converting the image to a 1-bit (black-and-white) version prior to running the algorithm.

The following text assumes you have some background in image filtering. If not, my suggestion is that you experiment with a GUI application such as GIMP to get a feel for what filters to use and how they can help you with basic image processing. Once you have the preprocessing figured out, that is, you know what filters you want to run on your image prior to the final algorithm, you can implement the filters with a Python script that makes use of PIL filters. (You might not even require a final algorithm if you select the proper filters.)

PIL provides us with the class `ImageFilter`, which supports a good number of filters. To use `ImageFilter`, import it as follows: `from PIL import ImageFilter` (or simply `import ImageFilter`). Once you've imported `ImageFilter`, call the `filter()` method that's part of the Image object (not ImageFilter object) to filter an image:

```
>>> from PIL import Image, ImageChops, ImageFilter
>>> img = Image.open('../images/nightsky.png')
>>> inv_img = ImageChops.invert(img)
>>> fil_img = inv_img.filter(ImageFilter.MinFilter(15))
```

In the preceding example, I've used the night sky images you've seen before and inverted the output so as to work on black stars over white background. I then filtered the image using a `MinFilter` filter (see Figure 9-10). The `MinFilter` works on a pixel-by-pixel level. For every pixel, it returns the minimum pixel from the square of size n (in the example, 15) centered on the given pixel. As you can see, even from this small example, there's quite a bit to be gained by working with image filters.

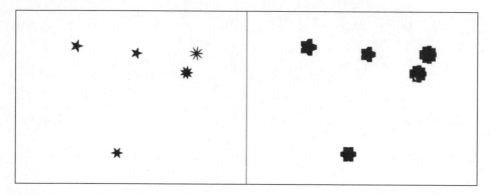

Figure 9-10. *Filtering an image: left is the original, and right shows the image filtered with a* `MinFilter` *set to 15.*

`ImageFilter` provides *fixed* image enhancement filters easily distinguishable due to their capitalized names:

```
>>> [filt for filt in dir(ImageFilter) if filt.isupper()]
['BLUR', 'CONTOUR', 'DETAIL', 'EDGE_ENHANCE', 'EDGE_ENHANCE_MORE', 'EMBOSS',
'FIND_EDGES', 'SHARPEN', 'SMOOTH', 'SMOOTH_MORE']
```

By the term "fixed" I mean that they accept no parameters. To use these filters, call the `filter()` method with the fixed filter, as follows:

```
>>> new_img = img.filter(ImageFilter.CONTOUR)
```

The names of these filters should provide direction as to what they perform.

`ImageFilter` also provides nonfixed filters (i.e., filters that accept parameters). Table 9-4 lists some additional filters supported by the `ImageFilter` object.

Table 9-4. *Some Image Filters*

Function	Description
MaxFilter(size=3)	For every pixel in the original image, returns the pixel with the maximum value from a square of width size placed around the original pixel. size must be odd (3, 5, 7, . . .).
MedianFilter(size=3)	For every pixel in the original image, returns the median pixel from a square of width size placed around the original pixel. size must be odd (3, 5, 7, . . .).
MinFilter(size=3)	For every pixel in the original image, returns the pixel with the minimum value from a square of width size placed around the original pixel. size must be odd (3, 5, 7, . . .).
ModeFilter(size=3)	For every pixel in the original image, returns the most common pixel from a square of width size placed around the original pixel. size must be odd (3, 5, 7, . . .).

Final Notes and References

Image processing is a large field and is gaining more and more popularity as computers increase in performance. And image processing is only two dimensional; nowadays we see more and more 3-D data processing as well, including video.

Armed with Python, the Python Imaging Library, and NumPy, even complex image processing tasks can be prototyped. However, image processing requires a great deal of memory and processing power; as you work with images you'll realize you may require faster tools, and you may even need to port parts of your code to a lower-level programming language such as C to gain performance. Nevertheless, Python is an excellent prototyping environment; it provides fast responses in an interactive environment and can help you define your image processing algorithm.

Additional information can be found at the following sites:

- The Python Imaging Library, http://www.pythonware.com/library/pil/handbook/

- GIMP, http://www.gimp.org/docs/

CHAPTER 10

■ ■ ■

Advanced File Processing
More on Files

A common task of programmers is working with files—not merely reading and writing files, but also organizing them, moving them around, deleting, compressing, archiving, and more.

I often find myself borrowing code from my previous projects, especially code that deals with reading and parsing files, typically via copy and paste. But that seems such a waste—why not come up with a library of functions that addresses most people's needs?

Other programmers must have felt the same way, and so they turned to writing modules, libraries of functions to perform these tasks. And many of these are now included with the Python Standard Library; more are added on a regular basis.

This chapter expands on ideas discussed in Chapters 4 and 5 and examines additional file-related topics. I also build on some examples from previous chapters as a way to introduce new topics and create more reusable code.

Binary Files and Random Access

The term *binary file* describes a nontext file: executable files, image files, or simply data files. In this section we'll show some methods of dealing with binary data files.

Working with text files, we've used readline() or read(n) to read chunks of data from a file. The function readline(), in a sense, splits the file into smaller chunks of data (i.e., lines of text).

With binary files, it's more common to see random access, that is, arbitrary reading of chunks of data from anywhere in the file. With text files, this is a bit harder because you don't know in advance how many characters and words are in a line, so randomly picking the nth line is not a trivial task. With binary files composed of fixed-length records, random access allows access to an arbitrary field.

The methods seek(offset[, whence]) and tell() are random-access file functions. To better understand what these functions do, you need to understand the concept of file pointers. A *file pointer* points to a location in the file: subsequent read or write operations will happen at that specific location (assuming the file was opened in a mode that allows random access read and/or write). Whenever we read or write data from the file, the file pointer is incremented accordingly.

The function seek() sets the file pointer to a value of our choosing; subsequent calls to read() will pick up from the newly "seeked" location. The function tell() returns the current file pointer value in bytes. Here's a short interactive Python session describing the works of seek() and tell():

```
>>> f = open('../data/example.bin', 'wb')
>>> f.tell()
0L
>>> f.write('0123456789')
>>> f.tell()
10L
```

■**Note** As in previous chapters, I assume you're running an interactive Python session in directory Ch10/src and that directory Ch10/data exists.

I've created a binary file. Once created, the file pointer associated with the file is set to 0, as shown by the result from f.tell(). After writing ten values, the file pointer is at 10.

```
>>> f.seek(5)
>>> f.write('0123456789')
>>> f.tell()
15L
>>> f.close()
```

I've changed the file pointer to point to location 5 and wrote again the same ten values. As a result, the file pointer has changed to 15. Let's print the contents of the file:

```
>>> open('../data/example.bin', 'rb').read()
'012340123456789'
```

As expected, the result is the string '0123456789' overlapped by another copy of the same string at location 5.

The argument whence in the function seek(offset[, whence]) instructs how the offset should be calculated. If whence is 0 (the default), seek() moves offset bytes relative to the start of the file. If whence is 1, seek() moves the file pointer offset bytes relative to the end of the file. Notice that in order to change the file pointer to n bytes before the end of the file, pass a negative value as an offset. On many systems, it's possible to seek past the end of the file (which is a feature, not a bug, as you'll soon see). If whence is equal to 2, seek() moves relative to the current location. Again, both negative and positive values are allowed. Negative values for seek() are not allowed if whence is 0. Continuing our previous example:

```
>>> f = open('../data/example.bin', 'rb')
>>> f.seek(-2, 2)
>>> print f.read()
89
>>> f.close()
```

I've set the file pointer to 2 bytes before the end of the file and printed the contents of the file from that point forward.

Example: Reading the Nth Field

The functions seek() and tell() are especially useful for accessing large binary files that contain fixed-length records. Unlike text files, with binary files of fixed-length records, you can calculate in advance the location of a field in the file. Combined with seek(), it's possible to read a single field. This is especially important in large files where reading the entire file or even reading the file a value at a time (without seeking directly to the required field) can take a considerable amount of time.

In this example, shown in Listing 10-1, we combine seek() and tell() with the struct module (see Chapter 4).

Listing 10-1. *Reading the Nth Field*

```
import struct
from math import sqrt
from random import randrange

# binary filename
bin_fn = '../data/large_file.bin'

Nfields = 1000      # number of fields
N = 766             # field to retrieve
fmt = 'cdL'         # format: char, float, long

fmt_size = struct.calcsize(fmt)

# create a random binary file
fout = open(bin_fn, 'wb')
for i in xrange(Nfields):
    data = struct.pack(fmt, chr(randrange(32, 128)), sqrt(float(i)), i)
    fout.write(data)
fout.close()

# read the nth value
fin = open(bin_fn, 'rb')
fin.seek((N-1)*fmt_size)
data = fin.read(fmt_size)
(c, d, l) = struct.unpack(fmt, data)
print "At location %d, I read:" % (fin.tell()/fmt_size), (c, d, l)
```

The first part of the script creates a binary file with some made-up data. The second part reads a single field at location 766 without reading the entire file. This is done by changing the file pointer to point to location (N-1)*fmt_size and reading only one field.

Here's the result from running the script:

```
At location 766, I read: ('"', 27.658633371878661, 765)
```

Example: Efficient Tail Implementation

In Chapter 5 you saw a possible implementation of head and tail functionality. The tail functionality was harder to implement for a very large file. The reason for this was explained in Chapter 5. In this example, we turn to implement tail functionality for large files with use of seek() and tell(), as demonstrated in Listing 10-2.

Listing 10-2. *tail() Function for Large Files*

```python
from os.path import getsize

def tail_large(filename, n=10):
    """Returns the last n lines of a very large file."""

    N, data = 1024, ''

    # open the file and retrieve its size
    f = open(filename, 'rb')
    fsize = getsize(filename)

    # seek to the end of file
    f.seek(0, 2)

    for i in xrange(fsize-N, -N, -N):
        # read the next chunk of data
        last_loc = f.tell()
        f.seek(max(i, 0))

        # store read data, reversed order
        data += f.read(last_loc-f.tell())

        # do we have enough lines?
        if data.count('\n') > n:
            break

    # print the last n lines
    lines = data.splitlines()
    for line in lines[-n:]:
        print line
```

The idea is this: read N bytes from the end and store the result in data. The parameter N is an arbitrary number and describes the number of bytes to read in one chunk. I've set it to 1024. If data contains more than n lines (by counting the number of times '\n' is encountered), break out of the for loop and print the last n lines of data. If data does not contain n lines, read the next chunk of N bytes (that is, backward) and add the read bytes to data. So in a sense, we're going backward from the end of the file, reading chunks of N=1024 bytes and counting whether we encountered enough line breaks. If we have, we print those lines; if we haven't, we keep reading more data until we either have read the required number of lines or have reached the beginning of the file.

This implementation is not as straightforward as the one presented in Chapter 5. However, there is a substantial performance gain for large files.

Example: Creating a Fixed-Size File

Dealing with binary files, at times there's a requirement to create a large file (of noninitialized values).

A trick I use to create a file is to seek past the end of the file to a location equivalent to the required length minus one, and then write 0 and close the file. This (in many systems) creates a file of the required size.

The following creates an uninitialized file of size 1GB (2^{30} bytes):

```
>>> f = open('../data/1gb_file.bin', 'wb')
>>> f.seek(2**30-1)
>>> f.write(chr(0))
>>> f.close()
```

Now to ensure that the file was indeed created:

```
>>> from os.path import getsize
>>> getsize('../data/1gb_file.bin')
1073741824L
```

■Note The ability to seek past the end of a file is system dependent and not supported by all systems.

Example: Recording Time-Based Binary Data

When recording time-based binary data, a method I particularly like is using the epoch notation (see Chapter 5). For this example, I'll be using functions from the time module and from Python's array module (not to be confused with NumPy's array object).

In case you're simply recording a variable as a function of time, it's easier if the recorded variable is in floating-point notation, because now both the time and the value use the same data type. This allows for a simple use of the array module, as shown in Listing 10-3.

Listing 10-3. *Writing Epoch-Based Data in Binary Form*

```
import random, time, array

N = 10
fname = '../data/binary_data.f64'
data = array.array('d')
```

```
# create data
for value in range(N):
    time.sleep(random.random())
    data.append(time.time())
    data.append(value)

# store data to file
f = open(fname, 'wb')
data.tofile(f)
f.close()
```

The script runs on average 5 seconds and generates timestamps and values. I've made use of the array method tofile() to store binary values to file.

Retrieving data from the binary file is simple as well, as you can see in Listing 10-4.

Listing 10-4. *Reading Binary Data Stored with Epoch Notation*

```
import random, time, array

N = 10
fname = '../data/binary_data.f64'
data = array.array('d')

# read data
f = open(fname, 'rb')
data.fromfile(f, N*2)
f.close()

# display data
L = data.tolist()
for t, val in zip(L[::2], L[1::2]):
    print time.ctime(t), val
```

Most of the work is performed in the line data.fromfile(f, N*2), which reads values and stores them in a Python array. I then rearrange the data and display the results:

```
Thu Dec 04 11:15:51 2008 0.0
Thu Dec 04 11:15:52 2008 1.0
Thu Dec 04 11:15:53 2008 2.0
Thu Dec 04 11:15:53 2008 3.0
Thu Dec 04 11:15:54 2008 4.0
Thu Dec 04 11:15:54 2008 5.0
Thu Dec 04 11:15:54 2008 6.0
Thu Dec 04 11:15:55 2008 7.0
Thu Dec 04 11:15:56 2008 8.0
Thu Dec 04 11:15:56 2008 9.0
```

I've used a trick to rearrange the data. When I convert the data from an array to a list, L, the values are interlaced: time, value, time, value, and so on. To print values, I can just iterate through L, converting to a time format every odd value. Instead I've opted to zip slices of even and odd values. The following code illustrates this:

```
>>> L = [1, 'Value', 2, 'Another value', 3, 'Last value']
>>> L[::2]    # these are the odd values
[1, 2, 3]
>>> L[1::2]   # these are the even values
['Value', 'Another value', 'Last value']
>>> zip(L[::2], L[1::2])
[(1, 'Value'), (2, 'Another value'), (3, 'Last value')]
>>> for i, s in zip(L[::2], L[1::2]):
...     print i, s
...
1 Value
2 Another value
3 Last value
```

Object Serialization

At times, working with an interactive session in Python, it's useful to be able to save variables to file. Prior to writing them to file, variables should be serialized, that is, converted into a stream of bytes. The stream of bytes can then be written to file and later retrieved.

Instead of creating dedicated file formats to deal with all sorts of variable types (lists, strings, NumPy arrays, and the like), Python provides us with a built-in object serialization module that is ideal for this purpose: Pickle.

The Pickle Module

Pickle comes in two flavors: the Pickle module and the faster C implementation named cPickle. With the better performance of cPickle comes a price: you can't subclass the module. Personally, I have not found this limitation an issue, so for me, cPickle is a better choice. To use Pickle, issue import pickle; to use cPickle, issue import cPickle.

The function cPickle.dump(obj, file[, protocol]) serializes an object and writes it to file. The protocol argument can take the values 0 for ASCII (the default), 1 for binary, and 2 to indicate support for new Python objects. Both protocols 1 and 2 create binary files. If you provide a negative value for dump(), the highest version protocol will be used. This is to accommodate for future protocol versions of Pickle and cPickle. The function cPickle.load(file) will read an object from file.

The function cPickle.dumps(obj[, protocol]) serializes the object and returns its string representation without writing it to file. Similarly, cPickle.loads(str) creates an object from a string.

Example: Saving and Retrieving Python Session Variables

The example in Listing 10-5 makes use of the cPickle module to write variables of varying data types to file.

Listing 10-5. *Pickling Several Objects to File*

```
import cPickle
from numpy import *

fname = '../data/mysession.pickle'
a = 3
b = "A string"
c = {'dict': 10}
d = eye(3)

fout = open(fname, 'wb')
for var in [a, b, c, d]:
    cPickle.dump(var, fout)
fout.close()
```

To pickle objects (i.e., serialize them) and write them to file, I've used the function cPickle.dump(var, file). You can issue subsequent calls to cPickle.dump() to store additional values to file as shown in Listing 10-5.

Now to read the objects from file (see Listing 10-6).

Listing 10-6. *Reading Objects from File*

```
import cPickle

fname = '../data/mysession.pickle'
fin = open(fname, 'rb')
var_index = 0

while True:
    try:
        var_index += 1
        exec "v_%d = cPickle.load(fin)" % var_index
        exec "var_type = type(v_%d)" % var_index
        print "Read v_%d, type is: %s" % (var_index, var_type)
    except EOFError:
        break
```

Whenever you issue a call to cPickle.load(), the return value is a Python object (unless the end of file is reached). However, the name of the object is not stored. Therefore, I've made use of the exec statement to create variables named v_1, v_2, and so forth to store the objects.

Here are the results from running the script:

```
Read v_1, type is: <type 'int'>
Read v_2, type is: <type 'str'>
Read v_3, type is: <type 'dict'>
Read v_4, type is: <type 'numpy.ndarray'>
>>> v_4
array([[ 1.,  0.,  0.],
       [ 0.,  1.,  0.],
       [ 0.,  0.,  1.]])
```

If you're using NumPy arrays, you can make use of the functions save() and load() provided by matplotlib. These functions accept a file name and read and write a NumPy array object to and from file:

```
>>> from pylab import *
>>> fname = '../data/session.npy'
>>> save(fname, eye(3))
>>> load(fname)
array([[ 1.,  0.,  0.],
       [ 0.,  1.,  0.],
       [ 0.,  0.,  1.]])
```

If the file name used in save() and load() ends with .gz, gzip compression is automatically used (see the section "File Compression" later in this chapter).

Command-Line Parameters

This section, which covers command-line parameters, is a bit of an off-topic discussion. (The reason I've decided to give an overview of command-line parameters before getting into the details of the FileInput module is that the FileInput module makes sense in the context of command-line parameters, as you'll soon see.)

A possible progression from an interactive Python session is creating a stand-alone utility or application—that is, a Python script callable from the shell, be it the command prompt in Windows or a bash shell in Linux. One of the options of interacting with such a script is by passing command-line arguments. For example, in the tail command-line utility, a command-line parameter could be the number of lines tail will display. So to list the last 20 lines of a file, you would write

```
$ python tail.py -n 20 filename
```

argv

The sys module enables command-line processing with the sys.argv variable, demonstrated in Listing 10-7. sys.argv is a list of strings containing the split shell command entered. The value in sys.argv[0] is the name of the Python script.

Listing 10-7. *Command-Line Arguments*

```
import sys
for i, cmd in enumerate(sys.argv):
    print "argv[%d] = '%s'" % (i, cmd)
```

Save the file as parse_args.py and run python parse_args.py 20 myfile in a shell. The results should look like this:

```
argv[0] = 'parse_args.py'
argv[1] = '20'
argv[2] = 'myfile'
```

Example: Creating a Fixed-Size File (Stand-Alone Script)

We turn to modify the code in this chapter from the section "Example: Creating a Fixed-Size File" to a stand-alone script callable from a CLI (shell or command window). The script, shown in Listing 10-8 (empty_file.py), accepts the number of bytes and a file name and creates a file of specified name and size.

Listing 10-8. *Creating a Fixed-Size File (Stand-Alone Script), empty_file.py*

```
from sys import argv, exit

usage = "Usage: python empty_file.py nbytes filename"

# we expect three arguments: script name, size, and file name
if len(argv) != 3:
    print "Improper number of arguments."
    print usage
    exit()

# is size an integer?
try:
    nbytes = long(argv[1])
except ValueError:
    print "First argument is not an integer number."
    print usage
    exit()

# retrieve the requested file name
filename = argv[2]

# can we create the file?
# here a failure could be due to a nonexisting path
try:
    f = open(filename, 'wb')
```

```
except IOError:
    print "Unable to create file", filename
    print usage
    exit()

# finally! create the file
f.seek(nbytes-1)
f.write(chr(0))
f.close()
print "Successfully created file %s of size %d." % (filename, nbytes)
```

I've carefully checked the parameters passed by the user to determine whether there are an adequate number of parameters and if those values are valid. I took special care to ensure the file can indeed be created. Finally, the code that generates the empty file is simple.

I've also introduced the function exit(), provided with the sys module. The function is especially useful when you're writing a stand-alone script, as it exits the script immediately.

OptParse Module

Enforcing a strict syntax for command-line parameters renders a script less user friendly. For instance, in the previous example, you might want the script to automatically create a file of default size, say 1KB, in case no length is provided. Or you might want to add additional parameters with default values, further controlling the behavior of the script so that it creates a path to the file name if it does not exist, for example.

Accommodating additional options as well as default options will cause the code in the previous listing to grow larger and less maintainable. When the number of options increases, consider using the OptParse module; the OptParse module is designed to address command-line parameters in an easy set of library functions.

■**Tip** The module getopt (http://docs.python.org/library/getopt.html) is an older module that also provides functions to parse command-line options.

To use the OptParse module, we follow these steps:

1. Create an OptionParser object.

2. Add options to the parser using the add_option() method.

3. Parse the command-line arguments using the parse_args() method.

The first step is simple: instantiate an OptionParser object by setting parser = OptionParser(). Adding options is a bit more complex as there are many possibilities to choose from (as you'll soon see). The last step is calling the function parse_args(), which returns a list of command-line options.

The return value of parse_args() is a tuple of options and arguments. The difference between an option and an argument is that options are, of course, optional, and arguments (positional arguments per OptParse documentation) are required.

Example: Processing Command-Line Parameters

We'll modify our previous example so that now the number of bytes per file is an option followed by the requested number of bytes (i.e., -n 1000), as in Listing 10-9 (empty_opt.py). Furthermore, we'll add an option switch, also known as an option flag, indicating whether a .bin extension should be added to the file name. The existence of the option flag -x instructs the script whether to create the extension: there's no additional value following it.

Listing 10-9. *Processing Command-Line Parameters Using OptParse, empty_opt.py*

```python
from optparse import OptionParser
from sys import exit

usage = "Usage: python empty_opt.py [options] filename"

# create an OptionParser instance
parser = OptionParser(usage)

# these are the options
parser.add_option("-n", "--numbytes", dest="nbytes",
    type="int", default=1000, help="number of bytes in file")
parser.add_option("-x", "--ext", dest="ext",
    action="store_true", default=False, help="adds 'bin' extension to filename")
(opt, args) = parser.parse_args()

# must have a file name
if len(args) != 1:
    print "Improper number of arguments."
    exit()

# append extension if switch is on
filename = args[0]+'.bin' if opt.ext else args[0]

# create the file
try:
    f = open(filename, 'wb')
except IOError:
    print "Unable to create file", filename
    exit()

f.seek(opt.nbytes-1)
f.write(chr(0))
f.close()

print "Successfully created file %s of size %d." % (filename, opt.nbytes)
```

First, I've imported the OptParse module. I then instantiate an OptionParser object and provide it with the default usage string. The usage string will be displayed as the first line whenever the user issues the command-line switch -h or –help, so: python empty_opt.py -h.

I then add options using the add_option() method. The add_option() method has many parameters to control how options should be parsed. In my first add_option() call, I've set how the user invokes this option: by entering either -n NBYTES or --numbytes NBYTES. I set the destination for this option to be named nbytes. This means that after the option is parsed, I can access the option value through variable opt.nbytes. The type of variable is int, as detailed by the type argument, and the default value is 1000 in case nbytes isn't provided by the user. Lastly, the help string associated with this option is detailed: help="number of bytes in file".

Similarly, I set another option named ext; this option is a switch, meaning the user will invoke the switch simply by entering -x or --ext; there are no additional values following the switch (in contrast, the -n option was accompanied by an NBYTES value). The action argument instructs OptParse to treat this as a positively acting switch: if -x is provided, set the flag to True. Lastly, I've set the default value to False and added a help string: help="adds 'bin' extension to filename".

Parsing the command-line options is performed with the call to parse_args(). Both options and arguments are then retrieved. The options are accessed via a class parameter, and the arguments are provided in a list. Following that is the actual creation of the file.

The following are the results from running the script with various options in a bash shell:

```
$ python empty_opt.py
Improper number of arguments.
$ python empty_opt.py -h
Usage: python empty_opt.py [options] filename

Options:
  -h, --help              show this help message and exit
  -n NBYTES, --numbytes=NBYTES
                          number of bytes in file
  -x, --ext               adds 'bin' extension to filename
$ python empty_opt.py file1
Successfully created file file1 of size 1000.
$ python empty_opt.py -x file1
Successfully created file file1.bin of size 1000.
$ python empty_opt.py -n 2000 --ext file1
Successfully created file file1.bin of size 2000.
$ python empty_opt.py -n 2000 --ext file1 file2
Improper number of arguments.
$ python empty_opt.py -n 2a --ext file1
Usage: python empty_opt.py [options] filename

empty_opt.py: error: option -n: invalid integer value: '2a'
```

The script expects an input as follows: [options] filename. Calling the script with command-line parameter -h or --help prints out the usage help message. This is implemented automatically when you use the OptParse module. Next, I've issued some valid command-line parameters and some invalid ones. OptParse handles the parsing of the values, while my code handles the number of arguments (only one: filename). I've also called the script with full option names (--ext) and abbreviated option names (-x).

Module OptParse is a rich module with many features. Refer to the online help at `http://docs.python.org/library/optparse.html` for a detailed description of the module.

■**Tip** As the number of options increases, consider using the ConfigParser module instead. See Chapter 4 for an introduction to ConfigParser and the online help (`http://docs.python.org/library/configparser.html`).

The FileInput Module

Closing our command-line parameters discussion is the FileInput module. The module provides an easy method for accessing several files (or streams) passed by the command line (i.e., `python somescript.py file1 file2 file3`). To use the module, issue `import fileinput`.

Using the module is straightforward: iterate over `fileinput.input()`. The result from the iteration is the next line in the current file. Once the end of the file is reached, the next file is opened automatically, and the process resumes until all lines from all files have been iterated over.

Table 10-1 lists some useful FileInput methods that can be used to further enhance scripts that make use of the module.

Table 10-1. *Useful FileInput Methods*

Method	Description
`fileinput.close()`	Ends the processing, closing all opened files
`fileinput.filelineno()`	Returns the line number in the current file
`fileinput.filename()`	Returns the name of the file currently being read
`fileinput.fileno()`	Returns the index of the current file
`fileinput.isfirstline()`	Returns `True` if this is the first line in a file
`fileinput.lineno()`	Returns the cumulative line number of all lines read from all the files
`fileinput.nextfile()`	Stops processing the current file and jumps to the next file

Let's turn to an example.

Example: Combining Data from Several Sources Based on the Epoch

Here we pick up on an example previously presented in Chapter 5 in a section with the same title as this one. This time we allow for more than two files to be combined, based on the epoch (see Listing 10-10).

Listing 10-10. *Combining Several Files Based on the Epoch,* `combine_epoch.py`

```python
import fileinput
from time import mktime, strptime
data = []
fmt = '%b %d %H:%M:%S %Y'
for line in fileinput.input():
    data.append([mktime(strptime(line[4:24], fmt)), line])
for line in sorted(data):
    print line[1],
```

The contents of the files are detailed in Chapter 5. Use the script as follows: `python combine_epoch.py file1 file2 ....` The source code should prove easy to follow.

Example: Searching for Text in Multiple Files

Again, building from an example previously shown in Chapter 5 in the section "Example: Searching Inside a Text File," we now search for text in multiple files. To use the script, `srchfile.py`, shown in Listing 10-11, issue the command `python srchfile.py search_string file1 file2 ....`

Listing 10-11. *Searching for Text in Multiple Files,* `srchfile.py`

```python
import fileinput, sys

# string to search is the first argument
for line in fileinput.input(sys.argv[2:]):
    if line.find(sys.argv[1]) != -1:
        print "File %s, #%d: %s" % (fileinput.filename(),
            fileinput.filelineno(), line.rstrip())
```

The main difference from the previous example is that now the first parameter is the string to search instead of a file. So I access the command-line parameters and pass the values from the third parameter onward (`sys.argv[2:]`) to `fileinput.input()`. Doing so will skip the script name (`argv[0]`) and the search string (`argv[1]`).

The fileinput module also provides support for modifying files as you process the lines via the `inplace` argument. Refer to the online help for more on this: `http://docs.python.org/library/fileinput.html`.

File and Directory Manipulation

Other than reading and writing files and processing command-line parameters, manipulating files is also a task commonly required of a developer. You've seen the os.walk module and some directory operations in previous chapters; here I expand on those, as well as file operations: deleting files, moving files, and more.

Module glob

The glob module enables searching for files given a file name pattern. The function glob(pattern) will return a list of all the files matching pattern; the function iglob(pattern) returns an iterator (as opposed to a list in glob()) of all the files matching pattern. I usually just use the list version, glob(pattern):

```
>>> from glob import glob
>>> glob('*.py')
['extract3.py', 'tail_large.py', 'cmp_dirs.py', 'cmp_files.py']
```

glob() accepts shell-like wildcards such as * (matches a string of characters), ? (matches one character), [chars] (matches any character from a list of characters), and [!chars] (matches anything but those characters listed). The following will match a file name that ends with py and contains a number:

```
>>> glob('*[0-9]*py')
['extract3.py']
```

This will match a file name that ends with py and does not start with c:

```
>>> glob('[!c]*py')
['extract3.py', 'tail_large.py']
```

Please note that glob expressions contain shell wildcards, and so are not regular expressions.

■**Tip**   See also module fnmatch (http://docs.python.org/library/fnmatch.html).

Additional os Module Functionality

You've already seen a considerable number of functions from the os and os.path modules (see the section "Moving Around" in Chapter 3). Table 10-2 lists a few more, not mentioned earlier, that are especially useful for manipulating files and directories. In the table, assume the current working directory is /home/user and the file in the directory is file.ext.

Table 10-2. *os Module Functions for Manipulating Files and Directories*

Function	Description	Example
os.chmod(path, mode)	Changes file permissions (in Windows, only read and write permissions are changed, all else is ignored).	os.chmod('file.ext', 0777) changes the file permissions to read, write, and execute for all.
os.chown(path, uid, gid)	Changes the group and user ownership of a file (not available in Windows). If you wish to change only uid, set gid to -1; if you wish to change only gid, set uid to -1.	os.chown('file.ext', 0, 0) will set the group and user ownership of file file.ext to root (assuming root has a uid of 0).

Function	Description	Example
os.remove(pathname) os.unlink(pathname)	Deletes the file specified in path-name.	os.unlink('file.ext') will delete the file file.ext.
os.rmdir()	Removes a directory if it's empty.	os.rmdir('/home/user') will remove directory /home/user if it's empty.
os.mkdir(path)	Creates a directory.	os.mkdir('another') will create directory /home/user/another.
os.makedirs(path)	Creates a directory as well as any intermediate subdirectories.	os.makedirs('dir1/dir2') will create directories /home/user/dir1 and /home/user/dir1/dir2.
os.rename(old, new)	Renames a path or file.	os.rename('file.ext', 'file2.ext') renames file file.ext to file2.ext.
os.renames(old, new)	Renames a path or file including the creation of intermediate directories and removal of empty ones.	os.renames('/home/user', '/home/user2/dir1/dir2') will rename the directory /home/user to /home/user2/dir1/dir2 as well as create subdirectories that do not exist and remove directory /home/user if it's empty.

Additional os.path Module Functionality

The module os.path provides functions that help manage file names and file paths. Table 10-3 lists some useful os.path functions. In the table, assume the current working directory is /home/user and the file in the directory is file.ext.

Table 10-3. *Useful os.path Functions*

Function	Description	Example
os.path.abspath(s)	Returns the absolute path of a file	os.path.abspath('file.ext') returns '/home/user/file.ext'.
os.path.basename(s)	Returns the file name, excluding path	os.path.basename('/home/user/file.ext') returns 'file.ext'.
os.path.dirname(s)	Returns the directory name of a path	os.path.dirname('/home/user/file.ext') returns '/home/user'.
os.path.exists(s)	Returns True if the path or file specified by s exists	os.path.exists('/home/user') returns True.
os.path.getatime(s)	Returns the last access time of a file	time.ctime(os.path.getatime('/home/user/file.ext')) will print the access time (ctime() is part of the time module).
os.path.getctime(s)	Returns creation time of a file	Similar to os.path.getatime() example.

Continued

Table 10-3. *Continued*

Function	Description	Example
os.path.getmtime(s)	Returns the last modification time of a file	Similar to os.path.getatime() example.
os.path.getsize(s)	Returns the file size in bytes	os.path.getsize('file.ext') returns the size of file file.txt in bytes.
os.path.isabs(s)	Returns True if the path specified by s is an absolute path	os.path.isabs('file.ext') returns False. os.path.isabs('/home/user/file.ext') returns True.
os.path.isdir(s)	Returns True if s is a directory	os.path.isdir('/home') returns True.
os.path.isfile(s)	Returns True if s is a file	os.path.isfile('file.ext') returns True.
os.path.join(base, seq)	Joins two or more paths, adding slashes as needed	os.path.join('/home/user', 'file.ext') returns '/home/user/file.ext'. os.path.join('/home', 'user', 'file.ext') returns '/home/user/file.ext'.
os.path.split(s)	Splits a pathname, returning the path and the file name	os.path.split('/home/user/file.ext') returns ('/home/user', 'file.ext').
os.path.splitext(s)	Splits a pathname returning the extension, including the dot	os.path.splitext('/home/user/file.ext') returns ('/home/user/file', '.ext').

Module shutil

The shutil module provides higher-level functions for copying, moving, and renaming files. Of those, we'll explore the following: copy(src, dest), copytree(src, dest), rmtree(path), and move(src, dst). For a full account of the module, refer to http://docs.python.org/library/shutil.html.

I assume a file named file1.txt exists in the current directory. If yours doesn't have this file, create one if you wish to follow along.

First, let's create a directory with subdirectories and copy file1.txt to the newly created directory:

```
>>> import shutil
>>> from os import makedirs
>>> from glob import glob
>>> makedirs('dir1/dir2/dir3/dir4')
>>> shutil.copy('file1.txt', 'dir1/dir2/dir3/dir4')
>>> shutil.copy('file1.txt', 'dir1/dir2/dir3/dir4/file2.txt')
>>> glob('dir1/dir2/dir3/dir4/*')
['dir1/dir2/dir3/dir4/file1.txt', 'dir1/dir2/dir3/dir4/file2.txt']
```

First, I imported several modules and functions: shutil, os, and glob. I then created a directory (as well as its parent directories): dir1/dir2/dir3/dir4. I made use of the function copy() in two ways: first, to copy the file file1.txt to the newly created directory, and second, to copy the file file1.txt to the same directory under a different name, file2.txt.

```
>>> shutil.move('dir1/dir2/dir3/dir4/file2.txt', 'dir1/dir2')
>>> glob('dir1/dir2/*')
['dir1/dir2/dir3', 'dir1/dir2/file2.txt']
>>> glob('dir1/dir2/dir3/dir4/*')
['dir1/dir2/dir3/dir4/file1.txt']
```

I've moved the file file2.txt to directory dir1/dir2. The results from glob() confirm the move.

Now I copy the entire directory leaf under dir1 to a new directory named Dir_1:

```
>>> shutil.copytree('dir1', 'Dir_1')
>>> glob('Dir_1/dir2/dir3/dir4/*')
['Dir_1/dir2/dir3/dir4/file1.txt']
```

And lastly, it's time for cleanup—I remove both directories as well as their subdirectories:

```
>>> shutil.rmtree('dir1')
>>> shutil.rmtree('Dir_1')
>>> glob('dir1')
[]
```

File Compression

File compression is the process of representing a file in fewer bytes. Compression is typically divided into two categories: lossy compression and nonlossy compression. In lossy compression, the compressed data is not identical to the original data; data is lost in the process of reducing the file size (hopefully nonimportant information is lost). Nonlossy compression uses clever schemes to represent data in a way that is more efficient. For example, instead of writing a hundred identical values to file, a nonlossy compression scheme might be to write the value 100, representing the count, and then the repeating value.

Python provides us with several compression and archiving modules. Archiving modules are used to create compressed files; compression modules deal with the compression itself and can be used on strings, not only on files. The distinction is somewhat blurred as some modules perform both compression and archiving. The modules bz2 (http://docs.python.org/library/bz2.html), gzip (http://docs.python.org/library/gzip.html), and zlib (http://docs.python.org/library/zlib.html as well as http://www.zlib.net/) provide nonlossy compression functionality; the modules tarfile (http://docs.python.org/library/tarfile.html) and zipfile (http://docs.python.org/library/zipfile.html) provide archiving capabilities. The names of the packages are also the import names, so to use gzip, issue import gzip.

There are some differences between the different modules in terms of compression ratio, performance, and popularity. They're all easy to use and provide excellent results. In this section we'll explore the tarfile module.

Example: A Compressed tar File

In the open source community, it's common to see files distributed with extensions .tar.gz or .tar.bz2. These are compressed *tar* files; tar stands for tape archive, but in reality there's no need for tapes. The example in Listing 10-12 creates several files, archives them, and then retrieves them from the archive.

Listing 10-12. *Creating an Archive*

```
import tarfile, glob

# create some files
for i in range(5):
    f = open('file%d.txt' % i, 'w')
    # write some data
    for j in range(100):
        f.write('Some data: %d\n' % j)
    f.close()

# archive the files using bz2 compression
tf = tarfile.open('files.tar.bz2', 'w:bz2')
for filename in glob.glob('file*'):
    tf.add(filename)
tf.close()
```

The first section of the script generates five files with some made-up data. Once files are created, I create a tar file for archiving. The file mode is specified as 'w:bz2', which stands for writing (creating) a tar file compressed with compression algorithm bz2. Other modes include 'w:gz' for gzip compression and 'w' for no compression. Similarly, opening an archive can be done by specifying 'r', 'r:gz', and 'r:bz2'.

Once the tarfile object is created, we add files to the archive using the add(path) method. If you provide a directory to add(), the entire directory is added to the archive. I've decided to add the files one at a time in case other files exist in the directory that I don't wish to include. Finally, I close the tar file, effectively creating the file files.tar.bz2.

Retrieving files from an archive is simple as well, as demonstrated in Listing 10-13. The method extractall() will extract all files from an archive. The method extract(member, path) will extract a file that is a member of the archive to a location specified by path. The method getmembers() lists the members (files) in an archive.

Listing 10-13. *Extracting All Files from an Archive*

```
import tarfile, os

if not os.path.exists('new'):
    os.mkdir('new')

tf = tarfile.open('files.tar.bz2', 'r:bz2')
tf.extractall('new')
tf.close()
```

Listing 10-14 shows how to extract just the first three files in the archive.

Listing 10-14. *Extracting Three Files from an Archive*

```
import tarfile, os

if not os.path.exists('new'):
    os.mkdir('new')

tf = tarfile.open('files.tar.bz2', 'r:bz2')
for member in tf.getmembers()[:3]:
    tf.extract(member, 'new')
tf.close()
```

I've made use of the method getmembers() to retrieve the list of files in the archive and then indexed only the first three files.

Comparing Files

Ensuring two files are identical is a common task. In case of input data files, it means we can remove the copy, and our script will both run faster and provide better statistics because now the data isn't used twice. The reasons for duplicate files can be numerous as discussed in Chapter 4.

A simple mechanism for comparing two files can be to open both files, read the entire files to memory, and then compare the values:

```
>>> data1 = open('../data/file1.txt', 'rb').read()
>>> data2 = open('../data/file2.txt', 'rb').read()
>>> data1 == data2
True
```

The main benefit of this method is that it's simple. However, there are several shortcomings:

- *Inefficiency*: Suppose one file is of size 10GB and other file is 1 byte long. By looking at the file sizes, it's possible to tell the files are not identical. On the other hand, reading a 10GB file to memory can bring the system to a crawl.

- *Lack of information*: If two files are not identical, what exactly are the differences?

Modules filecmp and difflib from the Python Standard Library provide us with functionality to compare files and find the differences.

Module filecmp

The module filecmp provides functions for file and directory comparisons. The method cmp(file1, file2[, shallow]) will compare file1 with file2. If shallow is not provided (or is True), files that have the same *stat* signature are considered equal. By this I mean files that have the same system information such as size, creation date, and more (see http://docs.python.org/library/os.html for an explanation of stat). If shallow is False, files are also compared for content.

```
>>> filenames = ['../data/file1.bin', '../data/file2.bin']
>>> for fn in filenames:
...     f = open(fn, 'wb')
...     f.write('some data')
...     f.close()
...
>>> import filecmp
>>> filecmp.cmp(filenames[0], filenames[1])
True
```

The class dircmp(dir1, dir2) enables the comparison of directories dir1 and dir2. The comparison includes all subdirectories as well. The method report() will print the result from comparing both directories.

For the following example, I assume you've created the file files.tar.bz2 in the previous compression example. Here, we'll create two directories, new1 and new2. Directory new1 will contain the extracted files from the archive; directory new2 will contain the extracted files from the archive as well as another subdirectory, new3, which will also contain the contents of the archive. We'll compare the directory contents (see Listing 10-15).

Listing 10-15. *Comparing Directories*

```
import tarfile, os, filecmp

if not os.path.exists('new1'):
    os.mkdir('new1')
if not os.path.exists('new2/new3'):
    os.makedirs('new2/new3')

tf = tarfile.open('files.tar.bz2', 'r:bz2')
tf.extractall('new1')
tf.extractall('new2')
tf.extractall('new2/new3')
tf.close()

cmp = filecmp.dircmp('new1', 'new2')
cmp.report()
```

The results are as follows:

```
diff new1 new2
Only in new2 : ['new3']
Identical files : ['file0.txt', 'file1.txt', 'file2.txt', 'file3.txt', 'file4.txt']
```

As you can see, comparing directory contents using the filecmp module is easy and simple.

Module difflib

The module difflib provides several objects and functions to help compare lists of strings (e.g., text files). Several functions provide a diff result in different formats. These include context_diff(), ndiff(), and unified_diff(). In this section we'll examine the context_diff(f1, f2[, fromfile][, tofile]) function; other functions have similar behavior.

First we create two files, ../data/file1.txt and ../data/file2.txt, with similar but not identical content, as shown in Listing 10-16.

Listing 10-16. *Creating Files for Comparison*

```
content = """A string
123, 456
789
some text\n"""
fname1 = '../data/file1.txt'
fname2 = '../data/file2.txt'

f1 = open(fname1, 'wb')
f1.write('before\n')
f1.write(content)
f1.close()

f2 = open(fname2, 'wb')
f2.write(content)
f2.write('after\n')
f2.close()
```

The two files differ in that the first file contains an extra line in the beginning, and the second file contains an extra line in the end. We call context_diff() to display those differences (see Listing 10-17).

Listing 10-17. *Comparing File Contents*

```
import difflib

fname1 = '../data/file1.txt'
fname2 = '../data/file2.txt'

lines1 = open(fname1).readlines()
lines2 = open(fname2).readlines()
for line in difflib.context_diff(lines1, lines2, fname1, fname2):
    print line,
```

I've included the name of the files as parameters to context_diff(); this will generate a report that displays the file names in the header information. Here are the results:

```
*** ../data/file1.txt
--- ../data/file2.txt
***************
*** 1,5 ****
- before
  A string
  123, 456
  789
  some text
--- 1,5 ----
  A string
  123, 456
  789
  some text
+ after
```

A section starting with *** means the report addresses the file ../data/file1.txt; a section starting with --- means the report addresses the file ../data/file2.txt. A line starting with a - sign implies that the line is missing from the first file; a + sign means the line is included in the first file but not in the second file. The output is similar to output generated by UNIX diff command-line utilities.

Additional difflib functionality can be found online at http://docs.python.org/library/difflib.html.

Final Notes and References

Python provides a wealth of libraries that deal with common programming tasks: file processing, command-line parameters, file and directory manipulation, compressing and archiving files, and many more. There are a great number of additional modules available with the Python Standard Library:

- The Python Standard Library, http://docs.python.org/library/index.html

APPENDIX

■■■

Additional Source Listing

This appendix is a collection of source listings that didn't quite belong in the chapters themselves, but nevertheless might be of interest to you.

Nudge Subplots

In generating subplots of size 2 by 2 for this book, I've noticed that the text for the x-axis of the top subplots clashes with the titles of the lower subplots. To overcome this, I've defined nudge_subplot(), a function designed to modify the location of subplots within a figure (see Listing A-1).

Listing A-1. *Source Listing of nudge_subplot()*

```
def nudge_subplot(subp, dy):
    """A helper function to move subplots."""

    sp_ax = subp.get_position()
    sp.set_position([sp_ax.x0, sp_ax.y0+dy,
        sp_ax.x1-sp_ax.x0, sp_ax.y1-sp_ax.y0])
```

To use the function, store the return value from subplot() and then "nudge" it by calling nudge_subplot(sp, dy), as shown in Listing A-2, where sp is the subplot and dy is the amount to nudge (a value of 0.02 for dy usually works well).

Listing A-2. *Using nudge_subplot()*

```
from pylab import *

# values to plot
t = arange(5)
y = array([1,  2, -1,  1, -2])

plot_cmds = [
    "plot(y)",
    "plot(-y)",
    "plot(y**2)",
```

```
        "plot(sin(y))"
    ]

figure()
for i, plot_cmd in enumerate(plot_cmds):
    sp = subplot(2, 2, i+1)
    if i == 1: nudge_subplot(sp, 0.02)
    if i == 3: nudge_subplot(sp, -0.02)
    exec plot_cmd
    title(plot_cmd, fontsize='large')
    xlabel('x values')
```

In this code, I've nudged the right subplots and left the left ones as is, as you can see in Figure A-1.

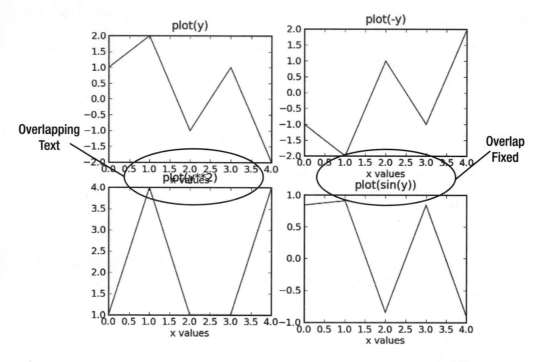

Figure A-1. *The left subplots are unmoved (the default), and the right subplots are nudged.*

The function nudge_subplot() is not backward compatible with older versions of matplot-lib. For example, with matplotlib version 0.91.4, the function set_position() accepts different arguments, and so the code needs revising. Nevertheless, the ideas are similar. Listing A-3 is an implementation that runs on matplotlib version 0.91.4.

Listing A-3. *Source Listing of nudge_subplot_old(), for Older Versions of Matplotlib*

```
def nudge_subplot_old(subp, dy):
    """A helper function to move subplots.

Works on matplotlib version 0.91.4."""

    sp_ax = subp.get_position()
    sp_ax[1] += dy
    sp.set_position(sp_ax)
```

Magic Square Arrows

In Chapter 7 I presented a figure describing the magic square algorithm. I used matplotlib patch arrows embedded in the algorithm to plot that figure. Listing A-4 is the source code used to generate the diagram.

Listing A-4. *Magic Square Diagram Creation*

```
from pylab import *

def magic_arrow(x, y, top_right, n, c=0):
    """Draws an arrow from point x, y."""

    d, my_colors = 0.15, 'rbymg'

    if top_right:     # top-right arrow
        mc = my_colors[c % len(my_colors)]
        ar = Arrow(x+0.5+d, n-y-0.5+d, 1-2*d, 1-2*d, width=0.2, fc=mc, ec=mc)
    else:             # down arrow
        ar = Arrow(x+0.5, n-y-0.5-d, 0, 2*d-1, width=0.2, fc='k', ec='k')

    # patch the arrow
    gca().add_patch(ar)


def show_alg(n=3):
    """Draws a magic square, n must be odd."""

    if n % 2 != 1:
        raise ValueError, "Magic(n) requires n to be odd."

    # prepare the figure, draw grid lines, hide ticks
    axis('scaled')
    axis([0, n, 0, n])
    for i in range(n):
        plot([0, n], [i, i], 'b')
```

```python
        plot([i, i], [0, n], 'b')
    xticks([])
    yticks([])

    # alternating color index
    altc = 0

    # initialize variables
    m, row, col = zeros([n, n]), 0, n/2

    # go through all the numbers from 1 to n**2
    for num in xrange(1, n**2+1):

        # assign the current number and display it on the figure
        m[row, col] = num
        text(col+0.5, n-row-0.5, str(num), va='center', ha='center')

        # store current row and col
        pcol, prow = col, row

        # increment row and col
        col = (col+1) % n
        row = (row-1) % n

        # if location (col, row) is nonzero, it means the cell
        # is occupied, move down
        if m[row, col]:
            col = pcol % n
            row = (prow+1) % n

        # if current location minus previous location is (1, 1)
        # draw a top-right arrow
        if col-pcol == 1 and prow-row == 1:
            magic_arrow(pcol, prow, True, n, altc)

        # if previous col location is identical to current
        # col location, draw a down arrow (unless it's the last cell)
        elif pcol == col and num != n**2:
            magic_arrow(pcol, prow, False, n)
            altc += 1

        # the following two elif sentences take care of drawing two
        # arrows in case of wrapping: one originating from the current
        # location, the other to the next location
        elif col-pcol == 1 and prow-row != 1:
            magic_arrow(pcol, prow, True, n, altc)
            magic_arrow(pcol, n, True, n, altc)
```

```
        elif col-pcol != 1 and prow-row == 1:
            magic_arrow(pcol, prow, True, n, altc)
            magic_arrow(-1, prow, True, n, altc)

        # last cell
        elif num == n**2:
            pass

        # if we've reached this point, there's a bug
        else:
            raise ValueError, "We should never be here."

def show_some():
    figure()
    for i in range(4):
        subplot(2, 2, i+1)
        show_alg(2*i+3)
        title('N='+str(2*i+3))

show_some()
```

I've defined the function magic_arrow() that draws an arrow at a given position using a matplotlib arrow patch. The arrow's direction is determined by comparing the current location with the previous location. Other than that, the code is similar to the one discussed in Chapter 7.

Fractal Function Source Code

In Chapter 9 I made use of a variation of the fractal script in Chapter 7 to create a collage by wrapping it within a function. Listing A-5 shows the function used in creating the fractal collage in Chapter 9.

Listing A-5. *Fractal Collage Function*

```
from PIL import Image
from cmath import *

def fractal(delta=0.000001, res=800, iters=30):
    """Creates a z**4+1=0 fractal using the Newton-Raphson method."""

    # create an image to draw on, paint it black
    img = Image.new("RGB", (res, res), (0, 0, 0))

    # these are the solutions to the equation z**4+1=0 (Euler's formula)
    solutions = [cos((2*n+1)*pi/4)+1j*sin((2*n+1)*pi/4) for n in range(4)]
    colors = [(1, 0, 0), (0, 1, 0), (0, 0, 1), (1, 1, 0)]
```

```python
    for re in range(0, res):
        for im in range(0, res):
            z = (re+1j*im)/res
            for i in range(iters):
                try:
                    z -= (z**4+1)/(4*z**3)
                except ZeroDivisionError:
                    # possibly divide by zero exception
                    continue
                if(abs(z**4+1) < delta):
                    break

            # color depth is a function of the number of iterations
            color_depth = int((iters-i)*255.0/iters)

            # find to which solution this guess converged to
            err = [abs(z-root) for root in solutions]
            distances = zip(err, range(len(colors)))

            # select the color associated with the solution
            color = [i*color_depth for i in colors[min(distances)[1]]]
            img.putpixel((re, im), tuple(color))

    return img
```

Index

You Need the Companion eBook